THE KING OF DIAMONDS

THE KING
OF
DIAMONDS

THE SEARCH FOR THE
ELUSIVE TEXAS JEWEL THIEF

RENA PEDERSON

PEGASUS CRIME

NEW YORK LONDON

THE KING OF DIAMONDS

Pegasus Crime is an imprint of
Pegasus Books, Ltd.
148 West 37th Street, 13th Floor
New York, NY 10018

First Pegasus Books cloth edition April 2024

Interior design by Maria Fernandez

Library of Congress Cataloging-in-Publication Data is available.

ISBN: 978-1-63936-605-7

10 9 8 7 6 5

Printed in the United States of America
Distributed by Simon & Schuster
www.pegasusbooks.com

For my intrepid granddaughters—Teddie, Cecily, Tiny, and Lula.

CONTENTS

She was young and privileged, a former debutante enjoying a few "victory laps" at parties for the new crop of debs. She got home well after midnight—again—and swayed woozily as she fell into bed.

She was sound asleep when something stirring in her bedroom awoke her. Though still groggy with alcohol, she rose on her elbow to look into the dark. She could see a man. He was going through the jewelry box on her dresser.

"You don't belong here," she said, slurring her words.

Without a word, the intruder turned and left the room. She fell back to sleep.

When she told friends about the incident the next day, she said she couldn't see the man clearly but had the distinct feeling he was someone she knew.

INTRODUCTION

How I Became a Detective

"Everyone loves a good thief... We like
talent more than we like morality."
—Sylvain Neuvel, *Crime Reads*

The King of Diamonds disappeared like a magic trick—poof!—just as I arrived in Dallas.

It was 1970. Fresh out of grad school in New York, I was starting work at United Press International. I drove into deeply conservative Dallas with everything I owned in a red VW convertible. It had a peace symbol on the back window and Simon and Garfunkel on the radio. At the time, I had long blonde hair and a sunny sense of possibility. Real life awaited.

Because I was the newest and lowliest employee in the office, the bureau chief put me on the overnight shift from eleven o'clock at night to six in the morning, the dreaded red-eye shift. That meant that I worked all night alone in a drab basement office. The only light came from sickly fluorescent tubes that flickered on and off at random intervals—like a prison code, I thought. I was never sure if the walls were painted that sallow shade of yellow or got that way from the ever-present fug of cigarette smoke. I took up smoking in self-defense.

Although the Dallas UPI bureau served as a major news hub, it was spartan as a warehouse. The only furnishings were gray metal desks that looked like army surplus. Clunky black phones and grimy ashtrays competed for space on desks with a clutter of press releases and newspapers. Décor wasn't important to the wire service—beating the Associated Press to news was. Reporters pounded out their stories on battered Royal typewriters, then headed for the nearest bar. I was twenty-three years old and to me, all this was glamorous.

For the next few years, I struggled to stay awake and keep the glass doors double-locked so street drunks wouldn't stagger in. I was supposed to deal with any news that came up in the middle of the night, which was generally killings, car wrecks, and tornadoes. Like your mother says, nothing good happens after midnight, sweetheart. But while everyone else in the bureau was at home sleeping, I was more or less in charge. I liked to think of myself as the Dawn Patrol, keeping watch over the city at night.

Part of my job was keeping the teletype machines filled with paper so they could crank out news day and night. The clattering machines were my only companions and my lifeline to the rest of the world. I was supposed to monitor them and strip off the streams of paper before they curled up like pasta on the floor.

Late one night, while I was skimming through the dispatches, I noticed a story about a jewel thief who got away with millions in jewels. No one could catch him, not the police, not the FBI, nobody. The thief had outfoxed them all and had a catchy nickname: "The King of Diamonds."

Hello there, Mr. King, I thought. *You sound interesting.*

And that was my introduction to the most famous jewel thief in Dallas history.

The elusive thief had sneaked recently into a mansion on Park Lane—and slipped out with $60,000 in jewels. That was ten times what I made a year at UPI. In those days, you could pay for a nice house with a yard and a garage and electric doorbell with $60,000—and still have money left over for a Cadillac. It would be equal to $400,000 today. The King had walked out with a bonanza.

The cagey thief had eluded police for more than a decade. He sometimes sneaked in while his victims were sleeping a few feet away or hosting a party downstairs. He climbed up trees and inched across rooftops. Somehow, he knew where to find the jewels.

With brazen skill, the thief had stolen jewels from heiress Margaret Hunt Hill, who ranked with Queen Elizabeth as one of the wealthiest women in the world . . . oil tycoon Clint Murchison . . . corporate whiz Jim Ling of LTV . . . Herman Lay of Lay's potato chips . . . and dozens more. These were not just the richest people in Dallas, they were some of the richest people of their time.

For months after I arrived, there was a tremor of anticipation. Everyone thought the burglar would strike again any day. He usually did. Reporters watched and waited. I scanned the wires every night, looking for a new incident.

But the infamous thief never resurfaced. The King of Diamonds had vanished.

And all the jewels with him.

Years passed, but I never stopped wondering: What happened to the mysterious thief? There was something beguiling, almost addictive about a jewel thief who couldn't be caught. It nagged at everyone who knew the story.

Who was he? How did he get away with the perfect crime?

A full account of his career seemed long overdue. Someone needed to reopen the case before everyone involved died.

"Why not me?" was my next thought.

After all, I was a lifelong fan of detective stories and had the bookshelves to prove it. I was drawn to the idea of solving a cold case, like coroner Kay Scarpetta, but without the scalpel.

True, nearly fifty years had passed since I first read about the jewel thief. I now had an AARP membership and Medicare card. My sporty convertible had been replaced by a sturdy Subaru. But I still had Nancy Drew's curiosity, if not the natural blonde hair. Since 1970, I had endured five publishers, one husband, two rambunctious sons, and a lifetime of newspaper deadlines—which meant, I reasoned, that I could look for the thief with seasoned eyes.

I had seen it all as a reporter—the demagogues, the wacko birds, the kooks, crooks, and chiselers of all kinds. Or, as Zorba the Greek would say, "the full catastrophe."

So, when it came to checking out some old jewel thefts, I thought, I can do this. No problem.

◈

Right away, I learned that burglars who steal jewels have a special mystique. Even in prisons, "second-story men" are considered a cut above ordinary burglars. That's because sneaking into bedrooms on the second floor is much riskier than a smash-and-grab on the ground floor.

Because he evaded police for so long, the King of Diamonds was a superstar in burglar ranks, the Houdini of thieves, invisible as a ghost, light-footed as Fred Astaire, and able to disappear into the night before anyone knew he was there.

Reopening the case after fifty years presented challenges. The trail was cold as a morgue for good reasons. Most of the victims and suspects were dead. And most of the records had been discarded. Though I could understand why the police might not keep burglary records for half a century, I was surprised the FBI destroyed its records after only a few years. When I asked a former agent why the files were tossed out so quickly, he suggested, "Someone powerful didn't want them around."

This was my first indication there was more to the story than I anticipated.

◈

To learn more, I headed to a place most detectives don't frequent—the public library. I spent hour after hour with the clip files in the Dallas Central Library, sorting gingerly through yellowed newspaper articles that flaked at the touch. By the time I left, my list of possible sources filled several pages in a legal pad.

But how would I find these people without a Ouija board? I turned to internet tools that the cops didn't have in the fifties and sixties—Ancestry .com, Facebook, LinkedIn, and Newspapers.com. No, I didn't have the skills of Lisbeth Salander, the hacker in *The Girl with the Dragon Tattoo*, but I knew how to navigate public records. Sitting in front of my computer, I could find the phone numbers of people to call along with their home addresses, email addresses, family members, college degrees, divorces, arrest records, zodiac signs, and even the model of their cars and their traffic tickets. I often felt like a window peeper seeing people in their underwear, learning more about people's lives than I really wanted to know.

I started making cold calls: "Hello, I don't think we've met, but I'm doing some research on the famous jewel thief called the King of Diamonds. Yes, the one in the 1960s. Is this a good time to talk?"

Several hung up on me, but most were just as fascinated by the thief as I was. Over the next six years, I interviewed more than two hundred people—relatives of victims, neighbors, policemen, and former reporters. Each one provided information of some kind—a name, a rumor, a recollection.

The biggest surprise was the dark side of the city. Dallas is a wonderful city to live in, full of big-hearted people. I was proud to call it home. But the convivial place where I spent most of my time was the upperworld, the world of art museums, churches, concerts, shopping malls. The underworld, the domain of nightclubs, gambling dens, and sleazy cocktail lounges held more sinister secrets than I knew.

Once I started digging, I found layers of intrigue that had been hidden from view. The subsurface of Dallas harbored sex traffickers, gangsters, and even a few spies. I began to think of that alternative universe as the under-history, the part you don't usually read about. A lot more was going on than sales at Neiman Marcus.

The assassination of President John F. Kennedy in 1963 had drawn attention to the right-wing politics in Dallas, but not even the glare from that tragedy captured the full story of that time—the good, the bad, and the very reckless. As one of the detectives put it, "There were a lot of strange things going on back then."

Getting to the rest of the story was sometimes uncomfortable. One woman threatened that if I kept asking questions, "you will be sorry." Several people said they couldn't talk out of fear for their lives.

This convinced me that I was onto something.

PART ONE
THE PHANTOM STRIKES

"I never stole from anybody who would go hungry."
—Cary Grant in *To Catch a Thief*

1

The Graf House

The crime that triggered all the excitement happened on a bone-cold night in 1959. A "blue norther" had blown across the barren stretches of Texas into Dallas. Rich women in Dallas turtled down into their mink coats and said, "Brrrrr!" to their husbands as they hurried out to cocktail parties.

Few realized it at that moment, but they were living in auspicious times. The country was entering a new era that year—and so was Dallas.

Dwight Eisenhower was finishing his last term in the White House. Despite Cold War tensions, he remained one of the most popular presidents of all time. He rarely spoke to his vice president, Richard Nixon, but didn't much want to.

Lyndon Baines Johnson, the arm-twisting, vote-counting Master of the Senate, had his eyes fixed on the presidency. He had the support of an armada of Texas oilmen who handed over envelopes of cash with a wink. Yet a junior senator from Massachusetts was preparing his own run for the White House. John F. Kennedy had the support of the star-struck media and, some said, the Mafia in Chicago.

So, yes, 1959 would turn out to be a hinge year, when the world turned a corner.

The fifties were an era of bobby sox, tuna casseroles, and home milk delivery. The world after 1959 would be a more dangerous place. The Soviets were launching satellite after satellite, while American rockets exploded like firecrackers. Civil rights protests erupted in the South. The first American soldiers were killed in Vietnam.

It would have a bearing on this story that Fidel Castro took over Cuba the same year. Castro's takeover forced mobsters Meyer Lansky and Benjamin "Bugsy" Siegel to shift most of their gambling operations to a godforsaken outpost in Nevada called Las Vegas. The first time Lansky and Siegel visited the dusty railroad stop, temperatures were 115 degrees Fahrenheit. The wires in their Cadillac melted. Yet the desert watering hole was their best hope for riches after Castro booted them from Havana.

Meanwhile, a little-known engineer at Texas Instruments, Jack Kilby, invented a miniature computer circuit in Dallas. It would become known as the "microchip" and usher in a digital revolution.

But the consequences of these events were as yet unknown. The new economic surge required oil and gas, so Texas became the gas station for America. And that meant Dallas, the banking center for much of the oil industry, was a boomtown. The lucky rich were celebrating in grand style. They were eager to show off their new wealth—and a master thief was happy to relieve them of it.

At first, people weren't paying attention when jewel thefts sprang up. They were throwing parties. Wildcatter Jake Hamon's wife Nancy flew in planeloads of snow for her "Christmas in July" party and cancan girls for her Paris party. As a former dancer, Nancy Hamon knew how to make entrances. She rode into her circus party on an elephant. For another party, she was carried in on a litter by four bare-chested men and wore a purple satin turban.

All the beautiful people of the day came to Hamon's parties—women with acres of diamonds and men with ranches the size of states. Landscaper Joe Lambert came in a cape. Opera patron Elsa von Seggern came in a headdress like Queen Nefertiti.

Other millionaires did their best to keep up. One brought in belly dancers from the Middle East for a Casablanca party. Another flew in Michelin-star chefs from around the world. One oilman's wife hired a full orchestra, a gospel choir, and a Dixieland band for her husband's birthday. This was not unusual.

What's surprising is that Dallas had a population of only 679,000 in 1959. The small cluster of downtown skyscrapers looked out over farmland for as far as you could see. An astounding amount of cotton—one half of the world's crop—was once produced within a three-hundred-mile radius of Dallas. The cotton millionaires had offices in New Orleans, New York, and London. They built fine homes and sent their children East to school. But many were left in ruins after the stock market collapse in 1929.

A prolonged drought did not help matters. As their farmland dried up and blew away, some West Texas families were reduced to eating cooked tumbleweeds. More than seven thousand people in parched areas died from "dust pneumonia." When Eleanor Roosevelt came to Texas on a political tour in 1939, a horrific dust storm brought her train to a standstill. She was so shocked by conditions that she urged her husband to speed money into soil conservation programs.

By the 1950s, more than a third of the state's population still lived below poverty levels. Yet Dallas thrived, thanks to wildcatters who bet big on oil and won. Dallas County did not have a drop of oil, but it had shrewd bankers. The city became an oasis in what was still a rural, agrarian state. Car dealers advertised, "If you don't have an oil well, GET one!"

When New York cultural critic Leo Lerman visited Dallas in 1958, he wrote in his journals of "the flabbergasting richness." Dallas was "parties, parties, parties," he said, noting that one host pointed out four of his party guests were billionaires and one made a million dollars a week.

The new fortunes fueled city ambitions of becoming a big-league player in the country. Civic leaders bragged that Dallas had the biggest state fair in the nation, the largest Rotary club, the biggest churches, the Cotton Bowl, and football stars like Doak Walker, Bobby Layne, and Don Meredith. Everyone was humming a song called "Big D" from the Broadway musical

Most Happy Fella. While the rest of Texas was a mess, the lyrics said, every home was a palace in "Big D, little a, double l, a-s!"

The song was terrific advertising for the city, but in truth, most people in Dallas did not live in a palace; far from it. The average income was less than $5,300 a year.

However, there was a glittering veneer of wealth that drew attention, like sparklers on a cake. The oil-rich were a small slice of Dallas, yet they became a big part of the city's gaudy image. Their conspicuous abundance was an irresistible attraction for opportunists—of all kinds.

❖

On the chilly night when the jewel thief made his leap into fame—Saturday, January 24, 1959, to be exact—Bruno and Josephine Graf were going to one of the year's most glamorous social events. For him, that meant black tie. For her, it meant jewels, cascades of them.

The Grafs were attending the Jewel Charity Ball in Fort Worth, where women were expected to sparkle. Mrs. Graf carefully selected some of her most beautiful jewelry to wear. Sitting in front of the big mirror in her dressing room, she put on a pair of stunning diamond earrings. Then she fastened a matching necklace around her throat and pinned a diamond-studded brooch to her gown.

Lastly, Josephine Graf slipped on her 20.4-carat diamond ring. The ring was a showstopper. People said in awe that it was "as big as the Alamo." Decades later, I would notice that celebrity Kim Kardashian had a ring not quite so big that was valued at more than $2 million.

Josephine Herbert Graf had been left with a fortune after the death of her first husband. She wore her wealth well. In photos, she is always exquisitely dressed, her face tilted up to the camera with patrician confidence. She went to the hairdresser several times a week to keep her hair in a fashionable mid-length flip, like movie star June Allyson. Her eyes were her most striking feature because they were an unusual pale blue, like the still Nordic sky in winter.

From what I could piece together about Josephine Graf, she joined oil society when she married John Warne Herbert III. "Jack" Herbert's family in New York had made a fortune in tobacco products like snuff. They lived in an apartment on Fifth Avenue, and when they attended the opera, the *New York Times* reported it. To his father's chagrin, John Herbert III preferred to spend more time on the town than with the family business. He was the kind of man who looked as if he slept in a tuxedo and, some evenings, did.

In the 1920s, young Herbert headed down to Texas to prove his worth. Texas was becoming known as a place where anyone with gumption and a bank loan could strike it rich. Some made it on gumption alone. When oil erupted like a pent-up volcano from the Spindletop oil rig in 1901, it spawned a black gold rush. Young men from all over the country were inspired to go to Texas and poke holes in the ground.

It was an exciting time. Children were let out of school to watch when word spread that a gusher might shoot up. Crowds gathered like tourists waiting for Old Faithful to spout.

That said, the fortune hunters who rushed into the state soon discovered the Wild West was still awfully wild. The roughnecks who did the hard, dirty work on oil derricks cussed like grimy poets and spent everything they earned in bars. The Texas Rangers were often called in to settle drunken brawls in boomtowns. And when the jails filled up, they handcuffed belligerents to light poles. The oil hands were easy to spot because they were missing fingers from wrestling with the massive, medieval chains that pulled drill pipes into place. Explosions and falls added to the risk. As one grizzled veteran put it, "I got blowed up twice and burned up once."

This was no country for the meek.

Jack Herbert arrived in the oilfields at the wheel of a white convertible. He wore jodhpur riding pants, looking as if he were on his way to a fox hunt.

"He was a wild Indian," fellow wildcatter Jake Hamon would say later. "If you went out with him for the evening, you had to plan on fighting your way out of a place or getting thrown out bodily."

Then Jack Herbert met Josephine Weaver. She had the kind of looks that made a man ambitious. So that was that. Jake Hamon later would credit strong-willed Josephine with helping to tame Jack Herbert.

Jack Herbert hit it big in the oil patch. Not something for the record books, like Spindletop, but big enough. It wasn't long before the Herberts bought a mansion near the Rivercrest Country Club in Fort Worth.

The colonial mansion had once belonged to cattle giant W. T. Waggoner. His 520,000-acre ranch in North Texas was second in size only to the 825,000-acre King Ranch in South Texas, so Waggoner built a mansion of appropriate stature in Fort Worth. His showplace had stately white columns in front and acres of lawn in back. Josephine Herbert remodeled the mansion and filled it with fine art and antiques that had been burnished to perfection by time.

When the Duke and Duchess of Windsor traveled to Texas, the Herberts received them with style. Josephine Herbert had royal jewels of her own.

These were glory days in Fort Worth as well as Dallas. Oil had created a surge of millionaires in the state, successors to the cotton barons and cattle kings. These were men who believed that if they dared much and got lucky, they could move up the ladder to an upper-class berth, to the world of country clubs, luxury cars, and expensive women.

In other words, the state was full of Gatsbys.

Some handled the great wealth—and temptations that came with it—better than others. The Herberts settled quite nicely into a life of privilege.

◆

Though she had a regal bearing, Josephine Herbert didn't grow up on Easy Street. She came from a family in Erie, Pennsylvania, that was prosperous enough to send her to a reputable boarding school, but when her father abandoned his family to seek adventure in South America, her mother was left with six children to feed. Instead of finishing her education, Josephine had to go to work. She got a job setting type on a linotype machine, a clanking contraption that dwarfed her in size. It was a relief when she found a job as a secretary. Yet when her father returned from his South American escapade, he was furious, saying she had disgraced the family by working. She never spoke to him again.

When a suitor from the prominent Pershing family came along, Josephine was more than ready to leave home. The couple went to New Mexico to go into the oil business. He struck out and the marriage did, too. Josephine decided to start over in Fort Worth, where her brother Parker was working as a geologist.

In Texas, it was said, people could get a second act, reinvent themselves and begin anew. Both Josephine and Jack Herbert did. Before he came to Texas, Herbert had been married to a *Ziegfeld Follies* showgirl. Josephine later would tell writer John Bainbridge she was working as her brother's secretary when she met dashing Jack Herbert, "And the next thing I knew, I was going through Europe with my diamonds and personal maid."

When the Japanese attacked Pearl Harbor in 1941, her near-golden life was upended. John Herbert enlisted in the Army Air Force at forty-two and was assigned to a bomber squadron in the Pacific.

While her husband was away, Josephine took over management of the Herbert oil companies. She went to the office every day and learned the business.

A few days before Christmas in 1942, she sat down at her desk at home to go through the holiday mail. It was late and quiet in the house, a welcome time to catch up. To her surprise, Mrs. Herbert discovered a telegram in the stack of Christmas cards. It was from General Douglas MacArthur, the Supreme Commander of Allied Forces in the Southwest Pacific.

The telegram read: *"The officers and enlisted men of the Third Bombardment Group join me in extending to you our deepest sympathy on the loss of your husband on November 24, 1942, while on a combat mission in New Guinea. Captain Herbert was one of our best officers, and we all share your sorrow."*

Only later, after two surviving crew members made it to safety in New Guinea, did Josephine learn her husband's crewmates pulled him from the shattered cockpit to the wing of the plane after it was shot down. He was so severely wounded that they could not save him. They had to leave dashing Jack Herbert with the plane.

Josephine Herbert was left with two young daughters, Joyce and Joanne, and an oil business. The widow Herbert was now the principal owner. "I had prepared myself," she said later. "I knew how to take over."

The business prospered in Josephine's cool and capable hands. Debts were paid. New wells were discovered. Though she didn't have a college degree, Josephine Herbert knew how to get things done.

❖

Five years passed before Josephine Herbert married again. This time, she chose Bruno Graf, an urbane European who pronounced his last name "Groff." Though born in Berlin, he went to school in Switzerland and preferred to say he was Swiss since Germany's reputation had been tarnished by two world wars. Bruno was no movie star, but he was good company and had the courtly manners needed for social circles. He kissed women's hands.

The Grafs drew attention wherever they went. Newspapers reported their Atlantic crossings on the *Queen Elizabeth* and *Île de France*. Society columns noted their dinners at the Colony Club in New York. They even mentioned the full-length, tourmaline mink coat that Josephine wore to a Fort Worth lecture, perhaps because it was the same tawny color as her hair, which she had magically transformed from brunette to blonde.

However, it soon became apparent that continental Bruno Graf did not fit comfortably in Fort Worth. The city had an informal Western style and was proud of it. It was called "Cowtown" because in the past, cattle drives brought droves of livestock from Texas ranches to the Fort Worth stockyards, where they were fattened up and shipped north to become steak dinners for the rest of the country.

Even after the stockyard business dwindled, the Fort Worth Stock Show and Rodeo remained one of the social highlights of the year. Men wore pricey boots and cowboy hats to watch the calf-roping and barrel races. Women showed off their turquoise jewelry from Santa Fe. It was great fun.

But Bruno Graf preferred reading and playing the piano. He spoke several languages fluently, yet as Josephine lamented, "There was nobody for Bruno to talk to." He wanted to move to a bigger city. However, her business, home, and closest friends were in Fort Worth. They divorced, and Bruno returned to Europe.

Josephine grew lonely in the mansion by herself. It was not proper to attend social events as an unattached woman—people would talk. Relatively young widows or divorcees like Josephine were in a bind because there were not enough widowers to go around. Constantly having to find a presentable escort was a chore.

Josephine decided to join Bruno abroad. They remarried and lived in a penthouse in Lausanne, Switzerland. It was "a beautiful life," she said later, but she missed the warmth of friends in the United States. Josephine sold her estate in Fort Worth so they could move to the more worldly Dallas in 1958.

They began construction on a house on Park Lane that would set a new standard for elegance. The modern showplace put the Grafs in the top tier of Dallas society—and into the path of a daring intruder.

On the night in 1959 that would prove so memorable, Josephine Graf was looking forward to seeing her old friends in Fort Worth. The Jewel Ball was held at the Ridglea Country Club because it had the largest ballroom in the area. Women wore their best jewelry, so the vast room sparkled with constellations of jewels. New York jewelers such as Harry Winston and Cartier added to the spectacle by bringing their most precious wares to show off. Women were invited to try on the jewelry. "You wore the jewels sitting on a pedestal to have your picture taken with guards all around you," one woman recalled. "People could come and look at you." And if their husbands had a happy evening of drinking, the women got new jewelry.

Because the Ridglea country club was a forty-mile drive from their house in Dallas, the Grafs began dressing for the black-tie ball earlier than usual.

On the way, they were picking up Algur Meadows and his wife, Virginia, to ride with them.

Al Meadows had made his own fortune in oil. At the time, his General American Oil Company had 2,990 oil wells in fifteen states and Canada—and he was drilling for oil in Spain. His new passion was compiling an art collection that would become the largest body of Spanish masterpieces outside of the Prado Museum. If there was a Velasquez or Goya to buy, Meadows bought it. He was what oilmen called "a big damn deal."

The two couples were good friends, so the drive to Cowtown would be an opportunity to catch up on art and political bumbling in Washington.

Because it was January and days were at their shortest, the sun was setting as the Grafs prepared for the ball. They had a vespers cocktail, maybe two, as they dressed. By the time they came down the elevator, it was dark and cold outside.

Yet inside, their house was bathed in an ethereal golden light. The lighting was amplified all around by gold-veined marble floors, gold carpeting, shining ormolu sconces, and gold-anodized columns that held up pale-gold ceilings. The interior glowed at night.

Their butler, a man of impeccable Swiss bearing, was waiting for the couple downstairs. He held open the door of their Rolls-Royce Silver Cloud and eased the car out the side driveway.

What the Grafs didn't know as they pulled away from their golden home was that someone else was watching from the shadows. A ten-foot-high wall protected the property, but apparently, it was not high enough. Someone who wanted to know when the Grafs left could hide unseen in a nearby creek, watching and waiting in the cold for the moment to climb in.

◆

The Graf house on Park Lane stood out in their neighborhood because it was a tour de force of modern architecture. Edward Durell Stone, the architect for the Museum of Modern Art in New York and the Kennedy Center in Washington, DC, designed the house. With typical frankness,

Josephine Graf proclaimed it was "a monument that Edward D. Stone built to himself—with my money."

The Graf house closely resembled the American Embassy in India that Stone had designed. Like the embassy, the Dallas home was designed to deal with hot weather. The second story was shielded by what architects called a brise-soleil, a sniffy French word for a sunscreen. Made of pure white terrazzo, the lattice-like screen added to the house's distinctive look. The Grafs' bedroom was located behind the brise-soleil on the second floor. A ledge four and a half feet wide encircled the upper level. It was wide enough for a person to stand on while looking into the house, although no one anticipated that somebody would.

By far, the most talked-about feature was the one-of-a-kind dining room. The dining table rested on a white marble slab surrounded by water four feet deep. The marble slab appeared to float miraculously on the water.

Guests had to be careful not to make a splash as they walked to the table. But on many evenings, they did. According to one account, banker Fred Florence was helping the hostess to her chair when he backstepped into the water. His hosts borrowed a tux from a waiter so he could continue the dinner in good form.

Falling into the drink at the Grafs' became a status symbol. When oilman Clint Murchison tipped in one night, Effie Cain, the irrepressible wife of oilman Wofford Cain, jumped in to keep him company.

Cocktail parties had become an integral part of socializing in Dallas. People were ready to entertain in a big way after enduring a drought of Biblical proportions. Seven years with little or no rain had taken a harsh toll on the state. Even the prickly pear shriveled up. Texas usually averaged thirty inches of rain a year. Fifteen inches was considered a drought—seven inches for seven long years was living hell. Cattle starved to death because there was no rain to grow grass and no money to buy feed. Hogs chewed on dying cattle in desperation. Farmers fled to cities by the thousands, and never went back to the land.

Many of the drought refugees came to Dallas, although the city was short on water, too. Dallas had to pump in water from the Red River—only to discover the water was so salty, it killed plants. To save the grass in the Cotton Bowl, the groundskeepers drilled a water well in the end zone.

When the dry spell finally ended in the late 1950s, people celebrated. Grass was growing again. Oil was flowing. And Big D was riding high.

Another kind of liquid fueled the celebrations: booze.

"There was a *lot* of drinking," recalled one social insider.

Tellingly, when party hostess Nancy Hamon lost a finger in a painful encounter with a blender, a prosthetic replacement had to be crafted. The designer asked what shape she preferred—bent, slightly bent, or straight. "Just make it look like I'm holding a drink," she instructed.

◆

The night of the Jewel Ball in Fort Worth, the Grafs stayed for the after-midnight dancing and drinks. By the time they got home, it was nearly three A.M.

Because of the late hour, Mrs. Graf placed her jewelry in a dressing table drawer instead of the safe. She was tired. She went to bed.

While she slept, a dark shadow slipped through the bedroom.

The next morning, Josephine Graf got up late. It was nearly noon. As she got dressed, she made a startling discovery:

The jewels she'd worn the night before were not where she left them. They were gone.

The best of her diamonds had disappeared. The diamond necklace. The earrings. The jeweled pin.

And the 20.4-carat ring as big as the Alamo.

2

Fannin and McCaghren

The Graf burglary was my introduction to the rarefied world of the Big Rich in Dallas. It was like getting a peek around the drapes of a private palazzo in Venice. The palazzos in Dallas were a cloistered world, furnished with the best money could buy and insulated from the prying eyes of outsiders—except for an intrepid cat burglar.

The Graf house was such a departure that newspaper accounts reported at length about its "Pompeian splendor." In awe, writers pointed out the master bedroom opened to a terrace three times the size of the bedroom itself. They marveled that the countertops in Mrs. Graf's bathroom were white marble, and the walls were covered in pink silk fabric. A small kitchen adjoined the master suite, and several maid's rooms were on the same floor.

At a time when few people could afford swimming pools, the Grafs had an indoor swimming pool. *Life* magazine published photographs of the pool, pointing out that the water level could be lowered six inches to prevent dampening the furnishings when guests stepped in. The house became the talk of the town.

◆

The thief apparently broke in while the Grafs were sleeping. To reach the jewels in her dressing area, he had to walk by their twin beds. He was close enough to hear the couple breathing. The intruder then tiptoed away with $215,000 in jewelry, the equivalent of $2.2 million today.

When the Grafs called the Dallas Police, word went hurriedly up the chain of command to Capt. Walter Fannin, the head of the burglary and theft department. The minute he heard how much had been taken, Fannin put one of his top detectives—Paul McCaghren—on the case.

A rising star, McCaghren had red hair and a John Wayne swagger. As a Marine in the Korean War, he survived the brutal battle at Chosin Reservoir in 1950. He didn't like to talk about it; in fact, he *wouldn't* talk about it. Records showed temperatures plunged to more than 30 degrees below zero Fahrenheit. The lubrication in rifles froze. Jeep batteries and radios failed. Syringes with morphine froze before the wounded could get relief.

It was so cold that men huddled in front of the exhaust pipes of tanks to find warmth. The parkas and boots that the Pentagon had issued were no match for the sub-zero temperatures. When the men hunkered down under enemy fire or tried to sleep on the icy ground, their feet froze. Eighty-five percent of the soldiers who survived suffered from severe frostbite. McCaghren's feet and legs were never the same, but police work seemed easy after that.

When he made detective, McCaghren still had the build of a high school football player, with broad shoulders and big hands. He exuded raw masculine strength.

If people asked how tall he was, McCaghren liked to say, "Seven foot five." He actually was six foot three. He seemed bigger because he carried himself with authority. He was a natural for police work because he had the kind of instincts a cop needs—a nose for larceny. And there was plenty of larceny around.

◈

McCaghren and Fannin made a good team. Fannin's no-nonsense demeanor tempered McCaghren's bravado. At forty-five, Captain Fannin had the wavy, silver-gray hair of a matinee star. His men called him "Gray Top." He had started as a squad car policeman, which meant a lot of nights rounding up deadbeats and hopped-up soreheads who had knifed or shot somebody. In his nineteen years on the force, Fannin had seen life in the raw.

His men generally respected and liked him. He had a seriousness that invited trust. Reporters described Fannin as even-tempered and well-spoken. One said he had a "gracious manner."

As head of the burglary department, Fannin insisted his detectives wear a suit and tie on the job. Some of the other departments allowed officers to wear western string ties, cowboy hats, and boots. Not Captain Fannin. He wanted his detectives to look more professional. This was not easy for men who came from hardscrabble, rural backgrounds. They had to scrimp to buy suits on sale at Sears, often their first.

Fannin was more fortunate. His wife, Betty, made hats at Neiman Marcus and was a gifted seamstress. She selected quality fabrics and hand-stitched new suits for him. He wanted to look like a man in charge, and he did.

Because of Fannin's strict dress code, his detectives resembled the cast of *Dragnet* when they walked up to the Graf house. On the TV show, tobacco-voiced Sergeant Joe Friday wore a suit and snap-brim hat as he tracked down criminals. Not to be outshone, the Dallas detectives wore fedoras with their suits and ties. They dressed like they thought cops were supposed to look, which meant they were easy to spot.

Knowing they were in upscale territory, the cops nudged Lt. Tyree Leonard forward to ring the doorbell at the Graf house. They thought he would make the best impression because he had attended college for a few years and was a neat dresser. Besides that, he was good-looking, "like a tall Alan Ladd."

A man in a double-breasted suit answered the door. He had a foreign accent and a crisp, highly formal demeanor. After a confusing exchange about whether they were expected or not, Tyree Leonard wasn't sure if he was talking to the owner of the house or the butler. He blurted out, "What are you?"

"I'm Swiss," Bruno Graf answered coolly. "What are *you*?"

"I'm a lieutenant," the flustered Leonard responded. "Nice to meet you, Mr. Swiss."

McCaghren winced as he remembered the moment many years later. "We were country bumpkins who didn't realize that there was a society out there that was so strange to us."

And with that, the detectives crossed over the marble threshold of the Graf mansion and into a world that was nothing like the mean streets they usually patrolled.

◆

Josephine Graf guided the detectives past the floating dining table, the eighteenth-century Chinese Fu dogs, the Ming lacquer armoire, and the Mondrians. Tyree Leonard, who had a habit of saying "Lovely, just lovely" about everything whether it was a flat tire or a good meal, fell back on his favorite phrase, muttering "Lovely, just lovely" as they walked through the house.

Mrs. Graf took the detectives up the spiral staircase to her bedroom on the second floor. "They were right *there*," she said, pointing to the dressing table. "Not all my jewels—just $215,000 worth—and now they are *gone!*"

At the time, it was the biggest jewel theft in Dallas history. The most valuable item was the 20.4-carat diamond ring. The big stone was flanked by two large, square-cut diamonds. When one of the detectives heard how big the center stone was, he whistled and said, "That's not a diamond, that's a skating rink!"

The burglar also took her platinum pin shaped like a bird on a twig. It contained fourteen marquise diamonds and 269 other diamonds. On top of that, he took a bracelet with forty-four marquise diamonds, 114 diamond baguettes, and seven round diamonds. And he grabbed several earrings and chokers, all studded with diamonds.

The cunning thief had hit the jackpot.

At first, police assumed the thief came in through the tall sliding glass doors on the first floor. Yet there was no sign the doors had been jimmied. Instead, to their surprise, the police found faint marks that showed the intruder had pried open a bathroom window on the second floor, near the Grafs' bedroom.

But that seemed impossible! To reach the window, the thief had to climb the ten-foot-high wall around the house and make a running leap to the ledge on the second floor.

It was a remarkable feat. Yet waffle-sole shoe prints on the top of the wall confirmed someone had indeed run along the narrow wall, then vaulted through the air to the ledge.

The intruder appeared to have carefully removed his shoes before entering the house. Vacuuming the carpet produced not a single trace of dirt. The thief must have walked through the master bedroom in his stocking feet while the couple slept nearby.

The police could find no fingerprints. The burglar apparently wore gloves, perhaps surgical gloves or thin leather golf gloves. He was as precise as a saboteur—and knew exactly where to look for the jewels that Mrs. Graf had taken off.

Mrs. Graf told police that she did not have on her hearing aids at the time, so she didn't hear the thief, but she had a feeling he was inside her closet when they went to bed.

"Isn't that odd?" she said, to no one in particular.

McCaghren asked to use a phone and called Capt. Fannin: this was no ordinary burglary.

3

The Hunt Begins

The Graf burglary made headlines as far away as California, New York, Wisconsin, South Dakota, North Carolina, and Missouri. Other newsworthy things were happening that week—the first NASA astronauts were announced and rigged quiz shows were causing a scandal—but the theft of a king's ransom in jewels made the front pages as well.

If I hadn't already been drawn to the case, reading the news stories secured the hook. *Who was he? Where is he?*

I will admit, at five-one with gray-white hair, I didn't look like a detective. Thanks to a West Texas accent, I didn't sound like one either. I considered this a great advantage. I wasn't a jaded private eye who spent most evenings alone with a bottle of Scotch and a jazz album. Nor would I be mistaken for the secretary-sidekick who tags along in a tight skirt and stiletto heels.

No, in my own way, I was as unassuming as Agatha Christie's rumpled Miss Marple, but without the hat and knitting. And as mystery readers know, it's always a mistake to underestimate someone who seems ordinary.

After years of newspaper work, I'd learned how to ask questions and read faces. You could say I'd been *around*—or at least nearby. When I covered the police beat, I learned the bad guys weren't all bad, and the good guys weren't all good. In this case, some of the victims weren't so innocent themselves.

◆

As I started my search, I wanted to make sure the King of Diamonds was as special as people thought he was, someone worth pursuing. I contacted policemen who investigated other high-dollar burglaries, starting with Cornell Abruzzini, a detective in affluent Greenwich, Connecticut. Abruzzini spent years searching for Blane Nordahl, who was known as the "Burglar to the Stars" because he stole silver from Ivana Trump, Bruce Springsteen, and other celebrities. Police estimated Nordahl committed 150 burglaries in ten states and got away with $3 million in silver. Abruzzini considered Nordahl a criminal genius, likening him to Lex Luthor, Superman's nemesis.

Yet, as good as Nordahl was, he was arrested eight times and served time in prison. "For your jewel thief to stay in *one* area and *not* get caught for that long is highly unusual," Abruzzini said. He explained that master burglars usually move from city to city to avoid arrest. And if they keep stealing, they usually get caught. Each burglar has a pattern, he said, and police get wise to the pattern. "You rarely catch them sneaking out a window," Abruzzini said. "Some detail trips them up, like a store receipt, a tool left behind, a footprint, a license plate—or an ex-girlfriend."

But nothing tripped up the Dallas thief, I noted. He got away.

Next, I talked to Kent McClanahan, a former Texas policeman who handles jewel theft cases for a national law firm. He agreed the Dallas thief was out of the ordinary. "Very few cat burglars could pull that off, walking into bedrooms while people were in there," he said. "You would have to have nerves of steel. Most people in Texas are armed. Walk on their carpet, and you might be looking at a gun."

At his recommendation, I checked with Scott Guginsky, a veteran from the New York Police Department. He's now the vice president of a security alliance that represents thousands of jewelry stores. Guginsky said most big-dollar jewel thefts these days are drug-related or carried out by organized gangs of "Colombians, Russians, Serbs, and Uzbekis." For example, the Serbian-led gang called the Pink Panthers got away with $10 million of Kim Kardashian's jewels in 2016 in Paris. Police estimate that "Les Pinks" have stolen more than half a billion dollars in gold and gems in thirty-five countries.

In contrast, the King of Diamonds appeared to be a solo operator who preyed on the same area over and over again. "It almost seems *vindictive,*" Guginsky said.

Then he told me a story that made me see the case in a new light.

Guginsky said his family went out to dinner at Burger King one night. He was supposed to turn on the porch light—and forgot. When his family returned, they discovered a burglar had taken the few pieces of jewelry they owned, items that had been passed down in the family. "I was ten," he remembered. "After all these years, I still remember that night. Every now and then, I will go online and look for a certain piece, with no luck. It was a unique snake ring from Germany that someone gave my father. It meant a lot to him. But it's still gone."

His story brought home to me that break-ins are not just about the things that are taken, but the scars that are left. Though burglary doesn't get the attention of violent crimes such as rape and murder, it takes a toll. As one of the cops put it, "Burglaries are traumatizing. People think, 'This man was in my bedroom, where I am with my wife, where I take my bath.' That has an effect on people."

Throughout history, violating a home and stealing a family's possessions has been considered a grievous offense. Well into the late 1800s, burglars were hanged, feet dangling, eyes bulging.

In Texas, burglary of a domicile is still considered a serious felony. That meant the King of Diamonds risked twenty years in prison or up to ninety-nine years for repeat offenses as a habitual criminal. Had he been caught, there would have been lifelong consequences.

◆

After talking with the burglary experts, I realized no one raised red flags to discourage me. Or yawned. They agreed the case was unique. So I went to work.

I photocopied all the articles about the jewel thefts in library files and spread them across the floor of my home in chronological order.

I see your path, Mr. King, I thought. *I am following you.*

From then on, I would spend more evenings with the jewel thief than my friends. He became a constant presence in my life. Many of the police felt the same way. Once you started puzzling about the thief, it was hard to stop.

Capt. Fannin put the entire burglary unit of the Dallas Police Department on the Graf case, more than fifty officers. Photos of the missing jewels were sent to police departments across the country. A nationwide manhunt was on.

The FBI put out alerts. Nothing turned up. Interpol flashed descriptions of the gems to diamond markets across the world. Stolen jewels usually traveled to diamond centers in Manhattan and Antwerp, or criminal entrepôts in Moscow, Marseille, and Istanbul. But no sightings were reported.

The DPD asked Scotland Yard and the Mexican Federal Police to keep an eye on international thieves—and their girlfriends. Again, nothing showed up.

Unfortunately, this was the norm. Although the FBI cited burglary as one of the most frequently committed crimes in the 1960s, police rarely recovered stolen jewels. In 1965 alone, insurance experts estimated $50 million in gems and precious metals were stolen, with only a 7 percent recovery rate.

Nevertheless, insurance companies put out the word they would pay—no questions asked—10 percent of the value of each piece of Josephine Graf's jewels recovered. Such offers were not usually ignored, but no one came forward.

Knowing the odds were against him, Fannin ordered his men to dig deeper. They checked parcel shipments. They pored over airline passenger lists for known criminals. They contacted car rental agencies. They checked guest registers at hotels and motels.

Fannin's team squeezed their informants, but none sang. They even tracked down a burglar who broke into Josephine Graf's Fort Worth home a decade before. Did he know who took the jewels? "No," he swore, "I have no idea who this joker is."

The police moved on. They investigated every servant who worked in the Graf house. They questioned every deliveryman, repairman, or recent visitor.

They even dismantled twelve feet of the metal covering on top of the wall around the Graf's house so it could be examined in the FBI crime lab.

What did it add up to?

A big fat nothing. The waffle-patterned footprints from the top of the Graf wall remained the only evidence the police had. Police guessed he wore pull-on galoshes of some kind to sneak up the creek behind the house instead of risking the street.

Leads poured in. The detectives checked out a former Rhodes scholar who stole pistols, a safecracker, and three guys peddling phony jewelry. Nothing panned out.

Fannin's squad was expending a tremendous amount of effort, yet every trail led to a dead end.

A week after the Graf break-in, an enterprising reporter from the *Dallas Times Herald* scored an exclusive interview with Fannin. But John Lingo Schoellkopf was not a typical police reporter. He was from an old-line Dallas family and was sent East to get an education. After the Choate prep school in New England, he came home to attend Southern Methodist University. But going to class was not his top priority. Schoellkopf was a maverick. Instead of playing the usual team sports, he took up Golden Gloves boxing and won more bouts than he lost. For a guy with country club manners, he fought hard and could take a punch.

Schoellkopf looked good in a tuxedo, but he was not drawn to the social life that he was born to. Instead, he was drawn to the gritty side of the city, the gamblers and grifters and drinkers who were great storytellers. He had dreams of writing a great American novel.

Thanks to family connections, he got a job at the *Dallas Times Herald*, the city's more liberal evening paper. A relative, Jim Chambers, was the publisher. As *Herald* veteran A. C. Greene put it, Schoellkopf was lucky to have been born into a "town full of uncles." He was on the fast track to becoming publisher, so Schoellkopf learned how to type in a hurry.

By taking weekend shifts and unglamorous assignments, Schoellkopf earned the respect of reporters who had derided him as the "staff nephew." They stopped by his desk to admire a photo of his winning boxing match; his opponent was on the mat.

When the paper's regular police reporter, George Carter, was off duty, Schoellkopf filled in. He had just turned twenty-one when he scored a scoop—an interview with Captain Fannin about the Graf burglary. The rookie reporter came away with fresh information on the hunt for the jewel thief. It was only later that some of his colleagues wondered if he could be the thief himself.

Schoellkopf was in his late seventies when I located him through friends. He agreed to meet at his North Dallas home. Although fifty years had passed, Schoellkopf remembered his interview with Fannin vividly. "It was a slow day," he recalled. "I decided to get as much as I could about the Graf case. I had a long interview with Fannin, who was working out his thoughts on what was going on."

Fannin confided that after seven days, the cost of the manpower on the nationwide hunt had already surpassed the value of the jewels. Though their search was fruitless, he was "more convinced than ever" that the thief was "a local house burglar who struck it rich."

For one thing, Fannin said, local newspapers had reported that the Grafs were attending the ball in Fort Worth. Anybody who could read would have known they would be dressed in their best.

Secondly, the thief left valuable items in the looted drawers. Fannin theorized that a more experienced "second-story man" would have taken everything. The pros tended to sweep everything into a bag or their pockets, Fannin explained. They sorted out the best items later.

Thirdly, the thief took an enormous gamble that he would not be heard as he tiptoed across their bedroom. An experienced burglar would prefer to go into an empty house. Or would settle for the silverware on the ground floor.

Fourthly, the thief swiped $25 from the handbag that Mrs. Graf left in the bathroom. Fannin didn't think an experienced jewel thief would have done so. Twenty-five bucks was penny-ante stuff.

It added up to an amateur who hit it big.

Fannin theorized the thief was already inside the home when the Grafs returned. Or he stood on the ledge outside and watched as Mrs. Graf put the jewels in the dresser.

Yet the simple truth was that after a week of the most intense manhunt of his career, Walter Fannin couldn't say anything for sure.

And he was not happy about it.

4

The Cat Returns

When detectives looked through their files, they discovered the Graf burglary wasn't the first by the wily jewel thief. Similar thefts had been occurring since 1954. None were large enough to trigger alarm bells like the Graf case, but there were dozens of unsolved thefts in the upscale areas of Highland Park, University Park, and Preston Hollow.

"He's picking those jewels like cherries," Fannin said in awe. The thief had snatched jewels from a wealthy widow, a cotton merchant, an insurance executive, and more.

There were indications the thief tried to get into other houses. Mrs. F. C. Dunn, who kept several thousand dollars' worth of jewels in her bedroom, was home alone when she saw a small light outside the bedroom window. She slipped from the covers and inched closer to look. A man was trying to open the screen. Mrs. Dunn tiptoed to her bedside table and dialed the police. The prowler must have heard the telltale sound of a rotary dial clicking. He fled, leaving waffle-sole footprints outside. Mrs. Sanders Campbell was also alone in her Preston Hollow home one night when she heard someone jiggling the lock of a glass door to the patio. Thinking quickly, she scared the intruder away by flicking the bedroom lights on and off. Once again, the prowler fled, leaving waffle prints behind.

The thief did better at the home of oilman Wofford Cain in Highland Park. His wife Effie was the spirited soul who jumped into Josephine Graf's dining room moat to keep their friend Clint Murchison company. Everyone liked Effie. She was fun and good-hearted. Yet while she and her husband were out one evening, the light-fingered thief helped himself to $45,000 of her jewels, the equivalent of $434,000 in 2022.

Then he hit the home of car dealer Felix Doran and got away with a bigger haul: $53,000 in diamonds. Fannin noticed the burglar seemed to take only the biggest and best jewels. He only took women's jewelry and ignored the expensive Rolex watches that men wore. In one burglary, he sifted through all the jewelry, then left without taking any of it. He was a very picky thief.

Police had not connected the earlier burglaries until the electrifying Graf burglary caught their attention. Yet after the Graf burglary, the biggest of them all, the break-ins seemed to stop. Police wondered if the thief had left town. Was he lying low because the Graf burglary generated so much heat?

Eight months went by.

Then the thief struck again.

◆

On Saturday, October 10, 1959, he broke into a home on Miron Drive, a wooded lane in Preston Hollow that was planted with well-appointed homes. This time, he got away with $53,000 in jewelry, a significant haul.

The owner of the house was surprising: Josephine Graf's daughter.

This was certainly unexpected.

Was the family connection a coincidence? Or part of a plan?

Joanne Herbert Stroud had the same blonde hair and pale blue eyes as her mother, but a gentler demeanor—Josephine Graf with fabric softener. She had made her society debut in New York as well as Fort Worth. And summered every year at their family home in Southampton.

Even so, sipping cocktails with the Social Register was not her end goal. Joanne Herbert was determined to earn an academic degree, something her mother had to forego. At the elite Foxcroft school in Virginia, students learned to ride, speak French, read Latin, and above all, to have poise. Joanne Herbert went on to earn a PhD.

On the afternoon of the burglary, Joanne and her husband, Ethan Stroud, an attorney, went to the annual Texas-OU football game. While the Strouds were cheering with thousands of fans in the Cotton Bowl, the jewel thief sneaked into their home.

Six people were inside: a fifty-year-old nanny, a cook, a laundress, and three children. None of them saw or heard the thief.

When Joanne Stroud returned from the game and discovered her home had been invaded, she was anxious about the safety of her family. Her children were seven, five, and nearly three at the time. As a mother, she said, it was chilling to think a criminal was inside the house with her children. "You feel vulnerable," she explained. "Your nest, your security, isn't so secure. We had a feeling of being violated. No one feels quite the same after that."

The thief took seven rings, including a unique engagement ring with a round diamond surrounded by petal-shaped diamonds, like a flower. The thief also walked away with several bracelets, clips, and earrings, a rich afternoon's work.

Fannin and McCaghren suspected advance planning. The thief took the jewels from an antique Chinese cabinet that would not have been readily apparent as a repository for jewelry. Had someone snooped around the bedroom during a social event? Or plied information from a servant?

The thief knew where to go. The master bedroom was at one end of the Stroud house, somewhat isolated from the other rooms and next to the driveway. He knew he could enter the bedroom without being seen.

Once again, the thief took only jewelry, no other valuables. There was no ransacking to indicate he had to search for the jewels. There were no fingerprints on sliding doors. Overshoe tracks were found—this time, they led to a nearby creek, but no mud or dirt was tracked into the house.

The Stroud burglary appeared to be the work of the same skilled burglar who slipped into the Graf house, perhaps a master burglar. And indeed, there was a master burglar in town that weekend.

◆

His name was Harold Hambleton Channell, and he had a record of more than forty arrests. After a 100-mph chase, Channell was captured the year before in Connecticut with cash and jewelry he took from a Greenwich financier. While his charges were on appeal, Channell flew into Dallas for the weekend, like stopping by an ATM. He let himself into the home of J. B. Orand, an automobile dealer who lived on Turtle Creek Boulevard, a scenic street lined with heritage oak trees.

While the Orands' daughter Nell went to the UT football game with her college friends, Mrs. Orand remained at home to wait for a telephone repairman. She was upstairs alone when she encountered a gray-haired man on the stairs.

At first, Mrs. Orand assumed the man was the repairman. As they talked, however, she noticed he didn't have on a uniform. And didn't have tools.

Growing increasingly anxious, Mrs. Orand told him, "I want you to turn around and leave this house right now!"

After the man backed down the stairs and darted out of the house, she called the University Park police. Chief Forrest Keene recognized the description of the intruder: Harold Channell, one of the most wanted jewel thieves in the nation. Keene called the FBI.

Channell had been stealing since World War I. Quick-witted and fleet-footed, Channel once pulled off a $5 million jewel theft. Between jail stints, he slipped into society soirees to scout targets. He got away with some of his slickest jewel thefts by boldly walking into homes and pretending to be the friend of a friend when interrupted.

When the FBI put out the word about his Dallas attempt, Channell was subjected to such an intense national hunt that he surrendered in Florida. However, he refused to answer questions about his Dallas trip.

Capt. Fannin wanted a crack at interrogating Channell. He was on the verge of flying to Florida when results came in from two faint fingerprints found on Mrs. Stroud's jewelry box. Fannin's hopes were pinned on those two prints. A match with Channell would solve the Stroud case and possibly the burglary at her mother's house. It would take the heat off Fannin and his department.

But the fingerprints did not match. Harold Hambleton Channell did not steal the jewels at the Stroud house. Someone else had—and he was still at large.

Deflated, Capt. Fannin ordered his team to go back through the list of unsolved burglaries. Perhaps there were clues they'd missed.

Lt. McCaghren put together a spreadsheet to track the King's methodology. He numbered each characteristic—#2 for overshoe tracks at the scene, #5 for some valuable items left behind, #15 for a nighttime burglary, and so forth.

A clear pattern emerged. The spreadsheet became the paper trail of one of the most skilled jewel thieves in the country.

Two months after the Stroud case, another burglary jangled bells. A thief jimmied a sliding door and broke into the home of Willard E. Walker, a financier and oilman who lived in Highland Park. Police realized the same thief had broken into the home earlier that year, but only reaped $300 in jewelry. He returned eleven months later, which was unusual. This time, he got away with $5,000 in platinum and diamond jewelry.

The Walker family assumed the thief was someone who worked for them because Mrs. Walker kept her best jewelry in a place that only a domestic worker might notice. She hid the jewelry under the removable seat of a fabric-covered chair at her dressing table.

Yet after interrogating the domestic staff and occasional workmen, the police couldn't tie any of them to the theft. They added the Walker burglary to their new spreadsheet: Overshoe tracks? Check. Some jewelry left behind? Check.

Police were getting a handle on the modus operandi of the thief. Now that they knew his pattern, they hoped to catch him in the act.

However, rather inconveniently, the burglaries paused again.

5

The Grand Hotel

M onths went by. Was the thief waiting in the shadows to strike again? Or languishing in prison somewhere?

The police were under intense pressure from city hall, the media, and the insurance industry to solve the Graf case. Fannin began to wonder if the same thief had pulled off several jewel thefts at the new Statler Hilton hotel.

Just as the Graf house was a shiny temptation, the Statler offered an enticing target for thieves. When the hotel opened in 1956, it was touted as "The First Modern American Hotel," an icon of mid-century design. Modern architecture had become increasingly valued as the city sought national distinction. Sophisticated architecture was costly, but it sent the desired message: money lives here.

The Statler architect, William B. Tabler, was credited with transforming travelers' tastes after World War II with his hotel designs. In contrast to older hotels that looked like European manors, Tabler created Hilton hotels in New York and Washington, DC, that looked like sleek office buildings. He sheathed the Dallas Statler in panels of glass and color-coated metal. There was nothing like it. It *gleamed.*

When the Statler opened, the celebration lasted four days and nights. The newly rich flocked to the hotel because it boasted so many "firsts." It had elevator music and a rooftop swimming pool. There were twenty-one-inch, black-and-white Westinghouse TVs in every room. And a landing pad on the roof so guests could arrive by helicopter. ("Can you imagine *that*?" people said.) The Statler ballroom could seat two thousand guests, big enough for a convention crowd, charity balls, or a performance by Elvis Presley.

Then jewel thieves spoiled the party.

In the space of fifteen months, thieves pulled off three jewelry heists at the Statler as well as thefts at other Dallas hotels. A growing number of guests went home without their diamonds.

And Walter Fannin's phone was ringing.

At first, Fannin thought the outbreak might be connected to a spate of hotel heists around the country. A ring of jewel thieves from Florida appeared to be involved. Then Fannin noticed that the Dallas hotel thefts mostly happened when society balls were held at hotels. A check of room registrations showed a handsome rogue was staying at one of the downtown hotels when $50,000 in jewelry was stolen from a room. Police learned the man was a frequent escort for society women—what used to be called a gigolo. He preferred the term playboy.

On closer inspection, it turned out the same gigolo-playboy was present in another hotel when $100,000 worth of gems were taken from a guest at a charity ball. He had an unusual name—Jasper Kirksmith.

I kept the name in the back of my mind. Months later, I ran across the same name while searching through FBI records online. It was the kind of late-night discovery that snaps you awake. A 1961 FBI report said a suspect named Jasper Karl Kirksmith might be involved in recent Dallas jewel thefts and hotel "prowls."

According to the FBI, Kirksmith also was a guest at a Florida hotel when a burglary occurred. The thief got away with $105,000 in jewelry, furs, and cash.

Called in for questioning, Kirksmith said yeah, he had heard about a Florida burglary, but no more. The acknowledgment wasn't enough to arrest him, but enough to keep an eye on him.

◆

The Graf house and the Statler hotel were not the only architecturally significant venues to figure in the burglary drama. Not far from the Graf house, famed architect Frank Lloyd Wright designed a home for a millionaire named John Alexander Gillin. Essentially, it was an 11,000-square-foot bachelor pad, built for entertaining of all kinds.

Gillin got rich by founding National Geophysical Co., which provided seismic services for oil exploration. Gillin was quirky, most people said, so it was no surprise he commissioned an unusual house. From the air, it looked like a spacecraft with wings. The wings contained the bedrooms. The extra-large swimming pool featured a shallow tanning ledge, where six-foot-four Gillin could stretch out in the water and get a tan. And, in keeping with the times, there was a bomb shelter big enough for a very tall man. These were not typical Frank Lloyd Wright features.

Though Gillin was socially awkward, he somehow got along with the temperamental architect. Retail genius Stanley Marcus had commissioned Wright to build a house but gave up in frustration. He called off the deal when Wright refused to include adequate closets ("for things you don't need," Wright said). Nor would Wright include air conditioning (not necessary in the "balmy" Dallas climate, Wright decreed).

The cancellation of the Marcus project left the Gillin home as the lone Frank Lloyd Wright house in the city. A copper dome crowned the exterior. Inside, an oversized stone fireplace anchored a hexagonal living area. To reinforce the geometric look, Wright designed a table for the dining room in the form of a parallelogram and used acute angles of 60 and 120 degrees throughout the house. Even the closets were oddly shaped. After a visit, socialite Nancy O'Boyle observed, "You would be stabbed if you leaned against the wall at the wrong angle."

All those angles meant custom millwork, which consumed time and money. When finally finished in 1958, the house was unique, even for Frank Lloyd Wright.

People began asking, "Who is John Gillin?"

Outside of the oil business and debutante events, where Gillin sometimes escorted society belles, few knew Gillin's name. However, they knew Frank Lloyd Wright's name, and they were impressed, which was the idea. Having a "statement home" meant people wanted to come to dinners, even though Gillin, who wasn't good at small talk, would sometimes leave the table before dessert and go to bed.

His private "stag parties" were another matter. Making conversation wasn't the point. Party girls were the appetizers. A PR executive who attended one of the parties noticed a lot of people going into the kitchen. He peeked in and saw that guests were dipping into saucers of cocaine. He whispered to his wife, "We need to go home." He was afraid the cops might come. But they never did.

Instead, John Gillin only came to police attention when he reported in November 1961 that a burglar took $330 in cash from his home. Because the thief pried open a sliding door and the house was near a creek, McCaghren added the burglary to their spreadsheet. Otherwise, the cash grab did not fit the King's pattern.

Yet John Gillin's name would come up again. One of Fannin's memos noted that a friend of Gillin's procured women for him. Though the gawky millionaire didn't have the kind of looks or charm that attracted women, he had enough money to pay someone to find "dates" for him. The name of the procurer rang a bell:

Jasper Kirksmith, the same man suspected in the hotel thefts.

I started a list of suspects and put Jasper Kirksmith's name at the top. Then I pinned it to the wall where I could look at it every day, just like the "murder boards" the cops had on TV.

6

The Red Scare

During the lull in jewel thefts, Capt. Fannin pressed his men to keep looking. "Get your butts out there!" Maybe in stronger words.

But nothing turned up.

There were other dangers to worry about. The jewel thief was pushed off the front page when the Soviet Union shot down an American spy plane. Then the Berlin Wall went up. President Kennedy advised all prudent families to get a bomb shelter.

Americans had been on edge since the Soviets sent their Sputnik satellite into space in 1957. Then the Soviets sent up a dog. And a man. Now Americans feared they were putting missiles in Cuba, just ninety miles from Florida.

A war of nerves was underway. Though the Soviet threat was real, people in Dallas went overboard. City leaders built a super-sized bomb shelter under the state fairgrounds so they could survive a nuclear attack. Thousands joined the John Birch Society, which claimed Harry Truman and Dwight Eisenhower were "dupes" of the Communist Party. Even the Dallas Junior League got involved, blocking a Picasso painting from a charity auction because of the artist's leftist views. Worse, radical elements of the Birch Society shouted down UN Ambassador Adlai Stevenson at a speech, rocked his car, and threatened his safety.

Considering the high anxiety, it should have been a minor event when the jewel thief reappeared in 1961. But when the King of Diamonds went back to work, he struck with greater daring. He hit the homes of the rich again and again and again.

The King was back.

He broke into the home of W. W. Lynch in April 1961. Lynch was a highly visible figure in those days because he was the chairman of the Freedom Forum, an elite anti-Communist organization formed by business leaders.

As president and chairman of Texas Power and Light, Lynch had a seat at tables of power. He was on the board of Republic Bank, the largest bank in the state, and a leader in the Dallas Citizen's Council, the city's council of elders.

Though the Lynches could be seen regularly at the Dallas Opera and Dallas Country Club, they seemed an unusual target for the jewel thief. They weren't part of the crowd that jetted around the world for a cocktail.

In fact, Martha Lynch won standing ovations as "Dallas's First Lady of Service" for her devotion to unglamorous causes. She volunteered in poor areas where club women in white gloves didn't normally venture. And when her sons went off to college, Mrs. Lynch cared for foster children in her home. She was known for her deeds more than her diamonds.

Yet while the Lynches were away that weekend, the artful thief climbed over the fence behind their white-brick home. As in other burglaries, he pried open a door and made his way to the master bedroom. He was choosy, taking just a few pieces of Mrs. Lynch's jewelry. The pretty necklace he singled out was valued at $1,634, not a fabulous sum, but the equivalent of $15,000 in 2022.

The necklace must have been exactly what the thief was looking for.

He took it.

The same weekend, the burglar climbed into the Preston Hollow home of J. Glen Turner. Turner was one of the top lawyers in the city. His peers had elected him president of the Dallas Bar Association and the Texas Bar Association.

Glen Turner's success had earned him an English country manor on Gaywood Road. With eleven thousand square feet, the house was big enough for five children. Yet Turner and his family preferred their ranch on weekends.

Turner was a horseman at heart. He bought the Circle T ranch for breeding Tennessee Walking Horses, the high-stepping steeds that pranced like a chorus line. Since the ranch was just twenty-eight miles from Dallas, it became a popular venue for entertaining. Turner added several barns, a racetrack, a boathouse, and a fifty-five-acre lake to the property. And since there was a Cold War going on, he put in a large bomb shelter.

With its manicured pastures and freshly painted barns, the Circle T looked like a movie set. Highland Park resident Guyanne Booth recalled driving to the ranch for a polo match with another couple: "I have never seen so many chauffeurs and so many Rolls-Royces in my life. Nobody drove their own Rolls, of course. We came out with some friends in their Lincoln Town Car, and they said, 'We can't park with the Rolls-Royces, we're not in their rank!' So we parked sheepishly at the other end of the lot. We laughed until we cried about having to apologize for driving a Lincoln.

"There was a lot of polo being played back then," she added. "Dallas had become a very sophisticated town. Too self-consciously sophisticated in some ways, but it *was* fun."

While the Turner family was at their ranch one weekend, the thief sneaked down a creek and over a fence into their backyard. A bay window in the bedroom of one of the Turner sons was not locked. The intruder climbed in like a teenager sneaking in after curfew.

However, as he stepped across the window seat, the burglar left a muddy footprint on the cushions. It had been raining, and he forgot to take off his galoshes. The thief left telltale footprints every step he took, the waffled tracks getting lighter and lighter as he headed down the hall to his target: the master bedroom.

"The guy didn't wander around. He knew exactly where he was going," remembered Glen Turner Jr. "There was a considerable amount of cash in a drawer, but he left that and picked through the jewelry," Turner said. "He got some good pieces and left. Nothing else was disturbed."

The thief walked away with $7,000 in jewels, the equivalent of $65,000 in 2022. Fannin's detectives ordered the domestic staff to take polygraph tests. They all passed.

In retrospect, the police did not understand the mind of the thief—not yet. Although it was true that house thefts are often committed by employees, it didn't make sense that a housekeeper or yardman would leave cash that could be spent without drawing attention, and take jewels that would be risky to sell.

It seemed more likely the thief was someone who just wanted the jewels, and only certain jewels at that. While the rest of the world was on Red Alert, the thief had a mission of his own.

In the months ahead, the thief struck at a relentless pace.

More than $14,000 worth of jewels disappeared from the home of N. J. DeSanders, who owned the Cadillac dealership. People were still talking about the DeSanders break-in when the thief took $16,000 in jewels from the home of Harry Rolnick, founder of Resistol Hats.

And in one of his most daring moves, the thief climbed across the roof to snatch $7,000 in jewelry from attorney Murphy Williams's home in University Park. After climbing up a tree, he inched across the rooftop, then dropped through an upstairs window into the dressing area of the master bedroom. No one in the house heard him. With three diamond rings and a diamond-studded wristwatch in hand, the thief made his way back across the roof, down the tree, and away.

It was a brazen feat.

No wonder people felt they were under siege, at home and abroad. Worrying about communists was one thing; having a thief on your roof was quite another.

7

The Safari King

W hen the thief broke into the Preston Hollow home of oilman
Herbert Klein, it must have been hard to walk through the dark
den without sensing someone was watching. Eyes glinted in the shadows.

Klein, you see, was a big game hunter, and the walls of his house on
Kelsey Road were covered with the heads of his victims. Klein was widely
considered "The World's Greatest Big Game Hunter." He had collected
more than 650 game trophies, becoming the only man to kill one of every
wild animal species in the North American continent—some that were
later extinct. He shot wolves, mongooses, fifteen species of owls, even a
rare Mongolian argali.

His house looked like a Madame Tussaud version of *Wild Kingdom*.
Full-sized lions and bears stood around the den, forever muted.

One horrified guest discovered when she used the guest bathroom that
even the toilet paper was held in place with truncated deer feet. She told
her husband she wanted to leave.

Yet a certain jewel thief wanted to come in.

On a cold January night, while most of Dallas was asleep, the thief pried
open the sliding glass doors of the Klein patio. He made his way through
the darkened house, step by step, quiet as snowfall.

Then he left.

What scared the thief away? The unblinking eyes of the deceased? A noise? No matter. The thief withdrew, leaving traces of mud and waffle prints where he entered. He shifted to another prospect not far away: the Ray Smith home on Audubon Place.

Like Herb Klein, Ray Smith was an oilman. He had one of those orphan-to-millionaire stories that were as common as Cadillacs in those days. After both of his parents died, Smith worked odd jobs, saving enough to buy a bobtail truck to haul fuel to oil rigs. That secondhand truck was the beginning of a trucking network in fifteen states and his own drilling company. Mr. Smith could afford to live down the street from mega-millionaire Clint Murchison Sr.

Smith and his wife, Mabel, were entertaining friends that weekend when the jewel thief sneaked into their house. The Smiths didn't hear the prowler remove the screen on a patio door. Their dogs didn't bark.

However, something scared the thief away. Perhaps someone walked by the bedroom where the thief was hiding, coming too close for comfort. The thief left, leaving waffle-print tracks outside the house.

Afterward, the Smiths found it odd that their dogs didn't alert them that an uninvited guest was in the house. They usually barked aggressively at strangers.

The burglar returned to Klein's trophy-filled house on a New Year's Eve. This time, he climbed through a bathroom window. And this time, he got what he wanted: five select pieces of jewelry valued at $75,000.

While the Kleins slept nearby, the thief gently opened the drawer where Mrs. Klein kept her jewelry. His take included a diamond bracelet with 216 diamonds and a $25,000 platinum ring with a large center diamond flanked by baguette diamonds. The ring alone would be worth $215,000 in 2022 dollars.

Mrs. Klein had worn some of the jewels that evening to a party. The thief must have banked on the probability that Mrs. Klein would arrive home at a late hour and place the jewelry in her dresser, not a safe.

A grandson and two of his college friends were sleeping in a neighboring bedroom. None of them heard the thief come and go.

After the Kleins reported the theft, police found partial footprints with the familiar pattern on top of a retaining wall.

Florence Klein was not a member of the flashy conga-dance crowd in Dallas, but she did have expensive jewels. Having a husband who was gone a lot had its compensations. While he went on business and hunting trips, she busied herself with teas and luncheons. And when her globe-trotting husband was available for social events, she got to wear the jewels he gave her to atone for his absence.

Like many wildcatters, Klein was rough-edged and happy that way. He did not consider finger sandwiches and petit fours a meal. He liked being called "Bwana" in places like Botswana. According to a natural history publication, Klein had "the face of a boxer and shoulders of a halfback." He kept his gray hair trimmed close long after flattops went the way of the Tasmanian tiger.

When Fannin's detectives arrived on the scene, they were impressed that the thief dared to return. A rack of expensive Weatherby rifles covered one wall, the kind of high-velocity weapons that could propel a shot through bulletproof glass.

The King of Diamonds took a big gamble that he could snatch the jewelry without waking up the dead-eye shooter. And he succeeded.

Fannin was a fisherman, not a hunter, so he hadn't heard of Herb Klein. McCaghren filled him in: Herbert Washington Klein learned how to drill for oil in Wyoming. The oil boom in Texas drew him to Dallas. His Dixie Drilling Co. did so well that he could spend time hunting critters as well as oil.

Klein's sense of adventure led him to pursue a drilling project on the island of Cuba. Drilling prospects were waning in Texas, so oilmen were looking farther afield for discoveries. Centuries before, Spanish explorers had reported an unusual substance seeping from the rocks in Cuba. The stories drew oilmen in the 1950s because the island also had 1) a corrupt dictator who could be bribed to do business, 2) gambling, and 3) beautiful women. It was irresistible. Klein and his partners bought up oil leases in Cuba, and so did mega oilmen like Clint Murchison and Everette DeGolyer.

But when Fidel Castro kicked out dictator Fulgencio Batista and began nationalizing American interests, the Dallas oilmen were out of luck. They had to hightail it home. As Klein ruefully put it, "We left some assets in the ground."

Dallas oilmen now had personal as well as political reasons to dislike Fidel Castro and his communist friends in the Soviet Union.

Because so many of the King of Diamonds' early victims—Josephine Graf, Wofford Cain, Willard Walker, Ray Smith, and Herb Klein—had oil fortunes, Fannin and McCaghren began asking, could the thief have a connection to the oil business?

More than a third of the homes hit by the jewel thief belonged to oilmen. And his next victim was one of the biggest.

8

Clint's World

The year 1961 was the burglar's busiest. He hit six homes, one after another, boom, boom, boom—and got away with $155,000 in jewels, the equivalent of $1.4 million in today's dollars.

Police were knocked on their heels.

While they were investigating one burglary, a call would come from another home, and then another. Police cars were racing from address to address.

In mid-April, a call came in about a burglary in Preston Hollow.

This one sent shock waves.

A jewel thief had walked away with sixty-two pieces of jewelry from a home on Audubon Place. The insured value was $95,433—the biggest haul since the break-in at the Grafs' house.

Yet that wasn't the most remarkable thing about the burglary.

The home belonged to oilman Clint Murchison Sr., sometimes described as "the Richest Man in America." Actually, he was only among the top five. Two other Texas oilmen—his friend Sid Richardson and H. L. Hunt—were even richer.

While the thief was sneaking into their home, Murchison and his wife, Ginny, were relaxing in the piney woods of East Texas at their house in the Koon Kreek Klub. The exclusive hunting and fishing club was one of Murchison's favorite getaways.

The members-only haven had a long waiting list. Even Murchison had to wait for someone to die to get in. Over the years, Koon Kreek members included governors, publishers, developers, bankers, and of course, oilmen.

Herman Brown, the head of Brown and Root in Houston, one of the largest construction companies in the world, escaped to Koon Kreek, too. His company built many of the pipelines that kept oil money flowing into Dallas banks. Thanks to connections to powerful politicians like Lyndon Johnson, Brown and Root also got contracts to build roads, dams, and military bases around the world.

Men didn't go to Koon Kreek to make deals, but they certainly made relationships that paid dividends.

Besides the company of high-powered millionaires, Koon Kreek offered the simple pleasures of fishing, duck hunting, and total privacy. The 9,000-acre retreat had three lakes stocked with largemouth bass. Guides baited the hooks and cleaned the fish for guests. "You could be the world's worst fisherman," guests admitted, "and still catch a twelve-pound bass."

Koon Kreek reminded Murchison of the country life he enjoyed as a boy. He grew up in Athens, Texas, a small town ten miles away that was more Southern than Western. At Koon Kreek, the cooks prepared buffets of fried chicken, turnip greens, mashed potatoes, and plenty of pie—pecan pie, buttermilk pie, chocolate pie, and lemon pie with two-inch chiffon tops.

Best of all, Clint Murchison could play cards and dominoes all day and much of the night. At Koon Kreek, it was good to be rich.

◈

The Murchisons were particularly glad to be at Koon Kreek that weekend because a garden tour was scheduled at their home. They could avoid the crowd.

For weeks, local newspapers had printed write-ups about the décor of the home. Society decorator John Astin Perkins had designed the interiors.

Landscaper Joe Lambert terraced the gardens. The articles rhapsodized about the Persian rugs on the parquet floors, the Ming porcelains, the Chinese lacquer screens. The inventory of material richness included Venetian crystal, multiple sets of Royal Doulton china, and antique French tureens that Marie Antoinette would have admired.

No wonder thousands of people came to see for themselves.

When the Murchisons returned home, Ginny Murchison made a startling discovery: some of her best jewelry had been stolen.

When she tried to interrupt her husband to tell him, Murchison waved her away. He was playing cards with friends and wanted to finish his hand.

According to news accounts, his wife teased him, "Well, now you have to buy me some new jewelry."

After he completed his card game, Murchison finally reached for the phone. But instead of calling the Dallas police, he dialed someone else.

He called J. Edgar Hoover.

Murchison knew the FBI chief would take his call.

◆

J. Edgar Hoover had cultivated ties to Murchison and other rich men in Dallas during the Red Scare. He sent his top agent to speak at the Freedom Forum and became a familiar sight around town. People fawned over the FBI chief, offering drinks or dinner. They were starstruck.

With his pug face and protruding Peter Lorre eyes, Hoover looked more like the triggerman in a gangster movie than the nation's top G-man. Even so, the FBI chief had served under six presidents, and at sixty-six, he had no intention of retiring. The secret information he had compiled on politicians was his job security.

Few Americans knew that Hoover had become an oddly neurotic potentate who sent "goon squads" to field offices to ferret out anyone disloyal to him. Even fewer knew he accepted financial favors from people he should have been investigating.

When Hoover visited Dallas, he often stayed with the Murchisons. During racing season, the oilman pampered Hoover and his ever-present companion Clyde Tolson at the Hotel Del Charro in California, which Murchison owned. The FBI chief liked to bet on horses at the racetrack near the hotel. Quite conveniently, Murchison owned the racetrack, too.

Hoover's poolside bungalow at the Del Charro had three bedrooms, two baths, a living room, a fireplace, a kitchen, and two patios. The going rate was $100 a night, the equivalent of $1,000 by 2022, but the FBI chief didn't have to open his wallet. Murchison always picked up the tab.

Later on, Washington power broker Bobby Baker contended, "Murchison owned a piece of Hoover. Rich people always try to put their money with the sheriff because they're looking for protection. Hoover was the personification of law and order and officially against gangsters, so it was a plus for a rich man to be identified with him. That's why men like Murchison made it their business to let everyone know Hoover was their friend. You can do a lot of illegal things if the head lawman is your buddy."

◆

Being buddies with the nation's top lawman did indeed benefit Murchison. His racetrack purchase was a prime example.

As a boy, Murchison had dreamed of owning a champion thoroughbred. He bet on horse races all his life. As soon as he hit it rich in the 1930s, he built Blue Bird Farm in the Trinity River bottoms. The business plan was ingenious: Murchison acquired the land by paying the delinquent taxes, then hired men out of work due to the Depression. The grateful workers transformed the bottomland into a first-class thoroughbred center with stables and tracks. Other acreage was turned into a cotton farm and a cattle-grazing operation. Bunkhouses were made of baked asphalt bricks from the crude oil that flowed from Murchison wells. Even the sand and gravel from the riverbed was put to use for concrete.

Visitors who got a tour were impressed. The barn was so big it made the *Guinness Book of Records*. But they were taken aback when the foreman confided Murchison had some out-of-state friends in the racing business that were scary. He was a rugged old cowhand, but even he felt uncomfortable around them. It was a hint of questionable relationships to come.

When World War II broke out, horse racing was put on hold until a better time. Undeterred, Murchison transported eighty of his best horses to Mexico City to race and shifted his sights to a new dream: buying the premier American racetracks.

In particular, Murchison wanted the Del Mar track in California, thirty minutes away from the seaside resort town of La Jolla. The track was a special prize because of its history. Seabiscuit raced at Del Mar. Legendary jockey Willie Shoemaker rode there. As a bonus, movie stars drove down from Los Angeles for a day at the track. Singer Bing Crosby was an original investor, along with actors like Gary Cooper. Del Mar was one of the top racing venues in the country. And Murchison wanted it.

But there was a significant obstacle. After the original Hollywood owners sold their shares, the track went through a series of hands—and some of those hands belonged to mobsters. The current owner was Al Hart, formerly known as Alfred Harskovitz. A former beer runner for Al Capone in Chicago, Al Hart made a fortune running liquor companies in California. He could afford to open his own bank in Beverly Hills and became a director of Columbia Pictures. Al Hart was sitting pretty. So when Clint Murchison inquired about buying the Del Mar track in 1953, Al Hart said, "No."

Once again, Murchison came up with an ingenious plan. If allowed to buy the track, he promised to donate the proceeds to Boys Inc. Murchison's friend Hoover had inadvertently given him the idea. Hoover had been pressing Murchison to support the youth organization, a pet project. However, Hoover probably did not have in mind linking the boys' organization to a racetrack—and the questionable clientele that came with it.

When the deal drew criticism, Hoover went to Murchison's defense. He told the press that Murchison "would be the last person in the country to use such a plan as a clever tax or business subterfuge." Going a step further, Hoover claimed that the deal would make the nation "more sturdy" because communists were trying to penetrate youth organizations.

To make sure Al Hart got the patriotic message, Hoover sent a couple of FBI agents to visit him.

Murchison got his racetrack.

Some sources say Boys Inc. only received nominal sums from the deal; others say the organization got up to $4 million over the years. One thing is for sure, the arrangement created so much controversy that Murchison's goal of buying more racetracks never got traction.

In the meantime, Murchison went out of his way to keep Hoover's favor. During one visit to Murchison's Del Charro hotel, Hoover complained that he preferred his vacation retreat in Florida because he could reach out the window and pick fresh fruit. Not to be outdone, Murchison had an assortment of fruit trees—lemons, limes, peaches, oranges—flown in overnight and planted around Hoover's bungalow.

And after Murchison bought the Henry Holt publishing house, what was the first book published? J. Edgar Hoover's *Masters of Deceit: The Story of Communism in America*. The profits went to a special FBI fund for Hoover's personal use.

The FBI chief also benefited from oil deals that Murchison set up for him. As journalist Bryan Burrough reported in *The Big Rich*, Hoover didn't share in the losses if the rigs didn't strike oil. But he enjoyed a share of the profits if they did.

So understandably, when Murchison called to report a burglar had broken into his house, his friend J. Edgar Hoover answered right away.

◈

The Murchison break-in added to the pressure on Capt. Fannin. He now had J. Edgar Hoover looking over his shoulder. Fannin knew the FBI chief's Machiavellian reputation. He was walking into a political minefield.

Gathering evidence at the Murchison home presented a dilemma because the theft wasn't discovered until days after the garden show. Footprints and fingerprints from three thousand visitors obscured any evidence. Finding the right fingerprints, Fannin told reporters, was like "looking for a needle in a haystack."

Still, Fannin put more than a third of his detectives on the case, the most intense investigation since the Graf burglary. But no hard leads turned up.

Fannin ordered lie detector tests for all the Murchison servants. There were no helpful results.

The U.S. Fidelity Casualty Co. offered a generous reward. No one came forward.

Police suspected the burglar knew somehow that the jewels were hidden behind a specially designed wall in the hallway. The sliding door covered a row of locked drawers that served as a vault. The burglar found a way to open the door. Then he pried open the drawers full of gleaming jewels.

FBI agents sent the drawers to Washington to be analyzed. The forensics team reported back that the thief used something like a 5/8-inch screwdriver to pry open the drawers. Fannin and McCaghren rolled their eyes—they had already figured that out themselves. Indeed, after an earlier theft, a screwdriver was found near a tree that the burglar had climbed like a ladder into the house.

In some instances, the thief appeared to use a larger tool called a pry bar, commonly found in hardware stores. Wider than a screwdriver, the edge of the bar left a fainter imprint on a door frame or window frame. In one case, Capt. Fannin said the entry marks were so faint, it looked as if the burglar had used a butter knife.

Fannin and McCaghren noticed that once again, the thief left behind more jewels at the Murchison house than he took. Though sixty-two pieces were missing, many more remained. The leftovers were worth $250,000.

Detectives were dumbfounded. *What kind of thief is this?* Who would pick through a fortune in jewels like chocolates in a box? Why would he leave so many valuable pieces behind?

The Murchison incident revived national interest in the Dallas burglaries. People might not have heard of Josephine Graf, but they had heard of Clint Murchison. He was on the cover of *TIME* magazine. *TIME* gushed that the oilman was the "biggest of the big rich," a financial genius who could "add $1 and $1 and get $11 million."

And now, somebody had invaded his house and plundered his treasure.

◆

I knew Murchison's name, but not much more. His unorthodox racetrack deal made me curious. What kind of guy was he? When I looked further, I found his career would make a good case study in business school—but theology school, no.

Young Clinton Williams Murchison started in the middle rather than the bottom because he was born the son of a banker. Even in a small town, or maybe especially in a small town, there are few sons of bankers who don't grow up with the sense that they are entitled because of their daddies.

A tendency to play by his own rules became evident early on when Murchison got caught playing dice at Trinity University. Rather than reveal the other players, he left school. He went to work at the family bank, but got bored with counting money, saying, the bills "stank."

Deal-making interested him more. Before enlisting in the Army in World War I, Murchison got a contract with the Army for East Texas pine. But there weren't enough workers available to do the logging. According to biographers Jane Wolfe and Ernestine Van Buren, Murchison leased several railroad cars and offered free booze at the railyard to unemployed men in San Antonio. Many of them passed out in the rail cars. When they woke up, they discovered Murchison had hitched the rail cars to a train headed to the East Texas timberlands, more than two hundred miles away. With hangovers and no money, the shanghaied men had to chop trees to pay their way home.

When he served in the Army, Lieutenant Murchison came up with another inventive scheme. He took scrap wood at the base, sold it for kindling, and gave the proceeds to the mess fund. He nearly got court-martialed for destroying government property. Still, Murchison remained unconvinced that he should follow rules he disagreed with.

◆

As a teenager, Murchison had learned the basics of cattle trading with his pal Sid Richardson. They made an unusual team. Neither one was a great scholar or athlete. And neither one had the kind of looks to make a Homecoming queen look twice. Murchison was five feet six, somewhat pudgy, and bandy-legged. His blue eyes might have been an asset, but he squinted and wore glasses. Richardson, taller at six feet, had a bull-neck and barrel chest, with a relatively small head perched on top. He walked with a limp from an accident and seemed middle-aged long before he was.

To succeed, both men had to rely on their wits and force of will. They scored their first success buying and selling oil leases. Murchison sold his holdings for $5 million in 1925. Though the country was headed toward a depression, he was a rich man at thirty.

Murchison multiplied his good fortune when he formed Southern Union Gas Company to pipe natural gas in five states. He scored a bigger bonanza when he drilled in the East Texas oil field that H. L. Hunt had uncorked. The giant oil field stretched through five counties and was booming. Murchison got his straw in.

From then on, Murchison's fortunes rose and fell with the oil price, but mostly they grew because he diversified his holdings to hedge against downturns in the oil patch. Besides Henry Holt publishing, he bought *Field & Stream* magazine, the Daisy rifle company, and a fishing tackle manufacturer. He also acquired life insurance companies, bus lines, and banks. By the 1960s, he owned 115 companies—uranium mines, taxis, outdoor theaters, and restaurants.

Murchison called his business method "financing and finagling"—which meant using borrowed money to buy one company, then using that company as collateral to buy another company, then another and another.

✦

Murchison liked to say, "Money is like manure—you have to spread it around to make things grow." That meant spreading around political donations as well as buying companies. Back when Murchison and Richardson were learning how to trade cattle, they discovered it paid dividends to invest in friends in high places, starting with the sheriff's office. For the rest of their lives, Murchison and Richardson courted men in positions of power to protect their business interests.

Toward that end, they funneled fat political contributions to Senator Lyndon Johnson, Senate Majority Leader Sam Rayburn, President Eisenhower, and Vice President Nixon. Sometimes the bundles of hundred-dollar bills were so thick, they wouldn't fit in a standard envelope. According to LBJ biographer Robert Caro, Johnson's lawyer John Connally once left a paper sack with $50,000 from Texas donors in an all-night diner. Another time, Connally hid $40,000 in donations in a drawer in his home, then couldn't remember where he put it. Washington was awash in oil money.

Murchison and Richardson also discovered they could buy sway by pampering politicians with vacations. Murchison transformed Matagorda Island in the Gulf of Mexico into a private retreat where his friends—and political leaders—could hunt, fish, gamble, and swap outrageous stories. To keep up, his friend Sid bought St. Joseph Island and entertained there.

Their hospitality apparently paid off. After President Roosevelt made a fishing trip in 1937 to the island retreats, he dropped his opposition to the oil depletion allowance.

Around that time, Murchison was facing criminal charges for pumping millions in "hot oil" in defiance of government limits. He got off with a $17,500 fine. Just a coincidence, perhaps.

✦

Though he did much to establish the image of a rich Texan, Murchison did not put on airs. He could have had Dom Perignon and caviar but was partial to Jim Beam and homemade chili. He certainly could afford the Brooks Brothers suits that his bankers wore but preferred to work in shorts that looked like lawn-mowing gear. He occasionally went to the Petroleum Club wearing short-sleeved shirts and sandals with no socks. At times, he used a necktie as a belt.

That said, Murchison had his own way of enjoying his fortune. He bought a ranch in the Sierra Madre mountains of northeastern Mexico and called it Rancho Acuna. His wife filled the twenty-room hacienda with antiques—finishing just in time for the Duke and Duchess of Windsor to visit. After the royals departed, Murchison groused that he would have paid $30,000 for them *not* to come. He was not impressed with royal titles, and he did not like to dress up for dinner.

Over time, Murchison acquired more than half a million acres in Mexico. It took hours to fly over the ranch by helicopter. For longer trips, Murchison revamped an army DC-3 with a wet bar. For fun, he liked to fly a planeload of friends to Cuba, where they could enjoy the gambling and floor shows. Showgirls danced under the palm trees, the conga drums pulsated, and the rum flowed all night.

Like oilman Herb Klein, Clint Murchison discovered Cuba's rich potential in the 1950s. He and his partners teamed up with mighty Standard Oil in the Cuban Venezuela Oil Voting Trust (CVOVT). Thanks to a cozy relationship with dictator Batista, CVOVT acquired oil rights to fifteen million acres on the island.

During the bargaining, Murchison was impressed with the work of two negotiators: Russian geologist Georges de Mohrenschildt and a Washington lobbyist named I. I. Davidson. Both were wily and fearless. So he hired them. Murchison knew they could do things behind the scenes without worrying about their consciences.

Every detective story needs a suspicious stranger, and de Mohrenschildt played that role with continental charm. The CIA suspected de

Mohrenschildt worked for German or Soviet or Polish intelligence services. But those countries thought he worked for the CIA. He was a figure of mystery—especially when it was revealed he had befriended accused presidential assassin Lee Harvey Oswald.

Though de Mohrenschildt would show up in the story later, I. I. Davidson had the greater role in Murchison's dealings. Davidson had developed a profitable relationship with Fulgencia Batista by selling him guns and tanks. He opened the door for Murchison's Tecon Construction Company to build a tunnel under the Havana harbor as well as military housing and a hydroelectric plant.

Those Cuban ventures were the beginning of a business relationship with "Irv" Davidson that lasted for decades. As a result, the Murchisons were drawn into associations that would prove problematic, if not illegal.

You see, Davidson's other clients included:

- The CIA
- Teamsters leader Jimmy Hoffa
- New Orleans Mafia boss Carlos Marcello
- Florida Mafia boss Santos Trafficante Jr.

On his tongue-in-cheek business cards, Davidson described himself as someone who could start revolutions, run governments, and quell uprisings.

He was only partly kidding.

On a typical day, he had lunch with White House advisers, helped Coca-Cola do business in Oman, and dined with J. Edgar Hoover. Davidson was so close to Hoover that he led fundraising campaigns for Hoover's foundation. It was no surprise when he sold the first Uzi machine guns to the FBI.

Davidson became an intermediary for the Murchisons in places where formal channels could not be used. Need to sell a pier in Malaysia? Done. Need to register a boat in Panama? Done. Need to build a facility for the CIA in Africa? Done.

Thanks to his relationship with Teamsters leader Jimmy Hoffa, Davidson arranged for Murchison's son Clint Jr. to get a multi-million-dollar loan from the union's pension fund for a development in Beverly Hills called Trousdale Estates. According to columnist Drew Pearson, young Murchison didn't want to ask his dad for the money. The project happened to include a lot for Vice President Richard Nixon at below market values. It proved highly profitable and led to more deals with the Teamsters union.

❖

When Murchison built the Del Charro in La Jolla, it became a convenient place to mingle with the rich, the famous, and the powerful. On racing days, a line of limousines pulled up like trains at the station. Murchison's oil friends—Wofford and Effie Cain, Buddy Fogelson and Greer Garson, Billy and Emily Byars—were regulars.

And on any given afternoon, the movie stars around the pool might include Joan Crawford, Betty Grable, John Wayne, or Gregory Peck. Between husbands, Elizabeth Taylor came by. So did Lucille Ball and Desi Arnaz. One star-studded evening, Hoagy Carmichael played "Stardust" on the piano by the pool.

Politicians gravitated to the Del Charro, too, including President Eisenhower, Vice President Nixon, Senator Lyndon Johnson, and Senator Joseph McCarthy. The politicians weren't officially fundraising, but vacations with the Texas oilman were beneficial.

Senator McCarthy traveled to Texas so often in the 1950s that he was considered the state's third senator. Dallas oilmen generously supported McCarthy's campaign to hunt down communists. In turn, McCarthy supported the depletion allowance that the oilmen banked on.

Oilman H. L. Hunt let the senator win at cards as a way of passing along money. Clint Murchison went even further. He lent McCarthy his plane to make speeches around the country and financed some of his political attack ads.

Murchison also gave McCarthy stock tips and profitable access to oil deals on the sly, just as he did for J. Edgar Hoover. "McCarthy was virtually on Murchison's payroll," Del Charro manager Allan Witwer said.

But McCarthy squandered his money gambling in Las Vegas and at race-tracks. He was often sloshed at the Del Charro. And crude. Even the men were embarrassed by his raunchy stories. Hotel manager Witwer recalled, "He'd get drunk and jump in the pool, sometimes naked. He urinated outside his cabana . . ." After McCarthy insulted his wife and shoved her into the pool, Murchison told the senator to pack his bags.

◆

You could say some of the other Del Charro guests had worse manners. On a stroll through the lobby, you were likely to run into some of the biggest mobsters in the country. Journalists in San Diego reported that the frequent guests included "Handsome Johnny" Roselli, the Chicago Mafia's main man in Hollywood and Las Vegas. Early in his career, Roselli looked after Chicago interests at the Del Mar track. The FBI said he was responsible for at least thirteen murders.

Local reporters also said Carlos Marcello, the New Orleans Mafia boss, stayed at the Del Charro. This got my attention. Federal authorities believed that Marcello was the puppet-master for organized crime in Dallas.

By all accounts, Marcello was cold-blooded as a cobra, and a cobra in a foul mood at that. I. I. Davidson warned clients about Marcello: "Look, when you deal with him, remember that loyalty and trustworthiness are everything to him. If you violate that, you can expect the worst to happen to you." As he spoke, Davidson slowly drew a finger across his throat.

Clint Sr. denied knowing Marcello. He would only acknowledge having dinner at Marcello's restaurant-casino in New Orleans, the Beverly Country Club.

This did not appear to be the whole truth.

A US Senate committee alleged in 1955 that Murchison companies had real estate and financial links to Marcello. In addition, the Commerce Committee reported that 20 percent of the Murchison oil leases in Oklahoma were financed by Gerardo Catena, a top associate of New York crime boss Vito Genovese.

Well, well.

Mr. Murchison's background was turning out to be more interesting than I thought. The Dallas press in the 1950s and 1960s had not paid much attention to Clint Sr.'s possible ties to mobsters. But the closer I looked at the Del Charro crowd, the more troubling connections I found.

◆

The frequent guests also included big-time gambling figure Ed Levinson, a "business associate" of Bugsy Siegel and Meyer Lansky. Levinson operated a bank for bookmakers and was a part owner of the Sands and Dunes casinos as well as the Fremont Hotel. He later partnered with Murchison interests in a business deal in Haiti that Congress investigated.

Then there was John Drew, aka Jacob Stein. A former associate of Al Capone, Drew ran the Molaska Corporation, an illegal distillery that produced five thousand gallons of bootleg booze a day—until Treasury Agent Eliot Ness busted in. When Drew was operating casinos in Reno and Vegas, the FBI went looking for him. He was hiding at the Del Charro at the time.

F. L. "Dub" McClanahan, a Texas oilman and gambler, also could be found at the Del Charro. McClanahan was said to partner with Carlos Marcello on oil deals. He did well enough at oil and poker to become part-owner of the Frontier Casino in Reno. J. Edgar Hoover enjoyed several breakfasts with McClanahan at the Del Charro before his FBI staff intervened. They advised Hoover to move to another table.

All these gamblers visited Murchison's hotel often enough to be considered regulars. That couldn't have happened without Murchison's notice and approval, because the Del Charro functioned essentially as a private hotel.

What did all this say about Murchison? Not much good.

I had been thinking of the jewel thief as the Bad Guy in the story and his burglary victims as the Good Guys. But maybe Murchison was a Bad Guy in his own way?

As Texas author Joe Nick Patoski put it, there was a "touch of the outlaw" in Murchison. All the oilmen griped about government regulations, particularly after a few Scotches, but Murchison defied the restrictions, often in the dark of night. He was widely known for pumping "hot oil" through his pipelines in defiance of federal limits.

"No one ran more hot oil than Clint Murchison, and no independent operator fought proration more fiercely than he," agreed biographer Jane Wolfe.

As a result of his reputation for flouting the rules, Murchison's peers in the oil business were leery of him. He did not have "clean hands," they said. As oilman J. R. Parten put it, he liked Murchison personally, but knew he had made a fortune disobeying the rules.

Part of me wanted to like Murchison because he had loyal friends who did. He took care to nurture them in business and life. He sent his friends sausage at Christmas, flew them to parties, wrote them thoughtful notes. They forgave his gruffness and questionable methods as "just Clint being Clint."

Murchison defended himself by saying, "If I had been guilty of all the things they say I have done, I'd be under the jail, not in it."

Whatever his transgressions in business, Murchison was a devoted family man. After the death of his wife, Anne, he bought the former Dallas Polo Club to create a dream home for his sons, with plenty of room for a menagerie of animals. When a fire destroyed much of the house, Murchison built a grander one, with seven bedrooms.

He added a pool so large that it became known as "the Gulf of Mexico." Murchison liked to station card tables around the pool for gambling marathons that lasted all weekend. Oil leases as well as money changed hands. To the wildcatters, gambling was just another test of manhood. "Are you in?" was the challenge for a card game, an oil well, or a company takeover. "Hell, yes," was the only manly answer. Murchison once settled a million-dollar business dispute with the flip of coin—and lost.

While he was unattached, Murchison did not lack feminine company; there were plenty of beautiful women who wanted a shot at marrying one of the richest men in the world. After Murchison met Virginia Long, the competition was over. She was twenty years younger and a dazzler. People said Ginny looked like Lana Turner but could hunt and fish with the guys. Even better, she liked to play cards.

Murchison showed his pride in his young bride by naming his plane *The Flying Ginny* and showering her with jewels. He wooed her with a 16-carat diamond engagement ring that cost $125,000 and moved up to bigger bijoux from there.

Murchison often relied on the taste of the J. Ortman jewelry firm in Manhattan for gifts. Ortman's partner, Jerry Blickman, usually brought samples to Dallas in person. To his bemusement, the multimillionaire met him at the airport in a 1953 Ford pickup truck, wearing rumpled khakis and an open-necked shirt. On one visit, Murchison bought everything Blickman had. The New Yorker was stunned.

As Murchison grew older and developed health concerns, he decided his house on the polo grounds had more space than he needed. He suggested a swap with his son John. He and Ginny moved into John's smaller, 9,000-square-foot house in Preston Hollow while John and his wife, Lupe, moved into Clint's 18,000-square-foot home.

As fate would have it, the swap moved Clint and Ginny Murchison into the jewel thief's favorite hunting ground—and he helped himself to Ginny's jewels.

◇

I had started looking into Murchison's background simply because he was one of the jewel thief's victims and I wanted to flesh out my description of him. What I found was much darker than I expected. His backstory drew me into unexpected territory—the underworld. This was the moment when I realized the story might be about more than missing diamonds.

I felt as if I had lifted a rug to look for a fallen earring and found a trap door. When I lifted the hidden door, there was a murky world below. From then on, organized crime showed up in surprising ways, along with political corruption and graft.

At this point, I wasn't sure what the web of connections meant. But one thing was clear: the jewel thief upped the ante considerably when he took Ginny Murchison's jewels. Clint Murchison Sr. was not just another oil man who got lucky and rich. He had very dangerous friends.

The jewel thief either didn't understand the multimillionaire's reach—or was trying to demonstrate his mastery.

Or maybe, he just wanted those jewels no matter what.

PART TWO
THE HUNTERS

"Of course, the detectives are cleverer than us. We expect them to be. But that doesn't mean they are paragons of virtue. Holmes is depressed. Poirot is vain. Miss Marple is brusque and eccentric. They don't have to be attractive. We don't need to like or admire our detectives. We stick with them because we have confidence in them."
—Anthony Horowitz. *Magpie Murders*

9

Fannin

The thief continued to run circles around the Dallas Police—and left more waffled footprints as calling cards. Many a night, the phone would ring while Fannin was in bed, asleep. After he fumbled for the phone in the dark, one of his detectives would say: "He hit again."

"Crap!" Fannin would yell.

The jewel thief had turned into Fannin's worst nightmare. The press had started calling him "the King of Diamonds," and the showy nickname was grating on Fannin's nerves. A local TV station had added to the thief's celebrity by broadcasting a special report on "The King of Diamonds—Gentleman Thief." Fannin had to endure thirty minutes of grilling from a trio of journalists. Worse, he had to share the stage with Harry McCormick, the cigar-chomping, potty-mouthed reporter who claimed credit for the thief's catchy nickname. When McCormick proclaimed the thief was getting away with the "perfect crime," Fannin had to grit his teeth.

Afterward, he complained to his wife that the publicity was getting out of control. Kids were even dressing up like the jewel thief for Halloween, like he was some kind of superhero!

Fannin stepped up the pressure to catch the thief. His men drove the streets of hard-hit neighborhoods night after night. No luck. He tried aerial surveillance, but the low flights were too noisy to be covert. Fannin threw everything he could into finding the thief, and it wasn't enough.

Though the jewel thief continued to elude him, the manhunt produced arrests on thousands of other cases. Fannin's dragnet snagged all manner of low-grade lawbreakers—window-peepers, pickpockets, hotel prowlers, holdup men, and other wayward souls. The burglary department recovered more than $1 million in stolen goods and cash while looking for the King of Diamonds.

As a result, the efficiency rating of Fannin's burglary and theft division soared. Fannin's team—usually one of the highest-ranked in Texas law enforcement—now ranked as one of the top in the country.

They just couldn't find a certain cat burglar in galoshes.

Although all the detectives felt the pressure to produce results, most of the burden fell on Fannin's shoulders. Fannin took the heat and lit another Philip Morris cigarette. As the King of Diamonds search wore on, he was up to two packs a day.

The seemingly unflappable Walter Charles Fannin devoted thirty-six years of his life to the Dallas Police Department. He had joined the police as a young man because his grandfather served with the DPD. Charles Abraham Fannin proudly wore Badge #5 for thirty years and was a figure of rectitude in the family. In contrast, Fannin's father, Walter, was a railroad engineer and away a lot. When he was home, he tended to drink heavily. So, when young Fannin chose a career, he did not work for the railroad like his dad; he became a cop like his grandfather.

When he joined the DPD in 1939, the uniforms were hand-me-downs from other officers. Because the pants given to Fannin were several sizes too big, even the drunks on the street could spot he was a rookie—and said so. Still, Fannin was glad to have the $100 a month. He served in the Navy in

World War II and rejoined the DPD when he came home. He had gained an air of command and rose steadily from motorcycle patrol to detective.

By the time Fannin was put in charge of the Crimes Against Property division, he had encountered every kind of crook you could imagine. He had arrested a one-legged burglar, not once but twice. Lots of fur thieves. Rare-coin thieves. A Bible thief. A dwarf burglar. A Blatz beer burglar. And a thief called "Zorro," who wielded a baseball bat.

Then the King of Diamonds case made Fannin a celebrity. When Fannin and McCaghren caught a shoplifter on their lunch hour, it made the news.

In 1962, the Dallas Press Club paid Fannin the ultimate compliment by spotlighting him as a "Newsmaker" in the club's satirical *Gridiron Show*. Two of the songs that spoofed people in the news were about Walter Fannin. Big-time swindler Billy Sol Estes only rated one.

In the first parody, the cast sang a ditty to the tune of "Hey Look Me Over!" that teased, "Hey, Captain Fannin, we've lost our rocks." When the burglaries were still going on four years later, the Press Club came back with another parody to the tune of "It Was a Very Good Year" that tracked the burglaries year by year, from Graf to Murchison and more.

Fannin, who was a special guest along with the top echelon of city leaders, laughed along with the others. He was a Newsmaker.

But uncomfortably so.

Would his grandfather be proud that his grandson was spotlighted in the *Gridiron Show*, or embarrassed he hadn't caught the burglar?

As time went on, the public attention became more annoying. When a newspaperman pestered him for fresh information, Fannin responded with a wave of his hand, "We're checking everything—including the horoscope." On cue, he pulled a copy of the daily horoscope from his inside coat pocket. He was actually kidding, but he knew the joke was on him.

Fannin was in his late forties when the King of Diamonds broke into his life. He was old enough to have seen his share of tragedy. His first child, a son, had been electrocuted in a home accident. The toddler was nine months old when he crawled over to a dripping air conditioner and touched an electrical connection.

"Fannin was devastated," a colleague remembered. "It nearly killed him."

When Fannin and his wife, Betty, were unable to conceive another child, they decided to adopt. The adoption agency suggested three siblings, two boys and a girl. Fannin later told McCaghren that when he and Betty went to meet the children at the adoption service, they were worried whether they could provide for all three on a policeman's salary. Yet they were concerned about the impact on the children if they were split up. The children must have sensed the couple's hesitation. One approached Fannin and asked shyly, "Do you think three is too many?"

That clinched it, Fannin said. He and Betty made up their minds. They would take all three, and make it work.

Fannin had been married several times before. He knew that police life, with its late nights and rollercoaster stress, can take a toll on families. So, while his detectives stopped by the Idle Rich lounge after work, Fannin usually went home for dinner.

He was determined to keep his family together—give or take a temptation now and then. He was a celebrity, with the wavy silver hair of a matinee idol, so ladies had an eye for him. If he returned the glance, he made amends by bringing his wife lingerie.

On weekends, he often went to church with his wife, and once taught a Sunday School class of sixth-grade boys. Though the boys loved his cop stories, Fannin didn't last long as a teacher because he hated praying out loud. He didn't talk about his churchgoing at work, but his faith helped him recover from the death of his son.

He could be a little vain; his favorite tie was a Valentino. For once in his life, Walter Fannin was an important person in town, and he wanted to look the part. Restaurant owners usually recognized him from newspaper photos. He rarely had to pay for a meal. "Look, it's Captain Fannin!" people said. Then they invariably asked, "When are you going to catch the King of Diamonds?"

◆

As I tried to find out more about Fannin, his daughter became an invaluable resource. She had the unlikely name of Delores Letart. Or as Raymond Chandler's private eye, Philip Marlowe, might put it, *"The dame's name was Delores Letart. Not what you'd expect for a copper's kid."*

We agreed to meet. In detective movies, such meetings are usually held in dark bars with a bartender who nods as he wipes the lipstick off a glass and says, *"If it's Miss Letart you want, she's in the booth at the end."*

But unlike the hard-boiled private eyes with hangovers and a weakness for dames, I was a hard-boiled grandmother with a weakness for detective stories, so we met at a Half Price Books store on a sunny Saturday afternoon. Delores Letart suggested there were quiet tables where we could talk.

In her early fifties with sandy-blonde hair, Delores had a down-to-earth manner that made me think she might be a teacher, the pretty and nice kind. But she said she had mostly worked as a secretary and event planner. The distinctive last name came with her husband Mickey. She was nice enough to bring several scrapbooks that her mother kept about her father's career and spread them out on the wooden table.

It took only a glance to see I had a treasure trove in my hands. The search for the jewel thief had dominated Fannin's career, so most of the yellowed clippings were about the case. Some were from the *Dallas Times Herald*, which had gone out of business before its back copies could be digitized. That made the clippings a rare find. Others were from detective magazines like *True Detective* and *Front Page Detective*, which the public library didn't dare keep.

I spent much of the afternoon with Fannin's daughter, leafing through the scrapbooks and learning about her dad. He doted on his kids, she remembered, and would tell her when he came in from work, "You are sweeter than the first load of watermelons in the spring!"

Fannin took the family on vacations twice a year, usually to the Texas coast, where he liked to fish. Later on, he took trips with his wife in their RV. One time, he and his wife went to Hawaii by using Green Stamps that merchants gave loyal customers. Mrs. Fannin saved the stamps year after year, patiently pasting them into coupon books until they had enough for a trip.

Fannin had an old-fashioned sense of propriety, his daughter said. When he mowed the lawn, he kept his shirttail tucked in so he wouldn't look slouchy. Although he enjoyed drinks with friends, he quit drinking around his children after he cursed in front of them. He promised it would never happen again. And it didn't.

Like many others of his era, Fannin was a chauvinist. He paid for his sons to go to college, but not his daughter. He loved her as much, but assumed she would marry a breadwinner.

"He didn't have a lot of tolerance for nonsense," his kids said. To teach one of his sons what would happen if he acted up and landed behind bars, Fannin locked him in a jail cell. And when his daughter, Delores, didn't know something, Fannin would drop her off at the public library and tell her, "Go find out what it is."

"He made you want to do better," his daughter remembered. The men who worked for him said the same thing. They did not want to disappoint Capt. Fannin.

When he got late-night threats, which he often did, Fannin would tell the callers he didn't give a darn what they threatened. His daughter heard him tell one caller that he could dig up all the blankety-blank skeletons he wanted, but he had a job to do.

I began forming a mental picture of the man who wanted to look respectable when he mowed his lawn, who made his kids toe the line, whose idea of a perfect vacation was fishing. He was a fifties kind of guy in a sixties world.

◆

Years later, Sgt. Detective John Chism remembered meeting Captain Fannin on his first day in the burglary department. "He told me right off the bat, 'We don't interrogate people and put them under lights. We *interview* them and listen.' He advised me to get to know my informants and people on the streets, to treat people nice. He said, 'If you get a burglary assignment, make sure you talk to the victims in person. Leave your cards on the front door and back door. If you don't hear from them, call them. Let them know you are really trying.' I was impressed with that."

Some of Fannin's men liked to razz him for being such a stickler about looking and acting professional. One detective recalled that when he joined the department, Fannin said, "Where's your hat?"

He replied, "I ain't had time to get one."

Fannin waved him to the door and said, "Get a hat."

When Fannin teed his team off, they retaliated by wearing cowboy hats instead of fedoras to work. Fannin would remind them they were supposed to be out catching burglars, not playing Roy Rogers.

As head of the burglary department, Fannin was the face of the King of Diamonds investigation for most of the 1960s. That meant he had to deal with reporters from around the country. Wire services like UPI covered the case extensively, which was how I first learned about it. Even the *New York Daily News*, fifteen hundred miles away from Dallas, printed two full pages about the jewel thief.

Many of the reporters noted in their news stories that Fannin's phone rang constantly while they interviewed him. One reporter observed that Fannin dutifully jotted down the information from each phone call that interrupted their interview. Fannin nodded his head repeatedly as he listened and answered, "Yes, ma'am. No, ma'am. Thank you, ma'am."

It was frustrating work. One tipster reported a man who looked suspicious because he was driving a sports car in the burglary area. Another pointed to a guy who went to Mexico a lot. Another claimed the thief was a fellow country club member who was unemployed but always had money. None of that panned out.

One day, Fannin received a call from a man who claimed someone in the penitentiary told him he knew who the jewel thief was. This time, Fannin personally went to interview the man. The inmate admitted sheepishly, he was just kidding.

And so it went.

Fannin needed a lucky break, a solid tip. Sooner or later, the thief would slip up, he thought. Sooner or later, a witness would come forward.

Fannin often sat at his desk and flicked his Zippo lighter on and off, on and off, while he sorted through the burglary reports.

Who is it? Click. Who is it? Click.

It didn't help.

❖

So far, the thief's footprints were the only physical clues Fannin had. He figured the thief wore galoshes so he could sneak down creeks and avoid streets where he might be spotted. Fannin called in Johnny Miranda, the owner of a shoe repair shop. He asked Miranda to estimate the thief's shoe size from plaster casts made at the burglary scenes. Fannin hoped the shoe size might help determine the thief's height. Miranda estimated the overshoe print was comparable to a size 12 shoe. From that, he theorized the thief was "at least six feet tall." Or someone shorter with big feet.

Fannin called his team into a huddle and laid before them fifty names of top suspects. He called it a sort of "popularity meeting." Which suspect did the detectives think was most likely the thief?

To his dismay, the detectives weren't 100 percent sure about any of the suspects on the list. They could only agree that the thief was "highly unusual."

It didn't help his mood when the *Dallas Times Herald* ran a front-page story that week with the banner headline: DIABOLICAL GEM THIEF STILL LOOSE.

10

McCaghren

McCaghren and Fannin became close friends during the King of Diamonds investigation, although their personalities were very different. McCaghren was the power batter on the team: raw, talented, raring to hit one into the stands. Fannin was the catcher: calm, steady, analyzing everyone's moves. They complemented each other and enjoyed each other's company. McCaghren's office was next to Fannin's.

When calls came in late at night about a new break-in, Fannin would tell other detectives, "Go track down McCaghren, wherever he is."

Most likely, he was playing cards. Paul McCaghren was a night owl. He told me he played poker every Thursday night—"and sometimes other nights, too."

Some nights, he "socialized." Fellow detectives liked to tease McCaghren about the evening they were patrolling an affluent neighborhood and saw his car in the driveway of an imposing house. They drove back to see if he needed assistance—or so they claimed. They knocked on the door.

An attractive woman opened the door. She gave the detectives a knowing smile and said, "I bet y'all are hunting for Paulie."

When they walked inside, they saw McCaghren sitting on the sofa with his shoes off and his feet on a coffee table. He had a drink in his hand and a smile on his face.

McCaghren had his own way of getting information.

◆

When I called, McCaghren suggested we meet for lunch. Our meeting at an Italian restaurant seemed straight out of *Goodfellas*. McCaghren was seated at a corner table, where he had a clear view of the restaurant and the door. I was surprised to see that he'd brought his business partner, Brad Smith, with him. At first, I assumed McCaghren wanted Smith as a witness to the conversation; he didn't trust me. Only later did I realize that McCaghren had trouble walking because of the injuries he suffered during the Korean War. He didn't want to be seen struggling with his walker, so he asked Smith to help him get to the table before I arrived.

Despite his physical difficulties, McCaghren was in command at the restaurant. The waiters called him "Sir Paul" and slathered him with attention, extra garlic bread, more wine, and a complimentary side dish.

McCaghren pronounced his name the Scotch-Irish way—*Mah-care-on*—and once had the carroty-red hair to confirm his heritage. Now in his mid-eighties, his hair had turned a faded ginger. Big boned and tall, he still projected authority.

At first, he maneuvered around hard questions about the King of Diamonds by telling mildly amusing anecdotes, like a yawner about a cat attracted by the infrared light on his camera during a stakeout.

I got the feeling McCaghren was testing me, gauging how much to reveal. As our conversations continued in the years ahead, he shared more, bit by bit. But at that first awkward meeting, he held back enough to keep me guessing.

◆

My take on McCaghren was that he was smart and tough—the kind of alpha-male cop who didn't mind breaking the rules. He had his own code of honor, which started with 1) catch the crook, and 2) be loyal to your team.

He came across as a Texas version of Robert Mitchum or Lee Marvin, gruff and sardonic. It was easy to see he would fit nicely into noir detective stories, so I began to think of him that way. You know the type—the imperfect guy who manages to do good despite himself. I immediately thought of Raymond Chandler's Philip Marlowe. He fortified himself with Camel cigarettes and doses of Old Forester. He was known to slap women. Dashiell Hammett's private eye, Sam Spade, usually had a smoke and a drink in his hand, too. He was known to slap *men*. Spade slept with his partner's wife and had a bad case of greed.

In comparison, McCaghren did not smoke, although he did know his way around a beverage. He only slapped a killer who earned it. But he had the flavor of the fictional gumshoes. He had an eye for beautiful dames and a nose for phonies. He talked like the pulp detectives, too. When I asked him what one of the burglary victims looked like, he growled, "She looked like a woman who had a fifth of vodka every day."

I actually was seeking details like her hair color and size, so I tried again: "I mean, what did she *physically* look like?"

"She looked like a woman who had a fifth of vodka every day."

I gave up. "Okay. How do you know?"

"Her maid told me she brought her a tumbler full of ice and vodka every morning. That's how she started her day."

This was a typical McCaghren exchange. Many of his stories sounded like scenes from *Naked City*. Late one night, he said, Capt. Fannin called him at home. It looked like the King had struck again. A blonde socialite had reported that $200,000 worth of diamond necklaces, earrings, and other adornments were missing. She wore them the night before to a social engagement, she said, and now they were gone.

Fannin and McCaghren drove to her home, a mansion in North Dallas with a circular driveway, sweeping staircase, the whole works. When they arrived, they found the woman weeping.

Her life, she said, was falling apart. She was from a wealthy oil family and left her husband for another man. Her new lover talked her into investing in his business—and now he was jilting her for another woman.

"He had to be a *fool*," McCaghren said, shaking his head.

"You mean she was attractive?" I asked.

"Ohhhhh yes, she was," McCaghren said.

The woman told Fannin and McCaghren the burglar took all her jewelry. "Now I've lost everything," she moaned. She was sobbing.

Yet something about the story didn't sound convincing to McCaghren. Whatever she was selling, he wasn't buying.

McCaghren asked if he could look around. The woman's bedroom was upstairs. As he checked the bathroom, his attention was drawn to a closet where the door was slightly ajar. He looked in and spied a large Kotex box on the floor that had been opened. Out of instinct, McCaghren picked up the blue box. It felt surprisingly heavy. He reached in with one hand and pulled out a diamond necklace.

McCaghren walked down the grand staircase with the Kotex box in hand. He described the scene: "I have the box and I'm walking toward them. Fannin was sitting on the sofa trying to put the woman at ease. I say, 'Want to guess what's in here?'"

Fannin couldn't believe what he was seeing. His lieutenant had discovered a box of sanitary pads? He blurted out, "Have you lost your mind?"

McCaghren turned the Kotex box upside down. All the sanitary pads and a tumble of jewels fell out at the woman's feet. "Here are your stolen jewels," he announced.

"My goodness! How did that get in there?" the woman said.

Case closed.

Many other theft reports didn't pan out but kept the burglary team busy. In one incident, the woman who called in a burglary report had placed her jewels in her safety deposit box and forgot about them.

In another, the family seemed oddly agitated and evasive. McCaghren sensed they were hiding something. The parents eventually confided that the man who stole their jewels also raped their daughter. They were distraught and worried the press might report the incident. They didn't want anyone to know.

McCaghren kept the burglary quiet to protect the girl. The rape didn't fit with the King of Diamonds' pattern anyway. He wasn't violent. As far as they knew.

♦

As months went by, the police intensified their nightly patrols in hopes of catching the burglar in the act.

"We had stakeouts all over the place," McCaghren remembered at our lunch. "There were men out there in the dark nearly every night."

Many times, FBI agents joined the night patrols. Agent Jim Bookhout looked like a straight-arrow G-man, with his dark hair trimmed short. Trained as a lawyer, he was meticulous about his work, sometimes to an extent that his police contemporaries found amusing.

"During one of our stakeouts, Bookhout saw a porch light blinking on and off," McCaghren remembered. "He was convinced that someone was tapping out a code about the burglaries. He kept trying to figure out the code. But it was just a flickering light bulb."

When stakeouts were held in Highland Park, McCaghren often partnered with Sgt. Henry Gardner, the lead detective there. One night, Gardner and McCaghren were hunkered down in an alley near the Dallas Country Club. McCaghren got a call on his walkie-talkie from one of his men. He said, "Lieutenant! How big do Dobermans get?"

McCaghren radioed to him, "As big as a small pony."

The panicked policeman replied, "Okay, we're about to get stomped by a Doberman or a small pony."

McCaghren chuckled at the memory, but I could tell this was another well-worn yarner. I tried to nudge him back to the crux of the matter: Who did he really suspect was the jewel thief?

McCaghren looked a little annoyed, as if I asked him to clean out the garage. He'd heard the question a hundred times before. He took another sip of his wine before rattling off the possibilities.

The main suspect was one I already had on my list: Jasper Kirksmith, the good-looking gambler who tried to cash in on the social scene. He was the kind of scoundrel that fathers warn their daughters about. Most of the social crowd thought he was up to no good, and McCaghren agreed.

The police pursued other leads, he assured me, but they didn't pan out. At that point, McCaghren paused as if weighing whether to continue. He poked at his crab salad with his fork. Speaking carefully, he added, "But there was *another* lead . . ."

I sensed something important was coming.

I leaned in to listen as McCaghren continued. There was a time, he said, when "We thought we had him. We thought we had him cornered."

He gave me a guarded sideways look to test my reaction.

"Tell me about it," I said.

One day, McCaghren said, he got a call from Highland Park detective Henry Gardner. "I think we've got something here," he said.

"I'll be right over," McCaghren said. He ran from his office to his car. The case was finally heating up!

The burglar had broken into a house not far from the Dallas Country Club, McCaghren said. He remembered seeing the club as he drove to the house. The break-in had most of the hallmarks of the King's style: the thief left waffle footprints, took only select jewels, and climbed a tree to get in the house.

The policemen followed the footprints down the alley and over a block or more. The tracks stopped in back of a house. The policemen went to the front and knocked on the door.

No one answered.

"We've got company," whispered Bob Waters, a Dallas cop who was with McCaghren and Gardner. He pointed to the second floor. They could see someone in a window. He was watching them. They knocked loudly again. KNOCK. KNOCK. KNOCK.

No answer. Gardner said he would find out who lived there.

Gardner called McCaghren later to say the house belonged to someone from a hardware store family.

I pressed McCaghren, "What was the name of the family?"

"I don't remember," he said.

"How about the name of the hardware store?"

"I really don't recall," he said.

I threw out a few names. Elliott's Hardware?

No, not Elliott's.

Sharp Hardware?

"That sounds familiar," he said. But again, he claimed he wasn't sure.

I sensed McCaghren was not going to volunteer anything more.

"So why did the thief quit? Why did the burglaries stop?" I pressed.

"Obviously, we got too close," McCaghren said. "We pretty well decided who it was. We just could never get to him."

He would say no more. Like the good poker player that he was, McCaghren wasn't ready to reveal all his cards.

That night, when I looked back at my notes, I realized he mentioned several times that progress was impeded by "jurisdictional issues."

So, I called him to ask what he meant. "You would think that three police departments could work together," he said, apparently referring to the Dallas department and the adjacent suburbs of Highland Park and University Park. "That's not the way it was."

That was all he would say. He was finished with answering questions. "I've got to go," he said. "I'll talk to you some other time." He hung up.

I sat there by the phone for a while, thinking about everything he had said. McCaghren clearly thought he and Sgt. Gardner had gotten close to the King—right up to his doorstep, in fact. But something held them back.

I wrote in my notes: Whose house was it? Which hardware family? What got in the way?

◆

After that, I talked to McCaghren on the phone or in person dozens of times as I tried to pry more information out of him. He was a challenging interview. But I came to enjoy sparring with him, me trying to get answers, McCaghren revealing only what he wanted—and nothing more.

He was good at dodging me. Once when I called him, he teased, "I've got a couple of people here who have big ears. I think they might be reporters. Why don't you call me back tomorrow?"

I worried at such times, was he playing me? Could I believe what he said about the case?

My instincts told me most of what he said was true. The trouble was deciding which parts. McCaghren was the classic unreliable narrator, whose recollections were sometimes self-serving or patchy. Not that McCaghren was a liar, but he was loyal to his friends and careful what he volunteered. He also was in his late eighties and struggled at times to remember details. The memories faded in and out, like signals on an old radio. When he told different versions of the same story, I stuck with the version that he repeated most consistently.

◆

When I tried to learn more about McCaghren's personal background, he brushed off most of my questions. He didn't want to talk about his past.

It took persistent probing to find out that McCaghren, like many of his colleagues, came from hard times. His father lost his dairy farm during the Depression and had to take jobs away from his family. For a while, he worked as a streetcar driver. By the time Paul was born, "a late, late child" as he put it, the other six siblings had left home. His mother, a diabetic, was often in poor health. Because his father was gone much of the time, he and Paul were not close. "He wasn't a bad guy, but he wasn't a good guy either," McCaghren said.

Somehow, his parents scraped together enough money to buy a small farm near Bristol, a town of a few hundred people in East Texas. Paul attended high school in nearby Ferris, where he was a gritty tackle on the Yellowjackets football team. The team selected him as captain.

Unfortunately, the Bristol farm produced more problems than profits. His parents moved to Dallas, where his father could get work. But Paul didn't want to transfer to another school. Being captain of the Ferris team was important to him. So, he got up before sunrise every day and rode the bus from Dallas to Ferris, twenty miles away. If he missed the bus back when practice ran late, he hitchhiked home in the dark. When paying for the bus fare became too difficult for his father, Paul had to drop out of school. "For financial reasons," he emphasized, to make it clear he did not flunk out.

Without other options, McCaghren told his father he wanted to join the Marines. Because he was still a minor, his dad signed the papers for him to join. McCaghren was seventeen when he headed out. Like a scene from a movie, he had a lump in his throat as he waved good-bye to his father, who simply nodded and walked away.

"That was the beginning of my real life," he told me. He was grateful for the order of military life, the regular meals, the manly camaraderie. Almost immediately, however, he was sent to Korea. McCaghren had never been out of Texas. Now he was on the other side of the world, trying to stop communists from taking over the Korean Peninsula.

As his unit marched north toward China, they were confronted with some of the lowest temperatures ever recorded in Korea. Soldiers froze to death with their rifles aimed at the hills. Their frozen bodies were stacked like logs in convoy trucks.

When I asked McCaghren about the brutal weather, he replied, "I'm still paying for it," and would say nothing more. He was from the "Marines don't cry" school and downplayed his injuries. He was wounded in the arm but dismissed it as "a minor wound." Still, he had to march out of the mountains on frozen roads while under heavy fire. He had just turned eighteen.

As a survivor of the horrific battle for Chosin Reservoir, he became one of the "Chosin Few." He received the Purple Heart and went on to serve a six-year tour of duty, which gave him the opportunity to earn his General Education Diploma (GED).

When he left the military, McCaghren joined the Dallas Police. In record time, he got married, had two daughters, and moved up to detective. He was a man in a hurry.

◆

That was about all I could get out of McCaghren about his background. I still wasn't sure what to make of him, especially whether to trust his version of things, so I sought out views from people who knew him during his police career.

"Good guy, tough and smart," said Hugh Aynesworth, who went from the *Dallas Morning News* to *Newsweek*.

"One of the best," said Darwin Payne, a police reporter at the *Dallas Times Herald* who became a historian of note.

"Smart as they come—100 percent," echoed Jim Ewell, the *Dallas Morning News* police reporter for many years.

Benny Newman, who went on to become police chief in the suburb of Irving, said, "Paul was a natural leader—if you walked into a room of one hundred people and asked, 'Who do you want as leader?' they would pick McCaghren."

Jack Davis, another police colleague, agreed McCaghren had a kind of charisma. "He was a good-looking guy back then, except he had that red hair. I used to call him, 'You redheaded son of a bitch.'"

Although they liked to razz him, detectives told me they admired McCaghren. "He was as fearless as anyone I've ever seen," one said.

As an example, they pointed out that McCaghren dared to take on the ruthless "Dixie Mafia." The gang was notorious for stealing and murdering across the South and Southwest. Sometimes they were called the "Cornbread Cosa Nostra" or the "Crossroaders," because they met at intersections before pulling off a job.

When they weren't hijacking trucks, robbing bars, or selling drugs, the Dixie Mafia stole jewels—often in Dallas. This added another complication to my search. Fannin suspected the outlaws pulled off some of the thefts attributed to the King. He told the press, "We know the gang have made some of our Preston Hollow jobs. I can't prove it, but we know they were there."

McCaghren went after the Dixie bandits. And sent their leader to the slammer.

11

The Dixie Mafia

I n the 1960s, the Dixie Mafia operated below the surface in Dallas, like scorpions under a rock. Since I felt duty-bound to check out every possibility, I peered into their dark world.

The group's leader in Dallas, Kirksey McCord Nix, had an unusual background for a career criminal: His father was chief judge of the Oklahoma Court of Criminal Appeals. Having grown up in a family of some means, Nix attended college. In early arrest photos, he has well-trimmed brown hair and is wearing a conventional suit. He could have passed for an insurance man. But Nix was a sociopath, a cold-blooded killer. In later mugshots, he is bloated, balding, and scowling.

Law enforcement officials believe Nix directed attempts to kill Tennessee sheriff Buford Pusser, who was cracking down on the Dixie Mafia's bread and butter—moonshining, prostitution, and gambling. Then he instigated a gangland-style murder of his rivals that resulted in twenty-five people dead in six states.

While in Dallas, Nix operated the Dixie gang like a guerrilla army. When police raided his apartment, they found a complete set of burglary tools, a police radio monitor, two-way radios, a window-fogging device, gas masks, lock-picking devices, three sets of handcuffs, a shotgun, and a .45-caliber automatic pistol.

◆

Paul McCaghren proved a worthy adversary. To catch Nix, McCaghren put together the Atlanta Metropole Criminal Intelligence Conference—a twenty-one-state network. As chairman, McCaghren was able to gather enough evidence to convict Nix for a host of crimes.

When McCaghren confronted Nix in the lobby of a Dallas motel, Nix unleashed a torrent of abuse and ridiculed McCaghren for not having an arrest warrant.

That was a mistake.

McCaghren's Scotch-Irish temper flared. Fists flew. McCaghren declared Nix had assaulted a police officer, giving him grounds to hit back. To punctuate his point, McCaghren threw Nix down some stairs.

"McCaghren beat the livin' crap out of him," another detective summed up.

McCaghren got into hot water at headquarters for the fracas, but was unrepentant. "He gave me a lot of lip," McCaghren said.

Nix ended up in the Angola prison in Louisiana, a maximum-security prison known as the "Alcatraz of the South." From his cell, Nix put a $50,000 bounty out for anyone who could kill Paul McCaghren.

When McCaghren heard about the bounty, he called Nix's lawyer and teased, "Couldn't you have made it $100,000?"

But this was no joking matter. Nix had arranged the killings of two people while in the prison hospital feigning health issues.

Nix came up with a scheme to get out of Angola. He set up a blackmail scam by placing photos of attractive young inmates in homosexual publications. The ads claimed the inmates were about to be released and looking for a new partner. When men replied to the "lonely hearts" ads, they were threatened with exposure. Victims from all walks of life were blackmailed—professors, mail carriers, politicians. One had to mortgage his house to keep his name quiet. The scheme raked in $867,000. Nix planned to use the money to buy a pardon from the Louisiana governor. Before he could, Nix was convicted for an earlier charge of gunning down a judge and his wife. The new sentence meant Nix would be in prison for the rest of his life.

Stuck behind bars, Nix confided to a Dallas pen pal that at the time of his arrest, he was on the verge of a major jewel theft in Dallas. His target? Algur Meadows, the oilman who attended the Jewel Ball in 1959 with Bruno and Josephine Graf. Meadows's mansion was the largest estate in University Park. It had white Italian marble floors and an indoor swimming pool with chandeliers. Nix had heard that Meadows's wife, Virginia, had "important jewels." His team cased out their home for weeks, peering through the gates, recording the schedules of security guards, diagramming entry points.

But before Kirksey Nix got the chance to grab Mrs. Meadows's jewels, he had a close encounter with Paul McCaghren's fist.

◆

With Kirksey McCord Nix in prison, George Albert McGann was more or less in charge of the Dixie Mafia in Dallas. Some say he was responsible for as many as thirty killings. McGann was a road gambler, which meant he went from town to town to cheat at card games. To make up for his losses, he stole jewels.

When he was flush, McGann liked to flaunt his success with flashy suits, expensive shoes, pinkie rings, and new cars. His nickname was "Cadillac," because he had a preference for the big shiny cars, like Elvis. One of them was red on the bottom and white on the top, which he considered a classy touch. He also bragged that he bought one of the first Mark II Lincoln Continentals in town.

McGann's sharp outfits were what attracted Beverly Oliver to him. She was singing at the Colony Club when he showed up with some of his pals. She noticed him right away. McGann was tall, around five foot eleven, and trim. His black-framed glasses gave him a Buddy Holly look.

"I wasn't attracted to the good-looking guys with hair on their chest," Oliver recalled. "I fell for the guy in a pretty suit who was clean shaven. He looked successful."

When they got married, a couple who owned the Sky Knight Club volunteered their house for the wedding. The wedding party was a who's who of local crime: Hitman R. D. Matthews served as best man. Guests included hitman-hijacker George Fuqua, hitman Stanley "The Creeper" Cook, bookmaker Johnny Ross Patrono, Fort Worth bookmaker Bill Jerden, and local Mafia leader Joseph Civello.

It was a cobra party.

The gathering showed how interwoven the Dixie Mafia, the Italian Mafia, and powerful bookmakers had become. They cooperated when convenient. As one bookie put it, the informal alliance was more like disorganized crime than organized crime, but it was still dangerous.

Most nights, the McGanns and their outlaw friends hung out in places like the Ali Baba Club or the Cotton Palace bowling alley. The Cotton Palace was a perfect clubhouse. It had forty-four bowling lanes, air conditioning, pool tables, a barber shop, and a bar.

Beverly McGann recalled the guys paid her $100 to $400 each time she sang "Ace in the Hole." They never tired of it and sang along. To her, they seemed like overgrown frat boys, renegades out to beat the system.

The outlaw life was heady stuff for McGann's young wife, who came from a family of limited means. When she was fourteen, she got a job singing with a musical troupe at the new Six Flags Over Texas amusement park. Beverly stood out with her blonde bouffant, cute figure, and a smile that would stop a truck. It didn't take her long to land a higher-paying gig singing at Abe Weinstein's Colony Club downtown. "My name was on the marquee," she marveled. She was sixteen years old.

When she took the stage, men in the audience would whistle. They slipped a few bills to the bartender and asked, "Who's the new parakeet?" More often than not, they would invite her for a drink between sets and hide their wedding rings. Some nights, after performing at the Colony Club, she served as a hostess for after-hours parties at the Carousel Club next door. Jack Ruby had persuaded her to mingle with the customers. The drunker they got, the more tips she got.

When she married McGann, Beverly thought her dreams had come true. He bought expensive clothes for her to show off as they rolled up to nightclubs in his newest car. The drugs came later, and the meanness. When she tried to leave him, McGann ordered his gang to drag her to Mexico, tie her to a hotel bed, and inject her repeatedly with heroin. She was comatose for days and nearly died. McGann gave her an ultimatum: stay with him—or turn tricks to pay for her heroin habit.

She stayed. After he was shot and killed, she married an evangelist. In her new life, she sang gospel songs.

When I met Beverly Oliver for lunch, she strode into the restaurant as if she were stepping on stage. Tall, striking, and statuesque, she exuded flashy glamour even at a grandmotherly age. She had on a black knit top, black skinny-leg pants, five-inch heels, and a lot of jewelry, including a dime-sized diamond ring. In sum, more Tammy Faye than Maria von Trapp.

Much of what Oliver told me was in a book she wrote, but she was more candid in person. She confirmed that the couple who hosted her wedding to McGann were killed a few months later by her husband and his buddies, who took over the Sky Knight Club. People who got in their way usually regretted it, she said. Some got taken for a late-night swim in Lake Texoma.

Her husband's name had come up as a King of Diamonds suspect, partly because he sold a bag of diamonds to another gambler that he swore were from the celebrated jewel thefts. The diamonds were so hot, McGann told the buyer, they should be hidden for a decade. But they turned out to be fakes.

Not all of McGann's jewels were fakes. In 1968, police arrested McGann at Love Field with $50,000 in "expensive jewelry." A judge sent him back to his West Texas hometown, with the proviso he get a job there. He returned to Dallas anyway.

When I asked Beverly if McGann could have pulled off some of the King of Diamonds thefts, she smiled coyly. McGann stole enough jewels, she said, to keep a large saltshaker filled with loose diamonds. He and his buddies stole jewels to finance their gambling, she explained, and were good at it. They bought the newest burglar alarms, figured out how they worked, and disabled similar alarms when entering homes. Then they fenced the stolen gems with pawnshops or sources in Dallas and Las Vegas.

McGann often hinted to poker-playing friends that he had dangerous connections. Those connections apparently caught up with him in 1970, the same year the jewel thefts stopped. McGann was shot to death in a Lubbock gambling house. His widow believed it was a gangland killing because the autopsy showed he was shot three times in the back and once in the abdomen. Someone wanted to make sure George McGann didn't walk away. He was thirty-four years old.

◈

At the time, most people in Dallas were largely unaware of the multiple layers of crime in the city that included bad guys like the Dixie Mafia. People were busy taking their kids to Six Flags Over Texas or taking in the latest James Bond movie, not suspecting there were real villains closer to home.

After McGann was murdered, Stanley Lee Cook took over the Dixie Mafia in Dallas. Cook was known as "the Creeper" because he liked to walk silently behind his victims before killing them. If you looked around at night and saw a guy with a cruel mouth and a bad Elvis haircut, you were as good as gone. Over the years, "the Creeper" was credited with twelve killings but never convicted for any of them.

After being shot in the abdomen, Cook had to wear a colostomy bag, so he switched to wearing jumpsuits. He later survived a gun battle with a former FBI agent who was on the trail of—wouldn't you know it?—stolen jewels. The Creeper was good at stealing jewelry, too. That is, until someone nailed him with a rifle shot from a billboard platform as he left a lunch with Houston drug smugglers.

Though Kirksey McCord Nix, George McGann, and Stanley Cook had been removed, remnants of the Dixie Mafia continued to make trouble in the region.

And Paul McCaghren was still tops on their hit list.

While McCaghren appeared unbothered, some of the men who worked with him grew concerned. Afraid they might get caught in the crossfire, they went to an assistant chief and asked what they should do.

"Don't get in the damn car with him," he told them, poker-faced.

Otherwise, McCaghren's pursuit of the Dixie Mafia made him a hero in Southern law enforcement. Though he could be unorthodox, McCaghren was driven to succeed—and did, moving steadily up the police department ranks. He got a bachelor's degree at Sam Houston State University and took night classes at Southern Methodist University to earn a master's degree.

During one of our sessions, I asked McCaghren about his SMU studies. What was it like, going to class with preppy students after a day of chasing criminals?

"Oh, I enjoyed it," he said, in his offhand way. "I learned a lot."

What were his favorite courses?

"Comparative religion and philosophy," he said, without hesitation.

This was a bit of a surprise. The great faiths of the world? *Philosophy?*

"That's right," he said. As usual, he would not elaborate.

But in an odd way, this made sense. For the police, the streets of Dallas were a laboratory of the good, the bad, the unhinged, and the unrepentant. It was enough to drive anyone to look for the meaning of it all.

12

Two Different Worlds

As time went by, people began to wonder, Why haven't the cops caught the thief? Were they incompetent? Keystone Kops?

No, Fannin's team was generally well regarded, and McCaghren was a rising star. So, why couldn't they find the thief?

McCaghren offered to set up a meeting so I could talk with other detectives who worked on the case. They met regularly at a Golden Corral restaurant in the suburb of Mesquite, so I joined in. The buffet offered all the chicken fried steak, mashed potatoes, and pie you could eat for $8.69. I had two helpings of fried okra in the line of duty.

I enjoyed talking with the cops. They were all in their eighties, with hearing aids and slow steps. But they remembered the search for the jewel thief—especially that they had to work overnight patrols for weeks without extra pay. Some nights, they drove as much as a hundred miles through the target areas, peering through their windshields for anything that looked suspicious—with no luck.

Some of them thought the thief was a shady playboy, which sounded like Jasper Kirksmith again. Others suggested a thief who stole so many spark-plugs that the price went up. They remembered he was nice-looking—but not his name. Several agreed there was talk about a guy from a hardware family. What was his name, I asked? No one could remember.

I started worrying: Were the cops being vague because they really didn't remember? Or were their hazy suggestions an effort to throw me off?

At that moment, McCaghren excused himself. He announced, rather showily, that he was leaving so the other detectives could "talk freely." They seemed to know he was going to do so; no one looked surprised. I had the unsettling feeling that the meeting had been orchestrated. Was I being led down paths that went nowhere?

Though the cops didn't provide names of suspects, they provided other information that was helpful. They remembered Captain Fannin turned the third floor of the Municipal Building into a military-style command center. He put an enlarged aerial photo of the burglar's target areas on the wall and rolled out a battle plan:

- Patrols and stakeouts were stepped up. One weekend, ten DPD detectives teamed up with ten FBI men to monitor ten Preston Hollow mansions between midnight and dawn.
- Wires with bells and tin cans attached were strung along creeks as a trip alarm in case the thief came sloshing through.
- Electric-eye cameras were installed near houses to snap photos of the thief in action.
- A high-tech company lent night goggles for after-dark searches.

When none of those efforts produced results, one of the detectives threw a dart at the map in frustration. He joked the King would strike there next. He came amazingly close: the next break-in was half a block away.

❖

As I spent more and more time with the detectives, I could see the divide between the haves and have-nots in the case. The cops shopped at Sears, while the victims shopped at Saks. The cops had used cars, the victims had private planes. Bank accounts segregated the city like race.

Though many of the wealthy residents came from the same small-town backgrounds as the cops, the wheel of fate had rewarded them with oil wells or wives with rich daddies. They had the benefit of compound interest. They could send their kids to good schools. Their wives didn't have to take jobs to make ends meet.

In contrast, the policemen's wives worked as checkout clerks in grocery stores, salesladies in department stores, teachers, and nurses. If the cops' kids went to college, they went to smaller state schools, not big-name universities.

Still, the policemen *thought* they were living the American dream—a house, a car, two kids—until they walked into the massive homes in North Dallas with Persian rugs, French paintings, and Russian chandeliers. They came face-to-face with the difference. Suddenly, they became aware that their shoes were the worse for wear, their suits ill-fitting.

As McCaghren put it when he was in a bitter mood one day, "Those people lived in a different world than we did. Here we only had pennies, scratching out a living, and we would have to go out to these fancy homes. You could tell they really did not want us around."

Even though most of the burglary victims were polite, the cops said, they were clearly uncomfortable having policemen in their homes. Many worried what their neighbors would think if they saw a patrol car in the driveway. Instead of calling the police, some called their lawyers to report their losses. And others just kept quiet.

The tensions brought home that most citizens didn't understand the people who kept them safe or what their life was like. As it was, the pay for policemen was low and the divorce rate high. At the time of the Graf burglary, the base pay for Dallas policemen was $326 a month, twenty bucks below a schoolteacher's salary. "If I bought a refrigerator, it was used," Detective Benny Newman remembered.

To make ends meet, two-thirds of the police force had second jobs. They umpired little league games, patrolled bank lobbies, guarded liquor stores. Detective John Chism worked as a security guard at the elite Hockaday School for Girls and did cabinetry work. Benny Newman moonlighted as a plumber's helper. And before he was shot and killed by Lee Harvey Oswald in 1963, Officer J. D. Tippit had two part-time jobs to support his family. He provided security at a barbecue place on Friday and Saturday nights and a movie theater on Sundays.

Then there was the emotional cost. Before the term "post-traumatic stress" came into being, cops struggled to deal with the violence they encountered on the job. It was hard to forget the sight of a head blown open. Or a child who had been tortured with cigarettes by a hopped-up parent.

In the 1960s, patrols became increasingly dangerous as more drugs and guns flowed into the community. "You get attached to the work, and you don't want to leave, but you can only step over so many bodies," Officer Gus Eberhardt told me.

Alcohol and pills became painkillers of choice for some officers. Promiscuous sex provided another outlet. Policemen didn't have to look very far for women to provide stress relief. There were always women around who were drawn to the police.

The combination of temptation and stress contributed to a 60 to 70 percent divorce rate. Fannin had been divorced twice. McCaghren was separated from his wife in the 1960s before reconciling.

When they began their careers, most of Fannin's men had been assigned to poor minority neighborhoods where the streets were full of trouble and animosity toward the police. Yet when they were sent to search for a jewel thief in neighborhoods where the streets were full of money, they felt even more out of place.

Often, the detectives drove up to the manicured mansions in police cars with missing hubcaps. One of Fannin's detectives remembered with a wince that when he was called to an elaborate mansion, a valet insisted on parking his car for him. He was grateful he had been issued a blue Ford from the motor pool that day and not the Studebaker Lark, which was pint-sized and pea green.

Even when the burglary victims were gracious, the detectives felt like strangers in a foreign country. After the King took $100,000 in jewels from a woman, she remarked to Captain Fannin, "Thank goodness, he didn't get my good jewelry!"

Fannin asked, "Your *good* jewelry?"

"Yes, I keep it there," the woman replied, motioning toward an open box on a bedside table. At least $250,000 in jewels was scattered inside, more than $2 million worth in today's values.

Fannin diplomatically urged the woman to put her jewels in a safe at the bank. She agreed and called her chauffeur to take the box to her bank. Fannin sent a detective with the driver. "Not that I don't trust him," he reassured the woman. But by this time, he didn't.

As more reports came in, the police suspected that some incidents blamed on the King were faked by homeowners to reap insurance money. In one instance, detectives found some "stolen" jewels hidden in the top of a toilet. "You would think people with buckets of money wouldn't do that," one detective said, "but they did."

Fannin kept fifteen of his fifty detectives on the King of Diamonds case for several years. Like the cop squads on TV, they were a colorful bunch:

Tyree Leonard, the lieutenant who looked like Alan Ladd, was deceptively handsome. He could muscle even the meanest guys into a squad car. And played golf with hard-nosed bookies.

Gus Eberhardt was the rash one. He became famous for driving over a suspect, who had fled an armed robbery at a dry cleaners by running out the back door. Eberhardt plowed through a fence and a chicken coop to run him down.

Jim Behringer was the uptight one. When we met at another Golden Corral—more fried okra—he wore a thick leather belt plus black suspenders to keep up his pants. A cautious man, I guessed. Sure enough, when we sat down in a booth to eat, Behringer repeatedly asked me to turn off my tape recorder. Reaching across the table for the Stop button, he would say, "Turn that thing off a minute!" After dueling for the button several times, I gave up and turned the recorder off. Still, Behringer remained guarded.

Jasper Kirksmith? "Some people thought he was the thief, but they couldn't get anything on him."

Did he remember a suspect from a hardware store family? "I heard talk like that, but nothing seemed to come from it." He shrugged. "There was also some talk about a gay hairdresser."

Did he remember their names? No. And so it went.

Sgt. Charlie Dellinger was central casting's version of a world-weary detective. He was balding and had the hangdog expression of a man with a sour stomach and unpaid bills. He always seemed to have a cigarette in his hand. Everyone called him Charlie—Charles sounded like someone with a better car.

During World War II, Dellinger served as an Army MP in what was left of Japan. Drawn to policing, he became known for his dogged pursuit. One time, he peeled off his shoes and shirt to dive into a lake to look for a stolen safe—and swam up with it.

Joe Cody was the mouthy good ol' boy on the team. He had a knack for giving the press catchy quotes about the King of Diamonds, like "Don't worry, we'll get him—if we don't run out of diamonds first!"

When Cody claimed the thief was a "way-out weirdy, a real nut," a reporter challenged him, "Then why can't you catch him?" Cody shot back, "The guys's a way-out nut, but a *smart* way-out nut."

Cody did not look like anyone you would want to tangle with. He played hockey when he was younger and had muscular forearms the size of Popeye the sailor. When he joined the DPD, Cody had been excited by the prospect of patrolling near his old high school in south Dallas. He soon discovered the neighborhood was going through a violent transition.

When Black families moved into the all-white area, they were greeted with bombs.

One day, as Cody drove through streets he used to know, a blast lifted a nearby house fifteen feet off the ground and blew out the windshield of Cody's patrol car. He survived with a bloody nose and cuts; the house did not.

Cody worked his way onto the safer territory of Fannin's burglary team. He was so eager to be on the hunt for the King of Diamonds that he went to the library and read up on diamonds.

Following that example, I went to the Sixth Floor Museum to learn more about Cody. The museum had hundreds of oral histories about the 1960s. When he was videotaped in 1999, Cody was working as a private investigator. Dressed in a short-sleeved Banlon shirt that showed his muscled arms, he looked like a guy who just came from the bowling alley.

On the tapes, he remembered how he first met nightclub owner Jack Ruby. "When we got off at eleven P.M., there was no sense going home with your wife already in bed," he said. So, the cops went to Ruby's club, where they could get free beers and a gander at the strippers. After running into Ruby again at an ice rink, where they both skated for exercise, Cody struck up a friendship with Ruby. Cody claimed he cultivated Ruby as an informant, although it was just as likely Ruby cultivated Cody.

"I knew Jack Ruby better than anybody," Cody bragged in his taped interview. He went to Ruby's club enough to know "the strippers were like prostitutes."

When Ruby decided to buy a gun to protect the cash he carried, he asked Cody to buy the gun for him because police officers did not have to pay tax. So Cody paid for a .38-caliber Colt Cobra at a sporting goods store, saving Ruby $18.

Cody then forgot about the purchase. He was running a scuba business on the side and business was busy.

Cody was not the only cop to hang out at Ruby's club. His partner, Gus Eberhardt, told the FBI that he visited Ruby's club nearly every night when he worked the late shift. Some policemen estimated that more than fifty cops had ties to the club owner. Others said the figure was much higher, perhaps one to two hundred of the thousand or so on the force. A former vice officer told the FBI, Ruby "knew just about everybody."

Patrolmen on the beat considered schmoozing with shady characters like Ruby part of their jobs. They needed to cultivate sources, and they couldn't do it from their desks in the Municipal Building. But fraternization had its risks if policemen got too close or complacent with lawbreakers.

Some got very close. Policeman Gene Stansell dated several strippers, including Penny Dollar. Harry Olsen married stripper Kathy Kay Coleman. Roscoe White's wife was the cashier at the Carousel Club. One cop even invited Ruby to his child's christening.

Ruby courted the cops by bringing sandwiches by the dozen to police headquarters and giving out bottles of booze as Christmas gifts. At times, Ruby "comped" as many as eight policemen to Sunday night steak dinners.

It was easy for cops to give in to such inducements—and hard to get rid of those who crossed the line. The internal review process was notoriously ineffective. Fannin sometimes got rid of bad apples by recommending them to other departments.

◆

Officer Charles Sansone was a prime example of internal problems. Like others, he had a second job: he was a bookie. And took bets in police headquarters. Gambling while on duty was against department rules, yet Sansone's bookmaking continued for years. FBI records showed he went almost daily to a service station owned by bookmaker Philip Bosco and local Mafia boss Joe Civello.

Reporter Warren Bosworth told me that when he was discussing the Mafia one day with an intelligence officer, the officer told him, "Come on, I'll show you the Dallas Mafia." He took Bosworth to a memorial service being held for the teenaged son of a reputed Mafia member. As they walked up to the funeral home, Bosworth was surprised to see Charlie Sansone "working the door." When he looked around, "the local members of the Mafia were all there."

So how did Sansone keep his job?

He did his work, policemen said. "Maybe Sansone was a bad guy," one explained, "but he wasn't a bad cop." He was smart, colleagues said, and spoke five languages so well that he served as an Army linguist during World War II. Sansone also ran fast enough to qualify for the Olympics. His colleagues marveled, "He could jump out of a patrol car going 35 mph and catch up with a suspect."

Sansone was open about the betting in the office, Sgt. Gus Eberhardt said. "He told officers if anybody asked about it, to say yes. He didn't care. He would come in and say, 'Anybody want to bet?'"

Sansone liked to buck the rules, wearing sandals to work and tossing beer cans out the window of the municipal building. On weekends, he sold hot dogs that he grilled on a rotisserie at his desk. When Police Chief Carl Hanson came by and noticed the smell of roasting frankfurters, he ordered Sansone to stop selling hot dogs. Sansone saluted. "Yes, sir!" A few weeks later, Hanson came by to check on Sansone. True to his word, Sansone was no longer selling hot dogs. He was selling pizza by the slice.

Several police chiefs tried to force out Sansone, with no success. In the early 1950s, he was suspended by the internal review board as part of an "honesty probe." The review board did not mention Sansone's bookmaking—that would have been awkward for too many guys on the force. Instead, the board cited him for minor infractions like swiping hubcaps from a stolen car and appropriating three bottles of beer while investigating a burglary at a lounge.

Sansone appealed the suspension and hired Charles Tessmer, a criminal lawyer known as "the devil's advocate." A snappy dresser, with wavy red hair and a whiskey-cured voice, Tessmer knew that trials were part theater. He once brought a bed into the courtroom to recreate a crime scene. During his career, Tessmer represented 175 people facing the death penalty, and never lost a client. He even won the day for a woman who admitted in court, "That son of a bitch just needed killin'."

True to his reputation, Tesmer out-lawyered the police attorneys. When the appeals board threw out Sansone's suspension, a contingent of off-duty cops cheered in the courtroom.

Concerns persisted about Sansone, but as one cop put it, "the guy had so much on everyone else, they couldn't touch him."

In 1966, Sansone was charged by federal authorities with violating the wagering tax stamp law by taking bets without registering or paying taxes. Just as the hearing was set, Sansone resigned. He received his full pension and went to work at a restaurant owned by Joe Ianni, a known La Cosa Nostra figure. Later, Sansone got a job manning a toll booth on the turnpike between Fort Worth and Dallas, taking payments from motorists and handing back their change, which few had time to count.

◆

Like most people, I like to believe the majority of policemen are dedicated practitioners even if they weren't as perfectly straight as the marble columns in front of their building. But every law enforcement agency has its bad apples, including the FBI and CIA.

When District Attorney Will Wilson cracked down on crime in Dallas in 1947, the house-cleaning included corruption in the Dallas Police Department. But vestiges remained. In the mid-1950s, a burglary ring was discovered *inside* the department. And in the 1960s, several of Fannin's detectives were known to be heavy gamblers who could be compromised.

A willful blindness persisted for many years about the corrosive effect of gambling in the department. In 1972, FBI wiretaps at bookmaker Bobby Joe Chapman's car lot captured the voices of more than a dozen Dallas policemen talking with the bookies.

"That doesn't mean they weren't *good cops* just because they placed bets," one detective insisted. "That's not in the same category as murder or taking a bribe."

But I had learned enough by this time to know that the fraternizing with lawbreakers normalized lawbreaking. And compromised investigations.

When East Coast journalists Jack Lait and Lee Mortimer came to Dallas in the 1950s to research their book *U.S.A. Confidential*, they noticed something else about the police department: the police turned a blind eye to illegal gambling and other infractions by VIPs because "the town's big shots run it."

"Mustn't arrest the son of a millionaire," they wrote. "The mayor, a businessman's choice, attends to that."

Such things—the tendency to wink at or hush up problems—became important as more came to light about the jewel thefts.

13

The Cat on the Prowl

There were more than a thousand burglaries a year in Dallas in the sixties, yet something about the King of Diamonds break-ins continued to haunt people. Someone—possibly someone they *knew*—was sneaking into their bedrooms while they slept, defenseless. It was the most intimate kind of intrusion.

The break-ins left people on edge. "It's not the kind of thing you forget," they said.

A few people refused to talk about it. One prominent woman came to the phone and said, "I know what you want to talk about, and I will not talk with you."

Click.

A former deb from a wealthy ranch and oil family answered the phone with a pleasant "Hello," but after I explained why I was calling, she became silent. I could tell she was still on the line by faint noises in the background. "Hello," I said. "Are you there? Hello?" Without a word, she carefully eased the receiver down on the phone.

Click.

I took a breath and moved on to the next person on my list.

Luckily for me, most people were still so fascinated by the case that they wanted to talk about it. I went to their homes, invited them to lunch, met them for coffee. Sometimes, I drove by houses that were hit and took cell phone photos. How did the burglar get on the roof? How did he get from a tree to that window? How far was the house from a creek?

With every break-in, I found new clues to add to my list. At first, the burglary at the Bee house looked like the other burglaries, but there were details worth notice.

Phil Bee was one of four Murchison associates targeted by the King of Diamonds. As senior vice president of Clint Murchison's Investment Management Corp., Bee kept the millionaire's diverse dealings in order. This was not easy since Clint Sr. often made deals on the phone or on scraps of paper.

The Bees had noticed the burglaries were getting uncomfortably close but never imagined they would be targets. By Dallas party standards, the Bees were ho-hum. Yes, Bee belonged to Idlewild, the group that hosted events for debutantes, but he preferred taking his family to their ranch on weekends. Joyce Bee kept busy with her church group and her children's schools.

The couple had three young children, two boys and a two-year-old girl named Jill. They worried about Jill because she walked in her sleep. They didn't want her to get hurt in the dark.

On the night of the break-in, the children were asleep in their beds when the thief walked from a creek to the Bee home. Since their house didn't have sliding doors, he removed glass panes from a downstairs window, working silently in the dark. Then he made his way to the Bees' dressing room and gently closed the door to their bedroom so they wouldn't hear him going through the jewelry drawers.

He selected three rings, a gold coin bracelet, and a pearl necklace with forty-four diamonds. One ring—a pear-shaped, seven-carat diamond ring—was valued at $15,000. Another was a sentimental favorite, Joyce Bee's engagement ring.

The thief worked so quietly that no one woke up, not even the family's Irish Setter. When Mrs. Bee discovered the missing windowpanes the next day, she rushed to check her jewelry. Some of her favorites were gone.

The FBI came with the Dallas police to investigate. They were acutely aware that J. Edgar Hoover was personally following the case—and Bee worked for Hoover's friend Clint Murchison.

McCaghren and Charlie Dellinger spotted the familiar overshoe pattern on the ground beneath the broken window. McCaghren asked Joyce Bee, had she worn the jewelry recently? Yes, she said, to a social event the night before.

Did anyone know they were going out? A pushy woman in social circles came to mind. There was something suspicious about her, and she had been in the Bee home. However, Mrs. Bee didn't want to stir up trouble by giving her name. Instead, she mentioned that society reporter Ann Draper had written an article about her recently that included their home address.

Many years later, Jill Bee remembered her parents saying what upset them most was that the thief was so near their children. What if Jill had been sleepwalking? And bumped into the burglar? The thought horrified them.

The Bees got a burglar alarm as soon as they could. And Mrs. Bee never allowed newspapers to print her address again.

Another aspect of the case intrigued McCaghren and Dellinger: Mr. Bee had received a jewelry delivery at his office that week from the J. Ortman firm in New York. Bee bought jewelry from the company sometimes at the recommendation of his boss, Clint Murchison.

An Ortman representative personally delivered a $10,000 diamond necklace to Bee on consignment. Bee wasn't sure his wife would like the design, so he put the necklace in his safe instead of bringing it home. Had he given it to his wife, it would have been in her dresser drawer the night of the burglary.

McCaghren wondered: Did the thief have "inside" information about the delivery? Other wealthy figures in Dallas did business with

Ortman, including Murchison executive Frank Schultz, landscaper Joe Lambert, Lay's potato chip founder Herman Lay, and a socialite named John Higginbotham. Had word circulated that Ortman was in town for a delivery?

McCaghren interviewed the New York jeweler and Bee colleagues. Nothing turned up, but the possibility remained that someone knew about the shipment.

The thief continued to keep the police off-balance. He pulled off five burglaries in three days, then remained inactive for months. He doubled back to some homes. The Otis family set the record of three visits from the jewel thief.

The first occurred in spring of 1961 when the thief broke into the Preston Hollow home of Herbert C. Otis. He had the good fortune of owning an engineering company that was sold to Halliburton, one of the world's largest oil field service companies. His two-story, brick home on Deloache Avenue was one of the loveliest in the area, in part because landscaper Joe Lambert sculpted the six-acre lot into a parklike setting.

The Otis family was cruising on their yacht in the Caribbean that spring. While they were away, the cat burglar scaled the wall around their home and climbed through a window. Once inside, he must have been disappointed, because most of the family's valuables had been put away for safekeeping. The thief left with only $5,000 in jewels, a portion of what he knew they had.

He waited until fall to try another family member. This time, he broke into the home of Otis's daughter Margaret, who had moved into a house of her own on North Versailles in Highland Park. She was stylish and smart, her sister Sally told me. Some of Margaret's jewelry was custom made by her favorite hairdresser, who was known as "Mr. Jack." When she went on a tour of Asia, she brought back gems for Mr. Jack to fashion into one-of-a-kind jewelry.

Like many former debutantes, Margaret Otis had graduated from playing the ingenue to a starring role as a charity ball chairman. When she was chosen to orchestrate the exclusive Crystal Charity Ball in 1961, it was a testament to her social standing. If there was a "must-go" event for the richest of the rich, the Crystal Charity Ball was it. When debutante Nancy Ann Smith and her friends created the gala in 1952, her father, Howell Smith, underwrote the first event with a check for $25,000, the equivalent of $260,000 today. The annual ball went on to become one of the most successful fundraisers in the city, pulling in millions for children's causes.

Margaret Otis worked all year to make the 1961 gala a success. She oversaw everything from the decorations to the donations. Miss Otis wanted to make sure everything went perfectly, with no regrets.

To her shock, a few days before the ball, someone broke into her home. The thief took a relatively small haul—$8,000 worth of jewelry—but some pieces were her favorites. She had worn the diamond wristwatch, cocktail ring, and diamond necklace a few nights before. Now they weren't in her dresser.

McCaghren rushed to her house. The two had met when he investigated earlier burglaries. As the hunt went on, they became closer. It was an odd-couple kind of friendship—he was a cop who grew up on a farm; she was a debutante who grew up in a mansion. He was gruff; she was warm. He played poker; she played in a handbell choir. Still, they enjoyed each other's company.

When her jewels were stolen, McCaghren suspected the King of Diamonds had come to call. The meticulous way the jewels had been lifted looked familiar.

McCaghren asked Miss Otis: Who knew she was going out? She ruled out her parents, and she trusted her hairdresser. (Her sister Sally Otis Cassidy seconded that in an interview with me. "Margaret was very decisive in her feelings. She would not have gone back to Mr. Jack if she thought he was involved in any way.") That left the social set. Margaret Otis thought immediately of a playboy who hung around the edges of the social crowd.

She didn't trust him. It might be him, she told McCaghren. It could be Jasper Kirksmith.

Ah, but McCaghren already knew about Jasper Kirksmith. And now he had an extra incentive to catch him, helping his new friend Margaret and her family.

A few months later, her family had another brush with the thief. When her father took his dog out for a walk at ten thirty P.M., he saw a figure run from his front yard. Otis hurried back into the house and called police. Captain Fannin arrived within minutes because the biggest debutante event of the year—the Terpsichorean Ball—was taking place that night and the burglary team was on alert. One of the police dogs picked up a trail right away and took officers to a series of rippled footprints. The tracks led across several boards placed over a nearby creek, then ended at a street. The dog lost the scent there, leading police to believe the shadowy figure fled in a car.

Plaster casts showed the footprints matched those at other burglary sites. The King had come to call on the Otis family, again. And slipped away, again.

I pondered these incidents for some time, looking for anything that added up to something. In both the Bee and Otis incidents, the burglar seemed familiar with their activities and neighborhoods, so it couldn't be someone who occasionally dropped into town. I put that on my suspect board: *Wasn't a visitor. Must live in the target area.*

Several more break-ins added to the picture. The thief broke into the home of oil producer J. Lee Youngblood on Belclaire Avenue in Highland Park. Youngblood told police he discovered the theft at dawn, two hours after he let the family dog out of the house into the backyard. Since the hour was early, he didn't lock the door when he returned to bed. Someone apparently was watching and let himself in.

The break-in had the hallmarks of a King of Diamonds burglary: The thief left overshoe tracks. He entered through a sliding glass door. He took some jewelry and left some. He climbed over a wall to enter the house, which was near a creek.

Though there was not much new to go on, the Youngblood burglary provided another clue: the King was out before dawn, waiting in the dark for the right moment to strike. I put another Post-it on my board: *He's a night owl. Must not have an eight-to-five job. And probably not married.*

♦

I also noticed that the Youngblood dog, like the Bees' Irish Setter and the Otis dog, didn't bark when an intruder was nearby. This seemed odd, so I started keeping track of family dog responses. Sure enough, pets did not sound off during burglaries at the homes of Frank Schultz, Margaret Hunt Hill, Alfred Heck, Wann Hill, Dean Guerin, Ray Smith, and others. Did the thief bribe them with treats? Or spray them with a calming substance?

Detectives in other parts of the country, who had investigated similar incidents, told me that the whiff of a person's sweat, triggered by fear and adrenaline, is often what alerts dogs. It was likely the Dallas thief had experience with dogs, they said, so he didn't panic.

Fannin's team had not included the reaction of dogs on their spreadsheet, so I added it to my growing list of clues: *Familiar with dogs.*

One family dog did raise an alarm in a break-in, yet the incident was troubling in a different way. Edward Wilson, an attorney, and his wife were entertaining friends at their house on Broken Arrow when an intruder broke in. As Mrs. Wilson walked by the stairs, she noticed the beam of a small flashlight upstairs. She knew all her guests were still downstairs, so who was upstairs? Just then, the Wilsons' dog Sheila, who was in a bedroom on the second floor, barked.

As the couple went up to investigate, Mrs. Wilson heard a male voice saying, "Hush, Sheila!" When they entered the bedroom, no one was inside. The intruder had gone out a sliding door. Though nothing was taken, the Wilsons were unnerved. How did the intruder know their dog's name? Who was in their house?

❖

As word about the burglaries circulated, people grew more apprehensive, even Beatrice Haggerty. Bea Haggerty had a good head on her shoulders, people said, a master's degree and common sense. She seemed unflappable. Yet the burglaries near her home made her uneasy.

Her husband had been working at an exhausting pace, so Mrs. Haggerty was thinking about going away for the holidays. Pat Haggerty was playing a critical role in the transition of Texas Instruments from an oil-services company into a high-tech pioneer, which meant longer hours at work.

As a Navy procurement officer during World War II, Haggerty was impressed by a small Dallas company called Geophysical Services Inc. The company had shifted rapidly from tracking oil to tracking submarines. When CEO Erik Jonsson offered him a job, Haggerty said yes. Renamed Texas Instruments, the company continued to reinvent itself at high speed, introducing the first portable transistor radio and the first handheld calculator. Then in 1958, engineer Jack Kilby figured out how to imbed a tiny circuit for computers on silicon. The microchip was born.

TI went into overdrive to focus on new technology, which meant Pat Haggerty did, too. Worried that he might exhaust himself, Bea Haggerty decided to go away for Christmas in 1962 and avoid the party circuit.

Before they left, she had the persistent feeling that she was on the King's list.

She chided herself that she was overreacting to the publicity about the thief. Their house in Preston Hollow seemed secure. It was walled on three sides; a lagoon fed by a creek made the fourth side inaccessible. And they had a guard dog.

Still, Mrs. Haggerty worried the thief knew they were going out of town. She sensed, "He is coming." She asked her daughter and son-in-law to stay in the house while they were gone. And she put her best jewels in a safe.

As she feared, the thief jimmied open a sliding door while they were gone. He went straight to the Haggertys' bedroom and her jewelry drawer. But Bea Haggerty had foiled him by removing her best jewelry. The thief was not interested in leftovers. He left empty-handed. Neither her house sitters nor her dog noticed him.

The Haggerty break-in confirmed that people were changing their habits because of the thief. They were arranging for house sitters, buying safes, and getting burglar alarms—all because of one mysterious intruder. The King of Diamonds had touched a nerve.

PART THREE
THE CULTURE OF COMPLICITY

"Despite the smug, pious, self-righteous image that Dallas had courted for the past half-century, there has always been a lascivious twinkle in the old girl's eye."
—Gary Cartwright, "Benny and the Boys"

14

High Society and Low Company

To my surprise, gambling came up in nearly every interview I did. Gambling permeated the King of Diamonds era. Most of the suspects gambled. Most of the victims gambled. The cops gambled. The press gambled.

In the 1940s, the Dallas FBI office reported to headquarters, "Gambling is presently operated in Dallas on such a large scale that the small fines do not appear to balance the tremendous scale of gambling."

Most Dallas citizens were like the *Ozzie and Harriet* TV show in the 1950s—except Ozzie had a bookie and Harriet hit the slots.

The exclusive Brook Hollow Golf Club had slot machines. So did Northwood Country Club and the Dallas Athletic Club. The Cipango Club hid theirs behind revolving panels in the bar. Even the fusty Dallas Country Club had "one-armed bandits" downstairs.

One Brook Hollow member recalled an episode involving a woman who was feeding quarters into a machine. The man playing next to her, who had been drinking heavily, complained that he was losing because the woman's ugly hat distracted him. "That's a *ridiculous* hat," he said with a sneer, "and you look *ridiculous* in it!" The woman's husband overheard him and rose to defend his wife. Grabbing the man by the nose, he pulled him down to the floor. "It's a *Lilly Daché*, dammit!" he thundered, making it understood the hat was French. And expensive.

Such was post-war Dallas: Prosperous. Status-conscious. And wayward.

Most players didn't know that the slot machines could be set to guarantee 30 or 40 percent of the take off the top to the house. And a washer could be hidden in the gears to keep players from hitting jackpots.

Would the club members have fed so much money into the one-armed bandits if they knew most of the profits went to organized crime?

The odds were yes, although most people didn't know specifically that New Orleans Mafia boss Carlos Marcello dominated slot operations in the state and the Chicago Outfit manufactured most of the machines. The Dallas rich were married to the mob without knowing who they'd married.

By the 1960s, while the jewel thefts were at their peak, federal authorities estimated $10 million *a week* was being wagered in Dallas—illegally.

From its beginning, Dallas had tension between its better angels and gambling.

When the city was incorporated back in 1856, more than 15 percent of the residents were professional gamblers. A district attorney tried later to curb gambling, but business leaders resisted. They were afraid that reining in card games would be bad for business. Rival Fort Worth was offering gamblers free rent and $3,500 to move there.

As a result, authorities allowed so much gambling that Dallas became known as the "Monte Carlo of the Midwest." Neighboring Fort Worth was called "Little Chicago."

During World War II, more than 1.5 million servicemen came to train in Texas—and fool around in Dallas. City fathers wanted to make sure the boys in uniform had some recreation, so they allowed twenty-seven casinos and goodness knows how many brothels, although as Mae West would say, goodness had nothing to do with it.

By the time the war ended, gambling was thoroughly woven into the fabric of daily life. In 1947, reporter Harry McCormick wrote an article about the number of opportunities he found in a single day. He placed a $2 bet with a bookie on a horse race . . . put a nickel in a slot machine at a downtown club . . . bought two 25-cent chances on a punchboard at a cashier's counter . . . inserted a nickel in a marble machine that paid off in cash . . . and bought a 25-cent ticket on a policy wheel. McCormick said he declined a dice game in the Southland Hotel, because he was tired. McCormick tended to exaggerate, but this time, maybe not.

Many people in Dallas had learned to wink at the law during Prohibition. The great flaw of the Eighteenth Amendment to the Constitution was that instead of convincing Americans to stop drinking alcohol, it forced everyday people who just wanted a cold beer to deal with criminals. In fact, a good many of those who did business with the bootleggers were churchgoers. As the saying went, "Whenever there are four Baptists, there's a fifth."

When Prohibition was repealed in 1933, the bootleggers shifted from selling booze to gambling—same customers, different vices. In return for the freedom to operate, gamblers handed over fines—a $10 "civic contribution" for each customer. The revenues helped municipal government keep taxes low. City fathers winked at gambling because they gambled, too.

So, when Texas Rangers raided gambler Benny Binion's headquarters at the Southland Hotel, the room was empty when they smashed through the door. The boys in blue had tipped Binion that company was coming.

Benny Binion was the bridge between the city's Prohibition days and more widespread gambling. He had started out as a teenaged grifter, learning poker on the road with his father, a horse trader. Instead of finishing school, Binion graduated to bootlegging and running rackets. When gambling boss Ben Whitaker retired, Binion anointed himself the new crime lord.

With his cowboy hats and western shirts, Lester Benjamin Binion was an unlikely looking gangster. He was a tall man with a soft roll around his middle. His face was soft, too, a baby sort of face, but not a pretty baby. Binion's main asset was his personality. He entertained card players with so many colorful stories they hardly noticed he'd won most of the hands. He understood the psychology of keeping customers happy: "People want good whiskey, cheap; good food, cheap; and a square gamble. Make the little man feel like a big man."

Binion promised Dallas leaders he would keep the Mafia out if they let him operate freely. The city kept their part of that deal. Binion? Not entirely. The Maceo crime family in Galveston maintained a close relationship with La Cosa Nostra families in Dallas. The Chicago Outfit had warehouses full of slot machines in West Dallas. The New Orleans Mafia controlled the racing wire. Mafia families controlled vending machines and jukeboxes. They smuggled in untaxed cigarettes and booze. When more out-of-towners started muscling in, Binion realized the new sheriff wasn't going to protect him and scooted to Las Vegas.

His legacy was a culture of quiet complicity with gambling. Even though Binion was a cold-blooded killer—he shot several rivals and blew up another—he presided over a regular poker game on the sixth floor of the Adolphus Hotel. The men around the table included insurance executives, stockbrokers, top men at the Waggoner Ranch, and even a governor, James V. Allred.

By the 1960s, it was not unusual to see prominent men list their University Club membership in their obituaries as if it were on the level of the Yale or Harvard Clubs.

In truth, the University Club had nothing to do with the academic world. It was a nightclub.

And it was run by racketeer Bennie Bickers—the "other Bennie." His nightclub on Commerce Street was an underworld outpost in the heart of downtown.

Bickers had started as the bodyguard for gambling boss Ben Whitaker in the 1930s. He lived on the floor below Whitaker's penthouse and intercepted threats, sometimes by placing a shotgun through the transom when gunmen came to the door. If they looked up, the last thing they saw was Bennie Bickers's smile.

Whitaker taught Bickers how to run the "numbers games," in which winning numbers were drawn like today's lotteries. The games were highly popular in minority areas where customers dreamed a lucky number would be their ticket out of poverty. But the odds were against it: the racketeers kept 80 percent of the take and paid 20 percent to winners. State-run lotteries pay roughly the opposite.

When Benny Binion took charge as crime boss, Bickers became one of his top hands and learned to watch his back. High hedges surrounded his home in Oak Cliff. If anyone came near, floodlights snapped on, and Bickers armed up.

After Binion left, Bickers acquired the University Club. He envisioned a Dallas version of Toots Shor's saloon in Manhattan. The Persian Room offered fine dining on the second floor, while the ground floor featured entertainment in a red-carpeted lounge. For many years, a comic with the improbable name of Ukie Sherin got laughs with jokes like, "Hey, more men have landed on that broad's bed than Iwo Jima."

The club was a boozy male preserve, although women sometimes stopped by for a restorative cocktail after a day of shopping at Neiman Marcus a few doors away. Was there some gambling going on at the University Club? Of course, veterans said, discreet cards and dice. A shuttle took customers who wanted more serious gambling to secret casinos around the area.

A former policeman provided security at the University Club, but other than that, the cops didn't step inside. For many years, the leading bookies in town gathered at the club on Tuesday mornings to settle their bets. Sometimes, billionaire H. L. Hunt stopped by to see if his wagers had paid off.

More importantly to me, the club's regular customers included several of the prime suspects in the jewel theft case. And they all had gambling ties to organized crime.

In 1962, Bennie Bickers sold the University Club to a surprise choice: sports booster George Owen. Owen worked for the Dallas Cowboys and caroused with team owners and their rich friends. The party-hardy millionaires reportedly put up the money for the club, then put Owen in charge.

After the sale, Bickers moved to Las Vegas to become a vice president at the Dunes Hotel. When he died of lung cancer a few years later, local obituaries politely referred to Bickers as a "sportsman," suggesting a gentleman who shot gamebirds rather than a gambler who shot people.

I noticed in the obits that singer Frank Sinatra—who associated with mobsters like the Fischetti brothers—furnished the casket covers. The list of pallbearers included car dealer W. O. Bankston, baseball star Mickey Mantle, a Binion hitman named Al Meadows (not the oilman by the same name), and Desert Inn manager Cecil Simmons, another former Binion associate. The honorary pallbearers included Major Riddle, who brought the first topless shows to Las Vegas. Sportswriter Blackie Sherrod also made the list, as did Murchison partner Bob Thompson.

The name of another pallbearer caught my eye: Dudley Ramsden, the head of the jewelry department at Neiman Marcus. Was the vaunted jewelry salesman hanging out with racketeers? If so, he had plenty of company.

◆

Dallas businessmen, flush with prosperity, gambled every way they could. Besides betting on sports, they bet their friends on the weather or that they could get a pretty girl to look their way. "My husband would even bet on how fast the waiter would come to our table," one woman said. "It was ridiculous."

In fact, local businessmen were so accustomed to gambling as a social pastime that cultural organizations like the Dallas Civic Opera had to add casino games to their gala dinners. Roulette wheels and craps tables were rented. An opera executive explained, "The men wouldn't come if you didn't have gambling."

Some Dallas businessmen got so caught up in the gambling smorgasbord in Las Vegas that they bought stakes in the casinos, for business and pleasure. They invested in the Desert Inn, the Sahara, the Dunes, and the Castaways casinos. Even staid Republic Bank invested in Vegas properties.

On the surface, investing in the casinos looked like a good investment. The revenues supposedly averaged 8 percent a year. However, the FBI estimated the Mafia was skimming more than a million dollars from receipts every day.

And they weren't giving the money to the church.

Former US Attorney Andy Barr put it bluntly: "Gambling is a big part of the criminal nest, along with prostitution and drugs. Gambling helps bring in money, wash it, launder it. They all have a symbiotic relationship—they can't live without the other."

The Dallas people who gambled with criminals would never admit it, but they were helping finance a toxic ecosystem.

As early as 1951, the *Dallas Morning News* had raised concerns that members of the city's elite were hobnobbing with criminals. In an editorial headlined FOR THE NICE PEOPLE, the paper chastised: "Some of the night spots that thrive on gambling with expensive food and name orchestras as the front cover are swank. You see our nicest people there, visibly flattered to have the suave and elegantly tailored bossman stop at their table. He's in the money or he would not be operating a place that has to cash in big and get its protection somewhere . . . Too frequently his background has covered every racket from prostitution to dope and illicit liquor with all their accompaniment that may include banditry and murder. He and his like have made their mark and their pile the country over and Texas is no exception to his presence or to his apparent pleased acceptance by socialites who ought to feel and know better."

Wham! Most Dallas editorials of the day focused on the dangers of communism. This one cast stones.

Yet the cozy relationships did not end. When I asked a businessman if he felt any misgivings about socializing with hoodlums, he laughed out loud. "Well," he said, "they're not *officially* criminals." But that was exactly what they were. To be blunt, gambling was the Trojan horse that organized crime used to enter Dallas.

The extensive society connections to organized crime via gambling added more complexity to my search. The city was honeycombed with risky business.

15

The "Devil's Playhouse"

Tracing the path of socialites who gambled heavily led me to the Top O' Hill Terrace. From the 1930s to the mid-1950s, Top O' Hill was a hush-hush hideaway for millionaires and mobsters.

Most Dallas residents didn't know the casino existed. But the wealthy crowd did.

The casino was hidden beneath a house in the sleepy farming community of Arlington. The unincorporated area was best known for its cotton gins and mineral waters. Things changed after a Fort Worth plumber named C. Fred Browning realized he could make more money gambling than fixing toilets. He set up a gambling room in the Texas Hotel, offering whiskey and wagering.

Gambling had grown so rampant in Fort Worth that Baptist minister J. Frank Norris began a fire-and-brimstone campaign to drive the gamblers out. Fred Browning decided to relocate where he would be out of the crusader's sight.

He found a former teahouse with the quaint name of Top O' Hill Terrace twelve miles away in Arlington. Made from chunks of reddish-brown sandstone and rough-hewn timbers, the teahouse looked like a country cottage. It was perfect for what Browning had in mind—a secret casino.

◆

Browning had an ingenious plan. He hired workers to lift the teahouse off its foundation, construct a casino underneath, then move the house back. Though times were hard as the Depression set in, Browning had made enough money gambling to equip the restaurant with fine china, crystal glasses, and Irish linens. He wanted everything to be worthy of a top-drawer crowd. For the casino, he splurged on thirty-nine-inch roulette wheels, rosewood pool tables, and an oak bar of exceptional craftsmanship.

When Top O' Hill reopened, diners could enjoy an elegant meal on the main floor—or slip downstairs to gamble. To enter the subterranean casino, patrons had to pass through a series of doors with two-way mirrors or peepholes. When they were admitted through the last, a steel-vault door, they found a gambling room with crystal chandeliers and tasteful wallpaper. A hat-check girl took revolvers as well as hats. The dealers wore tuxedos, and a white-jacketed bartender took drink orders.

It was an underground Casino Royale.

Browning had assembled a roomful of ways to lose money—three pool tables, several slot machines, three blackjack tables, two roulette wheels, and two craps tables. In a shrewd touch, Browning installed a hidden mezzanine with a two-way mirror so he could see who was winning—or hiding a card.

As he had hoped, the casino was irresistible to wildcatters who were gamblers at heart. Clint Murchison rolled dice on the ground outside until the doors opened. H. L. Hunt brought actress Gloria Swanson and comedian W. C. Fields. Swashbuckling Glen McCarthy, who was portrayed by James Dean in the movie *Giant*, flew from Houston. Sid Richardson and Monty Moncrief drove from Fort Worth.

As word spread about the casino, caravans of celebrities trekked in. Actor Don Ameche flew from Hollywood. Comedian Bob Hope came by train. Millionaire Howard Hughes rolled dice while wearing tennis shoes with his tuxedo. He brought blonde bombshell Jean Harlow for luck. When Harlow kissed the dice, Hughes won so many chips that crime boss Benny

Binion had to join the table to win the money back for the house. Hughes ended up losing a million dollars.

Over the years, the famous visitors ranged from boxer Jack Dempsey to comedian Buster Keaton. Humorist Will Rogers came with Fort Worth publisher Amon Carter. Cowboy stars Gene Autry and Tom Mix moseyed by. After leading men like Clark Gable came to play, female stars followed suit, including Lana Turner and Marlene Dietrich. Mae West quietly married the casino's handsome talent manager. Actress Hedy Lamarr, a successful inventor off-screen, was so impressed by the high level of play that she returned several times to test her skill.

Crooner Frank Sinatra and his pal Dean Martin showed up, and so did Robert Young, who would become known to TV audiences as the perfect father on *Father Knows Best* and the do-right doctor on *Marcus Welby*.

◆

Why would so many travel so far to play games in a basement? Rich and poor were drawn to the mirage of winning easy money. Browning made the casino a year-round destination by installing a heated swimming pool for winters and a giant chiller for summers. To expand the gambling opportunities, he built a boxing ring.

Browning dreamed of taking a champion to the Kentucky Derby, so he added stables for twenty-five to thirty-five thoroughbreds and built a separate building for a single horse: his prize stud, Royal Ford.

Keeping up the stables and paying off his racing bets eventually drained Browning's finances. During its best days, the casino allegedly averaged a take of $50,000 to $100,000 a night. However, a significant portion went to police bribes, Mafia payoffs, and the stables. Eventually, Browning was forced to borrow money to keep the casino open, then got a $400,000 loan from customer Sid Richardson.

Those who defended Browning claimed that he gave money to charities and didn't allow anyone at the tables who couldn't afford to be there. Church leaders weren't impressed by the charity whitewash. They thundered that the hilltop Babylon was encouraging "moral slackness"—greed, illicit sex, and violence. Families were falling into poverty, they said, because breadwinners were gambling and drinking away their paychecks.

They had a point.

Casino employees knew the gambling wasn't as "straight" as promised. Jack Poe, who worked at the casino as a teenager, told reporters many years later that he had to keep quiet about his job. "If you worked on top of that hill, you knew you should keep your mouth shut. I blocked it out of my mind for years because I was ashamed. It was the devil's playhouse."

Married men took their mistresses there. Or utilized the brothel, where the ladies of the night dressed in black velvet capes. Although working at the casino may have seemed glamorous to the women who were lured from farms or menial jobs, they were branded as "soiled doves" from then on.

Some customers were just a roll of the dice ahead of the law. Bonnie Parker and Clyde Barrow dropped by when they weren't robbing banks. Mobster Bugsy Siegel checked out the casino and so did Mafia bosses from Galveston, Dallas, and New Orleans.

◆

A good many of the jewel theft suspects also spent time at the casino tables. Dealers learned to be wary of three of them: The Kirksmith brothers. They were good at gambling and looked like trouble, even though they sometimes brought their mother. One of the dealers recognized the unique ring that Netta Kirksmith wore, a "snake eyes" ring with two diamonds set in onyx and platinum. He had seen it before in Las Vegas. Word went out: The lady was a serious player, and her sons, too.

The trail of connections to the King of Diamonds case was strong enough for me to drive to Arlington to check out what remained of Top O' Hill.

The casino entrance wasn't easy to find. I doubled back on the street several times, looking right and left. Suddenly, I saw a nondescript sign in front of a large stone gate: ARLINGTON BAPTIST UNIVERSITY.

I had arrived. One of the most notorious casinos in Texas was now a seminary.

The Lord works in mysterious ways, people said, and in this case, Top O' Hill staggered and fell under the weight of Browning's debts and a rare raid by Texas Rangers that scared away customers.

❖

Vickie Bryant, the wife of the seminary's former president, had agreed to show me around the site. She has written an authoritative account of the casino's history and created a mini-museum by rounding up poker chips, ashtrays, and a roulette wheel that wandered off when the casino closed in 1956. She seemed fully aware of the irony of a Sunday School teacher saving the story of a licentious casino. But to her, the casino is a parable of faith. J. Frank Norris had vowed at tent meetings that "one day, we will own the place." And then, by golly, they did.

Norris had personal as well as religious reasons to crusade against the casino. At nine, he took a bullet in his back that was intended for his alcoholic father. He was left with a bent posture and the determination to clean up violence and vice in the area.

Church leaders and lawmen tried repeatedly to get past the shotgun guards at the casino, but failed. In desperation, Rev. Norris's son rammed his car into the iron gate, damaging the vehicle more than the entry. The guests could have escaped anyway by fleeing through tunnels under the casino.

To show how many tunnels were underneath the site, Vickie Bryant pulled out a modern version of a "dowsing rod," the Y-shaped twigs used to pinpoint water. As we walked the grounds, the tip jerked down: Secret shafts were beneath us.

We went downstairs to the cafeteria the Baptists built in the former casino space. Jumbo pots hung over industrial-size stoves. Gallon cans of beans and tomatoes were stacked against walls. Mrs. Bryant directed my attention to a door. With a flourish, she opened it—and revealed a seventy-five-foot-long tunnel to the hillside.

During casino days, gaming tables could be flipped over to become dining tables if an alert came in. Racks for pool sticks revolved so gambling gear could be hidden behind them. And just in case anyone was arrested, publisher Amon Carter promised Browning that his newspaper wouldn't print their names.

◆

As I stood on the terrace of the old hideaway, it was easy to imagine what a heady experience it must have been to relax in the garden as the sun set in the west. Guests could listen to the orchestras of Tommy Dorsey or Benny Goodman while nursing a glass of the finest hooch that bootleggers from Galveston could smuggle in. A young pianist with the unusual first name of Władziu played in the garden before he became famous with his last name, Liberace. And Virginia Katherine McMath tap-danced there before she twirled in movies as Ginger Rogers.

Owner Fred Browning fancied himself a celebrity. He posed for photos in slouch hats pulled down Humphrey Bogart–style. While the casino's neighbors worked in overalls, Browning wore double-breasted suits and spats. An attractive young secretary chauffeured him to the horse races at nearby Arlington Downs.

Vintage photos showed the top dealer, John "Scooter" Crow, wore pin-striped suits with a diamond stickpin, like a financier. However, he kept a leather blackjack called a "sap" in his pocket. It was reinforced with a chunk of lead. If anyone was a spoilsport, the sap could deliver a blow to the temple that was the end of the game.

Mrs. Bryant pointed out a wheelbarrow with metal wheels that was used to haul away bodies after disputes. Corpses were routinely wheeled to the pig farm across the highway, she said, where they became victuals for massive porkers. With more than one pig at work, a body could be reduced to bone scraps and broken teeth in a few days. Leftover skulls, which were difficult to devour, were picked up by the casino staff, crushed, and buried.

Otherwise, bodies were hauled to creeks or stuffed down wells. With a well-timed pause, Mrs. Bryant added that the wells were doused with sulfur and lye, "to kill the odor."

❖

Casino worker Jack Poe got in trouble once for telling others that some of the bodies were still moaning when discarded. As punishment, guards split his tongue with a knife. Gussie the cook sewed it together with her needle and thread. Another employee confided to his family that he heard security goons say after a customer was removed, "Did you put the gun in his mouth—or his ear?"

So, yes, the Texas Rangers had good cause to declare Top O' Hill "Public Enemy No. 1" in the state. In 1947, a crew of Rangers led by Captain M. T. Gonzaullas sneaked in through a hillside tunnel and caught the casino in full swing. They say that when the Rangers stormed in, the gamblers still had cards in their hands. The Rangers arrested fifty patrons and eight employees.

Within a few days, Browning had paid his fines and was back in operation. But business dropped off as customers became more fearful of being arrested.

Another blow came when gambling boss Benny Binion bolted to Las Vegas. He took with him a suitcase full of silver bars made from melted coins and jewelry from Top O' Hill. The suitcase was so heavy that Binion had to haul it to his car in the infamous wheelbarrow.

As Fred Browning's financial troubles grew and his health declined, he handed the casino to longtime customer Sid Richardson. The oilman's Lamar Life Insurance Company then sold the site to the Baptist seminary in 1956. The Baptists had won.

❖

The casino's closing might have been the end of the chapter if not for an unexpected postscript. As I lingered to chat with Mrs. Bryant, she confided that she had received a warning from two mysterious visitors. The men claimed they were "Kennedy researchers," and asked to see her presentation about the casino.

When she finished, the men pulled Mrs. Bryant aside and gave her a blunt warning: she must stop saying that two men with ties to the Mafia collected payments from the casino.

"You should take those names out," they said, repeating for emphasis, *"You need to take them out."*

It was clear this was not a mere suggestion.

Fearing for her safety, Bryant agreed to remove the names. She still believed the Mafia got a percentage of the casino profits, based on Browning's records and her conversations with employees, but she kept quiet about it.

She didn't seem like the type to scare easily, so the incident stayed with me. Why would anyone care about the Mafia names? What was being hidden?

◈

When Top O' Hill closed its doors, other casinos sprang up in the area. Dice maestro Fred Merrill opened a casino in Rockwall, twenty minutes from downtown Dallas. It had a gated entry and guard dogs, just like Top O' Hill. Other secret casinos sprang up in North Dallas and one on Peavy Road in East Dallas. Suspected Mafioso "Chicken Louie" Ferrantello ran a gambling den between Dallas and Fort Worth.

How did people know where the new casinos were?

"Somebody had to let you know," a Dallas judge told me, "but everybody who needed to know, knew."

That included the woman with a distinctive onyx ring—and her three handsome sons.

16

The Peelers and the Guys

L ooking for the jewel thief was giving me an education I didn't anticipate. A different, darker city had been hiding in plain sight. The search led me next to the strip clubs that were hot stuff in the 1960s.

Why strip joints?

That's where the suspects were. Several of them recruited women for parties with rich men.

So I looked closer.

Although Dallas had a reputation as a Bible Belt stopover between the coasts, X-rated clubs did a very robust business. The strip shows were poor second cousins to the burlesque houses in Times Square. Still, they made local celebrities out of showgirls like "Tempest Storm" and "Chris Colt and her 45s."

A small orchestra put out the beat for the bump-and-grind routines, usually drums, a sax, and a piano. With a teasing swish of the cymbals and a snap of the snare drums—ka-pow!—the last piece of apparel dropped to the floor.

The better clubs had a variety show formula: a singer, maybe a magician or ventriloquist, a stripper, and a comedian, badda bing, badda boom. As one showgirl told me, "It was funny guy and take your clothes off, funny guy and take your clothes off." Such was big-city entertainment in the 1950s and early '60s—paying to see women in false eyelashes and little else.

Abe Weinstein's' Colony Club billed itself as the premier after-hours club in downtown Dallas, which meant the restrooms and ashtrays were a little cleaner. A block away on Jackson Street, Weinstein's brother Barney ran a club called the Theater Lounge. Jack Ruby's Carousel Club was only a garage door down Commerce Street from the Colony Club but several rungs below. As Weinstein put it, he ran a cabaret; Ruby ran a joint. Though the clubs had pretensions of supper clubs, the dimly lit, smoke-filled rooms mainly offered watered-down booze and eye candy.

Many of the strippers adopted gimmicks to draw attention. Jack Ruby touted Torrid Toni Turner as "Dallas's first and only reptile charmer." Terre Tale had a patriotic theme—her breasts bounced up and down in time to a marching song, hup-two-three-four. Satan's Angel, who twirled flaming tassels on her pasties, was advertised as "The Ta-Ta Flambé." And Shane Bondurant could swing a ten-gallon Stetson from one of her attributes to the other while spinning two large pistols.

On the surface, these shenanigans may have looked like harmless adult sport, dirty fun. As I looked closer, an uglier side became apparent. The exploitation of women for sex became a reoccurring part of the King of Diamonds story.

◆

Candy Barr was the "It Girl" of the swinging club scene. Besides dancing on stages, she entertained at private "stag parties." Car dealer W. O. Bankston, who hosted parties featuring Candy Barr, bragged that men sometimes paid hundreds of dollars for the chance to see her.

Candy Barr's rise and fall deserved a close look because her story was a rhinestone allegory for those times—and she was linked to players in the King of Diamonds drama.

Her real name was Juanita Dale Slusher. She was nine years old when her mother was killed after "falling" from a moving car on the highway.

Abused by a relative, unwanted by a stepmother, Juanita ran away from her home in Edna, Texas, at fourteen. Many years later, she told the *Los Angeles Times* that her stepmother would make her father beat her if she asked for new shoes or sprinkled too much water on her dress when she was ironing it. "I couldn't take it anymore," she said. She walked away from the farm one morning and headed for town.

She had the bad luck to be picked up on the highway by a man recruiting girls for what was called "the Capture," a prostitution ring that preyed on runaways. Juanita soon was being sold for sex in motels while other girls her age were sipping cokes at the Dairy Queen.

The pimps, Juanita later recounted, expected the girls to service as many men as possible, seven days a week. Oral sex was $20, full intercourse $100. That added up to thousands of dollars a year, but the pimps took most of the money, she said, and insisted on their turn with the girls, too.

As she told it, the Capture's clients included the sons of prominent Dallas families, who were being introduced to the custom of paid sex. Their daddies, who enjoyed a naughty night out themselves, knew where to find girls.

So did the cops. It was not unusual, Juanita said, for patrolmen to stop girls who were part of the Capture and give them a choice: an arrest for vagrancy or sex in the back seat of the police cruiser. There really wasn't much choice. Spending a night in jail meant missing a night's work and a furious pimp.

In interviews, Juanita Slusher rarely went into detail about the abuse she experienced. She saved her anger for her memoir and aimed it squarely at the hypocrisy of the city's elite—the bankers, the lawyers, even ministers—who frequented the prostitution networks.

She felt like a caged bird, she wrote, while college boys exploited the girls on sale. "Many had been raised in privilege; their destiny was to be the next generation of leadership," she wrote. "Their family wealth meant they would rarely get arrested, almost never face adverse publicity for a run-in with the law. Their fathers arranged for a promotion here, an envelope of cash there, perhaps a job for the son of a police officer . . ."

People in Dallas claimed there was no corruption in the city, Juanita wrote, but it was there. She didn't name names, but the descriptions in her book must have made VIPs squirm.

She ran from the assembly-line sex of the Capture and found work cleaning rooms at a motel whimsically named the Trolley Court. After spotting Juanita, a burglar named Shorty latched on to her. Shorty was several decades older, but far from a father figure. Like Fagin, the "kidsman" in Dickens's *Oliver Twist*, Shorty taught runaways how to be criminals. He forced Juanita to distract attendants at gas stations or drive the car while he stole from the cash register. To reinforce his control, he raped her. She was fifteen at the time.

Thanks to a good cop who figured out what was going on, Shorty was arrested and Juanita freed. She thought she had escaped the sex trade when she took up with one of Shorty's other "students," a safecracker named Billy Joe Dabbs. He asked her to get married and promised to take care of her. Instead, he made her the getaway driver in his burglaries and pushed her to have sex with men that she met while dancing at juke joints.

When Dabbs landed in jail, Juanita got a job waitressing at a café. After work, she liked to dance, especially the jitterbug. It wasn't long before she was dancing in lounges around town, changing clubs every time the Liquor Control Board agents caught her being there underage.

She looked like a woman, and a voluptuous one at that, but she made mistakes like the mixed-up teenager she was. When she was sixteen, she got a job as a cigarette girl at the Theater Lounge, where generous tippers got sex. One of the patrons lured her into making a pornographic film called *Smart Aleck*. She said later that she was "sick with shame" for appearing in the movie, but she needed the money.

Though poorly made, the raw film made the rounds of fraternity houses, fraternal lodges, and servicemen's clubs. Juanita Slusher became a porn celebrity. Before long, she moved up to the Colony Club as a dancer. Club owner Abe Weinstein saw something special in the feisty teen. He suggested she'd be more attractive if she bleached her hair. And he gave her a new stage name—"Candy Barr"—because she liked to eat Snickers bars. The name became part of her mystique.

Candy Barr wowed audiences with her sensual dancing and preferred to think of herself as a dancer. She was especially proud that she was hired to teach sexy dance techniques to actress Joan Collins for a movie role, proving she was more than another blonde in pasties.

She was in the vanguard of sexual liberation in the late fifties, according to *Texas Monthly*'s Gary Cartwright. Her body was perfect, he rhapsodized, "but it was the innocence of the face that lured you on." She embodied the conflict between "sex as joy, and sex as danger," he wrote. She made carnality look like fun. But if any overzealous fans reached out to grab her, she was known to slap them out of their chairs—and keep on dancing.

She also was a master of the deadpan line, which endeared her to journalists panting for a good quote. Her new marriage to gambler-pimp Troy Phillips turned out to be another disappointment. Phillips hung out at Jack Ruby's Silver Spur lounge in the Cedars neighborhood and owned a rooming house nearby. He forced Juanita back into sex work as an "outcall" hooker, available on request. They had a daughter together, but once again, she felt like a prisoner.

After she fled, Phillips barged through her apartment door one night in a drunken rage. Juanita shot him in the stomach. As police took her to jail, she struck a pose for the photographers, saying, "Make it sexy, boys." Her defense was that she was aiming for his groin but missed. The charges were dropped.

The shooting made Candy Barr more famous than before. As she put it, "People came out of curiosity to see the girl who shot her husband to defend herself."

Her admirers grew to include college kids, the press, and, some said, Governor Price Daniel.

Even local FBI agents became fans. Since their office was down the street, the agents walked over for amateur nights at Ruby's place because beer was free—and sometimes Candy Barr came to watch before her own act at the Colony Club. "God, she was pretty!" an FBI secretary remembered. "She had not put on all the makeup to go on stage. Her skin looked like a jar of cream. She was just beautiful."

When police arrested her for marijuana possession in 1957, the dramatic scene created a sensation. As the police barged into the stripper's apartment, she pleaded with them not to arrest the man who was with her: George Owen, the same guy who worked for the Dallas Cowboys and briefly ran the University Club. She claimed he was just a "john"—a customer—and promised, "If you let George go, I'll give you the marijuana."

Though it was clear he was more than a customer, the officers freed Owen, and Candy handed over a packet of "grass" that another showgirl had given her for safekeeping. The stash was so small, she had hidden it in her bra. It was barely enough for two cigarettes, four-fifths of an ounce.

When it surfaced that the police had been watching Barr's house and had wiretapped her phone, the bust looked like a setup. The police had laid a trap, using the other showgirl to plant the evidence. Capt. W. P. "Pat" Gannaway, the feared head of the vice squad, wanted to get Candy Barr out of town. Too many wives had complained to city leaders about the stripper. Too many prominent men were worried her address book might fall into the wrong hands.

After her arrest, radio broadcaster Gordon McLendon found Candy Barr an attorney, who was joined by two future state senators. Yet having a high-powered defense team didn't help. The trial turned into a sideshow. Judge Joe B. Brown borrowed a movie camera to take photos of the stripper from the bench. The next day, he brought his own camera, so he could pose with the defendant in his chambers.

Then he sat by and let prosecutors vilify her.

When the prosecution called George Owen to the stand, the lead prosecutor made a point of asking Owen, who was visibly an Anglo, whether he was a white man or a Negro, repeatedly implying that Candy Barr had sex with Black men. In closing, prosecutor Bill Alexander told the jury, "She may be cute . . . but she's soiled and dirty."

The jury slammed her with a fifteen-year sentence.

While her conviction was on appeal, Candy Barr performed in Las Vegas for $2,200 a week, more than she made in a month at the Colony Club. Gangster Mickey Cohen became her new boyfriend. Candy Barr had hit the big time, sort of.

She created a sensation when her "pre-jail tour" took her to the Sho-Bar in the New Orleans French Quarter. The Sho-Bar was owned by Mafia boss Carlos Marcello and his brother Pete. Candy Barr brought a crush of publicity to the club, but the applause was over when the courts rejected her appeal.

She reported to Goree prison outside of Huntsville dressed like a *Vogue* model in a stylish black coat and black gloves. She took one look at the women's unit and dryly observed, "I always wanted a brick house of my own."

By all accounts, Candy Barr was a model prisoner. She performed in the prison rodeo, sang in the choir, and earned her high school diploma. After three years, she was released on April Fool's Day in 1963, thanks to good behavior and the help of influential friends. She walked out with a Bible, $5 in spending money, and a bus ticket to her hometown of Edna on the Gulf Coast.

Her strict probation translated to "Don't come back to Dallas." Under the terms, Barr couldn't travel thirty-six miles beyond Edna, which was 260 miles from Dallas. With a population of less than five thousand, Edna's most distinguishing feature was two grain elevators. There were no clubs where Barr could perform. And she couldn't work at cafés where beer was served, which ruled out waitress jobs.

Candy Barr wanted to go into social work to help troubled young people, but doing good wasn't what people wanted to pay her for. She tried to go into the dog-breeding business—her old friend Jack Ruby gave her one of his puppies to get started. But the dachshund market in Edna was not robust.

She struggled to get by under the punitive restrictions until Governor John Connally pardoned her in 1969. She returned to the stage a few times when she needed money and posed for a centerfold in *Oui* magazine in her forties. When she was a grandmother, she agreed to a "match date" with

Playboy magazine founder Hugh Hefner, who smugly told the press she "was wonderful."

Other than those limited forays, Barr tried to avoid her past. She retreated from the press. The curious found her anyway, including me.

◈

I had interviewed Candy Barr on the phone when I was a reporter at UPI and remember her distinctive, butter-soft voice. She sounded like she was sitting alone in a room, drawing long drags on a cigarette. At that time, she lived in Brownwood, a town of sixteen thousand known for its football teams and bass fishing. Her lakeside home had a sign identifying it as FORT DULCE and a fence to keep the world away. A rare visitor noticed she didn't have any photos from her glamour days on display, just a painting of Jesus.

In the summer of 1970, I called her after new marijuana charges hit the news. Having the state's most famous stripper as a resident had so inflamed Brownwood's constabulary that they stormed into her home at two thirty in the morning and hauled her to jail. But they forgot one thing: an arrest warrant. The charges were dismissed.

When I called and asked what she thought about the maladroit raid, there was a long pause on the line. I felt sure she was going to hang up. Finally, she seemed to sigh and said, "And I thought it would be *quieter* here . . ."

I called her again in 1972 when I heard that she had published a collection of poems called *A Gentle Mind . . . Confused.* She explained she read poetry in prison and was inspired to write freehand verses about "all the things that happened to me." Buyers who thought the poems would be sexy must have been disappointed. They were mostly stream-of-consciousness jottings, therapy for a hard-knocks life.

◈

Though it may not seem like it, Candy Barr was one of the lucky ones. Not all the strip club performers survived.

Bobbie Lou Meserole, who performed as "Shari Angel the Heavenly Body," got addicted to the alcohol and pills that were readily available in clubs, an occupational hazard. At thirty-five, she was working as a prostitute. "Jada," a sultry stripper that Jack Ruby recruited from the Marcellos' Sho-Bar, ended up a heroin addict and drug runner for the Mafia. Stripper "Tuesday Nite" committed suicide. After "Baby LaGrand" was arrested for prostitution, she was found hanged in her cell by her black toreador pants. Marilyn Moon Walle, who performed as "Delilah," was shot to death. Marcia McKittrick was only sixteen when she started stripping at the Theater Lounge. Barely five foot one, she looked like a child with bright pink lipstick. Hooked on heroin, she turned tricks at conventions and Vegas hotels to support her habit. She went to prison after she got involved with a murder-for-pay plot.

◆

This was the other side of the glittering King of Diamonds era. The women who entertained men in nightclubs and at raunchy stag parties rarely, if ever, found the Prince Charming or happy ending they were seeking.

Why didn't the police crack down on club owners—like Jack Ruby? Over the years, there had been multiple reports that he was involved in prostitution. Sheriff Steve Guthrie said Ruby prostituted women from the time he arrived in Dallas in 1947. Ruby's first club partner said he provided women for policemen. A disc jockey testified Ruby provided women for radio salesmen and "others." A cop reported Ruby was pimping women at a downtown café, going booth to booth. The owner of several go-go joints said Ruby provided girls who were the "cripples and culls" from his downtown club.

And yet Ruby, who was arrested nine times for charges like public disturbance and carrying a concealed weapon, was never arrested for prostituting women. Not once. His biggest fine was $35 for ignoring a traffic summons.

I felt sure Ruby's close ties to policemen had protected him, but when I asked a veteran vice cop why Ruby got away with trafficking, he added another reason. Choosing his words carefully, he responded that the police felt city leaders wanted some latitude. "Gambling will always be around, and prostitution, too. It's age-old," he said. "But you can try to keep it in the commode and keep it from overflowing. That was the attitude of the time—keep it in the commode."

What about the businessmen who hosted the stag parties? And the jewel theft suspects who rented women for millionaires? Did the cops look the other way?

Sometimes, he admitted. When VIPs went carousing, there was an unspoken agreement "not to know."

17

"Let George Do It"

P olice looked more closely at Candy Barr's friend George Owen when his name began cropping up as a jewel thief suspect.

On the surface, Owen was a back-slapping sports booster, the kind of over-friendly guy who could find game tickets for you. Behind the scenes, Owen was heavily involved in illegal gambling—and more.

When Owen became owner of the University Club in 1962, his main accomplishment was hiring a talented singer named Diane Wisdom. Cute and blonde, she zipped around town on a motor scooter in her off-hours. Owen became such a fan that he married her. A year later, his gambling losses sank the club. The marriage went under, too.

Although a bust at management, Owen was a master at hustling. In the 1940s, he won a place on the basketball team at SMU with more drive than talent. For the rest of his life, he used that same bravado to pursue money, women, and trouble.

During one of our talks, McCaghren told me that police stopped Owen one day to tell him that he was driving with a briefcase on top of his car. When they opened the briefcase, it was full of money. Owen claimed he was on the way to the bank. McCaghren was skeptical. Among other things, he suspected Owen had something to do with the jewel thefts.

"Why him?" I asked McCaghren.

"People told us to look into him. Sources in the underworld, good sources." He repeated for emphasis, "Good sources. They pointed the finger to him." He wouldn't elaborate except to add, "He was into a lot of bad things."

When McCaghren clammed up, there usually was something behind the silence. I decided to find out more about George Washington Owen Jr.

It was understandable why Owen was worth a serious look:

- He was athletic enough to climb trees.
- He knew his way around affluent neighborhoods from his SMU days.
- He had gambling debts to pay.
- And he definitely had criminal connections.

Having come from a single-parent home of limited means, George Owen had to charm his way up the ladder. He wasn't especially handsome, but he had a fun-loving personality, which enabled him to marry five beautiful women and carry on a "special relationship" with Candy Barr. Even after he two-timed them, his wives tended to say he was a nice guy.

"He made me laugh, and I was always a sucker for that," one of them explained to me. "He had a way about him. He was just fun to hang with."

Owen had a knack for attaching himself to powerful men as well as beautiful women. Car dealer W. O. Bankston was his lifelong mentor. When Owen got out of college, Bankston helped him start a maintenance supply company called Mustang Chemical. However, Owen didn't let his new company or marriage to a pretty schoolteacher interfere with his party life. Before long, his party life became his job.

When Clint Murchison Jr. and his attorney friend Bedford Wynne were putting together a pro football team in 1960, they needed someone to help recruit players and keep them happy. Owen's title was player relations, but it would be more accurate to say he was the "Guy Friday" who scouted out women for athletes and team owners. Owen knew the prettiest women and darkest clubs in town. He was the straw that delivered the drink.

Owen immediately became part of the party crowd that sportswriters dubbed "the Rover Boys." Most of the revelers were associated in some way with Clint Jr., who was riding high as the founder of the Dallas Cowboys. According to team chronicler Joe Nick Patoski, the Rover Boys included Murchison business partners Bob Thompson and Bedford Wynne along with radio mogul Gordon McLendon, PR man Mitch Lewis, horse breeder Fritz Hawn, and oilman Steve Schneider. And from time to time, a wolf pack of monied men—bankers, real estate developers, stockbrokers—played along.

Money, that great deceiver, had led the millionaires to believe they were like gods and, unfortunately, the misbehaving kind. The middle-aged wild bunch set a new standard for carousing. There were X-rated parties at Bedford Wynne's apartment at the Maple Terrace and Gordon McLendon's Cielo Ranch. Some crashed the bacchanals at John Gillin's futuristic house.

Several sources told me the Rover Boys called their party girls "footballs" because they were passed around. Less charitably, Clint Jr. called them "half-whores."

Besides women recruited from the nightclub scene, the party girls included stewardesses and secretaries who were flattered by the attentions of rich men. Clint Jr. liked to attend graduation ceremonies for flight attendants so he could single out prospects. He reportedly kept a list. After a night out, a pretty girl might receive an expensive stereo and TV console. "You could always tell if a girl had been out with Clint," a business associate told me. "They all had the same hi-fi." Those who were invited to travel on his private plane got fancier fare.

Hugh Hefner's notion that any man could become a playboy had caught on in a big way. Men who once prided themselves on being straight-arrow family men now fancied themselves Romeos. They thought their wives didn't know.

"Oh yes, there were a bunch of them who got it into their heads that they were playboys," one wife told me. "They just needed that thrill. It was always the chase, in business and poker—whatever." She dismissed the philandering as a midlife fad, "harmless stuff." She advised friends whose husbands were on the prowl, "Just forget about it and get a new Galanos gown."

❖

When he wasn't out with the Rover Boys or scouting women, Owen played cards with rich men at their country clubs. And some complained he cheated.

"He was really bottom of the barrel," recalled a former accountant from Highland Park. "If we were playing gin rummy, George would slip one or two extra cards into his hand, which gave him an advantage. When he laid his cards down and said 'gin,' he would turn his discard over facedown—and hide an extra card under the discard. Once I figured that out, I quit playing with George. He would call me and say, 'Hey, let's go play cards,' and I would find a way not to."

"He put on a good front, hail-fellow-well-met and all that," the accountant added. "Some of the rich guys loved him because he ran errands for them. He enjoyed the notoriety and the power that came from working for people like W. O. Bankston. They never looked at him real close."

The FBI looked close and reported that Owen was setting up rigged card games with a gambler named Billy Ray Davis, who lived part-time in Florida. Davis was mean, a bookie told me, so mean that he avoided him. He shuddered at the thought of Davis. The FBI said that Owen and Davis had hitman R. D. Matthews call players they had suckered with an ultimatum when they didn't pay up. It was a portent of bad business ahead.

❖

In 1963, a Dallas police memo noted unusually heavy sports betting in the city. An informant tattled that Green Bay Packers superstar Paul Hornung and others were betting on NFL games and George Owen was involved.

The press took notice. But they were more interested in Paul Hornung than George Owen. Hornung was the "golden boy" of pro football—envied by men, desired by women. Could he be colluding with bookies?

A few months later, Hornung and Detroit Lions tackle Alex Karras were suspended for betting on NFL games and associating with undesirable persons. Hornung admitted publicly that he kept company with a Chicago nightclub owner and bookmaker Gilbert "the Brain" Beckley. George Owen was overlooked.

After Hornung was traded to the New Orleans Saints, his roommate turned out to be—George Owen. Cowboys minority owner Bedford Wynne had acquired an interest in the Saints and encouraged majority owner John Mecom Jr. to hire Owen. Hornung described Owen as a "character who knew lots of girls." He wrote in his memoir that whenever the Packers played Dallas in pre-season games, Clint Murchison Jr. and Bedford Wynne would instruct Owen to get Hornung and wide receiver Max McGee "a broad, thinking they would wear us out before the game." It never worked, he said. The Packers beat the Cowboys anyway.

In the 1970s, a federal grand jury questioned Owen about the transmission of wagering information between Dallas and Las Vegas where Owen spent a lot of time. The grand jury also subpoenaed restaurant owner Joseph Campisi, millionaire builder James L. Williams, and two police officers. Yet once again, nothing resulted. Owen seemed to be perpetually under investigation but never charged.

After McCaghren began making inquiries about Owen, Owen found out and confronted the detective in the lobby of the Maple Terrace, where they were both living at the time.

"I hear you've been asking people about me." Owen warned, "You need to lay off. Stop saying I'm a jewel thief."

"If you don't have anything to hide, don't worry," McCaghren shot back.

Ah, but that was just the problem.

Hiding seamy business was Owen's job. As one of his wives put it, "He knew every maintenance man and CEO in town—and every pimp and whore and judge."

McCaghren kept trying to determine what Owen was up to besides illegal betting. Rigging games? Recruiting call girls? Fencing jewels? All of the above?

Owen complained to McCaghren that someone had bugged his car. "Every time I look in the rearview mirror, I see the same car behind me," he said. "Did you guys put some kind of bug in my car?"

McCaghren claimed not to know.

"How can I find out if there is one?" Owen pressed.

"Just take it to a garage and have them put it on their lift and check the underside," McCaghren advised him. "The mechanics could find it pretty easy."

Owen took the car to a garage, but McCaghren was a step ahead of him. He had the DPD pull off the tracking device before Owen got there.

Nothing came of the surveillance. Or at least nothing that McCaghren was willing to share. Owen remained known as a card cheat and womanizer. His five wives included a Playboy Bunny and flight attendant Maureen Kane, who went on to marry White House Counsel John Dean. Maureen Dean became famous as "Mo" Dean, the striking platinum blonde who sat loyally behind her husband during the Watergate hearings in 1973.

And this was where George Owen's story got stickier.

George Owen didn't give many interviews. However, he agreed in the late 1980s to talk to Washington journalist Len Colodny, who was writing a book about the Watergate scandal. Colodny wanted to know how Owen met Maureen Kane. Owen said he met her when she roomed with Heidi Rikan, a woman he was dating. He had gotten involved with Rikan, he explained, when he and Bedford Wynne visited Antigua in 1963 or '64 to see about buying a hotel-casino on the island, the Hotel Mirador.

As Owen told it, he was dressed in a white Palm Beach suit on his way to the casino. It was raining, so the hotel put up an awning to keep people dry when they entered. As he walked up, Owen saw a blonde with a white poodle. Owen was so stunned by her looks that he sat down with a splash in a mud puddle, white suit and all. When the blonde looked his way, he told her, "I've never seen a son of a bitch as pretty as you, and if you jump on my back, I'll take you around the world barefooted."

This improbable but creative pickup line led to dinner with Heidi Rikan and an extended friendship, although Rikan had many other extended friendships. When Owen tired of Rikan, he introduced her to a Texas seed millionaire who provided an apartment for her in Bethesda, Maryland, for many years.

"She was dynamite," Owen told Colodny, "built like a brick shithouse." Almost everyone who met Rikan said the same thing, but in more elevated terms. She was Miss Universe beautiful, they said, smart and smooth. As Raymond Chandler would have put it, Rikan was the kind of dame who could make men "crawl over her shoes" for more. In Owen's case, she could make a guy sit down in a puddle.

But those kinds of descriptions in detective stories are always a red flag. There's trouble ahead. And the woman won't end up well.

I would not have discovered Heidi Rikan's mob connections if I had not been looking into George Owen's background.

As a stripper-turned-call-girl, Rikan made $1,000 a customer. She could afford sable coats and drove a Jaguar XKE. Her icy good looks earned her the nickname "the Countess" and brought her to the attention of Joseph "Possum" Nesline, the gambling and prostitution boss in the nation's capital. He used Heidi to relay money and messages to his casino interests in places like London and Antiqua.

When the Watergate scandal erupted, Heidi's address book became public because it contained the names of high-level Washington politicians. They included Nixon aide Jeb Magruder; Secretary of Commerce Maurice Stans; Connecticut Senator Lowell Weicker; Fred LaRue, a key aide to Attorney General John Mitchell; and even Watergate counsel Sam Dash.

Less noticed were the names of several football team owners—Art Modell of the Cleveland Browns as well as Clint Murchison Jr. and Bedford Wynne of the Dallas Cowboys. Some other Dallas names made the list, including broadcaster Gordon McLendon and restaurant owner Joe Campisi.

Several Mafia figures were listed in the address book along with Alvin Kotz, a Maryland gangster who ran an offshore gambling operation from the Caribbean. Adding to the intrigue, the CIA may have taped some of Rikan's trysts.

The publicity made Heidi Rikan damaged goods, too radioactive for her VIP clients. Tossed out by a "sugar daddy," she reportedly resorted to picking up men in DC bars and charging $50 for sex, barely enough to cover her drinks. After she moved in with a man in her Pennsylvania hometown, she fell down some stairs and died. Hospital records said she was drunk.

❖

And here's where the story gets sticky in another way. George Owen's introduction to Heidi Rikan in Antigua revealed other disturbing relationships.

According to Owen, the man who wanted to sell the Antigua casino had a familiar name: Gilbert "the Brain" Beckley. Yes—the bookie implicated in the Paul Hornung betting controversy.

People often described Gil Beckley as a charming and brilliant man who would have been a top CEO if he had gone to college. Instead, Beckley became the protégé of New York bookmaker Frank Erickson. Beckley inherited Erickson's clients in Dallas—like H. L. Hunt—and became the preferred bookie of celebrities like Bob Hope, George Raft, Frank Sinatra, and Rocky Marciano.

The FBI considered Beckley a criminal mastermind. His name surfaced in rigged boxing matches and heroin smuggling. He excelled at bribing referees and players. He blackmailed coaches who bet on their games. Everyone has their price, Beckley figured, and he could outbid their conscience.

When FBI agents seized Beckley's records in 1966 in Miami, his files showed he made $129,000 on bets that day alone. As the wise guys would say, that was a lot of cheddar—the equivalent of a million dollars in 2022.

Beckley's underworld connections ultimately proved to be his undoing. After he was indicted in 1966 on wagering charges, Beckley reportedly spilled the tea about the Patriarca crime family in New England to the FBI. Not long after that, Beckley disappeared. He was "off the boards," bookies said, out of play, *gone*.

As I sifted through FBI documents about Beckley, I discovered his partners in the Antigua casino included:

- Charles Iannece, aka Charlie White, a big-time bookie, shakedown artist, and hitman. FBI documents say White was a member of the Philadelphia crime family. He was known for shooting a guy to death on the way to a wedding.
- Charles "the Blade" Tourine, a feared executioner for the Genovese family. He ran the Capri casino in Cuba for Santos Trafficante and owned casinos in Florida, the Bahamas, and London as well as Antigua. The casinos did double duty as ports for drug smuggling. The Federal Bureau of Narcotics considered Tourine an international heroin trafficker of considerable clout.
- Anthony "Fat Tony" Salerno, an underboss in the Genovese crime family. Supposedly the model for "Fat Tony" in *The Simpsons* TV show, Salerno was a senior member of the Commission, the ruling council of La Cosa Nostra. With his broad torso and thick neck, Salerno was big as a leather sofa. It wasn't wise to get in his way.

Good grief, I thought. This was *Sopranos* territory.

If the story Owen told Colodny about the Antigua trip was accurate, Owen and Bedford Wynne were dealing with people with blood on their shoes. It was deeply troubling company for guys associated with "America's Team." This was no longer just a matter of "boys being boys."

❖

Owen acknowledged in his interview with Colodny that he was well acquainted with Heidi's boss, Joe Nesline. A short and dapper man, Nesline had an explosive temper that scared bigger men. As the overlord of gambling in the nation's capital, he had the backing of the Genovese crime family.

Nesline used Heidi Rikan and others to establish relationships with pro football figures. "Nesline understood the value of having inside information on injuries or the personal problems of star players," journalist Phil Stanford reported. Anything that could influence the outcomes of games was "useful in setting the betting line."

So, it was no coincidence that the names in Heidi's little black book included players from the Washington Redskins, the Green Bay Packers, and the Dallas Cowboys. And of course, George Owen.

In 1986, Owen was exposed as one of the boosters who provided illicit support for SMU football players. As a result, the NCAA banned Owen from any involvement with SMU athletics for the rest of his life.

❖

Unfazed by the SMU controversy, Owen remained active in the sports world. Being part of the action made him feel important, friends said. He did not have great wealth of his own, but he rode on private planes with men who did.

The former wife of one of the Dallas Cowboys owners remembered Owen saying to her one day, "I bet you think I am just a valet for these guys." She laughed but knew there was some truth to what he said. "Whatever they needed, they would just say 'George will get it' or 'George will do it.'"

Friends go to great lengths to defend Owen as someone who was generous to others. Eulogists at his funeral said he was the kind of friend who would give you the shirt off his back. Everyone agreed Owen was always the most fun guy in the room.

That said, Owen also was the kind of guy who cheated at cards and on his wives. He promoted betting that enriched organized crime. He passed women around like door prizes to rich men. When asked why he stopped dating Heidi Rikan, Owen said he had "hundreds of them" [women] and "couldn't just date one." One of his wives discovered that he took his mistress to the same nightclub where she worked. Another found out he was seeing other women when she saw him on TV at a basketball game with a blonde.

In other words, Owen was a cad.

But was he a jewel thief?

When Owen was seen limping with a hurt ankle, rumors spread that he injured it while jumping out a window during a burglary. Owen claimed he pulled his Achilles tendon playing basketball.

He might have been telling the truth that time. Owen may have been the joker in the deck, a trickster and cheat, but I doubted he was the King of Diamonds.

For one thing, Owen reportedly didn't smoke. Evidence at several crime sites indicated the jewel thief smoked.

For another, the King of Diamonds had refined tastes and was highly selective. The King could tell a real Cartier from a copy. George Owen? Probably not.

Owen also didn't have the pedigree or high-gloss polish to be invited into the homes of the people being burgled. Rich men played cards with Owen, but they wouldn't have invited him to dine with the Baron de Rothschild, although he certainly would have livened things up.

Still, researching George Owen had opened my eyes to big-time sports corruption in Dallas that went beyond friendly bets. This gave me pause.

For years, I thought I was the kind of gritty reporter who saw the ragged sides of life and told it like it was. Now I realized I was square as a box. I had spent far too much of my career covering the school board and city council—and not enough time looking into the night world. The *real* stories in Dallas were happening in places full of smoke and temptation.

18

"Papa Joe"

There were enough shady figures in Dallas back rooms to raise the next question: Could the Mafia have been involved in the jewel heists?

Who had experience snatching jewels? They did.

Who had the best network to whisk hot stuff out of town? They did.

Although local authorities insisted La Cosa Nostra was never a significant factor in Dallas, they were only partly right. True, the Mafia never held the city in a tight grip. You didn't have to slip greenbacks to somebody named Rocco to get "protection" for your mom-and-pop business or get a building permit.

That said, La Cosa Nostra definitely had a presence.

◈

Throughout the King of Diamonds era, Joseph Civello was the acknowledged head of La Cosa Nostra in Dallas. Civello insisted he was just a grocery store owner, but he was arrested in a major heroin bust in the 1930s and spent time in prison. By 1956, he was the undisputed boss in Dallas. When police stormed a Mafia summit in Apalachin, New York, Civello was one of the big boys arrested.

The FBI believed that Civello was closely allied with Carlos Marcello, the powerful Mafia boss in New Orleans. When Civello died in 1970, Joe Campisi, a longtime lieutenant, was considered his successor as head of the Dallas family, though he was never tied directly to any crimes. Federal officials believed that Campisi continued the special relationship with Marcello, facilitating his enterprises in Dallas while the mob boss kept his hand hidden. With his jokey personality, "Papa Joe" was the perfect front man. Whereas Civello kept a low profile; Campisi was a glad-handing extrovert. Everybody knew "Papa Joe." He ran the best pizza place in town.

◆

Campisi's parents had emigrated to the US from Sicily in the early 1900s, joining a small but growing Sicilian community in Dallas. First they opened a small grocery, then they bought a bar with a small kitchen. After a visiting relative suggested they sell "pizza pies" that were popular in New York, the result was Dallas's first pizzeria.

In the 1950s, Joe and his brother Sam Campisi started their own restaurant. They bought the Egyptian Lounge on East Mockingbird Lane from Johnny Grizzaffi, a local hoodlum, then changed the name on the distinctive sign to THE EGYPTIAN RESTAURANT.

The restaurant was an immediate success. The pizza was good, with a crisp crust and plenty of gooey melted cheese. Most evenings, people lined up outside to get in. Yet when their eyes adjusted to the dimly lit interior, customers often noticed some unusual people around them. They looked like gangsters.

People whispered for years that Joe Campisi had ties to organized crime.

To counteract the rumors, he worked hard at being pals with the police, the district attorney, and the press. They could count on free meals when they came in, so they didn't ask many questions.

◆

Joe Campisi coyly denied he was a member of the Mafia. He sometimes showed friends his name in a book called *Brotherhood of the Mafia* and laughed. When asked if he knew certain mob figures in Kansas City and elsewhere, he would shudder, "Those guys scare me."

District Attorney Henry Wade, a regular at the restaurant, contended that if Campisi was the worst Mafia boss in town, "then we have nothing to worry about."

Still, the debate continued: Was he—or wasn't he?

As Detective Paul McCaghren put it, "Joe led people to believe what they wanted to believe. If they thought he was a big deal, he let them believe that. If they thought he was just one of the little guys, he let them believe that."

G. Robert Blakey, the federal prosecutor who drafted the Racketeer Influenced and Corrupt Organization (RICO) Act, had a different view. When I asked if Joe Campisi was associated with organized crime, he answered emphatically, "Yes!" He said Campisi's phone records showed he called Marcello as many as twenty times a week.

Not only that, Campisi played golf with Marcello family members, sent Marcello 260 pounds of sausage at Christmas, celebrated Marcello's birthday with him, and sent letters to him in prison. They were so close that Campisi attended the wedding of Marcello's son Michael in New Orleans—and Marcello's son Joseph attended the wedding of Campisi's son Corky in Dallas.

Campisi bristled when reporters asked him about Marcello. The Marcellos were "beautiful people," he insisted, and he didn't know "anything wrong" that they did.

The New Orleans Crime Commission would have disagreed. They could have told Campisi that besides running gambling, Marcello's billion-dollar criminal operations included holdups, prostitution, extortion, and smuggling stolen goods from cigarettes to jewels to cocaine.

In fact, Marcello had a fencing operation for stolen goods in Dallas. According to investigative reporter Jim Atkinson, the day after a ring member agreed to testify, he was found shot to death.

Campisi was smart enough not to acknowledge such things. Marcello's nickname was "the Little Man" because he was only five foot three, but he was much bigger in mob circles than Joe Campisi.

Dallas intelligence officers told me that when some cops stopped a speeding vehicle one night, they discovered a decapitated corpse in the trunk. After questioning the driver, the cops realized he was a Mafia figure of importance. They couldn't resist asking, "Is Joe Campisi the guy in charge here?"

"*Campisi?*" the mobster replied with a sneer. "Campisi is a *mascot.*"

❖

After I arrived in Dallas in the 1970s, I met Joe Campisi while I was having pizza at his restaurant with college friends. Olive-skinned, with slicked-back hair that had a Brylcreem shine, Campisi came over to our table. "How's your pizza?" he asked with a big grin. He chatted with us for a while, then asked my friend sitting nearest to him what time it was. When she looked at her wrist, she discovered her wristwatch wasn't there.

She was upset. The watch was a graduation present. We frantically looked under the table. Nothing but gum. All of us started sliding out of the booth to search in the parking lot. Then Campisi broke into a loud laugh and produced the watch from his pocket. He had learned the art of lifting watches from a Chicago pickpocket, he said, and liked to stay in practice. Enjoying a good laugh, he made his way to the next table and asked how they liked their pizza.

❖

Everyone in town seemed to have a Campisi story. A band singer told me Campisi pulled the same pickpocket trick on customers at his pal Jimmy Vouras's restaurant, the Chateaubriand. Like my friends, the diners were amazed but uncomfortable when he dumped their bracelets and watches on the table.

A TV anchor told me Campisi gave him free meals and "walking around money" when he was out of work. A bookmaker remembered that Campisi warned him to walk away from a rigged card game at the Sheraton Hotel. Campisi whispered in his ear, "You don't want to play here."

Sportswriters noticed he took pizza to the Dallas Cowboys office on a regular basis and chatted with the staff about the injuries, the starters—just the kind of information a sports better might value.

Campisi gambled heavily. According to local historian Jim Gates, he was a regular visitor to Top O' Hill and bet big on boxing matches there. Gates claimed that Campisi and some of his associates tried to fix some bouts. When they won, Gates wrote, Campisi hosted parties with "good food, booze, and broads."

In the 1960s, Campisi ran gambling tours to the Flamingo Hotel when mob heavyweights owned the hotel. An informant told Dallas police that during one of his gambling jags in Vegas, Campisi lost everything he had with him or could borrow. Dallas friends—including bookmaker Bobby Joe Chapman—came to his rescue.

In 1974, US attorneys subpoenaed Campisi to testify before a federal grand jury investigating gambling ties between Dallas and Las Vegas. Yet nothing seemed to come from the probe. Campisi still got to use a personalized golf cart at the Byron Nelson Golf Tournament hosted by prominent businessmen. The only others to receive a special cart? Comedian Bob Hope and former president Gerald Ford.

More surprising, county officials named Campisi to a seat on the grand jury in the 1980s. This meant a man who admitted he associated with criminals had a say-so in criminal indictments.

◆

Though Campisi wasn't a Mafia heavyweight, he made pizza for them. His restaurant was a clubhouse for nefarious characters that ranged from con men to "made men" in La Cosa Nostra.

The customers who trafficked in jewels were easy to spot. Johnny Tomano, aka "Johnny Tomato," usually showed up with the pockets of his sports coat stuffed with bracelets and rings. The small suitcase he carried with him was full of jewelry and loose stones, all for sale.

Friends say Tomano got his sports coat from Rocky's Pawn Shop. He never wore anything else and never had the jacket cleaned. When he took it back to the pawnshop to have a button fixed, the seamstress insisted on dousing the coat with AirWick first. Though he dressed like a deadbeat, Tomano did well enough selling jewels in the shadow market to acquire extensive real estate holdings in North Dallas.

Another regular, Milton Joseph, sold jewelry out of his Cadillac as well as Campisi's. People called him the "jeweler on the hoof." KLIF radio personality Ron Chapman remembered that Joseph showed up while he was hosting a teen "sock hop." He pestered Chapman to come outside and look in his Cadillac. The trunk was filled with watches, necklaces, rings, and bracelets, like a pirate's treasure chest.

Lots of people mentioned Milt Joseph to me as a King of Diamonds candidate. But this seemed unlikely. As Campisi told federal investigators, *nobody* liked Milt Joseph. Even Jack Ruby found Milt Joseph annoying. He was too obnoxious to have gained access to posh events where the best jewels could be scouted.

Still, the regular presence of people peddling jewelry gave Campisi's restaurant the reputation as a discount warehouse for questionable goods.

A reporter who hung out at the restaurant told me that if you were friendly with Joe, you could get a Rolex watch, or a TV, or a diamond ring at his place. Maybe even a new set of golf clubs. "There's no telling what came over his back dock," he said.

❖

Yet the oddballs selling contraband were not the worst of the lot. No, on any given night, the crowd at Campisi's included guys like R. D. Matthews, who killed for a living—and stole jewels on the side. I had not heard of Matthews until his name started coming up as hitman and a possible King of Diamonds suspect. Gamblers and policemen alike said he was the scariest man in town.

It was hard to say what turned Russell Douglas Matthews into a killer, but it may have been the US Marines. After the Japanese attack on Pearl Harbor, he joined the Marines and proved his fearlessness, earning a Navy Cross and a Purple Heart.

When he returned to Dallas, Matthews fell in with the Green Gang, the most extensive criminal network in North Texas. Lois Green pronounced his name "Loyce," and if you were smart, you pronounced it right the first time. Lois Green and his gang of "Forty Thieves" were involved in safe-cracking, drug smuggling, robbery, and burglary as far away as Tennessee, North Carolina, Utah, Colorado, and Kansas.

Many of the gang members were ex-convicts because Green used a unique recruitment method: he enlisted inmates as they were released from prison. He developed a reputation for ruthlessness by stripping victims naked and shooting them at close range with a shotgun. Then he buried them half-alive.

When Green was shot-gunned himself, R. D. Matthews became a freelance gangster. He ran several bars in Havana and worked in the Hotel Deauville casino for Mafia boss Santos Trafficante Jr. before Fidel Castro took over. Afterward, he took on jobs with the hoodlums known as the Dixie Mafia and removed problems for Trafficante and Carlos Marcello. In the sixties, Matthews owned a series of nightclubs in Dallas, including the notorious Redman Club and Sky Knight Club.

When he was short on cash, Matthews stole jewels, a skill he learned in the Green gang. In fact, he kept a kiln in his garage to melt gold from stolen jewels.

The FBI described Matthews as bad in dozens of ways. Besides being a jewel thief, he was a narcotics pusher, hijacker, and murderer. Agents were warned that Matthews was armed and dangerous.

Stories about Matthews reveal an icy, lethal man. When a customer in a nightclub kept talking loudly while the singer was performing Matthews's favorite song, Matthews pulled out his gun and fired a shot over the man's head. Others weren't so lucky. A reliable source told me that a man who owed money to Matthews came to his house one day. The man didn't have the cash with him, so he said as a joke, "I know I owe you $200—here's a dollar as a down payment." As he placed the bill on the coffee table, Matthews pulled out a gun and shot him. He left the man dying on the floor and walked down the street to a Denny's restaurant, where he ordered a tuna melt, staying just long enough to establish an alibi. Matthews ate half of the sandwich and took half with him. Then he called the police and said, "I just got home, and there's a body in my house." When police arrived, Matthews calmly asked, "Anyone like half of this tuna melt?"

Later on, Matthews wore an eye patch, the result, his wife said, of being shot in the eye by a rival. Others said a girlfriend shot Matthews when she thought he was asleep. Either way, the patch added to his fearsome image. He looked like a one-eyed crocodile. Word went out, "Watch out for the man with the patch."

Dallas police arrested Matthews for burglary, possession of cocaine, illegal bookmaking, and aggravated assault with a motor vehicle. When they couldn't nab him for another charge, they arrested him 57 times for vagrancy. Though he served two years in Leavenworth on drug charges, Matthews usually lawyered his way back onto the street.

There are very few photos available of Matthews, but if you wanted to see what he looked like, you could drop by Campisi's bar. He went to high school with Joe's brother Sam and knew them both very well.

I wanted to refresh my memory of Campisi's restaurant, so I invited a friend to meet me there for lunch. Business in the dining room was slow that day, so we were steered to the red leatherette booths in the bar. Since my friend was a longtime journalist, I asked his advice on my King of Diamonds research. As we talked, I noticed the bartender edging closer to listen to our conversation.

This should have been a signal to cool it, but I discounted the risk. I slid out of the booth to snap some photos of the autographed pictures on the walls. A little voice in my head warned, "Don't." But I wanted some photos of VIPs with Campisi. Suddenly, a woman rushed up to me. She appeared to be one of the managers and asked what I was doing. I stammered that I had come to the restaurant in the seventies, and the photos brought back memories. She didn't appear satisfied, but she faux-smiled and left, with a nod to the bartender. The bartender, who looked like he could go a few rounds with Mike Tyson, immediately brought our check and stood uncomfortably close to our table, looming over us, until we paid.

"That was strange," my friend said as we tried to leave nonchalantly.

I put the incident aside until a series of events followed that put me on guard. When I visited a food store run by a local Mafia family, one of the owners repeatedly demanded to know my name and where I lived. He was so hostile, I left with my heart pounding. Then my accounts were hacked on several websites where I researched criminal records. These could have been odd coincidences, but then I received an anonymous note saying, "Look somewhere else." And an FBI source gave me an unexpected warning. As we finished our conversation and were about to hang up, she added some advice:

"Ms. Pederson—(pause)—be sure to give a copy of your manuscript to a trusted friend."

At the time, I laughed.

Afterward, I wondered what kind of dangers my source had in mind. Who would not want me digging around the past?

Well, actually, plenty of people.

People who preferred to keep skeletons buried.

People who knew what went on with the "party girls."

And people who knew about the layers of crime in the city, the sex trafficking, the illegal gambling, the shady deals.

I had noticed that when the subject of organized crime came up in interviews, people close to the underworld often changed the subject. "Everybody knows what happens if you talk too much," one explained.

After a while, I started getting edgy when I was working late at night and heard noises in the house. I installed more security and, silly as it may seem, got a tattoo of a dagger. It was small, but the blade had a sharp point.

I know this was like putting up a sign that says BEWARE OF DOG when you don't have a dog, but the tattoo was reassuring to me, a sort of protective talisman. I suspect many tattoos serve the same purpose. I deliberately put mine where anyone who saw it would get the intended warning: "I am tougher than I look."

PART FOUR
THE BEAUTIFUL PEOPLE

"It was almost like some light-fingered Louie was thumbing through the Dallas social register."
—Police reporter Harry McCormick

19

The Cinderella Set

As the thefts went on, Fannin and McCaghren noticed the King was mostly active from October to April. He seemed to be a part-time thief. The detectives kicked around possibilities: Did he take summers off? Or live somewhere else half the year? "Maybe he's at the Riviera," officer Joe Cody cracked. At that point, it seemed possible.

After they learned more about high society, Fannin's team realized the King was simply following the social calendar. He operated from fall to spring, when the most elaborate parties—like debutante balls—were held. This made sense because women were more likely to have their best jewels at the ready rather than locked away in banks or home safes.

A quick check showed the families of more than a dozen debutantes were hit. Several lost jewels the night of their daughter's debut. They went to bed thinking it was the best night of their lives—and awoke to find someone had spoiled the moment.

It wasn't long before the press figured out the debutante angle, too. The *Dallas Morning News* ran a front-page headline warning, HIDE THE GEMS, IT's FALL AGAIN.

But how would a *burglar* know about the social season? How did he know who was attending the gala events, and where they lived?

This was unfamiliar territory for me. We did not have deb parties in West Texas, where I grew up. All I knew about polite society came from reading Jane Austen novels.

I invited several debutantes to give me a tutorial at the Starbucks in Highland Park Village, where fashionable women shopped. The first thing you need to know, they said, is the social season revolves around two balls that are sponsored by elite men's clubs. Idlewild, the oldest club, gets to announce the debutantes at a ball in October. The honorees then make their formal bow at the Terpsichorean Ball in late January. In between, there are dances hosted by the Calyx and Dervish men's clubs, plus dances hosted by the premier women's organizations, Slipper and Cotillion. That's six big events. On top of that, there were parties hosted by each deb's parents, plus teas, lunches, and parties hosted by friends. The celebrating lasted through spring.

As one deb summed up, "It was months of seeing the same people."

The marathon of parties also meant a glittering pageant of wealth. In the late 1950s and early 1960s, a debutante's father could expect to spend $25,000 on a ball, the equivalent of $205,000 today. The menu for one dance included oysters Rockefeller, roast suckling pig, lobster, pâté in aspic, assorted French cheeses, mushrooms stuffed with shrimp, and marinated tenderloin of beef. Midnight supper was beef Wellington.

The season also required a wardrobe to showcase the debutante as worthy of attention. A formal gown cost a *minimum* of $800–$1,000 at Neiman Marcus in those days. The store also lent jewels to the debutantes, a shrewd investment in the future. as the young women began upgrading their collections. One deb remembered her grandmother advising her that whenever a tornado warning was issued, "Put on your good jewelry and get in the closet."

The honored young women were born to shine; most had been admired since they were paraded in a pram. They had camera-ready smiles, and after years of dance recitals, they could have waltzed in Vienna.

The Dallas debs were famous for a deep curtsy called the "Dallas Dip." From a standing position, they sank straight down like the wicked witch of Oz melting into her dress, then bowed their heads and rose back up. As they rose, they beamed a triumphant smile to their parents—and the crowd cheered.

It was a princess moment. And indeed, newspapers fawned over the debutantes like members of a royal family. The papers reported their escorts, their schools, their family addresses, and what they wore to parties, including jewels. A 1958 article specified: "Miss Campbell was gowned in slipper satin, a Forever Pink tone. The strapless creation had a wide skirt draped above the hemline and was festooned with matching satin bow-knots. Her jewels were diamonds and her wrap was mink."

When oilman Sid Richardson's niece, Nancy Ann Smith, made her debut in 1946, the event was highly anticipated because society balls had been suspended during World War II. It was the first deb ball in five years. Landscaper and party designer Joe Lambert rose to the occasion, transforming the Baker Hotel into an Italian palace with thousands of crimson-red dahlias.

No family wanted to be outdone, so each deb had to have an elaborate motif for her ball. A White Christmas party featured white birds in white trees and white bunnies on snow-like grounds. Another party featured aquariums with live fish at each table. There were casino parties and Gay Paree parties, Arabian Nights parties, and Roaring Twenties parties. One deb's family recreated the Vienna Opera House with forty strolling violin-ists. Another simulated a blue lagoon with flowing "water castles" created by Peter Wolf, who designed sets for the Dallas Opera.

◈

At their best, the balls were ethereal affairs. Young women in elbow-length white gloves and flowing white gowns swirled around the dance floor with straight-backed young men in white tie and tails. As they waltzed by in a blur of white shoulders and pearls, the scent of perfume floated in the air—a floral whiff of Joy, perhaps, or the sexy incense of Shalimar. It was intoxicating.

For some lucky debs, the parties served as a "pre-honeymoon." After all, the end goal of the Cinderella Dream was a proposal, a home in the right area, children in the right schools. The future depended on attracting Mr. Right or Mr. Will Do.

The catch was that after they married, women had to give control of their finances to their husbands. Under Texas law in those days, women could not buy a car or sign a contract, even a teaching contract, without their husband's permission. They could not hold charge accounts in their own names, which meant their husbands received the bill for everything they purchased. And if a woman had a bank account, her husband could tell the bank not to let her withdraw her funds. This would change in the decades ahead, but in the meantime, it remained vitally important for women to look pleasing and to please—while developing a core of carbon steel.

◆

If one debutante's story captured the importance of money in social life, it was that of Sharon Rubush Blake Simons. Her family history had technicolor sweep. Her grandfather, Michael H. Thomas, made a fortune as a cotton merchant at the turn of the century. People called him Mike, and he was as solid as the name. When cotton markets tumbled, he insisted on repaying every debt in full to show he was a "friend and no ingrate."

With that kind of credo, Thomas did well enough to buy a Georgian mansion in Highland Park. It had belonged to Electra Waggoner, the daughter of ranching giant W. T. Waggoner. She named the house "Shadowland" and spent $500,000 adding art objects and rugs from around the world. According to *Texas Monthly*, one closet was filled with fur coats, another with 350 pairs of shoes, and a third with the latest gowns from Paris and New York.

Electra hosted one epic wingding after another at Shadowland. She sometimes took party guests by private train to her ranch in East Texas, where the guests could see a derrick exploding with oil, or cowboys roping and castrating bulls. Her guests included Anne Morgan, daughter of financial titan J. P. Morgan, and Teddy Roosevelt.

When cotton dealer Michael Thomas bought the house at 4700 Preston Road, he continued the grand parties. He was in "high cotton" and could afford to. He had offices in England, where the great cotton mills were located. That meant the Thomas family divided their time between Highland Park and London. Their daughter Inez had a date with the Prince of Wales and played tennis with Lord Beaverbrook.

Little Inez, known as "Nezzy," was Mike Thomas's favorite of his five children. She had blonde hair, blue eyes, and a turned-up nose. She was petite—"no bigger than a minute," people said—and sassy. She had silver buckles on her shoes and wore dresses by the House of Worth in London. With her silk flapper dresses and wide hats, Nezzy Thomas looked like a character in a Fitzgerald novel, and in a way, she was.

She fell for J. William Rubush, a Dallas bachelor who was so handsome that everyone suggested he should be in the movies. He went to Hollywood and had a fine time hobnobbing with stars like Errol Flynn and Rudolph Valentino. However, he had more profile than talent. He returned home to marry Nezzy, one of the prettiest—and richest—girls in town.

The Rubushes lived a charmed life. Most evenings, they dressed to go out—silk and pearls for her, a tuxedo for him. They danced the night away, then slept till eleven. The Top O' Hill casino in Arlington was a favored destination. Bill Rubush kept trying to beat the odds at the gaming tables, but often failed.

When Nezzy gave birth to their only child, Sharon, she refused to take off her pearls in the delivery room. Even then, she wanted to keep up appearances.

The charmed part of their story crashed down when Mike Thomas died. Market losses and the Depression had drained the Thomas fortune. Nezzy and Bill Rubush were in a bind. They couldn't afford the taxes on the big house. They sold it to a new oil millionaire. To pay their daughter's tuition at the Hockaday School for Girls, the Rubushes had to can and sell pickles from a family recipe. Handsome Bill Rubush struggled. He knew how to dine out in style and gamble the night away, but not what to do from nine to five. He committed suicide.

Nezzy and her teenaged daughter had to fend for themselves. Sharon fibbed that she was sixteen so she could get a job at Neiman Marcus with her mother. Her mother worked in couture, selling the kind of clothes she once bought. Sharon modeled and ran errands for Evelyn Lambert, the store's glamorous fashion director. She learned a lot at the store about living well, though she and her mother were scarcely getting by.

The two had been reduced to renting a small apartment in Oak Lawn, a less prestigious area close to Highland Park. While The Argyle had a cosmopolitan name, their apartment was a far cry from their house on Preston Road. Their old home had a paneled library, a sunroom, and acres of stately lawn. The Argyle barely had closets.

Because they couldn't pay fifty cents to park downtown, Sharon and her mother rode the streetcar to work. When the Idlewild Club invited Sharon to make her debut in 1949, she told them no. Her mother could not afford a new wardrobe, much less the expense of hosting the expected family dance. "I don't even have enough money for carfare," she told the club leaders. They offered to make an exception to protocols because they understood her family's financial fall. Nezzy Rubush pressed her daughter to say yes. She hoped the debut would preserve her daughter's position in society and lead to "a good match."

So, like Cinderella, Miss Rubush got to go to the ball. Her godmother provided a dress that was altered, just as Vivien Leigh refashioned her plantation drapes into a ballgown in *Gone with the Wind*. By day, Sharon rode the streetcar and worked at Neiman Marcus. At night, she danced like a princess.

After the deb season, she surprised her mother by announcing she was getting married. But instead of one of her escorts, she wanted to marry Tom Blake, a Houston oilman and lawyer who was twenty-two years her senior. Blake had seen Sharon Rubush's photo in the newspaper and asked to meet her. Marriage followed. She wanted stability; he wanted her. They divorced after two years and a daughter. Later in life, Sharon admitted dryly, "I might have been looking for a father figure . . ."

She met Pollard Simons at a party at his estate on Lakeside Drive, another millionaires row of mansions. After a whirlwind courtship, they married in Palm Beach. Once again, there was an age difference: he was forty-one, she was twenty-one. But this time, the marriage lasted years.

When the house next door to her childhood home came up for auction, Pollard Simons bought it for his new wife. Sharon Simons had come full circle—from a golden childhood at 4700 Preston Road to a second chance at 4800 Preston.

She could now hire local sensation Trini Lopez to sing at parties and kick off dinners with caviar, sour cream, and blinis washed down with vodka in ice-cold glasses. She mastered multitasking long before cell phones and laptops arrived. President Eisenhower came for lunch one day, and Governor Connally the next. Her husband once invited four hundred people to dinner and gave her a day's notice. She carried it off.

Sharon Simons and her husband came from opposite worlds: She started with everything and lost it. He started with nothing and made a fortune. As a freshman in college, Pollard worked at gas stations. Now he owned oil wells. By the time he married Sharon, Pollard Simons could buy companies like other people bought cars. He owned mines, real estate, insurance companies, and office buildings. A butler brought him breakfast on a silver tray.

Having learned to play golf as a caddy, Pollard Simons was a scratch golfer. He helped develop the Thunderbird Country Club in Palm Springs, where stars like Bob Hope and Bing Crosby played golf. Yet to his deep disappointment, he was turned down for membership in Brook Hollow Golf Club, where the Dallas elite played golf. Word had circulated that Simons was "Middle Eastern," a code word for Jewish. At the time, Jews weren't admitted to establishment clubs. However, Simons wasn't Jewish.

Simons rebounded by building his own country club. The members at his Preston Trail Golf Club included Dallas mayors, bankers, and newspaper owners. And when he developed the Tryall Golf Club in Jamaica, his partners included Senator Lloyd Bentsen and Governor John Connally.

Princess Margaret came to visit at Tryall and so did designer Ralph Lauren, composer Leonard Bernstein, and CBS owner Bill Paley. While Pollard played golf, Sharon shopped for the exact kind of gin the Queen Mother preferred.

Like they say, living well was the best revenge.

◈

I had interviewed Sharon Simons several times on the phone about the King of Diamonds era and always enjoyed the conversations because she was blunt and colorful. So, when I flew to Las Vegas to check out casino links to the burglary case, I added a short flight to Palm Springs to meet her in person.

The minute I left the airport, I felt as if I had stepped into a surreal movie set of palm trees and aquamarine swimming pools. Besides fifty thousand pools and nine golf courses, Palm Springs offered $50 martinis and wine massages. Frank Sinatra and his Rat Pack pals are long gone but people-in-the-know whisper that the Mafia is still around, just more diversified and better dressed.

Sharon Simons's home in nearby Rancho Mirage turned out to be a tasteful, mid-century modern compound. Inside, the house was filled with art—her prized paintings by Warhol and Degas were flanked by her partner Francois Lucet's African sculptures. Best-sellers were stacked on a table with an unfinished puzzle, evidence of ways to fill a day. The dogs looked well-loved and the pool little used.

Sharon Simons entered in tailored slacks and a blouse accentuated by a necklace of oversized blue beads. It was easy to see why the *New York Times* described her as a "dazzling creature." Even in her eighties, she looked ready for a photo shoot. In earlier days, she would have been the kind of tough-talking dame that noir detectives matched wits with. Operatives like Philip Marlowe would have understood the price was too high, but the sport was good. Rich ladies always made things interesting, especially the ones with green eyes.

That kitchen was closed now, as Simons might say. Her party days were behind her. Arthritis limited her mobility, she said, and I could see she walked with difficulty. Filling in details about her life, she said that after her husband's death, she had a brief, turbulent marriage to an oilman. She went to Paris to recover. While there, she met Francois Marie Lucet, the son of a French Duke, an art connoisseur, and artist. After she returned to Dallas, they opened an art gallery together. It didn't last, but the relationship did.

She asked Lucet to drive us to a favorite restaurant, a Belgian bistro called Si Bon. The minute we entered, the owner rushed up to fawn over her.

A bit prickly at first—no, not this table, she insisted, that one is better—she soon settled in and warmed to old memories. When she chaired the Crystal Charity Ball, she recalled, she went to Spain and acquired two Lipizzaner horses to auction at the gala. She also hired two men to squirt wine from goatskin bota bags into guests' glasses. "Even Stanley Marcus was impressed," she remembered, "but I would rather eat bushes than do all that again."

She had a gift for using earthy metaphors, and like some women of her generation, she sweetened her conversation with coquettish phrases, such as "Sweet face, I am telling you . . ." Or "Angel, you wouldn't believe . . ." This was a woman who knew how to lay on the charm.

When her husband invested in Las Vegas casinos, she often went with him to the gambling mecca. She understood that her role was to look glamorous and support his business interests, even if that meant befriending people with a past, like Moe Dalitz, the owner of the Desert Inn. She had learned as a debutante how to make conversation with dull dinner partners, but making small talk with a gangster like Dalitz was daunting. "He had eyes like a lizard, just slits," she remembered. "They never closed, and he never changed expression."

In photos, I could see what she meant. Besides his heavy-lidded eyes, Dalitz had a battered nose that looked as if it had been in some arguments. Though not as well-known today, Moe Dalitz ruled Vegas in those days. As a protégé of Al Capone, he had commanded a navy of smuggling boats in the Great Lakes. Then he took over casinos and moved into the top echelon of the crime world. He became the largest landowner in Las Vegas by latching on to laundries, liquor stores, and prime real estate. When Pollard Simons suggested he add a golf course, he did. And used a gold-and-diamond ball marker.

When Sharon suggested Dalitz put in a lounge where women could drink Bloody Marys while their husbands played golf, he did that, too. Though still in her early twenties, she was a quick study.

Her husband sometimes handed her $100 so she could gamble while he went to more serious games. One night, she asked gambling veteran Jakie Freedman for advice on playing blackjack. She had asked the right man. For many years, Freedman ran the Domain Privee casino in a southern mansion on the outskirts of Houston. Only the rich and powerful were admitted. His staff turned away the rest by saying, "Mr. Freedman is not at home." During the Depression, Freedman reportedly saved Houston's First National Bank by not withdrawing his account.

When Texas authorities cracked down on gambling in the fifties, Freedman moved to the Sands casino in Las Vegas. His official partners were Jack Entratter and Carl Cohen of the famed Copacabana nightclub in New York. The unofficial investors included crime lords Meyer Lansky, Joe Adonis, and Frank Costello as well as gambling power Ed Levinson, one of the regulars at Murchison's Del Charro.

Freedman provided a friendly face for the casino. With his squash of a nose and big ears, he resembled entertainer Jimmy Durante. Many nights he welcomed customers in a Russian-Yiddish-Texas accent, "Jou'all come to da Sands."

Sharon Simons found Freedman easier to talk to than Dalitz. When she asked for his gambling advice, Freedman took her to the door and pointed to his shiny new Cadillac. "I didn't get that sitting on the *outside* of the table," he cautioned. "I got that sitting on the *inside*. Save your money. Buy some jewelry." She understood.

◆

Living with a high-powered businessman like Pollard Simons, who liked to drink and gamble and get what he wanted, was never dull but not always easy. Whatever their difficulties, she said, she relied on him, and he relied on her. When Simons had a heart attack, she brought three meals a day to the hospital—escorted by the Highland Park police chief.

She lived well, and she knew it. She had a Rolls-Royce and a driver. Landscaper Joe Lambert liked to tease there wasn't "a pillow too soft or a mink coat too white" for her. She told the story often and laughed every time because it was true.

Because of their style and frequent trips to different corners of the world, Pollard and Sharon Simons were declared the "jetsetty-est of Dallas" in social columns. When she lunched with Mamie Eisenhower in Florida, it made the news. If she danced with the band at her lawn party, it made the society columns.

With that kind of publicity, I wondered, Why didn't the King of Diamonds steal Sharon Simons's jewels?

He apparently tried. She just didn't realize it at the time.

One night in the mid-1960s, an uninvited guest entered her home. When the couple returned from dinner with friends, Sharon Simons sensed something was amiss but put the thought aside. As Pollard walked upstairs toward his dressing room and she busied herself downstairs, they both heard an odd swooshing sound.

Following the noise, they realized someone had made a hasty exit from a second-floor window. It was a remarkable escape. The intruder slid down a copper awning over a bay window like a playground slide. He dropped to the ground with a thump and dashed across the lawn into the dark.

As the two searched the house, they discovered the intruder had opened a closet that held a safe. The thief must have been looking for her jewels, but she had hidden them under the fabric skirt of a dressing room chair instead of the safe.

Sharon Simons considered herself lucky. Nothing seemed missing. Still, she was afraid to stay alone in the house after that.

At the time of the incident, she thought the intruder might have been a man who worked for them. But Pollard Simons didn't want to give police the man's name. He was a good man when he was sober, her husband said. Better to let it go.

Still, the intrusion nagged her. Who else knew they were going out? Whoever broke into their house either knew their schedule—or watched their home. Either possibility was unsettling.

Sharon Simons didn't realize that one of the leading suspects grew up a block away and knew the family that previously owned the house, the Reagan Caraways. In fact, when Geneva Caraway made her debut in 1958, the suspect attended parties for her. He had been in the house.

When I tossed out his name as someone who might have attended one of her parties, Sharon Simons dismissed the possibility at first. "I ran with an older crowd because my husband was older," she said.

But after some thought, she mused, "He might have been to *one* party . . . and yes, he might have known the family that lived there before . . ." She remembered the man had invited her to come to his home to see a painting she might like to buy. But when he warned that he kept snakes in his house, she told him she was terrified of snakes. "If you have snakes, I won't even drive down your street," she said. She never went to see the painting.

Could he have held a grudge? Maybe, she said. "But there was no way I was going in his house."

Plenty of others would have known Sharon Simons had expensive tastes because she was frequently honored as one of the "Ten Best-Dressed" women in the city, a competition that rivaled the World Cup. She was on a first-name basis with designers like Bill Blass and Oscar de la Renta. And she was good friends with Dudley Ramsden, the head of the Neiman Marcus jewelry department.

◆

Dallas women had a reputation for being fashionable. They deserved it. Women dressed up for shopping, bridge games, airplane trips. Jewels were an essential finishing touch, although custom decreed that women should not wear their heavy-duty jewelry before five P.M. To avoid being labeled a "daytime diamond person," tasteful women wore toned-down jewelry to club lunches and church. They selected "patio jewelry" for outdoor parties—and saved their dazzlers for society balls.

Such was the demand that several Fifth Avenue jewelry firms established full-time representatives in Dallas. One New York jeweler, Julius Cohen, did so much business in Dallas that he was known as "Sparkle Plenty."

The fame of the city's fashionable women spread. In the 1960s, several airlines commissioned posters to advertise their top destinations. The ads typically featured local landmarks—the Golden Gate bridge for San Francisco, the Empire State Building for New York. But what did airlines choose to depict Dallas?

A beautiful woman, fashionably attired and decked out in jewels.

Since the thief seemed to be singling out women who were featured in society coverage, police asked local newspapers to stop printing the home addresses of debutantes and party hosts.

The papers did. Yet the burglaries continued.

When the social season opened, women grew more apprehensive. They wondered if someone was watching them at the parties. Perhaps the thief was on the dance floor with them. Or next to them in the buffet line. He might even be standing close enough to smell their Shalimar. It was unsettling.

As one debutante put it, "It was a very peculiar business."

The Kadane burglary added to their fears. When Jack Kadane and his wife got home from their daughter Judy's deb ball, they discovered a burglar had beaten them in the door.

Kadane's family had emigrated from Lebanon and went from selling sundries out of a wagon to drilling for oil in the Texas Panhandle. An oil field and a town were named after them. When the Kadanes moved to Dallas, they thought they were living the American dream. They had a tasteful house in Preston Hollow with a wide lawn. Then the thief entered their home and the Kadanes realized how vulnerable they were.

"I don't remember how much the thief took, but I do remember my father was not happy about the whole situation," recalled Judy Kadane. "My mother was not a fearful kind of person, but she was very anxious about it. I think it was the fear of someone dangerous being in the house, rather than the loss of the jewelry itself," she said. "That's a scary thought."

Adding to their anxiety, her family still faced a full schedule of social events. That meant they would be away from their home on many nights. Her mother worried: What if the thief came back? Her father hired an off-duty policeman to babysit their house while they went out.

"Dallas used to be the kind of place where you didn't need to lock your doors when you went out. You could leave your keys under the car seat," Judy Kadane remembered. "Now, we had a policeman in the house, and a police car in the driveway."

20

Social Work

For a while, police thought the thief might be someone at Brook Hollow Golf Club, where the most glamorous events were held. Fannin's detectives gave polygraph tests to all the employees, including waiters. No connection turned up.

Next, the police wondered, Could the thief be a valet parker? A valet knew when people were at fancy parties. But that didn't explain thefts while victims were having a quiet dinner at home.

Suspicions turned to society reporters. They had access to party schedules and invitation lists. They attended many events. Could one of them be the eyes and ears of the thief?

Several names cropped up, but Ann Draper's name came up most often. When she was a society columnist at the *Dallas Morning News*, she was known for reporting that was as crisp and no-nonsense as she was. She worked her way up to society editor the hard way, party after party after party.

Mrs. Draper had an unlikely background for a social arbiter. She came from modest beginnings in Ovilla, Texas, which was so small it didn't have a high school. She finished school in nearby Midlothian, a town known primarily for its cement industry. Young Ann Bryson was popular enough to become a cheerleader and was selected "Miss Midlothian." She dropped out of college to marry Jim Draper and went to work as a newspaper reporter in what were called the "women's pages," the section for fashion, food, parties, and weddings. In 1955, she became the society columnist at the *Dallas Morning News*.

When she moved up to society editor, Ann Draper monitored the party scene during the most intense period of the jewel thefts, from 1959–1963. A sturdy woman with a broad face and knowing eyes, Mrs. Draper watched from the sidelines at hundreds of events. And she wasn't afraid to perch her glasses on her nose to see who was dancing with whom.

In 1963, she left the *News* to take over Party Service, a business operated by socialites out of their homes. Mrs. Draper turned Party Service into a full-time business that was indispensable and modestly profitable. In her new role, she controlled the social calendar, sent party invitations, and arranged catering. She also compiled the 1,200 names in the Dallas Social Register, certifying who was in and who was out.

During deb season, Mrs. Draper coordinated as many as 135 events in four months and was den mother to each year's crop of debs. That meant matching debs with escorts and advising them about the required clothes and etiquette. Though she was known in the newsroom for her salty language—"Oh, hell!" being a favorite—Draper advised the young women, "Never use swear words in public."

As manners relaxed in the sixties, more social starlets needed to be reminded: Don't chew gum at events. Don't ask for seconds. Do *not* put on lipstick at the table. Don't point at people. Only one glass of champagne. Cross your legs at the ankles, not the knees. Don't smoke on the dance floor. And for God's sake, *never* drink out of a bottle!

◆

Ann Draper called herself "the Social Secretary of Dallas," and she was. Newcomers often came to her for advice on how they could move from unlisted to A-list. One of those times, she was unwittingly drawn into an epic scam. It became a painful parable about social striving.

The trouble arrived with Margaret and Ernest Medders in 1962. Only a few years before, they had been scraping by in Memphis, Tennessee. Margaret worked as a practical nurse, helping patients with meals, baths, bandages. Ernest had only finished third grade, so he worked as a mechanic's helper and pumped gas at a filling station.

In an astounding transformation, Mr. and Mrs. Medders moved to North Texas. They had heard about the glamourous life in Dallas and wanted to join the whirl of parties. They announced they were heirs to an oil fortune and had an unlimited checkbook. They bought a 185-acre ranch right away and built a house with fifteen rooms, a swimming pool, and a horse barn stocked with Appaloosas. Another barn called "the Coliseum" doubled as a ballroom and could hold up to a thousand guests.

The Medderses were ready to have grand parties. But they didn't know anyone to invite and Dallas was sixty miles away. The couple asked a public relations firm in Dallas, How can we get important people to come to our parties?

They were advised to contact Ann Draper, who could introduce them to people who mattered. And she did. Among others, Mrs. Draper introduced the couple to Evelyn Lambert, who gave them advice on which arts groups conveyed the most status. It didn't take long for word to get around that Mr. and Mrs. Medders were an untapped source of money. Arts and charity fundraisers came running.

The Medderses learned how to entertain like rich Texans. They flew in Guy Lombardo's Orchestra, then brought in Ike and Tina Turner and the Beach Boys. They hired top caterers. They set up champagne fountains. And in a crowning touch, their PR firm hired helicopters—with pilots outfitted in tuxedoes—to ferry guests to their ranch.

At first glance, the couple seemed unlikely society figures: Mrs. Medders was a plump woman with a perky personality but little polish. While she chattered on, her husband, Ernest, rarely spoke. As one observer said, "He was the sort of man who, when you asked him a question, his wife answered." Still, he looked the part of a lanky Texan in his boots and cowboy hat.

Though most of the party guests had never met Mr. and Mrs. Medders before, they trekked to the ranch so long as the $50,000 barn parties continued. "The sixties in Texas was such a go-go, opulent time that people would do almost anything," society columnist Val Imm Bashour wrote later. "Nowadays, I doubt social unknowns could draw that kind of crowd. It shows what can be done with a good press agent and what appears to be endless resources."

The problem was Ernest and Margaret Medders did not have endless resources.

In fact, they did not have any resources at all.

They had borrowed $3 million to fund their dreams. They got $2 million from a small Roman Catholic order in Indiana called the Poor Sisters of St. Francis Seraph and the rest from three banks. The Medderses convinced them they were part of a lawsuit filed on behalf of three thousand relatives of Pelham Humphries, who had owned the land where the historic Spindletop oil well erupted. A lawyer told them that they would get part of a $450 billion claim. So, they started living like millionaires.

But when the lawsuit was thrown out of court in 1965, Margaret and Ernest Medders got nothing. Not a nickel.

Still, the Medderses continued to host parties with their borrowed money. Governor John Connally and Attorney General Waggoner Carr showed up. Lyndon Johnson invited the couple to the White House. They flew home on Air Force One.

Their sudden popularity went to their heads. Margaret Medders began describing herself as "the fashion arbiter of North Texas." Neiman Marcus sales staff drove stacks of clothing in limousines to the ranch so she could select what she wanted. Even after their money from the nuns ran out, Mrs. Medders treated herself to a spending fiesta. She charged a $65,000 ring, an $80,000 necklace, and a $75,000 mink. The tab was $350,000 before the store froze her account.

Undeterred, the Medderses bought radio spots to wish their friends a Merry Christmas. They held a party for Maria von Trapp of *Sound of Music* fame and another for clairvoyant Jeanne Dixon, who apparently didn't foresee her hosts were dead broke. In a final spree, they hired a train to bring their daughters' classmates to a ranch bash.

Then the Medderses admitted the party was over. They declared bankruptcy in 1967. Their charade had lasted five years. Some two hundred creditors were left with large unpaid bills, including caterers, florists, liquor stores—and Mrs. Draper. The biggest losers were the Poor Sisters, now considerably poorer.

The Medders fraud remained a sore subject for years. Money—or rather, the mirage of money—had blinded the *fête set to reality*. Worse, they were duped by a real-life version of *The Beverly Hillbillies*, which happened to be the most popular TV show at the time.

Even the astute Mrs. Draper had been taken for a ride. But she remained indispensable in social life. Perhaps it was inevitable that gossipers would speculate whether she was involved in the jewel thefts. If you had a suspicious mind, and everyone did by that time, you couldn't help but notice that Ann Draper had the kind of information a thief would need: who had jewels, where they lived, and when they were going out.

But the gossipers didn't know that Mrs. Draper was secretly helping the police.

Fannin's detectives had gone to her for advice, just like the Medderses, so she sat them around her kitchen table and explained the social world. She suggested women who had jewels that made them likely targets—and which men might be likely suspects. She was well acquainted with the men in social clubs because she managed all the organizations and kept their membership rolls.

As the thefts continued, Mrs. Draper went further to help the police. She wrote fake news items to trap the King. She reported in her society columns that certain wealthy couples were going away for the weekend, knowing that detectives would be waiting in the houses for the thief.

The thief never took the bait, but the police remained convinced he was someone who attended deb parties. When *Times Herald* reporter Warren Bosworth stopped by the burglary department, he couldn't help laughing when he saw "all the detectives were reading the society pages at their desks."

McCaghren took the research a step further by suggesting some detectives attend debutante events undercover to see what they could learn. Fannin agreed, but there was one problem: none of the detectives owned a tuxedo.

Debutante Margaret Otis volunteered to rent tuxes so detectives wouldn't have to pay out of their own pockets. She and McCaghren had become friends during the investigation. She wanted to help.

Unfortunately, the cops stood out at the fancy balls. They didn't know anyone. And they looked visibly uncomfortable in their rented tuxedoes. No one had told them not to wear brown shoes.

"I didn't even know what a cummerbund was," Detective Benny Newman remembered with a wince.

Some partygoers mistook the police officers for waiters and asked them for a drink. If the King of Diamonds was there, he was probably laughing.

And within a few weeks, Margaret Otis became one of the victims herself.

21

Sid and Nancy

O ilman Sid Richardson inadvertently became a factor in the jewel thefts—or rather his money did—when his niece Nancy Ann joined high society in Dallas.

Richardson was fond of his niece and proud to show her off. She was pretty and blonde. *LIFE* magazine featured a photo of him giving her an affectionate peck at the grand opening of the Shamrock Hotel in Houston in 1949.

Since he never married, Richardson stayed close to his sisters and their families. He liked to joke that he had been "thinkin' about a wife for forty years now." Friends theorized that the girl he was sweet on as a young man chose someone else. Late in life, he drily observed that the richer he got, the more women were interested in him. When Joan Crawford tried to sit next to him at the Del Charro, he squirmed until Ginny Murchison tactfully sat between them.

Richardson remained a bachelor, he said, because he had settled into a lifestyle of working long days and gambling long nights. He told a friend, "Any wife of mine would end up hating me. While I miss the companionship, I know better."

The news media dubbed Richardson "the Billionaire Bachelor," but even he did not know exactly how much he was worth. As he and his friend Clint Murchison would say, "After the first hundred million, who gives a damn?"

Some ranked Sid Richardson second only to H. L. Hunt in wealth and ahead of his friend Clint. Richardson owned millions in oil reserves, refineries, several ranches, an island off the Texas coast, part of the Texas State Radio Network, and half of Hotel Texas in Fort Worth.

He had been friends with Clint Murchison since they worked in his father's peach orchard as teenagers. Classwork bored Richardson, so he started trading cattle in high school and learned how to borrow and bluff. He attended two Baptist colleges, probably due to his mother's influence, who had named her son after an evangelist. However, young Sid was not cut out for the hymn-singing crowd—or the magna cum laude crowd. A teacher advised Richardson that he was wasting his time in college. He agreed. He preferred a livestock auction.

Richardson retained an interest in cattle-raising all his life, but gravitated to the richer prospects in the oil business. He was not an overnight success. He did odd jobs in the oil fields for eight years, including the hard, grubby work on rigs. He made his first fortune buying and selling oil leases with Murchison. A few years later, he was broke again, having lost at wells and cards. Richardson borrowed $40 from his sister Annie to run a "poorboy" operation. That meant buying equipment and leases on credit and persuading crews to take small pay in cash and a share of profits later. His first two wells were dry holes. By Christmas, Richardson didn't have enough money for a postage stamp and his crews didn't have food for their families. Richardson bought a truckload of groceries on credit and had it delivered to the roughnecks. His next wells paid off.

When his luck went dry again, he conducted his business in a drugstore. To visit a drilling site, he had to borrow money from the conductor. But he didn't give up.

While other oilmen were wrestling over oil leases in East Texas, Richardson turned to the desolate stretches of West Texas. He borrowed $30,000 from a friend and drilled in the sand dunes of Winkler County.

This time, he hit a mother lode of oil. Richardson drilled eighty straight wells in the Keystone Field without a dry hole. And kept drilling. His holdings brought in $2 million a year during the Depression.

Richardson amassed more resources than the Rockefellers—yet lived in a small room at the Fort Worth Club. His main personal indulgences were collecting Western art, raising quarter horses, and gambling. If there was a card game or craps table at hand, Sid Richardson was generally in.

♦

Like his friend Murchison, Richardson cultivated people in high places, but he wasn't a fan of Red-baiter Joe McCarthy. Richardson was a good enough judge of livestock to peg McCarthy as a jackass.

He preferred down-to-earth people, whether they were roustabouts or bankers or presidents. He had been friends with Dwight Eisenhower since 1941, when they shared a train ride together. Richardson changed parties to support Eisenhower when he ran for President and remained one of his most generous supporters. Though there were political reasons to keep up ties, the two genuinely seemed to enjoy each other's company. In photos, they are always laughing.

Richardson was loyal to his friends, and they returned the favor. He spoke on the phone with his friend Clint Murchison nearly every morning. Both marveled that they shared deals for decades but never had a disagreement.

According to Murchison's secretary, Ernestine Orrick Van Buren, Richardson once stepped away from a poker game at the Thunderbird Country Club to take a call from Murchison. When Richardson returned to the table, someone asked what Murchison wanted. He wanted to buy a railroad, Richardson said.

"What railroad was it?" the other players asked.

"Hell, I never asked," Richardson said. If Clint wanted him to buy in, Richardson didn't need the details.

When Murchison decided to buy the Del Mar racetrack, Richardson ponied up his share. He spent weeks at a time at the track, betting on races all day and playing cards at night. When FBI Chief J. Edgar Hoover was their guest during racing season, Richardson liked to rib the powerful FBI chief by hollering, "Goddamnit, Hoover, get your ass out of that chair and get me another bowl of chili!"

Although he was longtime friends with evangelist Billy Graham, Richardson was not a churchgoer. Late in life, he donated $100,000 to build a Baptist church in Athens in honor of his mother. When Murchison heard about it, he wrote his old friend a surprisingly tender letter. The gift, he wrote, would "instill love and respect for you and your family name." He closed, "May God put an aura around your head."

A short time later, Richardson died at this home on his San Jose Island. True to habit, he had put in a full day of deal-making when he had a heart attack. He was sixty-eight.

At the time of his death, Richardson controlled more petroleum reserves than three major oil companies. In his will, he stated that he did not have any direct descendants, but just in case someone showed up and claimed to be a descendant, he left a bequest of one dollar.

Richardson left the bulk of his estate to his foundation and the rest to his immediate family. He bequeathed $13 million to each of his sisters, Annie Bass and Fayrene Smith, as well as generous bequests to his nephew, Perry Bass, and his niece, Nancy Ann Smith.

The bequests had a significant ripple effect. His Bass heirs boosted cultural institutions in Fort Worth and helped revive thirty-five blocks of the downtown area. His niece, Nancy Ann, founded a major charity in Dallas—and became an accidental player in the King of Diamonds drama.

◆

The Smiths became part of the jewel theft story when they moved to Dallas. They had been dividing their time between their ranches near Wichita Falls and Fort Worth. Nancy Ann's father, Howell Smith, was partners with Sid Richardson in three ranches, managing thirty thousand to fifty thousand head of cattle. Though Howell Smith had ample money of his own, it was no match for Richardson's wealth, so he was generally identified as Sid Richardson's brother-in-law and his wife as Sid Richardson's sister, like small towns identified by the largest town near them.

Fayrene Smith wanted her daughter Nancy Ann to make her debut in the bright lights of Dallas. As soon as the Smiths got settled on prestigious Park Lane, she sought out social opportunities. However, she was still considered a bit folksy in circles where folksy was not fashionable. As one society matron put it, "Fayrene was a good ol' girl."

The Smiths' two-story brick home was catty-corner from Josephine Graf's house. But unlike the ultra-modern Graf house, the Smith home had a more traditional look. The house had large bay windows on the ground floor and lattice-trimmed balconies on the second floor, which gave it the appearance of a country house. ("Fayrene tried to French-ify it on the inside," one socialite said, "but it was still a lovely house.")

People forgave Fayrene for her rough edges because her daughter balanced the social scales. Nancy Ann had star quality, people said, like Princess Grace. When men said she was "a tall drink of water," they meant it as a compliment. Tall and willowy, Nancy Ann wore clothes like a swan-necked New York model.

She also had a daring side. Growing up in ranch country, Nancy Ann became an expert horsewoman. She won her share of rodeo ribbons, racing her horse around barrels at breakneck speed, blonde hair streaming from her cowboy hat.

While her friends settled down with husbands and toddlers, Nancy Ann showed her independent side, mingling with movie stars in Hollywood, even staying in step with dancer Dan Dailey on the dance floor.

When she finally married in 1957, Nancy Ann didn't choose someone from an established Dallas family. She chose an outsider who was tall, good-looking, and danced as beautifully as she did.

Jim Kirksmith had shown up in Dallas in the late 1940s with his brothers, Jasper and Jack. All three looked good in their tuxedoes and became popular escorts. As time went by, people noticed that Jim was on the dance floor with Nancy Ann Smith more and more. When he accompanied Nancy Ann on a trip to Europe in 1956, her ever-attentive mother, Fayrene, went with them. And paid Jim's bills. When the group returned, Jim Kirksmith and Nancy Ann Smith were engaged.

Their marriage was one of the most glamorous weddings in a glamorous era. One thousand guests were invited to the reception. Joe Lambert redecorated Brook Hollow Golf Club to look like a grand English garden. The entrance was lined with hundreds of hurricane lamps mounted on steel rods and placed at intervals of eighteen inches, creating a wall of light. Six people were assigned to relight the lamps if they blew out.

Inside, Joe Lambert transformed the ballroom into a garden by bringing in 193 dozen camellias, 1,170 Easter lilies, 43 dozen gardenias, 1,000 bride's roses, 650 sprays of white stock, 15 dozen white freesias, 1,000 snapdragons, 100 strings of hothouse smilax, 1,500 stems of peach blossoms, 500 bunches of violets, 2,000 azaleas, 14 dozen white lilacs, a dozen pink magnolias, 5 flowering white peach trees, and a dozen flowering crab apple trees. Approximately 4,000 beeswax candles were placed on the tables, with two men assigned to keep them lighted.

As far as fairy-tale moments went, Nancy Ann Smith's wedding was the tops. Sid Richardson beamed all night long.

Jim Kirksmith was thirty-nine when they married; Nancy Ann was thirty-three. She had thoroughly enjoyed the spotlight as a deb and post-deb; now she wanted to have a family.

Then, ugly rumors began swirling. People whispered that Jim Kirksmith was involved in the outbreak of jewel thefts, partly because he was an outsider and partly because he didn't seem to have a means of support other than Nancy Ann.

Had the jewel thief married one of the most celebrated debutantes in the city? Was he stealing from her friends, the crème de la crème of Dallas?

The potential for front-page scandal was enough to keep Capt. Fannin up at night.

I added Jim Kirksmith to my suspect list, along with his brother Jasper.

22

The Fabulous Cipango

F ollowing the Kirksmiths' trail led me straight to the Cipango Club. Everyone said the brothers went to the posh club a lot. It was the clubhouse for Dallas society, the place to see and be seen.

On any given evening, you could see members looking warily over the rim of their cocktails, wondering if one of the other diners had made off with their diamonds.

Their suspicions were well warranted. As it turned out, all of the main suspects frequented the Cipango.

The Cipango was the favorite watering hole of the rich from 1947 until it closed in the 1970s. People said it was a Texas version of the Stork Club in New York. Like the Manhattan nightspot, some of the owners were men on the wrong side of the law. It was certainly the kind of joint a crime writer would die for. Money was plastered all over the place, not all of it legit. White-gloved waiters glided from table to table. Millionaires sipped Scotch older than their dates. Debutantes danced dangerously close to men who were hoping to get closer.

And the bar? Filled with dolled-up women and guys with trouble on their minds. In the cinema world, this would be the cue for Humphrey

Bogart and Lauren Bacall. The main topic of conversation? Missing diamonds.

◆

At the time of the jewel thefts, private clubs were the only place where you could legally buy a mixed drink in Texas. Otherwise, people had to bring their own bottle in a brown bag and order a "setup" like Coca-Cola or tonic water. The legislature finally approved the purchase of liquor-by-the-drink in 1973, but until then, people in Dallas had to join clubs like the Cipango to get a good martini.

Originally, the Cipango was the home of an insurance businessman named John T. Trezevant. He built the twenty-room mansion on a slight rise near Highland Park in 1907. It was the first in a row of mansions built along scenic Turtle Creek. After World War II, when people had money to celebrate, the Trezevant mansion offered the perfect place for an exclusive club. With its walnut paneling, billiard rooms, and wide terrace, the Trezevant mansion was a place where millionaires could feel at home—or enjoy being away from home.

There was something exotic about the Cipango Club from its beginning. The name came from a mythical island sought by the explorer Marco Polo. Cipango was said to be a place of untold wealth and pagan splendor. According to Marco Polo, the people there "are dependent on nobody, and their gold is abundant beyond all measure." The streets of Cipango, he claimed, were paved in gold "like slabs of stone, two fingers thick."

The poorer streets of Dallas weren't paved at all, but many of the Cipango members *did* have abundance. The initiation fee was $1,000, a pricy sum in the 1940s. Members were supposed to have a net worth of $100,000 and no criminal record, the former enforced more than the latter.

The Cipango offered strong cocktails, hearts of palm, fillet of sole—and discretion. The man in the next booth might be with someone other than his wife. The woman dancing with abandon might be your mother's best friend. A well-muscled bartender—some recall his name was Jim—stepped up quickly to catch anyone who fell while dancing on top of the bar.

Many a night, couples dallied until the wee hours. Some liked to say the club was "where the elite meet to cheat."

Gambling was part of the attraction. While others enjoyed dinner or drinks downstairs, high rollers were playing cards and rolling dice upstairs. Men routinely whispered to their wives as they slipped away from the dining table, "I'm going upstairs for a while."

Snobs at old-line country clubs sniffed that the Cipango was created by "a bunch of oil guys who couldn't get into a *real* country club." But they eventually joined, too, because the Cipango was where things were happening.

Initially, the Cipango was open seven nights a week—sometimes until six A.M. As one socialite proclaimed, "Gin don't know what time it is." Many mornings, bandleader Ray Herrera had to play "When the Saints Go Marching In" to get patrons to *please* close their tabs and go home. He would march members out the front door in a Conga line to their cars. Women often would forget their furs or their purses—even shoes tossed aside on the dance floor. The next afternoon, a steady stream of servants picked up whatever their bosses left behind.

Marjorie Moore, the house piano player, came for a two-week booking—and stayed thirty-four years. She was famous for remembering everyone's favorite tune. As they entered, Moore would play their special song. Winthrop Rockefeller once tipped her $100 for every time she played "La Vie en Rose"—and requested it seven times.

Her real name was Mary Ann Meyer, and she grew up in Wahpeton, North Dakota, a small town close to Fargo. Miss Meyer was only medium pretty with brown hair in a business that favored sexy blondes. Still, Mary Ann Meyer was so good at singing romantic ballads that she got bookings in venues like the Fairmount Hotel in New Orleans. Along the way, she changed her name to Marjorie Moore, which sounded more worldly. In

1952, she was given the choice of a gig at the Desert Inn in Las Vegas or the Cipango Club in Dallas. She chose the Cipango.

The Cipango became her home and the members became her family. Despite offers from Joan Crawford and Arthur Godfrey to promote her career, Marjorie Moore stayed put. She never married, and people suspected from her wistful ballads that there was an unrequited love in her past somewhere. Yet when the stage for the piano rose up each evening, and the spotlight snapped on, Marjorie Moore from Wahpeton, North Dakota, was a star.

One night, actor John Wayne invited her to dance and twirled her across the floor. "In fact, he *threw* me across the dance floor," she remembered. "I ended up sliding across it. I'd seen that in movies, but I never thought it would happen to me."

Another night, Judy Garland was in the audience. Two men in the audience shouted repeatedly for Moore to sing, "Over the Rainbow." She ignored them until Garland stood up and said, "Honey, go ahead and sing it. I'll help you." Such moments became part of the club's allure.

◈

Membership at the Cipango was limited to one thousand and full of VIPs. Whenever movie star Greer Garson and her husband, E. E. "Buddy" Fogelson, dined at the club, they were treated like royalty. The Fogelsons divided their time between Hollywood, their ranch in New Mexico, and their new penthouse at 3525 Turtle Creek. Their penthouse had high ceilings and a dramatic view of downtown Dallas—the city was literally at their feet. And the Cipango Club was a few blocks away.

Instantly recognizable with her titian hair, Greer Garson had an imposing presence, much like the resolute characters she played on screen. Actor Robert Mitchum called her "Big Red." Yet she had a disarming sense of humor. She once brushed aside an inquiry about her age by replying, "I do wish I could tell you my age, but it's impossible. It keeps changing all the time."

Most people didn't know the actress had earned degrees in French and eighteenth-century literature in England—and was smart enough to walk a step behind her husband when they entered the Cipango, so *he* was the star, not her.

Buddy Fogelson was remarkable in his own right. Always meticulously dressed, with a thin, Clark Gable mustache, he was not cinematically handsome but looked polished and prosperous. In his twenties, he proved he had backbone after being badly injured in an auto accident. While recovering, he read law. At the time, you could become a lawyer without attending law school. Fogelson passed the bar exam handily—and wrote his friend Jack Herbert's will.

When war came, Col. Fogelson directed oil procurement for the Allied Forces, no small assignment, and helped establish a pipeline to fuel the Allied advance in Europe.

He remained such a patriotic man that he insisted on leaving 10 percent of his estate to the US government.

For all the material excess and misbehavior that oil wealth spawned, men like Fogelson presented a more positive image as an environmentalist and philanthropist. He liked to gamble as much as other oilmen, but he maintained the reputation of a gentleman. Not all the oilmen did.

Most evenings, the Murchison oil clan was well represented at the Cipango. In fact, Clint Murchison Jr. said he developed the idea for the Dallas Cowboys football team in a booth in the bar.

That said, it was the Murchison women who stole the spotlight. Though she grew up a tomboy, Clint Sr.'s wife, Ginny, wore glamour with ease. People remember with awe that her jewels were so big, you could see them in the dark. Lucille "Lupe" Murchison, the wife of John Murchison, was more interested in art than social life. Still, she could hold her own at the Cipango. She had an apricot-sized, 29-carat diamond ring, designed by artist Salvador Dalí. As for Clint Jr.'s wife, Jane, she had such a dazzling smile that she was the dream girl of every fraternity boy at SMU. But when the short, bespectacled, introverted son of one of the richest men in the world proposed to her, she said yes. Most evenings she wore her favorite hoop earrings to the club; they were covered with diamonds.

The Murchison women were often joined by up-and-comer Evelyn Lambert, who could be counted on to have the hottest gossip and latest fashions. Watching Mrs. Lambert dominate the talk at the table, people across the room sniffed, "Where does Evelyn get the money to keep up with the Murchisons?"

That was the Cipango code: you had to put on your best face—and watch your back.

The people-watching at the Cipango was part of the attraction. Looking around, you might spot some Fords and some Rockefellers. Or you might see comedian Bob Hope dining with Cipriano Andrade III. Like Jack Herbert, Dick Andrade came to Texas from a New York family of distinction. Determined to make his own name, he triumphed as a cotton and oil broker. He went on to build a pipeline, a refining company, and one of the world's biggest sulfur companies in Mexico.

Andrade enjoyed the fun that money could buy. He palled around with actors like Errol Flynn and Tyrone Power. During the Kentucky Derby, Andrade hosted parties for a week at his hotel suite and once brought a horse up the elevator to the festivities. He made life a party, people said, and picked up the tab. When a thief broke into his home in Preston Hollow and walked out with some of his wife's jewels, he did not report it to the police. He could replace them.

If you peered into the bar area, you might see sports great Mickey Mantle, who was building a giant bowling alley in Dallas. "The Mick" often bent elbows with football star Bobby Layne. Their capacity for alcohol was the stuff of legend. Mantle once floored a bar patron who was annoying him with one punch. Witnesses said he knocked the man out without leaving his seat or spilling his drink.

Actor John Wayne started coming to the Cipango during the filming of *The Alamo* in Texas in 1959. Wayne had been trying to make a movie about the historic battle for nearly seventeen years, but he needed money to finish the project. The Murchisons and other oilmen stepped up to help. Since tensions with Russia were heating up, they considered the movie a patriotic statement about American courage.

When reporter-socialite John Schoellkopf walked in, diners took notice. Word had circulated that he was keeping company with stripper Candy Barr, so people whispered he might be the mysterious thief. Some of Schoellkopf's colleagues at the *Dallas Times Herald* began to tease him, "Are you the King?"

"Absolutely *not*," his newspaper friend Jim Lehrer said when I mentioned the rumors. Schoellkopf wanted to make his name *writing* about crime, not committing it, Lehrer insisted. Capt. Fannin, who had gotten to know the reporter well, agreed. Schoellkopf wasn't on his list. But everyone else at the Cipango was.

That was the charm of the Cipango: The place was a mix of El Morocco and Rick's Cafe. At one table, you might spot slippery Russian Georges de Mohrenschildt, who was whispering about oil in Haiti—and jewels, the favored currency of people operating in the shadows.

Betty Blake, a Philadelphia heiress, might be at the next table. She had come to Dallas with Jock McLean, whose family owned the Hope Diamond. When they divorced, she stayed because she liked the city's energy.

She had partied in London with Noel Coward, spoke French fluently, and owned Picassos.

At another table, you might spot car dealer W. O. Bankston. He had no idea who Picasso was and partied with strippers. The maître d' once turned Bankston away for not having on a coat and tie. He returned in a tuxedo and top hat, but no shoes. He got all the way to the bar before anyone noticed he was barefoot.

As one of the members put it, the colorful auto dealer stood out in the fashionable club "like a hair in a biscuit." Bankston was partial to loud sport coats that looked like plaid car seat covers and wore a Rolex watch encircled by diamonds. He usually carried $1,000 in bills with him, rolled up and secured with a rubber band. When he needed money or wanted to impress someone, he pulled out the wad of bills and peeled off some greenbacks.

A born salesman, Bankston had more personality than a Shriner convention. He liked to open conversations by asking, "Guess how much money I made today?" The answer was plenty. Bankston made enough money to bid for the New York Yankees in 1947 and came close to buying the Dallas Cowboys in 1984.

Bankston got away with bragging about himself because he went from nothing to something. As he told it, he lost his job as an undertaker's assistant in Brownwood, Texas, on Christmas Day during the Depression. He was seventeen. Hoping to find work, Bankston hitched a ride in a boxcar to Dallas. He got caught at the railyard by a young constable named Bill Decker. Bankston persuaded the constable that he was not a vagrant because he had a dollar in his pocket (not true) and a referral for a job (also not true). Impressed by his spunk, Decker gave the kid a bunk for the night at the jail, a donut breakfast, and a lead on a real job.

Bankston was grateful the rest of his life. After he became a successful car dealer, he gave Decker a new car every year. Bankston also helped Decker win election as sheriff and made sure District Attorney Henry Wade won his first race. Over time, Bankston gained enough political clout to become chairman of the Dallas County Grand Jury—while keeping company with gamblers and hitmen.

As friends put it, W. O. Bankston "was bigger than the room," whether the room was a football stadium or the Cipango Club. Bankston didn't just befriend cops, he tagged along on their calls. He had a police radio and a car siren so he could speed to crime scenes with the siren blaring. Cops were always welcome to drinks in Bankston's office. And if he happened to be hosting a stag party that featured his friend Candy Barr, the lawmen returned the favor and did not spoil the party.

Friends defended Bankston's more questionable activities by saying he was the most big-hearted man they knew. Before his buddy Benny Binion left town in 1946, Bankston convinced the gambler to give his homesite on Northwest Highway to a church. The move enabled the church to expand its outreach to alcoholics like Bankston. Bankston regularly promised the minister that he would stick with the Alcoholics Anonymous program, which he did until he didn't.

Bankston was the friendly uncle of people in trouble. If you were down on your luck, out of a job, or behind bars, Bankston was the first to say, "I'll hep ya." When Floyd Hamilton, a member of the Bonnie and Clyde gang, got out of prison and couldn't get a job, Bankston hired the murderer as a night watchman. When baseball great Babe Ruth found out he had cancer, Bankston took him to get drunk. He helped Mickey Mantle buy a house when he moved to Dallas and bailed out George Owen when he flopped in business.

During times when he was "on the sauce," Bankston could be found at the Cipango bar with Owen and Mantle. According to *D Magazine*, the three won a bet one night by getting a Baltimore pitcher drunk before a game. Mantle and Owen rigged the contest by drinking tea instead of booze while daring the pitcher to match them drink for drink. The pitcher got drunk as a wheelbarrow. But so did Bankston, who forgot to switch to tea. He passed out after eighteen drinks.

◆

People drank at the Cipango with abandon. Perhaps it was the dark interior and the sense that they were in a hidden universe where the number of drinks or the hour didn't count. This usually meant trouble.

From the bandstand, the musicians could see who was cuddling and who was arguing. One married couple that drank heavily would routinely get into a fight at their table. "The funny thing was that she would throw a drink in his face every time—and then they would get up and dance," remembered singer Char Lovett.

Of course, many people came to the Cipango just to have a quiet, first-class meal—that would be the white-shoe lawyers, the pin-striped bankers, and the women in sensible Adele Simpson suits. But to tell the truth, they were the wallpaper for the chandeliers in the crowd.

As the night went on, party hostess Nancy Hamon was likely to sit on the piano and belt out show tunes. As a young girl from San Antonio, she went to Hollywood with hopes of becoming a movie star. After a few bit parts, movie mogul Louis B. Mayer told her the harsh truth: she didn't have the talent to be a star. But she stood out enough as a dancer on a promotional tour to capture the attention of oilman Jake Hamon. Thanks to Hamon's money, Nancy Hamon became the star of her own productions, the parties that were the talk of the town. For one party, she was Marie Antoinette; for another, a flapper. Between parties, the Cipango was her stage.

◆

When Nancy Ann Smith and Jim Kirksmith stepped onto the Cipango dance floor, they usually stopped the conversation. The two could dance like Fred Astaire and Ginger Rogers—or rather, Fred Astaire and Cyd Charisse, since Nancy Ann had long legs like Charisse. Nancy Ann had studied ballet and loved to dance. Jim was less schooled, but he knew how to show her off. They always drew applause.

"It was like magic," one woman said. "They could do the foxtrot and the rumba and the cha-cha. You name it, they could do it. And they looked gorgeous together. People just stopped what they were doing to watch them."

People may have put down their forks to admire the couple's style, but behind their hands, they were saying there was something shady about Jim Kirksmith and his brothers. Chances were good his brothers were upstairs gambling at the time.

◆

The loudest applause for Nancy Ann Smith's dancing often came from three stalwarts on the social circuit: John Higginbotham Jr., Gerald Hargett, and Currie McCutcheon Jr. The three had admired Nancy Ann's glamour since her debutante days and had attached themselves to her. When she was selected to appear at the Beau Nash charity ball in Chicago, they went along.

All three had been officers in social organizations: Higginbotham was past president of Idlewild. Hargett and McCutcheon were past presidents of Terpsichorean. They were "close as pages in a book," people said, and a handsome trio. John Higginbotham photographed well with his dark hair and blue-green eyes. He had escorted Hollywood actress Dorothy Malone when she was a Highland Park classmate named Dorothy Maloney. Gerald Hargett had curly brown hair and was noticeably short. His size was one of the first things people mentioned about him, as in, "Oh, the short one." When matched with a taller debutante, Hargett stood on higher ground to appear head-to-head in photos. He was clever and fun to be with, people said. Currie McCutcheon was tall and slender, with light brown hair and a pale complexion. His family lived in a Swiss Avenue mansion. He was a sweet guy, people said, and everyone liked him.

Altogether, the three knew how to put on the Ritz with dates drawn from the Social Register. They were well-dressed, well-mannered, and well-connected. Few would have ever guessed that one of them might become a suspect in the jewel thefts, but one did.

◆

I only went to the Cipango a few times, when it was in its last years. By that time, it had a shabby-chic, Gloria-Swanson-in-Sunset-Boulevard look to it. The stale smell of nicotine and Chanel No. 5 hung in the air.

It was so dark in the bar you had to feel your way to your chair until your eyes adjusted. I dimly remember seeing big phones on the tables. You could use them to call another table. Despite that attempt at modernity, the Cipango had the feel of years gone by, a time capsule.

When I asked Lt. McCaghren if he had ever gone to the Cipango Club, he gave me one of his withering, world-weary looks. "No. I. Did. Not. Go. To. The. Cipango," he said, accentuating every syllable. Cops were the last people members of the Cipango wanted to see. Besides that, a detective's pay didn't cover crêpes suzette.

People joked that the Cipango offered, "All you can eat for a thousand dollars." Despite the price, they remembered with fondness the steak au poivre, the "Itsy-Bitsy Salad" (which was not so bitsy), and the soufflé potatoes, which were french fries that magically puffed up in size.

Manager Eddie Zimmerman was the indispensable man at the Cipango for twenty-five of its best years. Without his demanding standards, it's doubtful the club would have enjoyed its elevated status for so long. He watched over every detail with hawklike vigilance: food must be served promptly at the proper temperature, glasses refilled without a spill, breadcrumbs whisked off the tablecloth. If Zimmerman thought the band singer was singing too loud for diners to converse, he would walk over and shut off the microphone.

Tall, with erect posture, Zimmerman had an old-world courtliness, like a displaced European royal. In reality, his father was a wholesale grocer, and Eddie grew up stacking crates of vegetables. He acquired his savoir faire working at the top-of-the-line Baker Hotel and Brook Hollow Golf Club. He was the perfect buffer between the silk-stocking crowd that dined downstairs at the Cipango and the rougher crowd that ran gambling upstairs.

The gambling was operated by racketeers Earl Dalton and Victor "Ivy" Miller. Both had worked for Benny Binion at Top O' Hill. As Damon Runyon might put it, Boy Scouts they weren't.

Ivy Miller did not fit anybody's idea of a posh club operator. He was tubby and had a boxer's smashed nose. According to Binion biographer Doug Swanson, Miller tried to improve his image by sporting a blue blazer, neatly knotted tie, and straw boater. He still looked like a street mug—and was. When a gambler named Sam Murray had encroached on Binion's territory, Ivy Miller fired seven bullets at him in broad daylight from the doorway of Dallas National Bank. He claimed Murray pulled a gun first, which Murray couldn't dispute because he was inconveniently dead. The district attorney dismissed the case for "lack of evidence."

As for Earl Dalton, he learned the nightclub business in New Orleans before joining Binion's gambling operations. Because he had less of a police record and more acceptable looks than Ivy Miller, Dalton was featured in Cipango publicity photos, with a neat handkerchief peeking out from his suit pocket. Dalton had learned how to handle well-heeled clients with finesse, as in "You're looking swell tonight—can I freshen that drink for you?" It wasn't long before he bought a house in Highland Park, and his wife became active in symphony teas.

Another guy with a past ran the gaming tables upstairs: Lewis J. McWillie. With his slicked-back hair and slightly hooded eyes, McWillie had the hard looks of George Raft in a mobster movie. But he wasn't acting. The FBI described McWillie as a "murderer." Underworld sources said he did "quality control" for crime boss Meyer Lansky.

McWillie testified to the Warren Commission that he came to Dallas in the 1940s to run dice games for Benny Binion at the Bluebonnet Hotel. Then he joined Binion's team at Top O' Hill and managed gambling at the Four Deuces Club in Fort Worth. At the Cipango, McWillie arranged "stag parties" with dice games, among other things.

His next stop? Cuba. McWillie served as a "key man" at the El Tropicana Casino, the largest casino in the world at the time. Santos Trafficante Jr., the Florida Mafia boss, personally recruited him to oversee the casino. And when Castro kicked Americans out of Cuba, Meyer Lansky made sure McWillie had a job in Las Vegas. Along the way, McWillie became friends with Jack Ruby, a relationship that still fuels conspiracy theories.

One thing for sure, "Chili" McWillie was more than a hired hand. After he left Dallas, he traveled in the highest circles of organized crime and was chauffeured to work in a limousine with a "torpedo" to protect him.

◆

As Binion's team moved on, majordomo Zimmerman became one of the Cipango owners along with "Judge" John Erhard, a partner in a downtown law firm. Erhard was not actually a judge, but he was a former US attorney and assistant district attorney. His legal status helped insulate the Cipango from problems.

Erhard and Zimmerman swore they put a lid on gambling after they assumed ownership. By that time, authorities were trying to crack down on illegal gambling. "I got tired of looking over my shoulder," Zimmerman said.

But when gambling was cut back, membership suffered. Zimmerman decided to bring it back in the guise of private parties. He set up a cocktail party to revive the fun and games. The rosewood tables and chips were pulled out of storage. Guests were getting into the spirit when the unexpected happened: the vice squad busted the Cipango Club.

It seems a pretty employee, who was having an affair with one of the bartenders, was married to a Dallas policeman. When he found out about the affair, he took action. As the police stormed in, the club receptionist raced upstairs to hide the cards and dice. By the time the cops got upstairs, she was sitting nonchalantly in a long mink coat, with telltale chips hidden under her.

It was precisely this kind of risqué drama that made the Cipango so chic, so much more fun than the tomato aspic at the Dallas Country Club. That is, until the King of Diamonds put a chill on the mood.

◆

As more homes were burgled, members of the Cipango Club grew understandably apprehensive. A member who lived on Park Lane, where multiple homes had been hit, worried that she would be the next victim. So, when she went to the Cipango, she kept her fur coat on. Underneath, she had hidden bracelets on her arms and necklaces around her neck. Her pockets were filled with rings and earrings. She figured her jewels would be safe if the thief came to her house, never realizing he might be sitting next to her.

Society columnist Val Imm Bashour remembered that people would look around the dining room and whisper, "It's one of us here." One grand dame wore her diamonds to the Cipango in defiance—and brought a guard to stand by her table, like a sentry at Fort Knox.

One night, the suspicion boiled over. Nancy Ann Smith's parents, Howell and Fayrene Smith, spotted Jim Kirksmith's brother Jasper on the dance floor. Howell Smith believed that Jasper was behind the thefts and got into a loud argument with him. After some pushing and shoving, Smith slugged Jasper in the stomach and warned, "You don't belong here. GET OUT!"

Witnesses say Jasper, who was taller, younger, and more athletic, taunted, "Is that all you've got?"

More blows followed and ungentlemanly words. Bystanders pulled the two apart before real harm could be done. Jasper Kirksmith calmly went to his table with his date. "Jasper seemed fine," a witness told me. "He wasn't rattled at all."

Everyone else, however, was unnerved. Tensions about the jewel thefts were getting out of hand.

Fayrene Smith, in particular, was hopping mad. She called Paul McCaghren at home and demanded that he get rid of Jasper Kirksmith.

"She wanted me to handcuff him, arrest him, get him out of town," McCaghren remembered.

McCaghren told her he was doing everything he could to catch the thief, but he couldn't arrest Jasper Kirksmith for the altercation at the Cipango Club.

"Why not?" she demanded.

"Because your husband threw the first punch," he answered.

This was not what Fayrene Smith wanted to hear.

PART FIVE

NIGHT MOVES

"There's the steal-from-the-rich-give-to-the-poor Robin Hood type hero, sure, but there are also plenty who just like to steal things."
—Sylvain Neuvel, *Crime Reads*

23

The King Goes to Cowtown

When there were lulls in the burglaries, the police were usually baffled. Had the King gone into hiding? Was he nursing an injury? The wait was nerve-racking, like sitting by a phone that doesn't ring.

Then the phone would ring.

Sometime in the wee hours of New Year's Day, 1963, the cat burglar broke into the Schultz home in Preston Hollow. A geologist trained at Stanford University, Frank Schultz got rich as a top executive with Clint Murchison's Delhi-Taylor Oil Company. Murchison believed that if you produced results, you deserved to be rewarded. Schultz produced results—and earned a 5 percent stake in Delhi Oil. He estimated that more than fifty people became millionaires working for Murchison.

While he was on assignment, the Schultz family lived in Canada and Algeria. When they returned to Dallas, they chose a house on Park Lane, never imagining the street would become a shopping strip for the thief. The King of Diamonds hit five homes near them.

The Schultz burglary was a bit of a surprise because the Schultzes were not bold face names in the city. Blonde and five foot ten, Betty Schultz was an elegant figure but not flashy. Her husband, Frank, wore horn-rimmed glasses and always seemed to have a suit on, even at home. He had an office in Paris and the Middle East, so he was often away. While he was gone, his wife oversaw their five children. The doors to the house were usually unlocked so streams of children could come and go.

That New Year's Eve, the Schultzes were going to dinner with four couples in their neighborhood. As they headed out, the homes around them were decorated for the holidays with movie-set perfection. The scent of wood burning in fireplaces filled the night air. The evening was a happy time, fueled by cocktails and the easy compatibility of friends. The Schultzes returned around midnight and went to bed.

When Mrs. Schultz awoke, the pleasant memory evaporated. Someone had taken $16,000 worth of her jewelry—including the diamond-and-gold wristwatch she wore to dinner. One minute the watch was on her wrist; then it was gone.

Though the thief selected some of her best jewels, he also took several pieces of expensive costume jewelry. He seemed to be shopping for items that he liked. It bothered Mrs. Schultz that he knew his way around the house. He had walked past the bedrooms of their children to get to the master bedroom. Their shih tzu dog, who usually yapped at visitors, stayed asleep on their bed that night. It was as if an invisible spirit had floated through the house.

From then on, the possibility that the thief might come back haunted Mrs. Schultz. She locked the doors every night and got an alarm system. As time would show, it wasn't enough to keep the thief from returning.

That same week, the burglar made a surprising zigzag: he expanded his franchise to the neighboring city of Fort Worth. The victims included oilman E. J. McCurdy; T. Fred Hodge, the president of Talco Drilling Company; and businessman Andrew T. Brown, whose wife was the widow of an oilman. All three lived in the affluent Westover Hills neighborhood.

The Fort Worth thefts raised a red flag in Dallas. Was the thief on the move? Fannin sent McCaghren to investigate. This was like being sent across the border into another country. The two cities were like siblings with similar DNA but vastly different temperaments. Fort Worth leaned west to the state's cattle empires. Dallas leaned east toward the culture of New York and Boston.

As a result, Dallas prided itself on fine dining in elegant venues like Ports O' Call, which served continental cuisine with a skyscraper view. Fort Worth bragged on Joe T. Garcia's, a family restaurant in a small white house that served enchiladas smothered in cheese and jalapeños. Dallas cheered for Cowboys on the gridiron. Fort Worth cheered for cowboys in the rodeo. Dallas had Neiman Marcus, where you could be fitted for a Balenciaga. Fort Worth had M.L. Leddy, where you could be fitted for custom boots.

In other words, it was never wise to refer to the two as "Twin Cities." Relations had been prickly since Dallas beat out Fort Worth for the Texas and Pacific Railroad line back in 1873. When Dallas elbowed its way into hosting the Texas Centennial in 1936, Fort Worth publisher Amon Carter was so steamed that he hired Broadway showman Billy Rose to put on a competing event. He calculated what would sell best during the Depression: games of chance and chancy women.

In contrast to the tame Ferris wheel rides and livestock exhibits in Dallas, Carter staged a "Nude Ranch Girls" revue with dancers who wore cowboy hats but no blouses. Sally Rand, the show's bawdy star, strutted her stuff behind peek-a-boo ostrich fans. She bragged to the goggle-eyed audience, "I haven't been out of work since the day I took my pants off." Amon Carter reportedly saw the show sixty times.

After he put up billboards that said DALLAS FOR CULTURE, FORT WORTH FOR FUN, traffic flows showed more people were driving to the show in Fort Worth than the other way around. Carter had made his point.

No one would ever say Amon Carter was humdrum. He once ordered a reporter to steal a train, slept in silk pajamas, and wore an oversized Stetson hat like cowboy star Hoot Gibson. Sometimes he added a bandanna with a diamond stickpin around his neck. Though Carter wore business suits in the office, he strapped on chaps and six-shooters for special occasions. The East Coast press found this irresistible.

Amon Carter could be brash, but like many of the new rich, he made his fortune by being brash. Carter had to earn his own way at thirteen after his mother died and his father remarried. He became a pint-sized hustler, selling picture frames door-to-door during the day and besting players in pool halls at night. To earn his keep in a boardinghouse, Carter waited tables and washed dishes. Sometimes he sold sandwiches to passengers on trains that stopped at the depot. When he was in his twenties, Carter talked his way into a job selling newspaper ads. Pretty soon, he owned the newspaper.

Few said no to Amon Carter. He could sell Tupperware to Cartier, people marveled. He persuaded Lockheed Martin and Bell Helicopter to move to the prairie outpost. He also acquired his own small forest of oil wells and could afford to gamble at Top O' Hill casino with the Big Oil boys. As his fortunes grew, Carter became a political power, making generous donations to Speaker Sam Rayburn and Senator Lyndon Johnson. He was, as they say, in the room when things happened.

Carter took particular pleasure in tweaking Dallas noses at every opportunity. When he attended business meetings on the Dallas side of the Trinity River, he brought his lunch in a paper sack rather than paying for meals in Dallas. He even put a gas can in his car to avoid buying gas in the rival city.

Despite the civic animosity, upper-crust residents in both cities enjoyed a Swiss-like neutrality for social purposes. The burglary victims in Fort Worth had memberships in Dallas country clubs. They attended charity balls and debutante parties in Dallas. They had accounts at Neiman Marcus, although Amon Carter's wife kept hers a secret from her husband. Now, they appeared to have the same jewel thief.

◈

The McCurdy burglary fit the King's pattern: a two-story home, waffle-shaped footprints, entry through a sliding door, some jewels taken, and some left behind.

The similarity was enough to prompt FBI agent Charles Brown to go with McCaghren to check out the McCurdy home. They reported back to Fannin:

Jim McCurdy and his family were watching TV after supper on New Year's Day. Margaret McCurdy heard a noise on the roof. Probably a squirrel, she thought. The following day, the McCurdys discovered that a thief had climbed a tree and vaulted over a railing to the roof. Working quietly, he used a glass cutter to make a small opening in the glass door to a sunroom. When he reached through to unlock the door, he knocked some glass onto the carpeted floor.

While the method initially seemed different, McCaghren remembered the thief had also removed glass at the Bees' house and some other homes in Preston Hollow. Once inside, the thief headed to the master bathroom, where he opened a draped panel in front of a dresser. With his soft-gloved hands, he opened the boxes inside the drawers. Before leaving, he carefully replaced the boxes and closed the draped panel, taking care to fasten the catch. He slipped out so quietly, the family didn't realize there was a break-in until they found broken glass on the carpet.

In response to the officers' questions, Mrs. McCurdy acknowledged that she had numerous friends in Dallas, including Josephine Herbert Graf and her daughter Joanne Stroud. She had attended a party at the Dallas Sheraton the month before that was hosted by Nancy Ann Smith. And yes, she knew Jasper Kirksmith, but said she had not seen him for a while, an indication the police had asked specifically about him.

Mrs. McCurdy added, almost as an afterthought, that she had received several phone calls in recent weeks from someone who hung up after she answered the phone. The calls made her uncomfortable, she said.

Was the thief calling to see if the McCurdys were in town? That suggested he didn't live in Fort Worth and wanted to make sure they were at home, with their jewels available.

◆

A few weeks later, Mary Hodge reported $10,000 to $13,000 in jewelry was stolen from her home, including jewels she'd worn the week before at the Jewel Ball.

The burglar had entered the Hodge residence by prying open a tall window. Once inside, he located a jewelry box on a dressing table and began sorting through it. He didn't know it, but Mrs. Hodge left the party early because she had rheumatoid arthritis that drained her energy. When she got to her home, it was not yet midnight. As she walked into her bedroom, Mrs. Hodge heard a sound. Someone was in her dressing room, a few yards away.

Startled, she said, "Oh!"

Hearing her, the thief bolted from her dressing room. He ran by too quickly for her to get a close look at him. Her heart pounding, Mrs. Hodge alerted their twenty-year-old son, who was asleep in his bedroom.

The thief got away with some of her best jewels, Mrs. Hodge told police, mostly those with large diamonds or emeralds. She assumed he was looking for big stones that he could fence, but found it odd that he split up several sets, taking earrings and leaving behind matching necklaces, or vice versa.

Like Mrs. McCurdy, she said she had many friends in Dallas. She had seen several at the Jewel Ball the week before, including Joe Lambert and his wife, Evelyn. And, of course, she knew Sid Murchison's niece, Nancy Ann Smith, who had lived in Fort Worth.

Since the Hodges were members of the Brook Hollow Golf Club, the University Club, and the Cipango Club in Dallas, police noted, there was a good chance the thief got a look at her jewels in those places.

◆

The next day, businessman Andrew Brown noticed the screen was off the sliding glass door on the patio of his house. Brown assumed the wind blew it off, and he reattached it. He didn't think much about it until he read about the Hodge burglary in the morning paper. He and his wife, Elizabeth, lived in the same Westover Hills area as the Hodges, so he became worried about her jewels. He called his wife, who was in the hospital, to determine if anything was missing. As they went over the contents, he discovered some of the felt-lined compartments were empty, others half-empty. They should have been full, his wife said. All told, some $50,000 in jewels were missing. The burglar had artfully hidden his theft by relocking the jewelry box and putting it back in place. He didn't leave fingerprints but left a waffled footprint on the living room floor.

◈

The Fort Worth incidents posed new questions:

Had the King expanded his operations? Or was someone copying him in Fort Worth?

And why didn't the thief strike well-known figures like Anne Windfohr, who lived in the same area and owned the most expensive jewels around? It was a good question, so I began asking around.

Everyone knew Anne Windfohr. People still talked about the deb party she threw for her namesake daughter "Little Anne" in 1958. "Big Anne" brought in Louie Armstrong's orchestra to play and placed a plexiglass cover over her Olympic-sized swimming pool to create a dance floor. The dancing went on till five in the morning. The next night, the cover was whisked off the pool. Swans floated on the water along with thousands of gardenias flown in from Hawaii.

Anne Windfohr was accustomed to doing things big. She had inherited the vast 6666 Ranch—more than 350,000 acres—from her grandfather, Samuel Burk Burnett. She went to Miss Porter's School for young ladies in New York and, when she came home, became steward of the family's cattle and oil interests. Her first husband, Guy Waggoner, was an heir to the Waggoner ranch. At 520,000 acres, it was even bigger than her ranch. Their marriage was comparable to the union of two European principalities. When her husband proved intolerably unfaithful, Anne left in cinematic style. She stormed out of their ranch house, crashed through ten gates, left the car running in the street at the nearest town, and walked to the train station. Like her ranch hands, she dusted herself off and moved on.

Windfohr was one of that special breed of Texas women who raised quarter horses, shot game without flinching, and bought art in New York and Paris. Her tastes were bold: Picasso, Gauguin, Matisse, Modigliani, Miro, and Leger. She collected jewels as well as fine art and could outshine her friend Josephine Graf.

In 1944, Mrs. Windfohr purchased a 48-carat diamond ring called the "President Vargas Diamond" from Manhattan jeweler Harry Winston. She paid $420,000 for the ring—an astounding sum during war years, and the equivalent of more than $7 million in 2023. The emerald-cut diamond was so large that Mrs. Windfohr had difficulty bending her finger. She tolerated the awkwardness because the ring made a statement: she was a woman of substance.

Jeweler Harry Winston often advised his clients, "People are going to stare—make it worth their while." Anne Windfohr did. Only one of her friends could boast a larger ring: Louisiana oil heiress Matilda Gray Stream. She had a 50-carat diamond ring that her husband gave her on her fiftieth birthday. Mrs. Stream wore it proudly and often. When she wore the ring to a ladies' lunch in New Orleans, one of her friends asked pointedly, "Matilda, don't you think wearing such a big diamond is a bit *vulgar*?" The table grew silent. Mrs. Stream replied with aplomb, "I did—before I had one."

Such was the spirit of the times. *New Yorker* writer John Bainbridge, who profiled the state's super-rich in 1961, revealed that Anne Windfohr also had an emerald ring nearly as large as her 48-carat diamond. It matched a necklace with five large emeralds. As a result, people buzzed after social events, "Anne was wearing the emeralds," or "Anne was wearing the big diamond."

Did the buzz reach the jewel thief?

Several of Mrs. Windfohr's friends told me that a thief had indeed broken into Windfohr's home. The thief had slipped through a jimmied door and made off with a number of jewels. He left no fingerprints and was never caught.

After the highly publicized burglary at Josephine Graf's home, Anne Windfohr confided to friends that the same thief might have struck her home. But she kept quiet, not wanting to call more attention to the break-in. "She was good about keeping things quiet," a friend told me. "She was a very private person."

Mrs. Windfohr suspected the thief was hoping to capture her President Vargas diamond, but she was wearing the ring that night. She decided to sell the gargantuan diamond, feeling it invited too much attention. When she had worn the ring to one of Nancy Hamon's costume parties, guests teased that the diamond glared like a locomotive headlight. Mrs. Windfohr discreetly sold the ring back to Harry Winston. She saw no need to invite further intrusions.

◆

When thefts in Fort Worth came to light, police immediately suspected the rough crowd that hung out on the Jacksboro Highway. Gambling and prostitution thrived on the six miles of highway between Fort Worth and Lake Worth that was called "Thunder Road," the "Highway to Hell," or the "Jaxbeer Highway." Bars and gambling dens operated side by side like a string of fast-food franchises.

The prime example: the Four Deuces at 2222 Jacksboro Highway. William Calvin "Pappy" Kirkwood built the white-stucco, Spanish-style house in 1934 and operated a gambling casino there until 1972. Like the Top O' Hill casino, the Four Deuces attracted the rich and famous. Cowboy singer Gene Autry was a fan, and publisher Amon Carter stopped by often. Oil kings Sid Richardson, Clint Murchison Sr., and H. L. Hunt were regulars, and so were politicians like John Connally, Lyndon Johnson, and Sam Rayburn. The big shots were usually joined by lesser big shots like judges and city council members. Some came for the two-inch-thick steaks, and some came for the Jack Daniels and card games. Mrs. Amon Carter brought her friends to play roulette after church on Sunday.

Even though the gambling was illegal, local law enforcement allowed the Four Deuces to operate freely. In fact, the club hired policemen as guards.

The best of the clubs, such as the Chateau, looked like mansions with gated entries. Special customers had access to private gambling rooms. And if a misguided Texas Ranger tried to bust in, guests could flee through tunnels, like Top O' Hill.

According to historian Ann Arnold, the worst gambling clubs had names like the Bloody Bucket and County Dump—and deserved them. Some put up chicken wire between the stage and the audience to protect entertainers from the beer bottles that drunken customers hurled at them.

Though the Jacksboro joints could get rough and raunchy, some provided a start for entertainers like Ray Charles, Trini Lopez, and Tina Turner. Willie Nelson sometimes played the honky-tonks on Saturday nights and the Baptist church on Sunday mornings.

The clubs also provided a base for crooks of every stripe—swindlers, card sharks, killers, pimps, drug dealers, and burglars. So, when a burglar made off with a batch of jewels in the prosperous part of town, Fort Worth authorities immediately guessed it was someone in the Jacksboro crowd who got ambitious.

◆

Some Fort Worth insiders suspected a local socialite, though nothing came of that. Reporters suspected a character named Walter Mark Flanagan. Flanagan started his rebellious ride with crime at the age of sixteen with an armed robbery. He took a break to serve as a tail gunner during World War II, then fell back into crime. His convictions ranged from watering his yard in defiance of drought restrictions to counterfeiting and transporting teenaged girls for immoral purposes.

Walter Mark Flanagan just couldn't do right, people said. He was bent toward trouble. By the late 1960s, Flanagan had racked up twenty-three federal offenses and was indicted multiple times for burglary in Fort Worth and Houston, where he was caught with $20,000 in stolen jewelry and furs. After one of his partners tipped police that Flanagan planned to unload some stolen jewels in Dallas, the loose-lipped partner was found in a cedar grove with a bullet between his eyes.

No doubt about it, Flanagan was a hardened criminal—he once admitted to beating a man senseless after dragging him from a hospital where he was recovering from stab wounds. But did Flanagan have the sophisticated tastes of the King? It did not seem so.

The Fort Worth families that were burglarized had their own theories about the culprit. Privately, they believed the intruder was a bachelor who attended the Jewel Ball and looked around. He was someone "on the ticket," they said, someone who had been on guest lists. And they suspected he was from Dallas.

That rankled.

The feeling that people in Dallas were too big for their britches was deeply ingrained. The possibility that someone from Dallas could be poaching jewels in Fort Worth did not improve matters.

24

The King Climbs a Castle

A few weeks after the Fort Worth burglaries, the press had a field day when the jewel thief made a quick grab from Jim Ling's palatial Dallas home. The King had robbed a castle.

Jim Ling was the prototype of the modern business mogul. He made "conglomerate" into a household word in the sixties when he combined an assortment of companies into Ling-Temco-Vought (LTV).

At its peak in 1969, Ling's conglomerate controlled Jones and Laughlin, America's sixth-largest steel company; Braniff, the eighth-largest airline; Wilson, the nation's largest producer of sporting goods and third-largest meatpacker; National Car Rental; Temco, which grew from making airplanes to making smart missiles; and Vought, the eighth-largest defense contractor in the country.

Even more remarkable, the former electrician built his mega-company by selling the first shares at the state fair like a corn dog vendor.

"Jimmy Ling had a presence," a company historian said. "Famous people like movie stars, presidents, even some striking stranger on the street, have a certain bearing," he said, "and Ling had that . . . When he was in the room, everyone knew it."

And when Jim Ling talked, you had to listen fast. Tape-recorded conversations showed he didn't speak in sentences; he talked in rapid-fire bursts of financial jargon that were hard to follow. He had five assistants who tried to keep up with him. At one point, *Inc.* magazine described him as a "financial Beethoven" who could hear a symphony when others heard only a tune.

Ling's backers said he was likable, brilliant, driven. Nearly six foot tall with broad shoulders, he projected vigor. But his critics claimed he was an upstart, an opportunist, and arrogant. Though Ling sometimes tried to project good-old-boy naturalness by wearing denim shirts and jeans, he owned an apartment on Fifth Avenue in New York and a vacation home in Palm Springs. He had a fleet of corporate jets and a company getaway called Eagle Ranch.

And then there was his chateau in Preston Hollow, the land of money royalty.

◆

The King of Diamonds must have found Ling's mansion on Gaywood Road irresistible. The house had previously been owned by Dick Andrade, the oil baron and bon vivant known for his two-week parties and racehorses.

After Andrade died in 1961, the Lings modernized his mansion and added a swimming pool, a Japanese pavilion, and a three-hole golf course. They furnished the interior with a king's fortune in antiques, including a mahogany table where twenty-four guests could be seated in gold Louis XV chairs.

The toilet fixtures were covered with gold, too, but it was the tub in the master bathroom that became the talk of the town. When the marble bathtub was being lowered by helicopter, it was so heavy that it fell through the floor with a resounding crash. Neighbors heard it blocks away. The floor had to be reinforced before the tub could be reinstalled. Annoyed by reports that the bathtub had cost $25,000, Ling made it a point to clarify that it only cost $12,000.

◈

James Joseph Ling had come a long way from Hugo, Oklahoma. His father worked as a fireman on locomotives, shoveling fuel into the boiler firebox. A devout Catholic, Ling's father was distraught after he accidentally killed a belligerent colleague in a quarrel. Though a jury ruled it self-defense, he retreated to a monastery in contrition. A short time later, Ling's mother died of blood poisoning. From the age of eleven, Jim Ling was shuttled between relatives and schools.

Ling did well enough in high school to skip several grades but got restless and left before graduation. He worked at odd jobs until he signed on as an apprentice to an electrician. It was a turning point in his life. Realizing he had an aptitude for electronics, Ling breezed through the journeyman process in six months instead of the customary two years. Racing ahead, he got married at seventeen, and had two sons by the time he was twenty-one. To support his family, he worked as a toolbelt electrician during the day and at an aircraft plant at night. During World War II, Ling spent most of his Navy tour of duty salvaging electrical equipment from destroyed ships.

When he was discharged, Ling sold his house to get enough money to set up a small electrical contracting firm in Dallas. His family lived in back of the shop. Working nonstop, Ling went from installing light fixtures in homes to wiring entire buildings. By 1955, he topped a million dollars a year in sales.

When he couldn't get financing from a bank to expand, he came up with the novel idea of selling shares at the state fair. He used that grubstake to buy a California company that made vibration-testing equipment for the aerospace industry.

Jimmy Ling was on his way. The press said he bought companies like boys collect baseball cards. One company led to another: Altec. Continental Electronics. Temco. Along the way, he and his teenage sweetheart divorced, and he married Dorothy Hill, his pretty and competent secretary.

Ling now rubbed shoulders at YPO with CEOs who had MBAs. *Forbes* and *Fortune* wrote admiring articles about him. The press called him a "boy wonder" and "Texas Titan." Like the Murchisons, he made the cover of *TIME*. He was running the fastest-growing company in the country.

When someone robbed Jimmy Ling's house while he was watching TV, it created quite a stir.

The thief had pulled off a spectacular feat. He made his way to the Ling house by going up a creek that snaked through the grounds. Moving cautiously across the wide lawn, he evaded a watchman who was patrolling with a dog. Then the thief inched up the side of the house like a rock climber. Brick by brick, he reached a second-story balcony. He got onto the balcony by swinging on a light fixture like a circus acrobat.

Footprints on the balcony showed that the thief paced back and forth, waiting for the right moment to slip in. Then he broke the latch on a bedroom window and climbed in. He must have forgotten to take off his shoes, because there were tracks on the rug of the guest room. Once he realized his mistake, the thief took off his shoes to walk the rest of the way to the master suite, where Mrs. Ling had a dressing area.

As his eyes adjusted to the dark, something shiny must have caught the thief's eye: a gold Rolex watch, sitting next to the bathroom sink. It was shaped like a cuff bracelet and decorated with 168 diamonds. He put it in his pocket.

The thief had just started to sift through the jewelry drawers, when he heard one of Ling's sons call down to his parents. To avoid being trapped, he grabbed a diamond ring and a gold wedding band, then vanished.

Jim Ling and his wife, Dorothy, were downstairs watching TV that night. Sometime after nine thirty, their teenaged son called down, "Are you guys going out?"

"No," they said. "Why do you want to know?"

"I heard a noise in your room," he said.

The Lings hesitated a few minutes, then decided to see if something was amiss. By the time they checked their bedroom, the King had made his exit. And Fannin's phone was ringing.

The police polygraphed more than a dozen Ling employees, including six gardeners, a cook, a laundress, an upstairs maid, a superintendent, two butlers, and a downstairs maid. Police reasoned the workers knew the layout of the home. The pattern of "take some, leave some" also was typical of insider thefts. A servant will sometimes take a few valuables, police say, so they won't be missed right away.

But no leads emerged from the interrogations. Not one.

The Ling burglary made the front pages of the *Dallas Times Herald* and the *Dallas Morning News*. As a result, Fannin and McCaghren were under renewed pressure to find the burglar—but he always seemed a step ahead of them. In one month, he had grabbed more than $100,000 in jewels, nearly a million dollars today.

When a reporter called for a comment, McCaghren sighed. "The words *King of Diamonds* hit with all the pain of a decayed tooth."

◈

After the Ling break-in hit the headlines, some neighbors expressed skepticism. Was it really a burglary—or staged? Gossips suggested that Ling had overspent on the house and faked the burglary to collect insurance. After all, the Lings were *new money*, the critics sniffed, as if illiterates had moved in next door.

It was a familiar reaction to new wealth. Like the Vanderbilts looking down on the Astors in Manhattan, the cotton rich had looked down on the cattle rich, and the cattle rich had snooted the rowdy oil crowd. Now, the oil rich complained about the upstart tech millionaires who seemed to come out of nowhere.

The newcomers had so much money they couldn't be avoided. But they were still considered parvenus who had slipped under the velvet rope into the ballroom. As one matron put it in a double uppercut, "The Lings were *nice* people. I liked them. But he married his secretary, you know. Their house *was* beautiful, but it wasn't *their t*aste—it was somebody else's."

◈

The taste came from John Astin Perkins, the interior designer for the Dallas Country Club, the Northwood Club, the Dallas Club, the Imperial Club, the Insurance Club, the Dallas Woman's Club, and the Hotel Statler.

If you wanted to look like "old money"—or just money—Perkins was your man. Perkins dominated the top echelon of Dallas design for five decades, fashioning a sophisticated look for new wealth in the city.

His signature touch included such things as parrot-green and white wallpaper or walls painted a rich persimmon. Perkins turned Oriental temple jars into lamps and brought in bold-patterned rugs. He put colors together in new ways, mixing apple green, pink, lilac, and mustard. He searched out antiques from around the world, like Coromandel lacquer screens. If a client didn't know what *chinoiserie* meant before she hired Perkins, she did soon after.

His fees were not for the faint of means. A client once pointed out the treillage that cost her thousands of dollars looked like an ordinary garden trellis. She asked what the difference was. "Money," the prickly Perkins replied.

As the burglaries went on, some victims wondered: Could the vaunted decorator be involved? He knew the layouts of many homes in the area.

The police doubted the designer would resort to burglary. For starters, John Astin Perkins was too vain to climb up trees and crawl down creeks. Even if he used a surrogate, Perkins would jeopardize his business if he broke into his clients' homes. Why stoop to stealing, when he could simply raise his prices?

The Ling house was Perkins's most ambitious project. He added eight thousand square feet to the 15,000-square-foot home. He put in marble floors, fountains, and Italian statues. By the time Perkins finished, the total price tag had soared to $3.2 million.

Despite his new success, Jimmy Ling had to borrow money to finish the project. The gossips had a field day.

❖

At first, insurance millionaire Troy Post was one of Ling's key allies. Post had a similar backstory: During his senior year of high school, Post had to go to work. Driven to compensate for his lack of a diploma, he went from working at an insurance company to founding one—with $130 in savings. He surged to success by offering policies to GIs who couldn't get insurance before they shipped out to fight in World War II. His Great America Corp. became one of the largest insurance companies in the world. Soon Post could buy other companies. And banks. He even bought an island in Hawaii.

Post and Ling had offices in the same building and served on each other's boards. Before long, their businesses coalesced. After Post's Great America Corp. bought Braniff Airways, Ling bought Great America Corp., which meant Braniff became a star in the LTV family.

Ling and Post transformed the regional airline by hiring bold executive Harding Lawrence to run it. Harding and his wife, Mary Wells, a New York PR star, turned Braniff into a trendsetter. Flight attendants were outfitted in uniforms designed by Emilio Pucci that flattered their figures more than the military-style uniforms worn by other stewardesses. Planes were painted in vivid colors by artist Alexander Calder. It was "the end of the plain plane," the airline announced.

Next, Post developed a $20 million resort called Tres Vidas de la Playa in Acapulco, which became a hip destination for "jet-setters." It featured two golf courses, tennis courts, surf-fishing, horseback riding, and an enormous swimming pool with barstools in the water. As a bonus, there were fifty casitas with private pools, in case guests wanted to forget about bathing suits and social conventions back home.

Just about everyone with money and suntan lotion wanted in. Memberships were a steep $5,000 but that didn't faze members like Warren Avis (yes) and Frank Sinatra. The board of directors included former Mexico

President Miguel Aleman, Giovanni Agnelli of Fiat, Prince Rainier of Monaco, and Count Ferdinand von Bismarck of Germany.

It was a heady time. Tourism to Mexico boomed. Margaritas became popular around the world. Airline stewardesses became chic—and traveled in dangerous proximity to businessmen away from home.

Owning the flashy airline gave Jim Ling and Troy Post much higher profiles, so the FBI figured Post's home in Preston Hollow might be the thief's next target. For several weeks, a team of agents sat all night in a van down the street.

Although the sprawling, three-story house signaled the Posts had piles of money, his wife told police she didn't have "piles of jewels." The cat burglar may have known that, because he never struck the Post home. Or perhaps he figured out the white van parked down the street every night was not empty.

In retrospect, you could say the Ling burglary revealed a tectonic shift in Dallas. The influence of Big Oil was ebbing. The brontosaurus discoveries that had pumped out billions in petroleum were giving way to discoveries in the Middle East. Future fortunes in Dallas would come from microchips and aerospace—Texas Instruments, Dallas Semiconductor, EDS, Raytheon, E-Systems, and LTV.

The lifestyles of the engineers with their white, button-down, short-sleeved shirts and pocket protectors tended to be more understated than the oil barons. They lived luxuriously, to be sure, but without the can-can girls and caviar. They drove Volvos.

The world of the King of Diamonds was fading fast around him.

LTV was at the forefront of the change. At its peak, LTV produced fifteen thousand different products—from tennis rackets to Mach-2 rockets. Who made the jet packs for NASA astronauts? LTV. Who made space cannons for the Department of Defense? LTV did, as well as surveillance systems for the CIA. Ling's company monitored the Vietnam war from space and equipped *Air Force One* with communications systems. Those were just some of the *unclassified* projects. Over time, LTV moved deeper into highly classified intelligence work. Even *60 Minutes* could not find out exactly what E-Systems, an LTV subsidiary, was doing.

◆

Jimmy Ling had created a global juggernaut with $6 billion in revenues. The toolbelt electrician could invite physicist Edward Teller to dinner. He could watch the Dallas Cowboys from the best seats in the stadium as a board member.

Even so, Ling remained hypersensitive about fitting in with the upper crust of Dallas. When he found out that his wife played poker with some friends, he exploded in anger. In his view, poker was not ladylike; she could play gin rummy or bridge, but not poker. He forbade his wife to join the poker game again—even though the hostess was a matron in the old-guard circles he aspired to.

Ling liked showing his pretty wife off. Trophy real estate was one way to advertise success; trophy wives were another. When other men cast admiring glances Mrs. Ling's way and said, "You lucky dog," that was status, too. That was being Somebody Among Men.

While people described Ling as intense, they described his wife, Dorothy, as nice. She had never imagined she would be thrust into the role of hostess in a palace, but she played the part with grace. She often surprised people with her modesty—when her husband gave her an extra-large diamond ring for Christmas, she donated it to her church. Later, people would note with admiration that when her husband's fortunes plunged, Dorothy Ling sold her jewelry to help.

◆

Ling's fall began in 1969. As the sixties were drawing to a close, Ling was increasingly jazzed about the potential of such things as laser weapons, holograms, and crystal technology. If new frontiers were being discovered, he wanted to own them. He poured himself into futuristic research.

Then his board gave him the boot.

Ling was playing cards at Preston Hollow Golf Club when he got a call from his office. The Nixon Justice Department had accused LTV of being "a force destructive of competition" and filed an antitrust suit to force Ling to give up Jones and Laughlin Steel. LTV stock plummeted from $169 a share to $4.25. Loans turned fragile. Shareholders bailed out. And board members rebelled. Jim Ling was forced to step down.

Just business, the board said. Ling was moving too fast, taking on too much. He ignored warning signs, they said, and was a poor manager. Besides that, they couldn't understand his rambling, convoluted financial explanations. Neither could banks.

Ling lost his seat at the table and his extravagant home.

His partner Troy Post was one of the leaders of the "palace coup." So was his banker, Robert Stewart III, who replaced Ling as chairman of the LTV board. It was nothing personal, board members said. They had to send a signal to the market, stop the death spiral.

Like a Greek chorus, local critics tsk-tsked that Ling bit off more than he could chew, stubbed his toe, and came a cropper, the Texas way of saying he was blinded by his ambition and flew too close to the sun. It wasn't long before business pundits were describing Ling as "sparsely educated" and said his business practices were a "shell game."

His defenders responded that Jim Ling was an idea man, not an operations manager. There were plenty of managers around, they said, but not many idea men who could see several chess moves ahead. Now there was one less.

Knowing Ling's difficult beginnings, I could understand the ambition that drove him to climb higher and higher. But what motivated the jewel thief to climb up the side of Ling's house? What drove him? Figuring out what made Ling tick was easy. Figuring out what made the thief tick was proving much harder. What compelled him to take such risks?

25

JFK

When tragedy rocked the city in 1963, the search for the jewel thief was thrown off course. The president had come to town—and was murdered.

President Kennedy's team had understandable concerns about venturing into Dallas that fall. They knew people were saying he was too liberal and too soft on communism. They knew about the hostile reception given to Adlai Stevenson.

Tensions were heightened when the presidential party arrived in Fort Worth for the first leg of the trip. It was dark and rainy as the president and first lady got to the Hotel Texas. The crowd pressed too close for comfort. The next morning, Kennedy mentioned the gloomy weather to his wife, Jackie. It would have been "a hell of a night to assassinate a president," JFK said. He pointed his finger like a gun and pretended to fire.

Still, he went on to Dallas, flashing a nonchalant smile for the press. When Dallas citizens greeted the Kennedys with exuberant cheers instead of jeers, the day seemed sunnier. Nellie Connally, wife of Texas Governor John Connally, turned to the president in the motorcade and said, "You can't say Dallas doesn't love you."

"No, you certainly can't," he replied.

Moments later, the bullets struck. And everything changed.

Compounding the tragedy, two days later, Jack Ruby—the same under-world wannabe who ran strip clubs and courted cops—shot and killed the primary suspect, Lee Harvey Oswald.

The wrath of the world turned on the right-wing millionaires and bombastic figures in Dallas who stirred up anger against the president. Although Oswald and Ruby were outsiders, many Americans blamed the city. Dallas was denounced as the "City of Hate," a label that would follow the city like an accusing shadow for years to come.

Dozens of King of Diamonds' victims were also caught up in the tragedy. Many were seated at tables in the courtyard of the Dallas Trade Mart, waiting for the president to address the luncheon. The attendees included Clint and Ginny Murchison, Mr. and Mrs. Herman Lay, Mr. and Mrs. H. C. Otis, Mr. and Mrs. Phil Bee, attorney Glenn Turner, Mr. and Mrs. Jim Ling, and many more.

John Erhard, the new Cipango Club owner, had a seat. So did oilman Jake Hamon and his wife, Nancy. Even flamboyant car dealer W. O. Bankston was there.

For the rest of their lives, the luncheon guests would remember the ripple of excitement as they waited for the president's arrival. Then some heard on their new transistor radios that there was a delay, perhaps an accident involving the motorcade. A murmur traveled from table to table: something is wrong.

J. Erik Jonsson, a co-founder of Texas Instruments, stepped to the podium. As chairman of the Dallas Citizens' Council, he was presiding at the luncheon. Jonsson announced there had been a mishap, but he had been told it was not serious.

Twelve tense minutes later, Jonsson came to the podium again. The ball-room fell silent. "I'm not sure that I can say what I have to say," Jonsson said, his voice breaking. "It is true that our president and Governor Connally in the motorcade have been shot." He asked the Rev. Luther Holcomb to say a prayer.

The minister later said he had attended countless funerals, but he had never seen such a large group of people so stricken with grief. Shocked beyond words, they left their food on the table and walked out, ashen-faced.

"We were sort of numb, and everybody just started walking out," philanthropist Ruth Sharp remembered. "People were sobbing everywhere."

◈

Everyone in the country would later have a story about where they were on that day, but many of the King of Diamonds players were in the thick of the events.

Two of Fannin's detectives, Joe Cody and Charlie Dellinger, had gone to a movie before their shift that Friday. The Majestic Theater was only a few blocks from the police station. When they clocked in, they learned the president had been shot.

As Cody remembered it, a car in the motor pool still had the keys in it, so they arrived at the Dealey Plaza scene within minutes of the shooting and parked in front of the Texas Schoolbook Depository. Sgt. Dellinger went to check the sixth floor, where a shooter had been sighted. Cody went outside to look around the grounds. He saw something unusual by the curb. It was a piece of head bone with reddish-brown hair on it. "I knew it was the president," he said later. Cody went back to tell the others that the president must surely be dead; part of his head was in the street.

When the two were back at police headquarters, Officer Nick McDonald brought in a thin man in handcuffs. He asked Cody to book him for shooting a police officer. Cody was one of the few detectives who knew how to type, so he often had to fill out paperwork for others. Cody asked the man his name and where he worked. When he said the Texas Schoolbook Depository, Cody was startled. He had been at the building minutes before. He asked, "Did you go to work today?" The man replied, "Yes."

Cody warned him, "Don't move, or I will kill you," and ran down the hall to where the police chief, FBI, and district attorney were meeting.

"Who are you hunting?" he asked from the doorway.

"Lee Harvey Oswald," they said.

"Well, I have him in my office," Cody said.

The top brass whisked Oswald away, but the confusion and chaos continued.

Cody being Cody, he went ahead with plans to attend a gar fishing rodeo that weekend in Louisiana despite the crisis. On Sunday, he stopped at a small grocery store to pick up some food. As he entered, a shooting on TV caught his attention.

Instantly, he recognized the basement of Dallas Police headquarters. Someone had shot the skinny guy he booked. Cody watched, transfixed. The shooter was only visible from behind, but he seemed familiar. When the TV newsman said the man's name was Jack Ruby, Joe Cody gasped. He suddenly remembered his trip to the gun store with Ruby. "Oh my God," he realized. "I bought him the pistol."

Again, Cody being Cody, he saw a business opportunity when he got over his shock. He began selling autographed photos of himself as the cop who booked Lee Harvey Oswald and sold Jack Ruby the murder weapon.

Jim Bookhout, the lead FBI agent on the King of Diamonds case, had rushed to police headquarters to represent the FBI. Within moments, he was interviewing Lee Harvey Oswald instead of burglary victims. Bookhout later recalled that Oswald avoided answering questions. He denied owning a rifle. When shown the invoice, Oswald said it was fake. When shown photographs of him holding the rifle, he said they were fakes. He admitted only to carrying a pistol and resisting arrest—and lied about where he bought the pistol. He remained an enigma wrapped in a tragedy.

Sgt. John Chism had just taken an injured robbery victim to Parkland Hospital. When he returned to his patrol car, he discovered it was blocked by a dark blue Lincoln convertible. The Lincoln had fresh blood all over the trunk and back seat. With a jolt, Chism realized it was the president's car. At first, he thought one of the Secret Servicemen had been run over. When he went back inside, Chism passed Mrs. Kennedy sitting outside the triage room with the governor's wife. The first lady's pink suit was splattered with blood. And suddenly, he understood.

Chism stayed to help wherever he could, radioing for more plasma, maintaining order in the hallways, pushing reporters off nurses' desks. Then dispatchers gave him the order: Go to Love Field immediately. A mob of people from the East Coast are flying in "to straighten Dallas out—with guns." Though he wasn't sure what he was walking into and how much support he would have, Chism drove to the airport and walked up to the gate, alone. To his relief, the deplaning passengers were "just normal people," unsure of what was happening next, like him.

Because of his quick thinking and cool head, Chism got a promotion. He was assigned to Fannin's department, where he would play a key role in the hunt for the jewel thief.

Fannin and Paul McCaghren were manning the control center at the Trade Mart that day. Three levels of balconies overlooked the atrium where the lunch was being held, adding to the risk, so 150 officers were assigned to guard the building. When an alert came on his walkie-talkie that a shooting had occurred, McCaghren ordered all the exits secured. Then he got word: It was too late. The president was dead.

McCaghren was not a churchgoer, but the assassination shook him. On Sunday morning, two days after the assassination, he loaded his wife and daughters into the family car and headed for a Church of Christ near their home in Garland. Overcome with emotion, the minister chastised the congregation, "We are *all* to blame! We *all* have to suffer!" Overcome with emotion himself,

McCaghren jumped to his feet and shouted, "BULLSHIT!" The minister stood stunned as McCaghren gathered up his family and left.

On their way home, he heard on the radio that Jack Ruby had shot and killed Lee Harvey Oswald in the basement of the police department. Though drained, McCaghren dropped off his family and went back to work.

In the days ahead, Police Chief Jesse Curry assigned McCaghren to a task force that would investigate how police security failed to protect Lee Harvey Oswald and forever lost the opportunity to resolve his motive. The post-mortem was a critical task. The King of Diamonds case would have to wait.

From then on, the enormity of the Kennedy assassination overwhelmed everything else. Rumors began swirling about Mafia involvement, Cuban connections, and right-wing plotting. The police department was wholly unprepared for the magnitude of the crimes before it.

The city went into shock. Schools were dismissed. Opera performances were canceled. Debutante balls were called off. One of the few events carried out was the game scheduled that weekend between the Dallas Cowboys and the Cleveland Browns in Cleveland. The mood was tense as the Dallas team ran onto the field. Advised not to mention the word *Dallas*, the announcer identified the team as "the Cowboys." The crowd booed them anyway. They taunted the players as "Kennedy killers" and spat on Dallas sports reporters. Cleveland won, 27–17.

People around the country continued to vent their anger on the people of Dallas. Residents were snubbed in restaurants when they traveled. They were told to get out of cabs. Long-distance operators hung up on them.

But the King of Diamonds was not in shock—or concerned about the city's reputation.

A few weeks after the assassination, he broke into a house in the heart of Highland Park. He slipped silently into the home of architect Wilson McClure on Beverly Drive, selected $25,000 in gems, and slipped back out.

Detectives at the scene theorized that the thief had tried to get into the same home the night before. They found indications he had climbed a tree and entered an upstairs bedroom. The McClures' three pet poodles had raised such a ruckus that he left. He returned the next night while the McClures were at a concert. This time, he jimmied a sliding door. And for some reason, the poodles remained quiet.

True to form, the jewel thief left some jewelry behind. And police found the print of an overshoe on a backyard step.

It was an audacious heist. The Highland Park police headquarters was a few blocks away.

26

The Do-Gooder

C ivic leader Ruth Collins Sharp remained deeply troubled by the tragic turn of events but tried to focus on her responsibilities. She was determined to do a good job as the first woman to serve on the grand jury. The panel had a new assignment: handing down an indictment for murder with malice to Jack Ruby. It didn't take long; everyone had witnessed the shooting on TV.

When not on jury duty, Mrs. Sharp began raising money for the family of J. D. Tippit, the policeman killed by Oswald. She wanted to help any way she could—and raised more than $600,000 for the Tippit children, an extraordinary sum. When Ruth Sharp asked, people gave.

Then the jewel thief broke into Ruth Sharp's house.

Mrs. Sharp seemed an unlikely target. Jewelry was not her passion—clothes were. Ruth Sharp loved dressing up and dominated the "Best Dressed" list of Dallas women for many years. She wore clothes well and was a striking woman. At five foot eight, she seemed taller because of the dignified way she held herself.

When city fathers started looking for women to sit on charity boards, Ruth Sharp was the first woman they turned to. She was known for giving generously to local causes like the Salvation Army and United Way. Scarcely a morning went by when she didn't slip a check under her doormat for someone who called during the night with an emergency. She would not be a troublemaker, business leaders reassured other executives. Ruth Sharp had roots in the city, they said, she knew her place.

But Mrs. Sharp challenged the status quo in her own way.

At a time when civil rights protesters were being sprayed with fire hoses in other cities, Ruth Sharp befriended Black people. When she read about a Black woman whose husband was killed in a car wreck, leaving her with three children, Ruth Sharp didn't just write a check. She visited the woman in the hospital, brought her home for lunch, found her a job, took her children to the state fair, and stayed friends for years.

Later, when HIV was stirring fear and paranoia, Mrs. Sharp raised money for the city's first AIDS treatment center. And championed a shelter for abused children.

People like Ruth Sharp were the load-bearing walls of the city. Stealing from someone who did so much good seemed petty, almost *spiteful*. Compared to other burglaries, the take was paltry. The diamond bracelet the thief stole was pretty, but not spectacular. The gold pin had mostly sentimental value. And the ring? Worth only $40. Why bother?

Something about the Sharp burglary had an odd feel to it. I wondered, Could the thief resent Ruth Sharp's do-goodness? Her status in the community?

I was forming a mental picture of the thief and tried to imagine what he was thinking. Did he begrudge people who were more accepted?

Hey, Mr. Thief, I wondered, *are you bitter about something? Why pick on someone so nice?*

❖

I looked into Ruth Sharp's background for anything that might explain the burglar's unusual visit. Unlike many of the King's victims, Ruth Elaine Collins Sharp did not come from oil money. She came from insurance money. Ruth was the daughter of Carr P. Collins, a hymn-singing Baptist who founded Fidelity Union Life Insurance Company. Though the oil families got more attention, a half-dozen families in Dallas made fortunes from the insurance business. Carr Collins also created the Vent-a-Hood Company to whisk away the smoke from charred meals. Then he bought a radio station. And a cemetery. And a hotel where movie stars came for mineral baths.

Collins's success meant his children grew up on Swiss Avenue, a wide boulevard with stately brick homes. Their house was surrounded by foundational families of the city. The Mungers, who pioneered cotton gin technology, lived down the street. So did the Neiman and Marcus families of retail fame. The Higginbothams, who owned a chain of hardware and dry goods stores, had eight homes on Swiss Avenue, by far the most dominant clan.

Ruth Collins was a Golden Girl. She grew up with a family nurse, summer camps, and Sunday dinners with luminaries like Helen Keller. As a teenager, she speeded through her neighborhood in her Ford convertible wearing a muskrat coat.

Still, the family's means did not insulate her from tragedy. When she was a junior at SMU, Ruth married a young Navy pilot. Eighteen months later, he was shot down in a bombing raid over Tokyo. Widowed at twenty-one, Ruth took a job at Love Field, guiding planes with hand signals. She was probably the only debutante on the tarmac.

After the war, she met Charles Sharp, who did not come from Dallas money. He had worked his way through law school and didn't even have a car. But Ruth noticed right away that he looked like the handsome man in Arrow Shirt ads.

They married in 1947 and started a family, two daughters and a son. To people who saw Mrs. Sharp in the society pages with her handsome husband, hers must have seemed a perfect life. In reality, Ruth Sharp shouldered a series of private difficulties. Her son, Stanton, was diagnosed with a mental illness that required special care the rest of his life. Then her husband, Charles, was struck with early-onset Parkinson's disease. When he could no longer care for himself, she fed and bathed him.

"I had my son running up and down the halls not knowing where he was, and I was up all night with Charles," she admitted in a reflective moment years later. "So, I had some lean years in there, shall we say."

Ruth Sharp rarely mentioned such troubles, and if others did, she brushed off sympathy by saying, "I wasn't always in a vale of tears." After all, she got to attend Queen Elizabeth's coronation, she would point out.

True, her life was not without glamour. She drove a Jaguar. Her admirers included Lord Mountbatten, and her friends included Sophia Loren.

When she was nominated to serve on the grand jury, it was a departure from business as usual in the county courthouse. The men who ran the county kept power by handing out contracts and favors to their friends. In contrast, Ruth Sharp wasn't interested in political patronage. She believed in duty. She showed up each day at eight A.M. and listened intently to the cases. After the traumatic November 22 lunch, she returned in shock to the jury room, then went home to comfort her children.

As social activities resumed after the holidays, Ruth and Charles Sharp decided to go to the Terpsichorean Ball on January 24. It would be an upbeat change. Yet while the Sharps were at the dance, someone removed a screen in the back of their house and climbed into their bedroom.

Around ten P.M., the Sharps' teenaged daughter Sally returned home from her first date. She didn't stay out late, as instructed. When she came in the front door, she heard a sound coming from her parents' bedroom. "I looked that direction and noticed the door was closed," she said. That struck her as odd because the door was usually open. She thought her parents had beaten her home and gone to bed.

But she was wrong. Someone else was in their bedroom.

The teenager turned on the TV to watch a movie before going to her room. She undressed and went to bed. Down the hall, the jewel thief eased out the window of her parents' room.

The next day, her mother reached into a drawer of her dressing table and discovered several things were missing. They included a small diamond bracelet her parents had given her and a gold pin of her mother's that she treasured.

Had someone noticed those were her favorites? She wore them often.

Yet how did the thief know the Sharps were attending the deb ball? That same night, he stole jewels from the Jack Kadane family across the street. How did he know both families were going to the ball?

Rather than being frightened by the close encounter, young Sally Sharp was thrilled that the coverage memorialized her first date. However, she thought it was odd her mother was targeted. "It was a little ironic," she told me years later. "He was called the 'King of Diamonds,' and she certainly wasn't dripping in diamonds."

◈

I was beginning to realize that the burglar was not just looking for jewels; he had something to prove. The fact that he did not try in the slightest to camouflage his footprints or his well-publicized technique at burglaries was a message:

He wanted everyone to know the King of Diamonds had been there.

That possibility made me remember a 1958 theft at the Preston Road home of W. C. McCord. As the president of Southland Life Insurance Company, McCord was a certified member of the Establishment. He was a former city councilman and member of the powerful Citizen's Council. He belonged to the Cipango Club, the Dallas Country Club, and Brook Hollow Golf Club, where the thief might have spied his wife's jewels.

Though there were seven bedrooms in the McCords' house, the thief apparently knew exactly where to find the jewels. He took what he wanted and left. Nothing was disturbed. Mrs. McCord did not realize there had been a break-in until she got a mysterious call at 4:15 in the morning, a few days before Thanksgiving. A man said some of her jewels had been stolen and he knew who did it. Yet he hung up without revealing a name. Mrs. McCord quickly checked her jewelry. The caller was right: some of her best jewels were missing, including two diamond pins, a diamond rope necklace containing 324 round diamonds, a bracelet with eighty-six diamonds, and a three-stone diamond ring.

Was the caller betraying the jewel thief? Or was it him? Did he want to let people know he had stolen from a city leader so cleverly that no one discovered it?

The Sharp burglary was likely to be in the news because Charles Sharp was a prominent figure as well as his wife. He was a member of the city council and a recent mayoral candidate. He and his wife had just pledged $400,000 to SMU. Sure enough, the Sharp robbery made big headlines.

Did the thief still want to be a story even after the Kennedy tragedy took center stage? Was he vain enough to want his burglaries in the news? I was starting to think so.

ABOVE: Bruno and Josephine Herbert Graf dressed for a night at the opera. *From the Associated Press.*
BELOW: The Graf house glowed in the dark. *Photo by Jason Franzen.*

ABOVE: The Graf's famous floating dinner table. *Photo by Jason Franzen.* BELOW: Capt. Walter Fannin and Lt. Paul McCaghren on the hunt. *From Jack Beers,* Dallas Morning News.

Oilman Clint Murchison Sr. looking at ease by a bar. *From the University of Texas at Arlington Library Special Collections.*

Fort Worth publisher Amon Carter (left) enjoys a lunch with Dwight Eisenhower (center) and oilman Sid Richardson (right) in 1950. *From the University of Texas at Arlington Library Special Collections.*

Top O' Hill casino owner Fred Browning dressed for success. *Photo courtesy Vickie Bryant.*

The Top O' Hill casino, hidden away in Arlington, Texas. *Photo courtesy Vickie Bryant.*

Stripper Candy Barr became a celebrity in Dallas. *From the Associated Press.*

Sportsman and suspect George Owen kept company with millionaires and gamblers. *From the* Dallas Morning News.

Sharon and Pollard Simons dressed for an 1890s theme Hamon costume party. *From the Nancy Hamon Papers, Bywaters Special Collections, Hamon Arts Library, Southern Methodist University.*

Mrs. Dudley Ramsden (left) and socialite Nancy Ann Smith stepping out at a Hamon costume party. *From the Nancy Hamon Papers, Bywaters Special Collections, Hamon Arts Library, Southern Methodist University.*

ABOVE: Oilmen Buddy Fogelson (seated at left) and Dick Andrade (seated to the right) watch the chef prepare crêpes suzette at the ritzy Cipango Club. Gambler and club part-owner Earl Dalton (handkerchief in pocket) looks on. *From* LIFE *magazine/Shutterstock.* BELOW: To reach the master bedroom of the Ling mansion (left), the jewel thief climbed up the side of the house to the balcony of another room and broke in. *From the Associated Press.*

ABOVE LEFT: Stanley Marcus (left) and jewelry executive Dudley Ramsden welcome Her Highness Maharani of Baroda to Texas in 1963. *From the Dallas Public Library/Texas-Dallas History and Archives Division/The Dallas Morning News Collection.* ABOVE RIGHT: Social maven Evelyn Lambert (right) and her husband Joe Lambert (far left) enjoy the party scene with oilman Jack Vaughn and his wife Mary Jo. *From the Nasher Sculpture Center.* BELOW: Nancy Hamon presided over the most glamorous parties in the city. *From the Nancy Hamon Papers, Bywaters Special Collections, Hamon Arts Library, Southern Methodist University.*

The handsome Kirksmith brothers—Jasper (top), Jack (below right), and Jim (below left)–became early suspects in the case. *Courtesy of Yearbook Photos.*

ABOVE LEFT: When he was twenty-one, John T. Higginbotham Jr. traveled first class on the RMS *Queen Elizabeth* to Europe. *From the Kevin Fox collection.* ABOVE RIGHT: Higginbotham was often featured in society coverage as an escort for debutantes. *Staff photo,* Dallas Times Herald. BELOW: Oilman H. L. Hunt (center) made a rare appearance at a Hamon costume party with his son-in-law Al Hill Jr. (left) and daughter Margaret Hunt Hill (right). *From the Nancy Hamon Papers, Bywaters Special Collections, Hamon Arts Library, Southern Methodist University.*

ABOVE LEFT: Police Detective John Chism continued the hunt for the jewel thief in the late 1960s. *From the Chism family collection.* ABOVE RIGHT: US Senator Joseph McCarthy took a break from investigating communists in the 1950s for a vacation in Puerto Rico with his look-alike, Dallas executive Robert Thompson. *From the United Press.* BELOW: Joe Campisi provided pizza for city officials as well as mobsters at his Egyptian restaurant. *From the collections of the Dallas History & Archives Division, Dallas Public Library.*

ABOVE: Socialite John T. Higginbotham Jr. at the age of thirty. *From the Kevin Fox collection.* BELOW: The Crystal Charity Ball—founded by oil heiress Nancy Ann Smith—became the premier social event in the city. *From* Town and Country.

In the 1960s, Delta Air Lines posters for flights to Dallas featured beautiful women in jewels. *From Delta Air Lines.*

ABOVE: Opera patron Elsa von Seggern wore her prized opal ring to pose with tenor Alfredo Kraus. *From the collections of the Dallas History & Archives Division, Dallas Public Library/ Phil Schexnyder.* RIGHT: Lt. Paul McCaghren and Sgt. Charlie Dellinger show some of the thousands of police files on the King of Diamonds case. *From Andy Hanson,* Dallas Times Herald.

Architect Frank Lloyd Wright with client John Gillin. *From the collections of the Dallas History & Archives Division, Dallas Public Library.*

Philanthropist Ruth Sharp (right), seen here with former First Lady Barbara Bush, became one of the jewel thief's victims in 1964. *From voly.org.*

Society editor and party planner Ann Draper helped police look for the thief. *From the* Dallas Morning News.

ABOVE: Like many of the thief's targets, Frito-Lay chairman Herman Lay's home was in the upscale Preston Hollow neighborhood. *From Candy's Dirt/MLS.* RIGHT: The jewel thief became a media star in the 1960s. *Dallas Times Herald, Dallas Morning News, Fort Worth Star-Telegram.* BELOW: To track the thief, the Dallas police drew their own map of Preston Hollow. The highlighted sites show the area was riddled with burglaries. *From the Paul McCaghren collection.*

$200,000 in Gems Taken At Palatial Dallas Home

SOCIAL CALENDAR:
Hide the Gems, It's Fall Again
'Tis the Season
For That Thief

Dallas Jewel Thief Another Socialite Robbing Friends?

REAL PUZZLER
Diabolical Gem Thief Still Loose

Dallas Jewel Thefts
A $700,000 Question: Where Are Gems Sold?

Master Jewel Burglar Eludes Police In Most Baffling Case During Decade

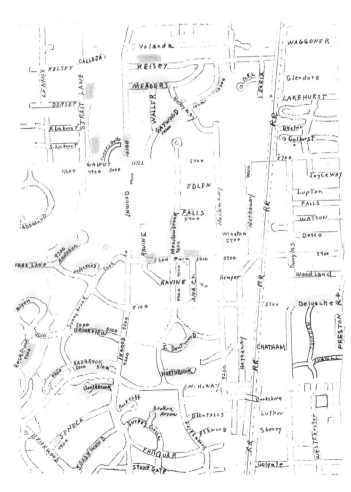

27

Phantom of the Opera

With annoying regularity, McCaghren stepped into Fannin's office to report, "There's been another one."

"Don't you *ever* have any *good* news?" Fannin would complain. "Get out of here!" Then, "Where was it?"

One morning, McCaghren filled him in: "Home of a lady named Elsa von Seggern. Owns a shovel and crane company. Made a *lot* of money. Lives in a big duplex in Highland Park."

"How did he get in?"

"Climbed a tree, pried open a window on the second story. The Highland Park guys said he took some rings, jewel pins, and some golf figurines. Rummaged around. Probably looking for something."

"Rummaged around? *Golf figurines?* Doesn't smell like the King," Fannin said. "Let's move on."

But Fannin may have been wrong to discount the von Seggern break-in. The thief had rummaged through several homes when looking for something in particular. For example, he pried open several closets at the W. J. Lewis home in Highland Park. The jewelry he wanted had been placed in a box in another room.

Something told me the von Seggern case deserved a second look.

People assumed from her exotic clothes and manner that Elsa von Seggern was a displaced German baroness. In truth, she was born Elsie Seggern on a farm in Nebraska. She became an opera lover not by sitting in a royal box but by listening to the Metropolitan Opera on the radio. Like many others in the story, she was determined to be something more.

Newspaper accounts described von Seggern as being darkly attractive with "piercing blue-green eyes." She told friends that she left her Chicago job to follow a man from Dallas. "I thought he was single—turned out he was married!"

She stayed anyway and found work as a secretary in an insurance company. Using $185 of her savings, she launched her own equipment company and built it into a major supplier of heavy machinery. By the 1960s, her Shovel Supply Co. had a Triple A Dun & Bradstreet rating and 175 employees.

Befitting the times, she signed her checks "E. F. von Seggern" so her customers wouldn't know they were doing business with a woman. She installed her friend L. C. Ferguson as president of the company. She called the shots but identified herself as the vice president. She made it clear that she preferred the company of businessmen to country club women and didn't want to be known as one of the "ladies who lunch."

Von Seggern accentuated her differentness by wearing silk capes and turbans to opera balls. After trips to Egypt, she became convinced that she was a descendant of Queen Nefertiti. She had replicas made of the queen's headpieces—including one covered with leopard skin—so she could wear them to gala events.

When she traveled, she went to remote locales. She flew through the peaks of the Andes. She trekked from Pakistan to India. She crossed Siberia by rail and studied Spanish in Mexico.

Von Seggern clearly had cosmopolitan tastes. She collected artworks by Tamayo, Leger, and Chagall—along with burial urns from China, water jugs from Egypt, and other artifacts. It seemed unlikely she would have "golf figurines," as the Highland Park police reported. I suspected the policemen misunderstood her accent and the figurines were something more rarified, like "Guelph" artifacts from Medieval Europe. Most Guelph art was German, like von Seggern, and included gold and jeweled crosses and reliquaries. It was a long shot, but a better guess than "golf" figurines.

The thief may have been looking for her oversized opal ring. The opal was big as a pigeon's egg, people said. It's possible von Seggern was wearing the ring that night—or had hidden it in a coat pocket in her closet. Her friends told me later that von Seggern often hid jewels in the pockets of her coats. When she died and her domestic helpers were invited to take any clothing they wanted, some may have walked away with more than they expected.

It was easy to see why von Seggern might draw the thief's interest. Her philanthropy and lavish style were well-known. During lean years, she paid the entire opera payroll several times. She underwrote fourteen productions by herself.

That's not to say von Seggern gave graciously. She once imperiously tossed a donation on the floor, forcing an arts staffer to bend down and pick it up. When she served as treasurer of the opera, she had such an autocratic way that the finance committee asked for her removal.

General manager Larry Kelly liked to tell the story that he once dreamed von Seggern died. While lying in state, she sat bolt upright in the casket and asked him, "How many pall bearers are there?" Kelly answered, "Eight." "Fire four of them," she ordered, and lay back down.

As I found out more about von Seggern, it dawned on me that many of the people targeted by the King were Dallas Opera supporters, at least two dozen. Besides von Seggern, that included Josephine Graf, Clint Murchison, Margaret Hill, Jim Ling, Herman Lay, Wilson McClure, W. W. Lynch, Joanne Stroud, Margaret Otis, Barbara Varel, Wofford Cain, Howell Smith, Frank Schultz, Charles Sharp, Lawrence Pollock, Glenn Turner, the Kleins, the Haggertys, and more.

I suspected that Fannin and McCaghren didn't consider that the thief might have rubbed elbows with targets at the opera. I added a new note about the thief: *May have liked opera and rare objects.*

◈

The search had taken longer than I anticipated. Six years had gone by. I chided myself that Agatha Christie's detectives could crack a case on a train ride or a showdown in the library. Still, my clue board was now covered with yellow squares of paper. As I stood back and looked at them, I thought, *I am getting to know you, Mr. Thief. I am getting closer.*

My list of the thief's characteristics had grown:

- Wants people to know it's him. Alerted a victim afterward. Doesn't hide clues like waffle prints.
- A social insider. Knew the Sharps and the Kadanes would be attending the same event, so he hit both houses the same night.
- Must not have a regular eight-to-five job, since he often stays out all night. May be self-employed. Probably not married.
- Lives in the area. Knows alleys and creeks far too well to be an outsider.
- Well-mannered and meticulous. Replaces drawers, avoids damage other than window glass.
- Can be cruel, taking sentimental items like wedding rings and family brooches of little financial value.
- Vindictive at times, spoiling matched sets.
- Knows how to control dogs. May have pets.
- Has sophisticated tastes; possibly an opera supporter.
- Cautious. He sometimes called victims—Schultz, McCurdy, Ling, and more—to make sure they were in town with their jewels at hand. Leaves windows open for a quick exit.
- Prideful. Shows off his prowess with daring feats of climbing and jumping.

A composite was emerging of a cultivated thief with a chip on his shoulder. I could almost see him: a man in a tuxedo with a knowing air.

PART SIX

THE SUSPECTS

"It is the psychology I seek, not the fingerprint or the cigarette ash."
—Hercule Poirot

28

Profile of a Thief

Many people said the same thing about the King of Diamonds: "He was just like Cary Grant!"

Everyone in town seemed to have seen the 1956 movie *To Catch a Thief*. Actor Cary Grant played a debonair jewel thief who stole from the rich on the French Riviera. The movie played in theaters just before the Dallas thefts hit the headlines, so Cary Grant became the image of the thief.

"Dallas had arrived—the Riviera had its jewel thief, and now we had ours," a burglary victim told me.

But catching the real-life thief was proving to be a lot harder than the movie version. Five years after the Graf break-in, the sensational burglary was still unsolved. The statute of limitations was running out. The clock was ticking.

Fannin and McCaghren had interviewed more than two thousand people and polygraphed two hundred suspects. They had filled several tall, gray file cabinets with hand-typed reports. They had compiled more than seventy thousand information cards on every person whose name cropped up.

But one thing was still missing: the burglar's name.

As conventional approaches failed, Fannin resorted to more unorthodox measures. He met with a fortune-teller who insisted she knew who the

King was. "He's a boilermaker who tends the furnaces at the homes of the rich," she told him.

Fannin listened patiently before telling her, "The only thing is, none of them have a furnace."

He asked a career burglar for advice on the theory that it "takes a thief to catch a thief." The former jailbird said the King of Diamonds didn't behave like any other thief, so he was stumped. But he had a point: The jewel thief was different. He acted like a considerate guest. He always put everything back in order. If he had to stand on a chair to reach a window, he put a handkerchief or hand towel on the chair. He was a gentleman thief.

◆

Fannin and McCaghren began to realize they were dealing with a *why-dunnit*, not just a *who-dunnit*. Why would someone leave so many jewels behind? Why would someone sneak into bedrooms and hide in their closets? What kind of person was this?

McCaghren got an idea: Why not invite an expert to make a psychological profile of the thief? It was a novel approach. Behavioral analysis of criminals had been around since the Jack the Ripper case in the 1880s, but the concept was not widely applied. The FBI didn't create its Behavioral Sciences Unit until 1972.

McCaghren believed a profile could provide a key to the unique case and knew just the man to do it from his graduate studies at SMU: Dr. Robert Stoltz, head of the psychology department.

Professor Stoltz studied all the burglary reports and went on night patrols with the detectives. Then he drafted a profile that shaped the search. Stoltz hypothesized the jewel thief was:

- A young man in his early thirties.
- Athletic, but not a contact sport player—more like a former tennis player, fit enough to climb trees and walls.

- Perhaps a "mama's boy" or latent homosexual, who took jewels to admire and covet, not to sell. He seemed to have an obsession with women's jewelry.
- A member of a family of means with access to social circles.
- A stylish and neat dresser with good manners.
- A person who feels he has been snubbed in some way or has a grudge.

So far, the thief had not demonstrated any violent behavior, but Stoltz warned he might panic if cornered. The police needed to find him before a tragedy occurred.

Fannin and McCaghren quietly checked out several young socialites who seemed to match the Stoltz description. They kept the vetting under tight wraps because they were reaching into some of the city's big-name families.

At the time, more than a half dozen men were active in elite social groups who fit the "mama's boy" description. They were considered latent homosexuals, but it was kept quiet because homosexuality was strictly taboo. The penalty for sodomy in Texas was fifteen years in prison.

Suspecting a socialite of being a jewel thief was one thing; suggesting he might be a "latent homosexual" added to the risk. Police had to tread very, very cautiously, like the thief.

29

The Face in the Night

O nly a few victims got a glimpse of an intruder who could have been the King.

One was Sam Wallace, who owned one of the largest mechanical contracting firms in the country. It was said the Sam P. Wallace company provided the air conditioning for every building over five stories in Dallas.

When World War II ended, someone needed to provide the plumbing, heating, ventilation, and refrigeration for the boom in construction, so Wallace's company expanded to forty-nine states and twenty-seven countries. His projects ranged from the Hilton Hotel in Hong Kong to the Astrodome in Houston.

Wallace's friends called him a glorified plumber, but he was a rich plumber. He did well enough to build a new home in Highland Park in 1962. It was so close to the Dallas Country Club that he could walk across the street for steak night.

The Wallaces moved into their rose-brick home a few weeks before the burglar climbed through the window of Mrs. Wallace's bathroom. Her husband's bathroom was located on the other side of the master suite.

The two were asleep when Wallace heard a noise in his bathroom. He glanced at his watch—it was 1:15 in the morning. Who could be in the house at that hour?

Sam Wallace got out of bed, still half-asleep. He padded in his pajamas and bare feet toward his bathroom—and saw a man rifling through the drawers.

A jolt of adrenaline hit Wallace. He was now totally awake. He was sturdy enough to put up a fight, but he worried the intruder might be armed. Wallace tiptoed back to the bed to pull his gun from under the mattress. He nudged his wife's shoulder and whispered: "Call the police!"

The intruder heard him. He sprinted toward Mrs. Wallace's bathroom on the other side of the bedroom. Operating on sheer reflex, Wallace lumbered after him.

Wallace thought he could corner the intruder in his wife's bathroom since there was no exit. To his amazement, the burglar vaulted head-first out the bathroom window like an acrobat.

Wallace leaned out the window and peered into the darkness, his heart pounding. He aimed at the figure on the ground and pulled the trigger.

His gun jammed.

Wallace could hear the burglar moaning. He had hurt himself when he landed on some garden tools.

"Lie still!" Wallace ordered as he struggled to get his gun to fire.

But the burglar didn't stay still. He staggered to his feet and limped across the backyard before Wallace could get off a shot. When Wallace finally fired his gun, the intruder was climbing over the fence. He got away.

Police later discovered the burglar had hit the ground so hard that he made a dent in the dirt. There were traces of what appeared to be blood. Footprints nearby had the familiar waffle pattern.

A check of the grounds showed the thief had unscrewed floodlights that might have exposed him. Then he carefully placed a lawn chair on boards so he could reach the high bathroom window.

Fannin ordered his men to contact hospitals to see if anyone checked in with backside injuries. None were recorded. They brought in several men they considered suspects. None of them had backside injuries either.

On top of the cuts and bruises he suffered, the thief must have been chagrined that he didn't find what he was looking for. Because his recent thefts had been widely publicized, Mrs. Wallace had stashed her jewelry in different parts of the house. She had $50,000 worth of jewelry hidden that night.

When I called her decades later, Mrs. Wallace was an elderly woman, yet she remembered that night well. "We had heard and read so much about this jewel burglar that we didn't want to take any chances that he might make us one of his victims," she said.

Her precautions forced the thief to take the additional risk of going into her husband's bathroom when he couldn't find what he wanted in her bathroom. He only had time to grab some money from Mr. Wallace's billfold before he ran out.

Police hoped Sam Wallace could provide the description they desperately needed. Wallace said the man was bare-headed and unmasked, but he didn't get a good look at his face. The man was short and somewhat stocky, he said. He wore a sports coat and pants that looked ill-matched, he said, as if the guy had dressed in a hurry—or was trying to disguise his appearance. Wallace couldn't say whether the thief was fair-headed or dark-haired. But he was white, Wallace said, which ruled out most of their domestic workers.

"How tall was he?" a detective asked.

"About five foot seven—like that fellow over there," Wallace said, pointing to a policeman standing nearby.

The policeman was actually five feet, eleven inches tall.

The discrepancy showed how difficult it is for witnesses to judge height. That's why convenience stores have color-coded strips posted on the sides of their doors, so clerks can gauge the height of robbers more accurately.

Fannin was deeply disappointed that Wallace couldn't give a more detailed description, but he had a hunch there would be other opportunities. "He'll strike again," Fannin predicted.

◆

Fannin was right.

A year later, someone else got a glimpse of the burglar when he broke into a house on Strait Lane. Strait Lane was an exclusive address, in the same league as Park Lane. The owner of the house, Charles M. Moore Jr., was vice president of Geophysical Service, the company that became Texas Instruments.

On a crisp March evening in 1963, Charles Moore and his wife Katherine were attending a benefit performance at the Dallas Theater Center. The Moores' teenaged son Marvin was asleep in bed when something awoke him.

"Something told me to get up," Marvin Moore told me years later. He walked out of his bedroom into the semi-darkened hallway.

"There was someone walking up the hall," Moore said. "Both of us were startled."

The teenager was so surprised, he couldn't speak. So was the intruder.

"Then, as if he knew where he was going, the man ran into my brother's room," Moore recalled. "He went out a side door and disappeared through the backyard." The man must have been familiar with the house, Moore said, because had he turned a different way, he would have been trapped in a bathroom.

Police asked Moore, What did the intruder look like?

Moore couldn't say. He couldn't see the man's face clearly because he didn't have his contact lenses or eyeglasses on. But he described the prowler as being around five feet eight or nine inches tall and about 150 pounds. He appeared to be in his midthirties, the teen said. He wore a dark shirt and pants and a "stingy brim" hat pulled low over his face. The press had reported it was an "Alpine hat," so Moore clarified when we talked that it was *not* an Alpine hat, just a sportier version of the kind of fedora that some businessmen wore. He also remembered another important detail: the intruder wore Hush Puppies, a casual shoe with crepe rubber soles.

After he determined the intruder was gone, Moore called the security service employed by the family. It took the guard forty-five minutes to arrive. He advised the teenager to call the police and left.

When the police arrived, they were furious the security service didn't notify them sooner, when the intruder's tracks would have been fresh. Nevertheless, their dogs were able to follow the tracks to nearby Bachman Branch. The man apparently used the creek to make his escape to a car parked out of sight.

Moore chuckled as he remembered how excited the police were to have him as a possible witness. "They said, 'You are the only sober person who has seen this guy!'"

The police brought in an artist to make a sketch of the intruder, but the teen's description was too vague to be helpful. They tried showing the teenager a book of mugshots, but Moore didn't see anyone who resembled the man he encountered. Many years later, Moore told me he kept telling the police, "These guys don't quite fit.

"I realize now the difference was this guy had class," Moore said. "The guy was so smooth and quiet and brazen. He had a different demeanor. The people they showed me looked like common criminals."

The man he saw was relatively well-dressed. In fact, Moore thought at first his parents had brought him home with them from their social event. "If you ran into him on the street," he said, "you would think he belonged in the neighborhood."

Moore didn't hear from the police after that night. However, he heard that authorities had confronted the jewel thief and told him to lay off.

When I asked Paul McCaghren about that possibility, he shrugged and said, "Well, I wouldn't be surprised about that. I wouldn't be surprised at all."

♦

The burglar only spoke to victims once. He usually protected his identity by running away when interrupted. But in 1964, he dared to speak.

The encounter occurred at the home of Chester Donnally, an oilman and investor. Donnally and his wife, Evelyn, lived on Baltimore Drive in University Park, a suburb adjacent to Highland Park and Preston Hollow.

Like many of the King's targets, the house was near a creek, this time, Turtle Creek.

At four A.M., Evelyn Donnally woke up. She saw a light in her bathroom.

The intruder sensed that she had stirred.

He shined a small flashlight in her eyes. "Get out of bed," he ordered.

"No," Mrs. Donnally answered.

"Get up!" he insisted.

"NO!" she replied again.

"Why?" he asked in exasperation.

"Because I just have on my nighty, and I don't know you," she said.

From there, the scene careened between a comedy of errors and a war of nerves. Chester Donnally, who went by "Chas," was listening from his side of the bed, pretending to be asleep. Growing concerned the intruder might be armed, Donnally rose up and ordered his wife, "Evelyn, get out of bed! He might have a gun."

The burglar did not appear to be armed, but he was clearly frustrated. Having looked through several drawers in the dressing table, he guessed the jewelry he wanted was in a locked box. He ordered Evelyn Donnally to unlock it.

Once again, she said no. The box contained special items that belonged to her mother, who had passed away earlier that week.

Once again, her husband urged her from bed, "Evelyn, *do it!*"

When she opened the box, the burglar began sorting through the jewelry. Chas Donnally tried to talk him into leaving. "You must have the wrong house," he argued. "We don't have much jewelry. You should go to Vassar Avenue. It's just a block away. That's where the *real* money is."

Donnally rattled off the names of neighbors who would be better prospects, knowing that he could warn them after the burglar left. Dick Bass's house was not far away, Donnally said. "He's got ranches and oil money. He owns ski resorts!

"Harold Byrd lives over there, too," Donnally went on. "He has a telephone in his car! And H. L. Hunt's daughter Margaret—she's one of the richest women in the world! You should try her house."

But the thief wasn't listening. He kept looking through the jewelry box. "I want your diamond ring," he commanded Mrs. Donnally.

"I don't have it here," she lied. While the thief wasn't looking, she had slipped her diamond wedding ring and some diamond earrings into her hand. She dropped them onto the carpeted floor and covered them with her foot.

Growing even bolder, she grabbed the thief's hand as he reached for some earrings. "Don't take those," she said.

"Why?" he asked.

"They are my mother's, and I could never replace them," she argued.

Once again, her husband advised her, "Evelyn, *let go!*" But she wasn't going to let go without an argument.

Although the burglar had been calm and deliberate much of this time, he chastised her in frustration, "I wish you would hush! You're making me nervous!"

She snapped back, "Well, *you* are making *me* nervous!"

Exasperated, the burglar ran out of the bedroom. In his rush to leave, he dropped an emerald necklace and a bracelet in the driveway.

The Donnallys happened to have relatives staying with them who had come for her mother's funeral service. As soon as the burglar left, Chas Donnally went down the hall and knocked on their bedroom door.

"Did you hear that?" he asked.

They nodded their heads, yes.

"Why didn't you call the police?" Donnally demanded.

"We thought you were having a fight," they said sheepishly. "You kept yelling at Evelyn to get out of bed."

Although the incident was unnerving at the time, it became a favorite anecdote for the family.

Unfortunately for the police, the Donnallys could not provide a good description of the thief. They claimed they didn't see him well because he shined his flashlight in their eyes. His face was obscured by the dark.

Fannin told the press he doubted the intruder was the King because he appeared to use some kind of tool to twist open the kitchen doorknob, something he hadn't done before. But the Donnally incident had strong similarities to the King's pattern: The thief knew where the jewels were kept. He only chose the best. He appeared to have seen some of Mrs. Donnally's diamonds before and asked specifically for them.

His conversation with the Donnallys was also revealing. A typical criminal would have said, "Shut up!" instead of "Hush, you're making me nervous." It brought to mind the burglar who broke into the Wilson residence on Broken Arrow. He told their dog Sheila to "Hush." If this was the same guy, he had manners.

30

"The Store"

The thief's hit list looked like the Neiman Marcus customer base, so people began speculating there might be a connection.

The luxury department store was such an integral part of Dallas life that it was known simply as "the Store." One of the first things that the newly rich wanted was to look rich. The *New Yorker* magazine captured that ambition with a cartoon showing a woman on the porch of a shack with an oil well spouting out back. She is saying to the telephone operator, "Neiman Marcus, quick!"

◆

If there was a single factor that created the Dallas image for riches, it would be oil money—followed closely by Neiman Marcus. When the Marcus and Neiman families opened the department store in 1907, they realized right away that a reputation for good taste sold a lot of merchandise. So, when the store unveiled its "Christmas Book" in 1916, it was nothing like the catalogs from traditional purveyors in the Midwest like Sears and Montgomery Ward. There were no flannel nightgowns or work boots to be seen, but you could order fashions from Paris and handbags from Milan. The store's reputation for elegance was established.

When young Stanley Marcus joined the team in 1926, he launched the first weekly fashion shows in an American department store. By 1938, "Mr. Stanley" had added the *Neiman Marcus Award*, which became the Oscars of the fashion industry. Dallas became fashion-conscious. Even in the 1940s, Neiman Marcus had nearly three hundred charge accounts that ran over $50,000 a year.

When Stanley Marcus awarded French designer Coco Chanel the store's fashion award in 1957, it was a coup for her and the store. After World War I, Chanel had revolutionized fashion with a pared-down style that freed women from corsets and long skirts. She had to shutter her couture house during World War II, and when she reopened in 1954, her fashion line was not well-received by the French press. Many could not forget that Chanel had gone through the war in relative comfort at the Ritz Hotel—or forgive that she had a German lover. Her career was stalled when the Dallas store honored her. Stanley Marcus thought her crisp styles were perfect for the modern American woman. At seventy, Chanel got the boost she needed for a comeback.

The vaunted Neiman Marcus marketing team staged a special welcome for the French icon. Chanel wanted to visit a ranch, so Stanley Marcus arranged a Western-themed party at his brother Edward's farm near Dallas. There were demonstrations of roping, riding, and square-dancing. The surprise was a unique fashion show: Instead of giraffe-thin models, cows and bulls paraded down the runway, displaying couture on the hoof. One bovine model featured a "mid-calf look." Another wore ropes of pearls, a spoof on Chanel's favorite accessory. The showstopper was a pair of unlikely newlyweds—a bull stuffed into evening clothes and wearing a top hat was hitched to a young heifer in white Chanel and veil. Chanel clapped her hands with delight.

After that, it was easy to get top designers to come to Dallas.

Marcus moved quickly to introduce "Fortnight" extravaganzas, which brought international fashion, art, and food stars to Dallas at a time when fewer people in Dallas traveled abroad and fewer people abroad came to Texas. For the France Fortnight, a model of the Eiffel Tower was erected in the store's lobby. The tower spouted from the top like—what else?—an oil well. Neiman Marcus spent $400,000 on the event; it produced an estimated $2 million in revenues.

When Marcus introduced "His and Hers" Christmas presents—matching planes, Egyptian caskets, camels, and robots—the outrageous gifts generated publicity around the globe. Selling costly wares to people who already had everything reinforced the perception that people in Dallas had the riches of maharajahs.

It was only natural that the Store became part of the drama when the mysterious jewel thief burst onto the scene. Almost all the victims bought jewelry there.

And three suspects had worked there.

◆

Since the thief singled out the best jewels like an expert with a jeweler's loupe, people wondered, Could the thief be a *jeweler*? Or someone working in tandem with a jeweler? Speculation turned to top jewelers like Richard Eiseman, who cut a Bond-like figure in his tuxedo. But most of the talk swirled around Dudley Ramsden.

Ramsden headed the precious jewels department at Neiman Marcus. He drew suspicion because he knew who had the best jewels; he had sold a lot of them. He could spot a fake from across a lobby. What's more, he and his wife, Alma, regularly appeared in society pages as part of the "in crowd."

Could Dudley Ramsden be exploiting his access?

His customers included everyone on the "Best Dressed" list plus movie stars like John Wayne and Joan Crawford. Ramsden painted the town with Wayne when he visited and provided peacemaking gifts for his wife. Crawford, who was born in San Antonio, shopped with Ramsden whenever she returned to the state. And when her fortunes ebbed between movies and husbands, Ramsden discreetly sold pieces of Crawford's jewelry for her.

Lesser known was the fact that Dudley Ramsden's other friends included gamblers like Bennie Bickers. When Bickers owned the University Club down the street from Neiman Marcus, Ramsden liked to stop by for a drink or two—and sell jewelry to Bickers.

To his prominent customers, Dudley Ramsden was known as a personable dinner partner. "A delightful man," they said. However, store employees said working for him was like suffering the demands of fashion editor Miranda Priestly in *The Devil Wears Prada*. When the magazine diva said in the movie, "Please bore someone else with your questions," she could have been channeling Dudley Ramsden.

❖

Ramsden came to Dallas from the East Coast in 1948, bringing with him several suitcases full of fine jewelry from New York and Europe. He convinced Stanley Marcus to let him sell jewels as a concessionaire on the first floor of the store. It wasn't long before he became a vice president.

As writer Skip Hollandsworth observed in a *D Magazine* profile, Ramsden "charged prices to make a millionaire blink," yet convinced customers they were getting a bargain. He set strict standards for his salesmen, ordering them to keep their suit jackets neatly buttoned. Like a drill sergeant, Ramsden regularly tested the salesmen to make sure they knew the price of every item in the display cases. If one bragged about selling an expensive diamond, Ramsden would snap, "Why didn't you sell them something else? Those people could afford it."

Dudley Ramsden did not suffer slackers or grousers. Neiman Marcus PR executive Tom Alexander remembered being in Ramsden's office when the phone rang. After listening for a while, Ramsden said to the caller, "I tell you what. I am sixty-five years old, and I am getting rid of all the nuisances in my life, and you are one of them." Then he hung up.

Still, the cranky Ramsden was a genius at selling. He convinced customers the jewels would appreciate in value and they would be missing a great opportunity if they didn't buy while they could. Wallets opened. If a woman worried that her husband might blow his stack about the size of her bill, Ramsden would let her put the jewels on layaway to spread out the cost.

Ramsden went to legendary lengths to make a sale. Stanley Marcus recounted in his book, *Minding the Store*, that after one of his salesmen lost a sale on a diamond necklace, Ramsden flew to the customer's ranch to convince the man he'd made a mistake buying from another jeweler. It was the day before Christmas and bitter cold. To reach the man's ranch, Ramsden had to charter a flight and drive for several hours. He found the customer talking to a veterinarian about a horse. "I've flown three hundred miles to keep you from making a mistake," Ramsden told him. "Please give me fifteen minutes." He placed the Neiman Marcus necklace on the tailgate of a truck and invited the rancher to put the other necklace next to it. The difference was evident. The rancher switched to the Neiman Marcus necklace.

Though his son teased that he only had a sixth-grade education, Ramsden had gone far with innate smarts and acquired charm. While his wife was tall, blonde, and striking, he was a rather nondescript, balding man. It was his personality that drew people to him.

Ramsden cultivated many of his high-end customers at Brook Hollow Golf Club. Stanley Marcus couldn't join the country club because he was Jewish, so Ramsden talked his way in. He was not shy about reminding his golf partners when their wives had birthdays coming up.

One day, after a round of golf with Clint Murchison Jr. and his brother John, Ramsden discovered someone had sprayed his Cadillac with garish red-and-green paint. Ramsden turned the same colors. He was livid. The culprit turned out to be Clint Jr., who loved practical jokes. Fortunately for all, the paint was water-soluble, and the car returned to good form. In retribution, Ramsden had the locker room attendant move Murchison's car to a different parking spot so he couldn't find it.

When Ramsden replaced his Cadillac with a Rolls-Royce, it fueled new speculation that he was involved in the jewel thefts. Ramsden had purchased the Rolls secondhand, but the pricey car still triggered talk. Could Dudley Ramsden be retrieving jewels he once sold? Since the victims would need new jewels, he could benefit again.

Most people didn't know that Ramsden, like society editor Ann Draper, was secretly helping the police. He provided the names of women who might be likely targets so the police could stake out their homes. His first suggestion? Nancy Hamon, the party hostess with plenty of party jewels. When a waiter handed her a drink with a sliver of lime in it, she chided, "I have emeralds bigger than that." And she did.

In fact, Mrs. Hamon had so much jewelry that she referred to it as her "life's work." When she went to style citadels such as New York, Paris, and San Francisco, she brought a rolling Zero Halliburton aluminum suitcase that was full of jewels.

Dudley Ramsden gave Fannin's team a heads-up that Mrs. Hamon was attending the Jewel Ball in Fort Worth. Police stationed an officer in her house. The burglar kept his distance.

While he may have seemed a likely suspect, there were good reasons to think Ramsden was not the King of Diamonds.

For one thing, his wife, Alma, didn't suspect him. According to friends, when Ramsden went on a trip to New York and didn't invite her, she was miffed. Then she thought of a way to make her husband regret not taking her: She put her best jewels in a cardboard box and left them in the hall of their house in case the burglar dropped by. She attached a note: TAKE ALL YOU WANT.

Like her, the Dallas detectives didn't believe her husband was the thief. Why?

He would never risk losing his membership at Brook Hollow, or his Rolls.

31

The Marvelous Mrs. Lambert

The notion that *someone they knew* could be breaking into their homes fueled constant gossip. The worm of suspicion crept into everyone's thinking.

As one socialite put it, "Fingers were pointed."

Everyone had a theory about who "the King" could be. Was it the man who glanced overlong at your necklace and not your bosom?

Or perhaps the furrier with the unctuous demeanor?

For a while, there was talk about a doctor who was athletic and a developer who was a social climber. People in the art crowd suspected a gallery owner named Renato Mazzo. An elegant man from a pedigreed Italian family, Mazzo supplemented his gallery income by making busts of wealthy patrons. Because his clients posed in their homes, people speculated that Mazzo used the access to map out thefts, then smuggled the stolen jewels to Italy by hiding them in plaster casts of heads. This should have won a prize as the most creative theory. The rumors ruined Mazzo's business, yet I could find nothing substantial to tie him to the thefts.

One of the names that came up often was a woman. Could the King have been a *Queen*?

Though people who encountered the thief described a man, some theorized a female mastermind could be calling the shots for a nimble male assistant. This would explain how the thief knew the interior of dressing rooms: a woman could enter such private areas to "freshen up" during a dinner party while men could not.

The woman whose name surfaced repeatedly was one of the most flamboyant figures of the era: Evelyn Lambert.

Evelyn Lambert could have starred in an Agatha Christie murder mystery, the kind with a countess, a conman, some newlyweds, and a detective, all gathered in a remote location when jewels go missing. Evelyn Lambert was a natural to play the countess; she was a cross between Auntie Mame and Lady Macbeth. People either liked Evelyn for her dash and style, or they did not.

Mrs. Lambert had a prominent, pointed nose that gave her a dramatic profile. She accentuated those sharp lines by wearing her hair pulled into a large bun on top of her head. Her friends teased that pulling her hair back so tautly saved the cost of a facelift. Too taut or not, the distinctive coiffure became Evelyn Lambert's "look."

In later years, she added oversized round glasses, which made her look like an owl with a topknot. You certainly could not miss Evelyn Lambert in a crowd. She was tall and had a preference for bold colors.

One socialite recalled seeing Evelyn walking through the tony new NorthPark shopping mall as if she were promenading on the Champs-Élysées, dressed to the nines in a wide-brimmed hat with several standard poodles on a leash.

"Evelyn made entrances," agreed society writer Val Imm Bashour. "She was stunning in a dramatic sort of way, not conventionally beautiful. The first time I saw her was at a gallery opening. She swirled in. She didn't sweep in. She swirled in wearing a shocking pink chiffon that absolutely floated around her. It was very effective. I thought, 'My word! *Who* is this woman?'"

That was a good question.

Evelyn was a woman with a past, and some suspected it wasn't exactly the past she described. A Dallas woman who visited Evelyn at her Venetian villa said the Italians had a word that fit Evelyn perfectly: *"Furba,"* she said, making a slow, slicing motion down her cheek with the back of her thumbnail. "It means smart in a sly, deceitful way. *Furrrr-ba.*"

When Mrs. Lambert's name began coming up, I noticed people looked around carefully to see if anyone was listening before they leaned in to say sotto voce, not to be overheard, "Evelyn Lambert. She was *very unusual.*" Their comments always came with a request that they not be quoted.

Even fifty years later, people feared repercussions because Evelyn Lambert was such a dominant figure. During her heyday, *Texas Monthly* proclaimed she "was one of the most influential forces on the Dallas social scene . . . her imprimatur could put any cause in the limelight."

Feedback about her was a checkerboard of vices and virtues: Charming. Calculating. Powerful. Mesmerizing. An opportunist who used people. A fabulist who made up things. Vivacious. Vindictive. Dynamic. Talented. Generous. A world-class hostess. A fraud.

But was she also a thief?

◆

Though her husband, Joe Lambert, owned a highly successful land-scaping business, people questioned, Was it profitable enough to pay for a lifestyle that included a Rolls-Royce, a penthouse, and a sixty-two-room Italian villa?

Vogue magazine devoted several pages to the Lambert villa, and so did *Architectural Digest.* Mrs. Lambert had turned the sixteenth-century manor into a showplace, commingling antiques and rare tapestries with bold modern art.

"She loved themes," one guest remembered. "When she served German food, she would deck out the serving staff in lederhosen." Other times, the servants wore colorful handcrafted caftans that were so artistic that Evelyn hung them on the walls. She set her dining table with silver goblets and Crown Derby china. Her guests included the Queen Mother, the Shah of Iran, and a steady stream of jet-setters from Dallas.

As one wag put it, "If seven people ruled the world, Evelyn would have had all of them to dinner."

Evelyn Lambert's social overdrive took her to an international stage. But like the Americans who sought refinement abroad in Henry James novels, the umbra of her past followed her. People suspected something was fishy about Evelyn's grandiose posturing, but they generally went along for the ride.

After her husband, Joe, died in 1970, Evelyn gave up their Dallas penthouse and lived in Italy. Twenty-one years later, when she turned eighty-four, she arranged for the villa to become a music conservatory. She shipped her art and furniture to Cuernavaca, Mexico, where she transformed a sixteenth-century hacienda into a stylish compound by adding a swimming pool and pink bougainvillea. She chose the house partly because it was near a historic church and she had become more religious in her later years. Still, she liked to tell visitors the house was once the site of the Black Cat brothel, a detail she relished.

The walled hacienda was perfect for entertaining. Photos from those days show Evelyn presiding over parties in her garden, wearing white slacks, a bright lemon-yellow tunic, and a matching sun hat about three feet wide.

Within no time, Evelyn became known as "Mother Goose" for gathering around her an eclectic group of artists, musicians, celebrities, and millionaires. As writer Turtle Bunbury put it, she was "a room-lighter," even in her nineties.

And she was. Although she fabricated—or hid—large parts of her life, much of what Evelyn Lambert did was remarkable. At a time when many of her contemporaries settled for tulip tours with their garden clubs, Mrs. Lambert went to Kashmir to live on a houseboat. She fished for marlin in Cuba. She dined in Venice with Clare Boothe Luce, Mrs. Cornelius Vanderbilt Whitney, and cosmetics king Charles Revson. Her zest for life was contagious, people said. You wanted to be with Evelyn because she was where the action was. "She was *fabulous*," they would say, "simply *fabulous*."

That said, Mrs. Lambert ruffled some fine feathers by daring to be culturally liberal in a highly conservative city. Once, she invited dozens of society women to a house party in Cuernavaca with the caveat that they bring a gay friend rather than their husbands. This was quite avant-garde for the Bible Belt. When people said Evelyn was *different*, they didn't mean it as a compliment.

Others objected to her incessant self-promotion. She was pushy, they said, so overbearing, so annoying. Even Virginia Nick, a lifelong friend, admitted Evelyn made enemies because she was blunt and said exactly what she thought.

I wondered, Did Evelyn's name keep coming up because she had rubbed too many people the wrong way? Or because she always needed money?

People noticed that Evelyn sometimes asked guests at her Italian villa for donations. To compensate the help for the extra work, she said. Sometimes she sent bills to guests after she had invited them to visit.

"She had a silver bowl on the table, and you were encouraged to leave something," recalled one wealthy visitor. "The house was a small palace with a swimming pool and avant-garde art. It wasn't finished—they were still working on it. But she preserved this wonderful place—they didn't have money to do it all without help. I didn't see anything wrong with that."

When Evelyn relocated in Cuernavaca, she followed the same pattern and pressed guests to chip in or buy art that she was selling. One guest remembered, "She would single out the people that she knew could afford a painting and tell them, 'You *love* this, don't you? You *must* have it!'"

Another guest remembered, "She would suggest you fill the tank of her car. I didn't mind, but you couldn't help but wonder how she afforded everything."

Several prominent women told me that they suspected she skimmed some of the donations for charity auctions for herself. One woman went home from a meeting that Evelyn had dominated and told her lawyer husband, "I'm starting to worry how much is going to Evelyn and how much is going to the arts."

Others questioned her past. When Evelyn arrived in Dallas in 1948, she called herself the "Marquesa del Barrio." She claimed she was the widow of a Spanish noble, the Marqués Francisco Earl del Barrio y Dunbar, whose family owned Bacardi Rum in Cuba.

Not everyone believed her. As one socialite put it, "She was no more a marquesa than my housekeeper."

So, who was Evelyn Lambert, really?

Once I began tracking down the claims she made, it became evident Evelyn had a flexible relationship with the truth. Contrary to her claim that her Cuban husband attended Princeton, the registrar's office found no record of him. And his family was not associated with Bacardi Rum, other than as a tasty drink. The Bacardi historian said he had never heard of the del Barrio family.

I wondered, why was Evelyn Lambert so deceptive about her past?

Had deception become a way of life for her?

Records showed Evelyn Alicia Kelly was born in McMinnville, Tennessee, December 20, 1907, although sometimes she listed her birthdate as December 7 and sometimes spelled her name Kelley. Her mother and father were both teachers, so money was scarce, but learning was prized. After Evelyn's father died, her mother took a job as a math teacher in Durant, a town of less than six thousand in untamed Oklahoma.

In some accounts, Evelyn said she was twelve when they moved to Durant. Other times she said fifteen. She seemed to have a relatively happy high school experience—debate team, society reporter on the school newspaper. Then something changed.

Evelyn later said she left Durant as soon as she could. Throughout her life, she refused to discuss her years in Oklahoma other than to say she "hated it." She sometimes referred to the period as "the bad old days."

A well-to-do Dallas woman, who also grew up in Durant, told her family that she knew why Evelyn wouldn't talk about her Durant past: she had abandoned a child there.

If true, having a baby "out of wedlock" would have been a scandal in the small town—and a traumatic experience for a young girl. It would explain Evelyn's deep reluctance to discuss Durant.

When I tried to verify the birth, I ran into a bureaucratic wall. Local officials wouldn't release the record without permission from Evelyn, who was long gone. I was stymied until I found a commercial records site. There it was: a baby boy with the surname of Kelly was born in Durant on September 3, 1925—when Evelyn was eighteen. "It's her," the clerk confided. No first name was given to the child.

The birth occurred a year after Evelyn went to Chickasha to study at the Oklahoma College for Women. Afterward, she lived at home and studied at a local college. As soon as she earned a teaching certificate, she left town. Evelyn Kelly was eager to leave her mistakes behind her.

◆

At the age of twenty-one, Evelyn headed north to Chicago, where she talked her way into a job at the *Chicago American* newspaper and found a boyfriend, Enrique Alferez, a talented young sculptor from Mexico. When he won a commission to carve twenty-four art deco reliefs for the Palmolive Building, Evelyn posed for the wood carvings. She was his muse and more.

They married in the spring of 1929 and moved to New Orleans, where Alferez was captivated by the libertine French Quarter, perhaps too much so. Before they had been married a year, he divorced Evelyn in Mexico.

At twenty-two, Evelyn Kelly went looking for better prospects in Cuba, which was booming. As many as fifty cruise ships were docking in Havana every week, their decks brimming with Americans looking for a good time. To support herself, she worked as a translator at the *Havana Post*. Then she switched to a public relations position at one of the hotels and found the excitement she wanted.

Errol Flynn, Clark Gable, Frank Sinatra, and Ava Gardner flew in for daiquiris. International stars like Edith Piaf and Maurice Chevalier entertained at the hotels. It was a glamorous time—even the mobsters running the casinos looked sophisticated in white dinner jackets.

Cuba provided "a renaissance for my soul," Evelyn said later. She began collecting art, inspired by the artists she met with Alfarez.

In 1931, she married Havana businessman Frank del Barrio. When they went to the casinos, she noticed the people who were having the most fun—and had the most money—were from Dallas, Texas.

With typical daring, Evelyn found a novel way to visit Big D: she brought a troupe of Cuban voodoo dancers to the 1936 Texas Centennial in Dallas. Their scanty costumes and throbbing *Santeria* drumbeats cast a spell on audiences. As their impresario, Evelyn generated so much news coverage for her troupe that more performances had to be added. Evelyn had found her niche: she was good at putting on a show.

Her marriage to Frank del Barrio ended about this time. Though she claimed he had died and she was a widow, Frank identified himself on travel documents as "divorced" and was very much alive.

Evelyn made her way to Manhattan, where she found another beau. Though she rarely mentioned it during her Dallas years, Evelyn married Harry Fonda, a distant cousin of actor Henry Fonda. Their engagement announcement in the *New York Times* said he was a "cotton planter" with land in Tennessee and Arkansas.

Eight months after they left for a trip around the world, Evelyn returned to New York—alone. She told reporters that she left her bridegroom in Bali because he was more interested in the local women than her. "I have the title of BBB," she said, "'Bandoned Bali Bride."

Hundreds of newspapers, from Oregon to Orlando, picked up the story. The *Nashville Tennessean* devoted an entire page to her misadventure, being careful to note in the headline, "so she says." Evelyn identified herself as "the daughter of a wealthy sugar plantation owner in Cuba," a new twist on her story.

A few weeks later, columnist Dorothy Kilgallen published an item questioning Evelyn's account: "What Evelyn del Barrio forgot to tell reporters was the fact she and her husband, Harry Fonda, split up in Europe—not Bali, which was sarong story."

Once again, Evelyn recovered by leaving town. She went west to San Diego, where she got a job with a company that shipped fruit and vegetables from Mexico to military bases. It wasn't long before she switched to a job at the May department store. With typical flair, she staged fashion shows that had live music and dancing by Arthur Murray dancers. She also became friends with a Korean American designer named Alma Shon, who created artistic gift wrapping in department stores. The two were so close that Evelyn became godmother to Shon's son, the first of twenty-three godchildren she would consider surrogate children during her lifetime.

In 1948, Evelyn got an offer to direct sales promotion at Neiman Marcus. She drove into Dallas in a secondhand station wagon with her friend Alma and her baby, as well as a young interior designer named Bobby Waddell. Evelyn sometimes said Waddell was her nephew and sometimes her godson. Whatever the relationship, they all lived together in a prefabricated barn. With their combined talents, the threesome transformed what was essentially a storage facility into an ultra-modern home with Picasso prints in the kitchen. The design was so chic that it made the *Dallas Morning News*, perhaps with a push from Evelyn.

With her distinctive looks and self-assurance, Evelyn proved a natural as the narrator for Neiman Marcus fashion shows. She had a daring sense of style, and Dallas spent lots of money on style. Fashionable customers admired Evelyn's pizzazz, but her coworkers resented her bossiness and self-promotion. She had the subtlety of a panzer tank, they complained. According to a former colleague, when she and Stanley Marcus were not getting along, he had her office door boarded up and re-wallpapered while she was out of town. When she returned, her desk was still in her office, but the door was gone.

She left Neiman Marcus after two years, saying she had an offer back in Los Angeles. A store executive told friends the real reason was that she borrowed some fashions for herself. Evelyn told friends that she fell from grace after she took some models to Canada for a style show and charged it to the store without permission.

Whatever the last straw, it wasn't a surprise when the headstrong style maker parted ways with the Store. The surprise was that instead of going back to LA, she got married again. Evelyn claimed she met landscaper Joe Lambert when he arrived at a garden party wearing a white linen suit in a chauffeur-driven car. She ditched her escort and went to dinner with him instead.

At first glance, it did not look like a promising match. Both had made mistakes with early marriages, she more than he. She was sharp-edged; he had a happy charm. However, both needed a partner for the nonstop social life in Dallas. And both had artistic leanings. As a bonus, Joe belonged to elite organizations like Idlewild. He was a gateway to status.

Joseph Oliphant Lambert came from a family in Shreveport that owned a landscaping firm. In the late 1940s, Joe and his brother Henry set up their own business in Dallas, Lambert Gardens. Joe became famous for finding a way to grow azaleas in the punishing Texas climate. To trick the southern bushes into feeling at home, he reinforced the soil with several feet of peat moss—and voila! Pink and red and white congregations of color began appearing all over town. All you needed to do was look around to see who hired Joe Lambert. The azaleas were his billboards.

Rose Youree Lloyd, an heiress from Shreveport, became Joe's patron in Dallas. She owned a Greek Revival mansion across the street from the Dallas Country Club. As first commissions go, it was a catapult onto Money Street. Rose Lloyd had so much money that she once mistook a mailing with the town of Highland Park's annual budget for a bill—and sent in a check to pay the total. When the Dallas Country Club tried to buy her home for an expansion, she countered with a proposal to buy the country club instead. Eccentric as well as rich, Rose Lloyd wore different-colored wigs to match her outfits when she traveled on cruise ships. And when Joe Lambert did the landscaping for her mansion, she was so impressed by his good taste and Southern manners that she included him in her will.

Joe cut a striking figure. He wore a black eye patch because he lost the use of one eye when he was younger. He was a handsome child, so his mother tried to remove a birthmark on his face that she felt disfigured him. Instead, the radiation treatments ruined his vision in one eye and left him scarred. Yet on him, the eye patch looked debonair, an image he reinforced by wearing a black cape to parties.

◆

When it came to panache, Joe and Evelyn had it. They were among the first to move into the chic new apartment complex known simply by its address—"3525." When it opened in 1958, the twenty-three-story tower drew national coverage, even visitors from Europe. It introduced a new kind of living to the Southwest, the luxury high-rise.

By offering a sculpted swimming pool, hair salon, nightclub, and gourmet restaurant, 3525 lured the rich and famous out of their baronial estates. Designed by celebrity architect Howard Meyer, each residence had a terrace with sweeping views of the city. On top of that, 3525 had twenty-four-hour valet service and year-round air conditioning. The wealthy practically trampled the flowers to get in.

When movie star Greer Garson moved into one of the penthouses, 3525 was declared the city's most glamourous address. The Lamberts took the adjacent penthouse. They decorated their 5,000-square-foot apartment in avant-garde style, putting paintings on the ceilings as well as the walls. They placed a drawing of Evelyn by Sir Cecil Beaton by the door where every visitor could see it. Antiques were mixed with modern art by Picasso, Alexander Calder, and Salvador Dalí. Large copper pots from Africa held plants.

Guests were either mesmerized or appalled by Evelyn's tastes in art. A kinetic sculpture had two swords that crossed each other and rotated. In the bedroom, there was a robot with eyes on springs that would light up. And on a ledge in the hallway, a bronzed flip-flop sandal was enshrined on a pedestal.

Reinventing herself again, Evelyn Lambert became a champion for the arts. Though her wealthy friends provided the money, she provided the oomph to start a modern art museum, a liberal arts college, and an organization to support local theater. She put her impresario skills to new uses, organizing charity auctions with donated items and renting tents so larger fundraisers could be held.

"You have to give her credit," her friend Rob Kendall said. "She would find a good cause and then find somebody to support it. She got a lot of rich women to get up and get involved."

That was true—Evelyn Lambert managed to do good and have a roaring good time at the same time. *Cosmopolitan* editor Helen Gurley Brown came to dinner at the Lambert penthouse. An Italian baron got married there.

"Her parties were small theatricals," Val Imm Bashour remembered. "She staged them, choosing her guests like characters in a play. She didn't waste her invitations. She made sure whoever she invited had a reason to be there."

◈

Her defenders discounted the tall tales Evelyn Lambert told about herself as "Evelyn being Evelyn." They wrote off her manipulations as benign transgressions. They enjoyed her company and stayed friends, at least on the surface.

When I asked women who insisted that Evelyn was the jewel thief if they had ever mentioned their suspicions to her, they shuddered and said, "No. Never!" It was easier to go along with the fictions, avoid conflict, and safeguard their social positions.

Still, eyebrows were raised when Evelyn and Joe Lambert began arriving at events in a white Rolls-Royce. It prompted so much ribbing that Joe

Lambert put a bumper sticker on the Rolls that said, "Your Bushes Did Not Pay for This Car."

Joe Lambert could afford the Rolls—even in the 1950s, the bill for his landscaping projects or party decorations ran into five figures and beyond. Often, he would give customers his receipts and say, "Just pay me what you think I deserve." That always bumped his profits up.

When Evelyn took on the sixteenth-century villa near Venice, Joe landscaped the twelve-acre grounds even though he was struggling with leukemia. It turned out to be his last project. After he died in 1970, Evelyn moved full-time to the villa. Her enemies noticed the jewel thief was no longer a problem in Dallas—and neither was Evelyn.

She stayed busy in Italy. When money was needed to save Venice's deteriorating palazzos, she recruited money from her pals in Dallas and auctioned off a weekend at her villa with a picnic that included caviar, champagne, and an orchestra playing in the garden. Afterward, a friend told a journalist, "They call her the female pope here because she could easily run the Vatican."

◆

So yes, Evelyn Kelly Alferez del Barrio Fonda Lambert had come a long way from Durant, Oklahoma. Along the way, she reinvented herself. And she may have feathered her nest at the expense of others. But was Evelyn Lambert a jewel thief? Was Joe complicit?

There were understandable reasons why some people suspected the Lamberts—their access to fine homes, their expensive lifestyle, Evelyn's questionable past. Joe knew the targeted homes inside and out from his years of party planning and landscaping. Had the police noticed that, too?

Yes.

When I asked Detective McCaghren about the Lamberts, he confirmed that Lambert came to his attention. "People would say, 'Lambert put in my garden,' 'Lambert was in my house.' We checked him out, but didn't find anything."

Joe seemed an unlikely candidate to me, too. He had a limp and poor vision. Not only that, he had a business reputation to consider. Lady Bird Johnson had honored him. He supervised the landscaping for the governor's mansion in Austin. It didn't seem logical that he would risk that professional standing.

Besides, everyone liked Joe. "You wouldn't think of having a party and not inviting Joe," one socialite said. When he died, his ashes were flown back to Shreveport in a colorful Braniff jet full of friends—the perfect parting touch. The *Morning News* ran an editorial saluting his efforts to beautify the city.

So, Joe, no. Not the King of Diamonds. People liked Joe too much to believe he would do anything to harm them.

But did police investigate the wrong Lambert?

One woman was so convinced that Evelyn was the culprit that her words tumbled out in a rockslide of emotion. "There was *always* something very *suspicious* about her," she said. "I always thought she was stealing things, always. But I didn't want to say."

Others countered that Evelyn looked suspicious but wasn't. "Evelyn knew more ways to skin a cat to make money than anyone," said Sharon Simons. "But she would be last on my list of suspects."

To sort out the possibilities, I tried the test on TV cop shows: Did Evelyn Lambert have the means, the motive, the opportunity?

The means—Evelyn was middle-aged and had become caftan-sized, but some argue that one of the young proteges drawn to her style could have carried out the break-ins for her. "I would *not* put it past her," an arts executive told me. "She could con someone into doing what she wanted with such ease."

The motive—Those who knew her well agreed that she always seemed in need of money.

The opportunity—A number of people pointed out that Evelyn was in many of the victims' homes not long before the break-ins.

I still wasn't convinced, partly because the Lamberts had been burgled themselves in 1958, by someone who took $4,000 in jewels, enough to be included on the police spreadsheet.

Yet a number of people remain convinced Evelyn Lambert was involved in the thefts. They couldn't shake the thought, even after sixty years.

32

The Salon Set

After each burglary, the police checked to see if the culprit could have been someone who had done work in the homes. They searched out repairmen, caterers, bartenders, pool cleaners. No luck.

Next, the police narrowed their focus to anyone who might have known when the victims would be wearing their best jewelry—such as the elite hairdressers who prepped society women for special events.

This made sense. The hairdressers knew more about the women in their hands than their husbands did. The best hairstylists were confidants, escorts, decorators, and fashion advisers for wealthy women. While their husbands were out making money, Dallas women were having their hair done.

Hair stylists became more essential in the 1960s as hair fashions changed dramatically. Women across the country wanted the chic flip that "Mr. Kenneth" designed for Jackie Kennedy. *Vogue* models favored edgy Sassoon cuts. College girls adopted the long, straight hair that folk singers like Joan Baez and Joni Mitchell wore. Motown girl groups like the Supremes popularized the beehive and side-sweep. And after Annette Funicello and Sandra Dee wore their hair in a bouffant "Bubble" in beach movies, millions of teenagers did, too.

Dallas women became famous for their "big hair" look. They weren't the only ones in the country to backcomb their hair into a helmet-like bouffant, but they took the style to new heights. To answer critics, they shot back, "The higher the hair, the closer to God."

◈

When "frosting" came along—streaking hair with a lighter color—Dallas women discovered they could be forever blonde. Again, the trend didn't start in Dallas, but it reached its apotheosis there.

French hairstylist Antoine de Paris is often credited with creating the frosting fad. He preferred to be called Mr. Antoine. Some said he was the "greatest hairdresser of the twentieth century," so Neiman Marcus named its salon after him. The maestro periodically flew in from Paris to conduct coiffure workshops—always insisting that the salon be filled with white calla lilies for his arrival.

Mr. Antoine was grandly eccentric. Like Liberace and Lady Gaga, he marketed his flamboyance. He claimed to sleep in a glass coffin and played a wall-sized cathedral organ at home while wearing a white silk robe. Many evenings, he strolled Paris boulevards with a dog dyed mauve.

In truth, Mr. Antoine's name was Antek Cierplikowski. And he was Polish, not French. He shot to fame in the early 1900s when he created a short haircut for an actress who needed to look younger for a role. That bobbed hairdo evolved into the "shingle" cut of the Roaring Twenties. The bold look drew gasps. For centuries, women had tied back or bound up their hair. Long, lustrous hair was considered the ultimate in femininity, a woman's pride—and strictly for a husband's enjoyment when his wife let her hair tumble down in the privacy of her bedroom. The bobbed haircut challenged all that and became the rage among the young and rebellious.

Just as Chanel transformed clothing for women, Antoine of Paris revolutionized hair care by pioneering the first hair spray, modern hairdryers, and shampooing hair in the salon. When he opened salons at Saks Fifth Avenue and Neiman Marcus, they were instant triumphs.

Mr. Antoine coached the Dallas hairdressers to use psychology with clients. They should size up their customers, especially their insecurities about their appearance. Pretty women always worried that their looks were fading, he explained, and plain women always wanted to look prettier. As he put it, "Every woman is an abler and better person when she knows she looks well."

◆

The Dallas stylists learned his lessons well. Grateful women included them on trips and showered them with gifts. One woman gave her favorite hairdresser a new Corvette. Another offered to pay her stylist $10,000 not to pursue a hot romance in New York. He left anyway and came back chastened when the flame cooled.

The hairstylists at the Antoine Salon in Dallas were held in such high regard in the 1960s that women flew in from New York, Europe, Mexico, and South America to get their hair styled while they shopped at Neiman Marcus.

The best stylists made themselves indispensable. They offered advice on Broadway shows, wines, restaurants. They knew which colors were most flattering for each customer and where to find the best antiques. But mainly, they provided a listening ear, just as Mr. Antoine suggested.

Keeping a client's confidence required discretion. Stylists knew when their clients were going out and what they were wearing. Some went to customers' homes to give them a comb out and a spritz of hairspray before a big event. That meant the elite hairdressers were intimately familiar with the dressing rooms of burglary victims.

As calls increased that a hairdresser might be the thief, Fannin sent detectives to several salons. "We got an earful of gossip," McCaghren remembered. "They told us who was sleeping with who, who had a drinking problem. You would be amazed." Information even surfaced about hairdressers who sold drugs on the side. But substantial leads about the burglaries? Yes and no.

◇

One name came up often: Jack Weisenhunt, known to his clients as "Mr. Jack." Weisenhunt came to prominence in the 1950s as the lead stylist in the Antoine Salon at Neiman Marcus. Few customers knew his last name. You only had to say Mr. Jack, and women knew who you meant.

When Mr. Jack toured Europe in 1957 to survey the latest coiffures, it made the news. When Maria Callas performed in Dallas in 1958, Mr. Jack styled her hair for each of her stage roles.

"Jack was a *celebrity*," remembered Fred Stucke, who worked with Weisenhunt at the Neiman Marcus salon. "It was a different era. We wore suits at work every day. When a big customer flew in from out of town, a parade of salespeople would troop by the hair dryers with clothes and hats and purses for them to choose from while they were getting their hair done."

After nineteen years, Jack Weisenhunt left the Antoine Salon to start his own salon. He brought Myrtle B. Ross, a popular hair colorist, with him as a partner. Everyone called her "Brewster," her middle name. *Vogue* magazine spotlighted Brewster's genius for transforming dull gray hair into more flattering colors. Rose Kennedy and the Duchess of Windsor came for the Brewster treatment. One customer liked to have her hair dyed the color of her latest Cadillac convertible, so Brewster obliged with shades of pink, blue, and violet. She was a big part of Mr. Jack's success story and vice versa. Some say Brewster and Mr. Jack invented the color "champagne toast" for blondes. "Blondes really do have more fun," she would say.

When Mr. Jack moved, his loyal clients moved with him. Jack's salon was a second home. Some clients came several times a week. One came every day. And one confessed she slept at night with her head angled off the bed so she wouldn't ruin her hairdo.

"Back then, women had their hair done more often. Now they do their own upkeep," Weisenhunt told me. "Those days, they *depended* on you. A woman told me, 'I could get a divorce easily, but I could *never* change hairdressers.'"

The secret of his success, Weisenhunt thought, was that he took a personal interest in his clients. "If they wanted to find something, a house or whatever, you helped them with it. What they were interested in became important to you as well."

On the eve of social galas, Mr. Jack's salon looked like a pre-party. His "A-list" clients included Jane Murchison, Evelyn Lambert, Betty Blake, and Nancy Ann Smith. Renowned party hostess Nancy Hamon prepped for her costume parties at Mr. Jack's salon and so did her husband. He wore a leopard-print smock while his hair and eyebrows were dyed "Hearty Russet," the shade favored by Ronald Reagan.

Actress Greer Garson made the salon scene, and so did tap-dancing actress Ann Miller, who was married at the time to Dallas oilman Bill Moss. Miller later wrote in her autobiography that she left the marriage because she could not keep up with the parties that lasted two or three days.

"The glamour was mesmerizing," remembered hairstylist Fred Stucke. "I was so young at the time, in my twenties, just a kid from Ohio, and I was so impressed with these people. I remember someone gave me tickets to the opening of the opera. Nancy Hamon arrived in a limousine with a chauffeur. She had on an elegant black dress and a mink coat to the floor. I was awestruck."

As the burglaries went on, people noticed that a lot of the victims went to Mr. Jack's salon—Margaret Hunt Hill, Betty Schultz, Dorothy Ling, Barbara Varel, debutante Margaret Otis, and more. They wondered, could Mr. Jack be the King?

There was buzz about other hairdressers, but Jack Weisenhunt aroused more suspicion because he made and sold jewelry. He had taken a course at the YMCA to learn how to make jewelry and exhibited his work with the local craft guild. Pretty soon he was selling his creations to his clients. As one client remembered, "Jack always had some jewelry in his pocket."

Weisenhunt also stood out because he sometimes served as an escort for clients who had been widowed or divorced. Women who had suffered through social events with sodden or sulking spouses were grateful for his courteous manner.

A New York caterer who was flown in for a party weekend in oil-rich Longview told me he never forgot his introduction to Mr. Jack. The East Texas hostess had alerted him that one of the guests was a famous jewel thief. "People call him the King of Diamonds," she said, "but I like him."

The caterer was intrigued. He was even more intrigued when Mr. Jack drove up in a Rolls-Royce, the ultimate status signifier.

◊

Jack Weisenhunt had arrived. His success was especially remarkable for someone who came from a small cotton town with a population of 1,300.

His origin story showed what shaped him—his remarkable mother. Mollie Weisenhunt left an unhappy marriage in Tucson at a time when divorce was not common or easy for women. On her own, she faced a new quandary: How could she earn a living?

"She became a hairdresser," her son Jack remembered. "It was the only thing a single woman could do besides take care of children. She had two little kids of her own to raise, so she went to beauty school. When she heard the town of Hico didn't have a hairdresser, that's where we went."

Hico (high-coe) was only a two-hour drive from Dallas, but worlds apart. Though once a booming cotton hub, by the time the Weisenhunts arrived, the town only had one filling station, a Piggly Wiggly grocery store, a movie theater, and women who wanted their hair to look nice.

Jack grew up watching his mother work. In those days, hairdressing largely consisted of cutting hair, hiding gray with henna, or giving a wave to straight hair with heated curling irons.

Young Jack admired his mother's grace with customers and her determination to provide for her family. He remembered that after working all day, his mother cooked dinner for her children and washed and ironed their clothes. "She was a strong woman," he said. Even in his nineties, he remembered her birthday: January 2.

Mollie Weisenhunt taught her children to be polite to everyone. During the Depression, "showing class" meant showing character. Everyone in Hico was struggling to get by, so there was less stigma to being poor than in big cities.

When Jack Weisenhunt finished high school, college was an impossible dream. He went to a cosmetology school in Fort Worth instead. During the war, fewer men were available to work, which helped Weisenhunt land the job of his dreams: the Antoine Salon at Neiman Marcus.

He gained polish and contacts on the job, so by the time the jewel thefts started, Mr. Jack was a familiar sight at social events.

Then people started whispering that he was the jewel thief.

◆

I tracked Mr. Jack down in 2016 by finding a family member's obituary. I called the next of kin, one after another, until I reached a relative who told me Weisenhunt had retired in Laguna Beach, California.

I felt awkward calling him about the thefts after so many years, but Mr. Jack was gracious when he answered the phone.

"I guess you know your name came up a lot," I ventured.

After a pause, he responded with the kind of mild-mannered diplomacy that won him faithful clients. "Oh yes, I know, things were said," he said.

Did the police question him?

"Never did," he said. "We heard about all the people they were looking at. One woman supposedly told police, 'You haven't picked up Jack! He knows all of us! He has been in our house!'"

Some clients teased him with a fake pout when they came into the salon, saying, "Jack! I feel left out—you haven't come to my house! Aren't my jewels good enough?"

Rumors continued to circulate, not only about Weisenhunt but also his friend Evelyn Lambert.

"Some people said it was me, or it was Evelyn, or it was us together," he remembered. "We would laugh about it. She would say, 'Can you imagine me swinging on a balcony? I would break my back!'"

He and Evelyn were such close friends that she gave him a bust of herself. Constantly trying to augment her finances, she had commissioned sculptures of her distinctive profile. "She wanted to sell them," he remembered, "but she ended up giving them away." He was honored to have one. When his house in California caught fire, the bust of Evelyn was one of the few things he rushed to save.

Had it ever crossed his mind, I asked, that Evelyn could have hired someone to pull off the jewel thefts for her? Weisenhunt bristled: "She would *never* stoop to that!"

As for the accusations about him, his main concern was the impact on his family if they heard the talk. I could hear the emotion in his voice as he remembered, "What would my family think? What would they think?"

I asked him how he responded when customers suggested his salon employees might be helping the thief by eavesdropping on conversations.

"We didn't do that! These were women we knew as *friends*," he insisted. Once again, the emotion was palpable.

So, if it wasn't him or Evelyn or one of his stylists, who could it have been?

Weisenhunt hesitated. Choosing his words carefully, he said, "Most people thought it was someone who had been married for a short time to someone." I assumed he was referring to Jim Kirksmith's brief marriage to Nancy Ann Smith, but he shied away from naming names.

"It was definitely the talk of the town," he added. "Every week, it changed who it was. At Brook Hollow parties, everyone would look around and choose who they thought it was."

There were understandable reasons for suspecting Mr. Jack: His clients included a lot of the burglary victims. He made jewelry. Parts of the police profile applied to him because he was in his thirties and just under six feet tall. He was close to his mother. And he admired beautiful things.

But the suspicions didn't add up to a case—the glove did not fit. It was hard to imagine the low-key hairdresser climbing trees and crawling across rooftops. His main exercise was brushing hair. Theoretically, an agile colleague could have carried out the break-ins for him, but it didn't seem likely that he would risk his salon, his society friends, and his family's trust. Those who knew him said Jack Weisenhunt was a careful man.

Could he have been in debt? According to most accounts, he was a capable businessman. "He worked hard," a colleague said. "He stayed late for his clients."

When a client told Weisenhunt that US Attorney Barefoot Sanders was pursuing an independent investigation into the thefts, he decided to take action to protect his reputation. He drove to Sanders's office to assure him he had nothing to do with the burglaries. "It's not me," he promised Sanders. "I am not a thief!"

Sanders believed him.

❖

Yet the rumors returned in 1969 when a burglar broke into Dean and Jo Guerin's home. Dazzling Jo Guerin was one of Mr. Jack's star clients. He posted her photo in his salon. She had teal-blue eyes and a platinum mane that stood out in a crowded room.

The thief had broken into the house at 4747 Miron before. Joanne Stroud, Josephine Graf's daughter, lived there when her jewels were taken in 1959. Ten years later, the Guerins were living in the house with their two young sons.

The Guerins were a high-profile couple. Dean Guerin founded the investment firm of Eppler, Guerin, and Turner, one of the leading merger and acquisition firms in the Southwest. He liked to drive Ferraris and could afford to sail in the Caribbean on his fifty-seven-foot yacht *Arbitrage*. He was athletic—a scuba diver and skier—and a bon vivant, part of a men's gourmet cooking class taught by legendary Helen Corbitt of Neiman Marcus. Cooking was becoming a new competitive sport for men.

As for Mrs. Guerin, if you wanted an illustration of Blonde Glamour, she fit well. A beauty queen in college, Jo Guerin still turned heads. She regularly made the best-dressed lists and played the romantic lead in community theater productions.

That night in 1969, her mother was babysitting the Guerin sons while the couple went to a New Year's Eve party. The boys went to bed early and their grandmother soon followed. As the clock ticked toward midnight, the thief walked up from the nearby creek, just as he had years before. Then he pried open the sliding glass door to the master bedroom.

Jo's mother thought she heard a noise from that direction but didn't investigate because she didn't hear it again. Records show it was freezing cold outside—as low as 25 degrees Fahrenheit. The thief may have come in to keep warm and hid until the Guerins returned and went to bed. After the Guerins turned off the lights, and their breathing was regular, he made his move.

The thief located the small safe in their bedroom. Mrs. Guerin had placed the jewels she wore to the party in the safe before she went to bed, but she didn't lock it, thinking it wasn't necessary while they were in the house. The thief must have figured she wouldn't. Without a sound, he scooped up the jewels—about $12,500 worth, equal to $100,000 in 2023. Then he retreated to the creek, leaving his distinctive footprints outside.

The next day, the Guerins were stunned to discover her jewels were gone. Their family dog, a Labrador retriever, had slept throughout the intrusion.

"It affected my parents profoundly," their son Steve remembered years later. "They were creeped out that someone was in the room with them. My dad bought an alarm system right away and was very vigilant about the protocol of turning it on. And he got a handgun."

Though friends told Jo Guerin they thought Mr. Jack was the thief, she refused to believe it. She continued to go to his salon.

As it was, Mr. Jack endured the rumors for years before deciding it was best to retire somewhere else, with fresh ocean air. He moved to California and did not return.

The Dallas Police let him be.

By this time, they were pretty sure someone else was the celebrated burglar.

33

The Kirksmiths

When I started asking questions about the case back in 2015, social insiders all blurted out the same name immediately: the Kirksmiths.

"Everybody thought it was the Kirksmiths," they said.

Paul McCaghren agreed. "We suspected the Kirksmiths, but we never could make a case on them," McCaghren said.

When Jasper, Jim, and Jack Kirksmith arrived in Dallas in the late 1940s, they were looking for ready money and beautiful women, so they hit the debutante circuit. Before long, people noticed that they had no apparent jobs. Word got around that the brothers were involved with Mafia types in Las Vegas. They were up to no good, people said.

When the jewel thefts became a regular occurrence, the social crowd buzzed like a hive on high alert for predators: "It's the Kirksmiths!"

Were they right?

◆

The brothers had a pedigree that destined them for the Dallas drama—part ranch royalty, part Hollywood. They considered themselves above most people.

On their mother's side, they were descendants of a historic Texas family, the Nails. The Nails had settled in the untamed territory to the west of Fort Worth in the 1830s. Family lore said John Nail "killed a man in Tennessee" and fled to Texas to avoid the law. Destiny caught up with him: Nail was killed while leading a posse to catch an outlaw named Big Horn Smith. His grandson, James Henry Nail, enlarged the family's holdings by joining large landholders like Dan Waggoner and Burk Burnett in leasing tracts of land from the Comanches, who were losing ground to the influx of settlers. It was on these Native American lands that Teddy Roosevelt joined the cattle kings on hunting expeditions in the 1890s.

Over time, the Nail family ranchlands grew to 65,000 acres. Their holdings were largely concentrated around the town of Albany, not far from Camp Cooper, where Robert E. Lee bunked before the Civil War.

James Henry Nail increased the family's fortunes considerably by expanding into banking. Before long, rich oil deposits were discovered on Nail land. The Nails became prairie aristocrats. They vacationed in Europe. Some daughters went East to finishing school; some sons went to Princeton.

By the fourth generation, Nail heirs were preoccupied with quarrels over inheritances. One even wrote a book about the infighting. He called it *Per Stirpes*, a legal term meaning each branch of the family should receive an equal share of an estate. Family members joked: Where there was a will, everyone wanted in it.

The Pyle branch of the Nail family had more musical talent than ranching skill. Wynne Pyle became an internationally acclaimed concert pianist. For a woman who was born in 1881 in Ladonia, Texas, population 350, it was a singular achievement. The nearest music school—Kidd-Keye College in Sherman—was a full day's travel by horseback or buggy. Wynne Pyle's next stop was Berlin.

With her dark blonde curls and aquamarine eyes, Wynne Pyle created a sensation in the orchestral world. The Archduke Eugene of Austria was so smitten, he reserved the entire first row when she performed in Vienna. Rich men swooned when they heard her play Rachmaninoff, and sent jewels backstage. When she died, her bag of jewels fell into the hands of her three wayward nephews—and disappeared.

Though Wynne Pyle had the spotlight, her older sister Lou Netta set forces in motion behind the scenes. Netta was a striking brunette. She had studied voice but gave up her career to marry Karl Kirksmith, a renowned cellist. He, too, had grown up in a talented family. Both of his parents were music teachers. His unusual surname was a combination of their last names, which his parents thought would look more distinctive on marquees. By the age of fourteen, Karl Kirksmith was touring as the "Boy Wonder of the Cello." He went on to play with symphony orchestras in New York, Chicago, Cincinnati, and Philadelphia. Because female musicians weren't accepted in major orchestras, his six sisters played in vaudeville and Chautauqua circuits as "the Dainty Half-Dozen." Karl became an esteemed teacher at the Cincinnati Conservatory of Music. Critics hailed him as one of the best cellists of his day, second only to Pablo Casals.

Karl struck an impressive figure on stage, with blue eyes and dark blond hair. When she saw him perform, Netta Pyle was captivated. After they married in New York, they had three sons. Netta gave them names from her Nail family tree: Jasper Karl Kirksmith, Jim Buck Kirksmith, and Jack Nail Kirksmith.

While Karl taught in Cincinnati, the boys were sent to military school. As for Netta, she was not the type to stay home and iron shirts while Karl performed; she preferred the casinos across the river in Newport, Kentucky. Newport was the first city in the country to be known as "Sin City" because of its wide-open gambling, prostitution, and racketeering. The mob-run "carpet joints" that grew out of Prohibition offered floor shows, fine dining, and gambling. Netta became a regular at the gaming tables.

After Karl had a contractual dispute with the Cincinnati symphony in 1937, the family made a fateful move to Los Angeles, the land of beautiful people and bad behavior. Karl found a new position with the Hollywood Bowl orchestra.

His three sons welcomed the change of scene. They had film-star good looks and muscular physiques honed at military school. Women found them highly attractive.

Jasper, the oldest, joined the Army during World War II and got married while stationed in Texas. His bride filed for an annulment after thirteen days, an early sign Jasper was a bad risk in the romance department.

Jim, the middle brother, served as a B-24 pilot in the Air Force, flying a plane named *Tuff Titty* on bombing missions over Europe.

The youngest brother, Jack, got to skip the war. He claimed a disability because of a foot injury. He also had a music career to pursue. Jack was a gifted French horn player and had performed with the Washington Philharmonic. When the family moved to California, he played in the Los Angeles Philharmonic and studio orchestras that produced soundtracks for movies. If you listen closely during the film *From Here to Eternity*, you can hear the distinctive sound of Jack Kirksmith's French horn.

Before long, however, headstrong Jack Kirksmith got fed up with union restrictions on when and where he could play. He put away his French horn for the rest of his life and focused on something that brought in much more money: gambling.

◆

The Kirksmiths got more involved with gambling after they met Marion Hicks, a former Packard dealer from Oklahoma. Hicks did well as a real estate developer in LA, but did even better running gambling ships. Hicks and a syndicate of gamblers owned a floating casino called the SS *Caliente*. Customers took water taxis to the ship, which added to the air of adventure. The rich and the reckless climbed on board, along with professional gamblers like Nick "the Greek" Dandelos.

At the time, gambling ships like the *Caliente* anchored three miles off the coast of Long Beach and Santa Monica because gambling was legal in international waters.

One of the most famous ships, the SS *Rex*, could hold two thousand gamblers. It had French chefs, a full orchestra, and a squad of gunmen.

When California Attorney General Earl Warren cracked down on the floating casinos, Marion Hicks shifted his sights to Nevada, where wagering was legal. Hicks bought a stake in a Reno casino, then put together plans for a grander venture in Las Vegas: the El Cortez Hotel Casino. His casino partners included architect John C. Grayson, who had owned slot machines in Arizona and was arrested for gambling on one of the gambling boats. One of the other investors turned out to be gangster Moe Sedway, who fronted in deals for mob boss Meyer Lansky. Sedway supervised the racing wire, which was controlled by Lansky and his buddy Bugsy Siegel.

And oh yes, there was another partner:

Netta Kirksmith.

Mrs. Kirksmith owned two hundred shares of the El Cortez and served as vice president. The Kirksmiths were in the casino business—with people who carried their money in suitcases.

◆

When the El Cortez opened in 1941, it was considered the finest hotel-casino in downtown Las Vegas, although it only had fifty-one rooms. The row of brick arches across the front gave the El Cortez a hacienda look. Inside, the hotel featured a floor show and gambling. It became known as a place where serious gamblers came to play.

Local historians say the El Cortez also served as a beachhead for organized crime, a model for "skimming" money from daily receipts. Workers who trained there went on to bigger venues like the Flamingo, the Riviera, and the Desert Inn.

In 1945, Bugsy Siegel bought the El Cortez for $600,000. He had a squad of "business associates" behind him—mobsters Meyer Lansky, Gus Greenbaum, Dave Berman, and "Ice Pick Willie" Alderman. They reportedly paid cash.

◆

I had heard the Kirksmiths had Vegas connections, but I wanted corroboration, so I flew to Las Vegas. As the plane landed, the flight attendant announced, "Welcome to Lost Wages!" Signs in the airport showed happy visitors quaffing drinks over heaping plates of food, with the caption, "Self-control is overrated."

It was 108 degrees outside, so I took a cab straight to the El Cortez instead of walking around. The casino still had its hacienda façade, but a modern tower had been added, as well as a business center and a twenty-four-hour gym. Still, when compared to the 6,852 rooms in the MGM Grand, the 364-room El Cortez is dwarfed. Nostalgia is its main drawing card. The current owners boast the hotel is on the national historic register and play up its colorful history with vintage black-and-white photos. They've named the main restaurant "Siegel's 1941" and put a "Meyer Lansky Burger" on the menu. They even keep a shiny black '41 Lincoln coupe parked in the lobby.

Still, gambling fills nearly every inch of the place. Video poker games are crowded into the lobby and side rooms. Spellbound players hunch over the flashing, clanging machines, oblivious to everything around them. Earplugs were available in vending machines to shut out the noise, but when I put in a five-dollar bill, no plugs emerged. I considered this an omen and did not try the games. Instead, I walked around and took notes. After I had circled several times, I noticed the desk clerks were watching me. Time to go, I thought, and walked out into welcome sunlight.

I cabbed over to a lunch meeting at the Four Seasons, where the décor was in earth tones and the only noise came from splashing fountains. I was looking forward to meeting Bob Stoldal, an award-winning TV news director in the Lou Grant mold, professionally tough in a good way. Stoldal also was a history buff and head of the Las Vegas historic preservation commission. We had corresponded for more than a year but had not met. With his thatch of white hair, he was easy to spot.

Stoldal had offered to search for documents that might confirm the Kirksmiths' involvement with the El Cortez—and he delivered. He walked me through a stack of papers and pointed out where Netta Kirksmith signed the original El Cortez documents. "It clearly was an interesting sidelight for them—and maybe more," he said.

So the rumors in Dallas were true: The Kirksmiths had operated a casino in Vegas. With proof in hand, I left "Lost Wages" as fast as I could.

◆

Not long after the El Cortez sale, Karl and Netta Kirksmith divorced. He went to live with a sister in Seattle; she returned to Texas. The brothers opened a nightclub in Los Angeles. Jack handled the musical talent while Jim tended bar and Jasper tended the ladies. They called the club Billingsley's Bocage Room because it shared space with a restaurant owned by Sherman Billingsley, founder of the Stork Club in New York. As best I could tell, the name "Bocage" was homage to a blues performer.

The club had a prime location—5927 Sunset Boulevard, just a few blocks from the famous corner of Hollywood and Vine. Errol Flynn sat at the bar. Frank Sinatra and Ava Gardner came to openings. The Maguire Sisters got their start at Bocage. Nat King Cole and Mel Torme sang there, and so did Sarah Vaughn.

Jack and Jasper made the news when they were picked up in a gambling raid and charged with vagrancy. They laughed it off—*vagrants?*

They took it more seriously when their nightclub sank into financial trouble.

Singer Anita O'Day wrote in her autobiography that she opened a limited engagement at Bocage in 1947. She was getting a percentage of the receipts for her booking and hoped to make "some real bread." When a standing-room-only crowd greeted her opening night, she was thrilled. But the next night, a "labor dispute" caused the staff to strike.

The brothers struggled to keep the club running. A Nail family history shows that when their grandmother Mollie Pyle died in 1948, Jasper and Jim did not attend the funeral. Netta had to apologize that her sons had pressing matters in Los Angeles.

They certainly did. As Anita O'Day lamented, "The joint folded."

Out of luck and money, the brothers relocated to Dallas, where their mother had purchased a home in upscale Highland Park. Their names soon began popping up in society pages as escorts at debutante parties.

And that's when the trouble began.

◆

Though their first names all began with a *J* and they were all over six feet tall, the Kirksmith brothers had distinctive differences.

Jasper, the oldest, was a charmer and con artist. People checked their wallets after shaking hands with Jasper. He had blue eyes and wavy hair that was dark blonde when he was younger, like his father. His powerful build helped him become a swimming champion in high school.

When he moved to Dallas, "Jap" Kirksmith operated on the margins of high society. He developed a reputation as a gigolo, a man hired to escort society women. Behind their backs, he mocked them as "debu-trash." When he wasn't bumming expense money from them, he procured women for millionaires like John Gillin. Word got around that Jap Kirksmith was a reprobate, a lounge lizard who preyed on women. It wasn't hard to imagine him stealing jewels.

Jim was the easygoing middle brother, the one described as nice. He had dark hair and warm brown eyes, like his mother. At military school, he excelled more at sports than academics, playing football, baseball, and basketball, and competing in boxing and water polo. While he may not have been the smartest of the brothers, Jim was smart enough to pilot a plane during the war and get back alive.

Like Jasper, Jim developed a reputation in Dallas as a playboy/gigolo, since he had no apparent job. A former deb who went out with him remembered, "He was polite and well-mannered—because I guess that is what you do if you're a gigolo." Still, she thought he was so nice that she kissed him goodnight.

Jim was an appealing escort—he knew how much cuff a tuxedo should show, danced like a dream, and could mix a good drink. Although he had no radio experience, broadcaster Gordon McLendon was impressed by the handsome newcomer and gave Jim a job at his new Liberty Broadcasting System. Unfortunately, the job evaporated when the radio network collapsed in 1952. To start over, Jim Kirksmith set up an office and tried to get in the oil business, like everyone else.

Jack, the youngest brother, was rakishly handsome, too, but had reddish-blonde hair and blue eyes. He was considered the most intellectual of the three and taught himself German by listening to operas. Even while a high school student, he played French horn with national orchestras. He also lettered in tennis, played squash, and crewed. The school yearbook noted he was active in the Dramatics Club, with "famed dramatic ability as a lover."

After their nightclub went bust, Jack turned to gambling in Dallas. He gambled at Top O' Hill before it closed and at the Cipango Club. Other evenings, he played bridge on the twenty-sixth floor of the Adolphus Hotel and poker at the Petroleum Club.

Gambling gave Jack access to oilmen like H. L. Hunt, who became a gin rummy partner and oil leasing coach. In one of his oil ventures in Kentucky, the final negotiation for a lease depended on a shooting match—and Jack Kirksmith won.

He was a smooth operator, people said. His easy charm masked a foxlike cunning. "Jack was a *con man*," said a man who saw Kirksmith often at gambling parties. He remembered that Jack excelled at poker dice, a speedy form of poker, along with drinking. "He could finish a bottle of Seagram's V.O. in one sitting and it wouldn't faze him." The Kirksmiths reminded him of the Maverick brothers on TV, the man said, "handsome gamblers on the make."

◆

To everyone's surprise, it was Jim—the polite and placid middle brother—who hit the jackpot when he married Sid Richardson's niece, Nancy Ann Smith. After their fairy-tale wedding in 1957, the newlyweds seemed to have a swell life together. They moved into a home in Preston Hollow and adopted two children as soon as they could. Jim was named a member of the elite Terpsichorean Club.

But the gossip about the jewel thefts wouldn't go away. The rumors followed the newlyweds, surrounded them, marked them. Convinced that the Kirksmiths were involved, people theorized that Jim used Nancy Ann's social access to scout targets, Jasper carried out the thefts, and Jack fenced the jewels with his gambling connections.

Jim struggled to surmount the rumors and prove himself worthy of the affluent circles he married into. He told former classmates he was doing well in the oil business.

In reality, Jim Kirksmith couldn't find his footing in business. He gambled to get money, but usually lost. A gin rummy player remembered the time Jim Kirksmith lost so many hands, he ran out of money: "Jim asked them to hold the phone, so to speak, and ran out to get some more money. When he ran out of that, they said he could stay in the game if he took off one piece of clothing every time he lost. He ended up playing without his clothes."

As his resources decreased, his drinking increased. Oilman Bill Moss remembered that when he arrived for a dinner at the Kirksmiths' home one night, Jim was passed out in the bedroom. His marriage to Nancy Ann was in trouble. And the burglary rumors were in overdrive.

The Dallas police started tailing Jim Kirksmith. When he flew to a business meeting in San Antonio, police had his suitcase pulled from the luggage cart. The detectives broke the lock and checked the contents. Nothing was inside but a change of clothes.

When the rumors wouldn't subside, Jim volunteered for a lie detector test. He said he passed; police said the results were inconclusive. The whispers went on. Jim Kirksmith returned home one day to find his belongings on the front steps. The marriage had only lasted three years.

Jim moved into his mother's house on Edmondson in Highland Park. He tried to get back on his feet, but many evenings, he drank with his mother at home. Netta's doctor had advised her to only have one drink a night, but he didn't say what size, so she often poured a large tumbler full of vodka for herself—and one for Jim.

⬥

Suspicions that Jim might be involved with the burglaries were reignited when someone broke into the house belonging to his ex-wife's parents, Howell and Fayrene Smith. On November 13, 1961, a burglar climbed a tree into the Smiths' house on Park Lane and took nearly $35,000 in jewels from what used to be Nancy Ann's bedroom.

Did Jim or his brothers target Nancy Ann's family in revenge for the divorce? Some thought so.

The police spreadsheet showed that the burglary fit eight of the King's characteristics. The thief climbed up to a second-story balcony and pried open a window. He took some jewels and left some. It looked like the King of Diamonds, the police said.

The next month, on December 20, Jim Kirksmith was found dead on the floor of his bedroom in Netta's house.

His mother said she found Jim lying next to his bed. He was in his pajamas with his hair neatly combed. He appeared to have fallen out of bed, with one leg tilted up as if caught in the bedding when he fell.

The report from the medical examiner showed Jim Kirksmith had a blood alcohol concentration of .524. That was nearly seven times the .08 level considered too drunk to drive in Texas. According to medical research, a BAC of more than .30 could have put him into a coma. A count of .45 is usually fatal. Jim exceeded that.

Jim Kirksmith died at the age of forty-three. The medical examiner listed acute alcoholism as the official cause. Jack Kirksmith told others his brother's death was an accident. He theorized his brother had taken a Miltown tranquilizer and had a "toddy"—a potentially lethal combination.

If so, did Jim Kirksmith take a sedative accidentally—or deliberately?

When I asked Paul McCaghren about the death, all he would say was, "It was suspicious."

I asked a Kirksmith relative if someone could have tampered with Jim's drink. After some thought, she said it was possible. "Jim had a separate entrance to his bedroom," she said. "Someone could have used the back entrance to get into the house without Netta knowing."

I followed up, "Who could have wanted to kill Jim? Did he have gambling debts? Did he have enemies?"

"Hmm," she said, nodding her head slightly, "hmm." She would say no more.

Some in the social set believed Jim had committed suicide. They said the police were coming the next day to question him about the Howell Smith break-in.

Whether a suicide, an accident, or something else, Jim Kirksmith was a casualty of the jewel thefts. "He was a very tragic figure," a woman who had dated him told me. "He couldn't find the success that he needed. But he had a real kindness about him. He was just in the wrong family."

The burglaries continued after Jim Kirksmith's death, so the theory no longer held up that he was instrumental in the thefts. The focus shifted to his older brother, Jasper.

Life magazine offered Jasper $10,000 to write an article titled, "I Was the King of Diamonds." This was a tempting sum, the equivalent of more than $100,000 in 2023.

But Jasper turned down the offer.

Did that mean he was not the thief?

Or too smart to confess it in print?

McCaghren somehow got Jasper's datebook and tracked down his girlfriends for questioning. With help from the intelligence bureau, McCaghren also hid a video camera in a vent in Jasper's apartment. ("Did you have a warrant?" I asked McCaghren. Well, no, he said, we probably should have gotten one.)

What did the video surveillance show?

That Jap Kirksmith had a very robust sex life. And he was the kind of guy who pushed a girlfriend out of bed after sex and ordered, "Go earn some money."

Detectives began crowding up every morning to watch the steamy videotapes, so McCaghren put a halt to the taping. "Our job isn't watching Jasper in bed with women," he told them. "Go find some evidence."

Though his team investigated Jasper for months, McCaghren still couldn't pin anything on him. But their paths crossed again. "After I retired from the police in the 1970s, I set up my own security service," he told me. "I had an office out on Forest Lane with a big picture window. One day, I looked up and saw Jasper walking by. He saw me looking at him, so he came in. He thanked me for telling people that we were investigating him. 'You guys did me a big favor. Now all the women want to sleep with me—everybody wants to say they slept with the King of Diamonds!'"

McCaghren enjoyed a hearty laugh at the memory—until I pointed out that Jasper, who was six foot three and broad-shouldered, seemed too big to climb trees and slip through bathroom windows like the King did.

Annoyed, McCaghren gave one of his shrugs. "He was a likeable guy," he said. "You would probably like him if you knew him."

◆

I tried for months to reach the wives of the Kirksmith brothers. I dropped off a polite interview request at Nancy Ann Smith's apartment building. No response. So I asked her friends to relay my request. They said she shook her head no, no, no. The Jim Kirksmith chapter in her life was not a happy one, and Nancy Ann Smith had no desire to revisit the memories.

Next, I tried to reach Jasper's widow. I left dozens of phone messages. She didn't call back. So I left notes in her mailbox. I put poinsettias on her porch at Christmas. And lilies at Easter. No response. Finally, in desperation, I offered to pay her. (Sorry, Bob Woodward.) No response. Judging from the small brick home she lived in, she lived modestly. The money might have come in handy, but she wouldn't talk. Her drapes were always closed.

I had better luck finding Jack Kirksmith's widow. I stumbled across her name while searching online for information about the Kirksmith family. Tommie Kirksmith had posted a comment below a blog item about the musical Kirksmith sisters. It only took a little more searching to find her. She lived an hour away.

When I called Tommie Kirksmith and explained I was looking into the King of Diamonds thefts, she laughed and asked, "Are you *sure* you want to go down that rabbit hole?"

Still, she agreed to talk. We met one morning at a Dairy Queen near her home. Tommie Kirksmith pulled into the parking lot in a heavy-duty Dodge Ram truck that dwarfed my Subaru. When she climbed down from the cab, she turned out to be quite petite. The truck came in handy for her rescue work with the SPCA, she explained.

Tommie Kirksmith had a single braid of gray hair that hung down her back, and she wore jeans that looked as if they'd seen some saddles. Even with no apparent makeup, she was still a striking woman. Her eyes were a distinctive violet blue. When I asked her who people told her she looked like, she said, "Usually Elizabeth Taylor, sometimes Leslie Caron. I don't think I look like either one, but maybe a little of both." When Jack Kirksmith took her to parties in Dallas, he told her to beware of men like Bedford Wynne and his "Rover Boy" friends. He warned aggressive men to keep their hands off her—she belonged to him.

We talked until our breakfast burritos turned cold. Tommie Kirksmith recalled how Jack promised to marry her when she was just a young girl. He was seventeen years older and asked her grandmother to save her for him. He said he would come back for her after she turned eighteen—and did. He was divorced and the father of a young boy when he showed up at the oil company where she was working. "When he stepped off the elevator, he had on his Sam Spade jacket, looking all pretty," she remembered. She said yes.

Because of his business and gambling setbacks, their marriage was "chicken one day and feathers the next," she said. Cars and homes and jewelry came and went. But she stayed with him.

Did Jack have a drinking problem like Jim? Yes, she said, it was a family curse. All three brothers had drinking problems, and so did their father. Jasper sometimes came to her house to dry out or hide out during bad spells.

◆

As our conversations continued, I suspected Tommie wasn't telling me everything she knew, but I couldn't blame her. A lot of people weren't.

She repeatedly insisted that Jasper Kirksmith was *not* the jewel thief. "He didn't do it," she said with finality. "I know it for a fact."

Why?

"Because Jack said so," she answered. "And Jasper said so."

The brothers may not have been angels, she insisted, but they weren't jewel thieves either. In fact, she said, their mother Netta was so mortified by the accusations that she took to her bed.

The rumors wrecked her husband Jack's oil and gas efforts, she said. Who was going to invest with a guy who might be a thief? In mid-1963, she and Jack moved with their children to Corpus Christi to start over—just before the bank repossessed their home near Preston Hollow.

After more ups and downs, Jack received some money from the Nail family wills. They bought the property they had been renting in North Texas and called it Tranquility Base. Tommie became a church elder and sang in the choir. She wanted to leave her roller-coaster years behind.

As we continued to exchange emails and phone calls, Tommie Kirksmith never budged from her conviction that the Kirksmith brothers didn't take the jewels. "It wasn't them," she would say.

Could she be right and everyone else wrong?

When I sifted through police documents that Paul McCaghren had saved, I found Jasper was up to more mischief than Tommie Kirksmith knew. A memo written by Captain Fannin on January 13, 1963, provided a significant lead.

Fannin wrote that he had received two calls that week from Chief Criminal Deputy E. N. Buie in the Fort Worth Sheriff's office. One of Buie's sources, who lived and worked in Dallas, said Jasper Kirksmith had been trying to dispose of loose diamonds. His source, a woman married to a gambler friend of Jasper's, said Jasper was in a Dallas club when the vice squad raided it. He claimed that he flushed some loose diamonds down the toilet. Jasper had cut up and remounted some stones, the source said, and had some large pieces of jewelry for sale.

"We are attempting to determine Kirksmith's whereabouts," Fannin reported to the Fort Worth deputy, adding that he had shared the information with the FBI.

What happened?

Nothing. The police still couldn't tie Jasper directly to the thefts.

Yet if the tip was true, it meant Jasper Kirksmith was trying to get rid of hot jewels at the peak of the King of Diamonds' break-ins.

34

The Pawn Connection

What happened to the jewels? That was part of the enduring riddle about the case. Where did they go? Why were none of them seen again?

After each burglary attributed to the King of Diamonds, the DPD's property recovery squad made inquiries at pawnshops around town. They showed photos of the stolen jewels to the shop owners.

Nope, haven't seen them, the owners said.

However, as one detective confided, "I can't say they didn't take something under the counter."

The recovery team usually retrieved a million dollars in stolen goods a year, but the King's jewels? None. Not even the most distinctive pieces.

Could a duplicitous pawn broker have spirited the jewels out of town? It was certainly possible. Some shops were a back door to the underworld.

When I asked detectives if any of the suspects had a connection to pawnshops, one replied, "Yeah. Jasper Kirksmith. He played cards with Arthur Bishop."

Jasper, again.

But *who* was Arthur Bishop?

With a little digging, I found out Arthur Bishop owned a handful of pawnshops in the 1950s and 1960s. He took college courses to learn how to make jewelry and installed a workshop in one of his locations where he could transform hocked jewels into new creations and sell them at below-market prices.

Like many of the pawnshop owners, Bishop gambled on the side. And for several years, he ran a casino near downtown—with the permission of Sheriff Bill Decker. The way I heard the story, Bishop rescued the sheriff's son from an embarrassing scrape in the 1950s. In gratitude, Decker told him, "I owe you one."

Some months later, Bishop asked the sheriff to let him operate a casino on Knox Avenue near Central Expressway. Decker, who played poker regularly, said, "I'll give you one year."

After a year, Bishop returned and asked the sheriff, "Could you give me one more year? I am making so much money; it would be a shame to quit now."

Decker said, "I'll give you one more year, but you damn sure better not ask me for a third."

All this was illegal, but Arthur Bishop did so well, he could afford to take his wife to dinner at the Cipango Club. During his flush years, he donated money for jewelry classes at Tyler Junior College. And hired the students.

After gambling boss Benny Binion relocated in Las Vegas, he asked Bishop to make a ring for him to celebrate his success with the Horseshoe Casino.

Bishop designed a gold ring that was big as a jar top, people said. He shaped the ring like a horseshoe and covered it with diamonds, emeralds, and rubies that once belonged to someone else. The ring was worthy of a lord or pop star, and in a way, Benny Binion was both.

Arthur Bishop had a certain star power himself. At six foot one, Bishop was handsome enough to model the "dos and don'ts" of wearing Army uniforms for military publications. After the war, he tried acting, which wasn't profitable, and the mortgage business, which wasn't fun. Then he opened a pawnshop on East Grand Avenue and found his future. Like other pawn dealers, Bishop handled everything from drum sets to diamond rings. And maybe a little monkey business on the side.

"Arthur Bishop had a great personality," one of the detectives recalled. "He would say, 'I don't have to steal, I'm in a business that does steal.'"

◆

Something about Arthur Bishop's name sounded familiar. When I looked back through my notes, I discovered a friend had mentioned Bishop when recalling a burglary in Preston Hollow. It involved a woman who owned a popular children's shop called Young Ages.

In 1964, Mrs. Mary McLeod frightened away a burglar when she returned home from dinner around eleven P.M. The sixty-one-year-old widow lived on Seneca Avenue, a short street in Preston Hollow with only nine homes. As she prepared to go to bed, Mrs. McLeod noticed a side door had been pried open. She called a friend, who rushed to the house. They began to search room to room. Just as they reached a balcony in the back of the house, a man bolted from the shadows and fled down the stairs. He darted across the lawn into the dark.

Lt. Paul McCaghren came to the scene. "Looks like you got lucky," he told Mrs. McLeod. "You scared off the King of Diamonds."

She was less fortunate the next time. Another break-in occurred a decade later, after Mary McLeod had remarried and became Mrs. Floyd West. This time, the break-in didn't fit the King of Diamonds pattern, but it raised interesting questions about the pawn underworld.

At 10:15 P.M. on a Wednesday, two masked burglars broke into her house. They rousted Mrs. West, who was seventy-five by that time, and her eighty-six-year-old husband, Floyd, from bed. One of the burglars demanded, "Where is the big ring?"

When Mrs. West handed over a fake ring she used for travel, the intruder exploded, "I want the real thing!" He covered her face with a pillow and pistol-whipped her husband. Terrified, she agreed to get the diamond ring from a special box, but begged him, "Please not this one!" Celebrity jeweler David Webb—who created jewels for Elizabeth Taylor and Jackie Onassis—had designed the ring for her. It was one of a kind. The burglar grabbed it and found two other diamond rings, a set of matching emerald pieces, a pair of pearl-and-diamond ear clips, and a diamond-encrusted watch—altogether about $64,000 worth of jewelry.

The intruders attempted to shove the blood-spattered couple into a closet, but it was too small to hold both of them. Instead, they forced the two into a bathroom at gunpoint and warned them: "Don't call the police for fifteen minutes."

They needn't have worried—it took four hours for the police to arrive that time. Frustrated when the police were also slow to follow up on the case, Mrs. West took action herself. She placed an ad in *D Magazine*, offering a reward, no questions asked. For a year and a half, her ad appeared in the magazine every month.

Then one day, Mrs. West got a call from a man who had seen the ad. He said he could get her jewels back.

His name was Arthur Bishop.

Mrs. West paid him $5,000 in cash and got most of her jewelry back, including the David Webb ring and some earrings with jewels "the size of plums."

How did Arthur Bishop get his hands on the jewels?

He didn't say, and Mrs. West promised not to ask.

The incident suggested that tougher characters had started working the King's territory. It also raised uncomfortable questions about Arthur Bishop. How did he get the jewels? Why didn't he dismount the stones and repurpose them? Were they too hot to sell? Did he know who took them? And how did he hide such things from the police?

In 1966, Arthur Bishop helped his son Pat open a pawnshop in Oak Cliff, a former suburb south of downtown. The storefront on Jefferson Avenue was only seventeen feet wide and seventy feet deep, but young Bishop did well enough to add several adjacent properties.

By the time I began my search, Arthur Bishop had died, but I thought it might be worthwhile to visit his son Pat. Bishop Pawn stood out—it took up half a block and was painted bright red and white.

Inside, the shop was lined with glass display cases, each one full of cameras, harmonicas, watches, and knives. Along the back wall, locked cabinets protected an arsenal of rifles.

I stood there for a few moments in awe. *There's a country song in this somewhere*, I thought. Who parted with the ring inscribed "Always and Forever"? Who had to give up their guitar?

At that moment, a man with luxuriantly curly hair and a big smile walked up. Pat Bishop had a retro look about him that made me think of casino bosses in brocade tuxedo jackets. But his friends had warned me, Pat Bishop looked like a George Raft type, but wasn't. Newspaper articles praised him for professionalizing pawnshop operations. His pawnshop had been voted "Best in Dallas."

Knowing the topic was jewel thefts, Pat Bishop was understandably guarded but cordial. He said he didn't know anything about the King of Diamonds because he was in high school when the thefts took place. When I mentioned Josephine Graf's 20.4-carat diamond, he pulled out a calculator to check the value and raised his eyebrows.

Bishop said he learned after a few years in the pawn business that he could make more money from jewelry than anything else. Electronics got outdated overnight. Firearms were complicated to buy and sell. But *jewelry*? Jewelry retained value, he said, and took up little space. So Bishop enlarged his jewelry section and hired more employees to make new pieces from forfeited gems. "If you have an idea, we will make it," he said.

Like a host showing off his home, Pat Bishop pointed out the framed photos on the wall of his office. There were photos of his father and mother at the Cipango Club and photos of Elvis Presley, who ate a bowl of chili across the street.

To get back on subject, I asked if his dad gambled, as if I didn't know.

"Yes, he loved to gamble," Bishop said.

Las Vegas?

"He went to Vegas, but he liked the local casinos better."

"Where were the local casinos?"

"Oh, scattered around town," Bishop hedged. "They were kept quiet."

People also gambled *with* his father, he volunteered. "Dad placed bets for people who might approach him at his table at Campisi's," he recalled. "Everyone knew him."

Did his father gamble with a guy named Jasper?

"Maybe," he said. "My dad knew a lot of people." Then he asked, "Have you ever heard of Bobby Joe Chapman?"

Yes, I said. The biggest bookie in the Southwest, or something like that.

"That's right," he said. "My dad knew him."

I got the picture.

I checked out several more pawnshops after that. Before eBay, they were the best way to recycle things that had seen better days: Blenders. Banjos. Golf bags full of dusty clubs. All were ransomed by someone who needed cash in a hurry—like the woman who traded her husband's ashes for a gun. One man pawned a fake arm made out of cork every time he was out of work. He would slam the prosthetic limb on the counter and demand, "What do I have to do for twenty bucks—*give you my right arm?*" This went on several times until he wired money from Houston with the note, "Put my arm on bus. Got a job."

The pawnshops filled a need, former pawnshop owner David Goldstein insisted. "Where else would a guy with no legs or a lady with no home get money?" he said. "Republic Bank isn't going to loan them a *penny.*"

Goldstein was part of a family that owned a half-dozen pawnshops in the downtown area known as "Deep Ellum." His father, Isaac Goldstein, owned Rocky's Pawn Shop and a jewelry store. His aunt owned Molly's Tool and Gun. Another relative owned Uncle Sam's. But the most famous family member was his uncle, Rubin Goldstein, who called himself "Honest Joe." His shop was the Disneyland of detritus. Outside, every inch was covered with hubcaps and signs. Inside, the shop looked as if the city had been turned on its side and all the stray appliances tumbled in. Some say Joe slept in the shop and only took a bath once a month, which meant he made a strong impression. So did the Edsel station wagon he drove. It had ads on the doors and a machine gun on the roof.

The Elm Street pawnshops were Dallas's version of the back alleys of Cairo. Since some of the owners also operated jewelry stores, diamond salesmen from Israel came to call with briefcases handcuffed to their wrists. Local salesmen like Milt Joseph and John Tomano came with loose gems rattling in their pockets.

A lot of jewels changed hands, but shop owners insisted the King's plunder was not included. They didn't want problems with the cops, they insisted. It was a headache to take hot stuff. If they suspected something was stolen, they had to record who brought in the item and where they got it. If a thief was caught, they had to go to court to testify. "It was just not worth the trouble to take something suspicious," David Goldstein promised. "If I took something hot, I didn't know it."

Still, there were more than seventy pawnshops in town at the time. Could one of the owners have dirty hands? Fannin's detectives suspected a shop owner on Harry Hines Boulevard. He was known to fence jewels to pay for his cocaine habit. Then there was a secretive gem dealer with a downtown office. He had been cited by the IRS for not reporting his transactions. He was a *weird* guy, a detective told me, a little scary.

And there was the suspicious shop on Grand Avenue, which had not been grand in a long time. In the 1960s, one of the Elm Street pawn owners had opened a satellite location on Grand Avenue. He called it a "swap shop" to avoid regulations and put up a big sign that advertised, THE KING OF DIAMONDS.

The manager was a Native American who was tough enough to tell the meanest hoodlums "No deal" if their jewels were too hot to handle. People called him "Big Indian," because you could park a couple of Buicks on his shoulders. He always wore his shirttail out, presumably to cover the gun in his waistband. He also hung out at strip clubs and moonlighted as a "cleaner," a collector for gambling debts. Few argued with him. "The guy could collect from a graveyard," a bookie told me in admiration.

When I tried to find out more about the swap shop manager, people invariably got apprehensive. A nightclub performer who bought a used wedding dress at the shop changed the subject. "I probably shouldn't even mention him," she said. She didn't return phone calls after that.

I called a former pawnshop owner who told relatives that he knew who fenced the King's jewels. But when I asked him who it was, he became so nervous that he started stuttering. "I can't talk about it," he said.

Fannin knew all too well there were ways the King's jewels could have been spirited out of town. He told reporter Robert Finklea, "We were frustrated. We knew that jewelry should have shown up. But as we got into it more, we found that jewelry could be anywhere in the world. Once it was taken out of the settings, not even the owners would recognize it. It was untraceable."

With the advent of computer technology, it would later become possible to record the color, clarity, and facets of gems in databases. Lasers could inscribe identifying marks. But such things were not possible in the 1960s.

Paul McCaghren had his own theory why there was no trace of the missing jewels. At one of our lunches, he introduced a tantalizing thought: the King might not have been stealing for financial gain.

"He could have kept all the jewelry for himself, like some men collect naughty photos," McCaghren said. "They were his trophies."

Then he threw a grenade into the possibilities: "It's entirely possible the jewels are still here."

"Where?"

"Who knows?" he said, then went back to jabbing at his crab salad with his fork. "You tell me."

"You mean he was like the millionaires who buy masterpieces and put them in the safe?"

"Something like that," he answered.

PART SEVEN
CASE CLOSED

"Very few of us are what we seem."
—Agatha Christie

35

Following the Footsteps

Finding the jewel thief had become a real-life game of *Clue*. One by one, I had ruled out George Owen, interior designer John Astin Perkins, society editor Ann Draper, jeweler Dudley Ramsden, Mr. Jack, and eventually, Mrs. Lambert.

A lot of local thieves were suggested—and discarded. One used an armed team that wore jumpsuits and ski masks. Not the King's style. Another lived in a hotsheet motel next to a pawn shop. As one of the cops put it, he wouldn't have known which fork to use at fancy parties.

That left two people who were mentioned most often:

- Jasper Kirksmith—the gigolo, pimp, and gambler
- And the mysterious man from a hardware store family

While Jasper remained a strong possibility, I still needed to find out more about the mystery man from the hardware family.

After McCaghren told me he followed the burglar's footprints to a house in Highland Park, he dodged my efforts to get his name. He would only say the family owned hardware stores.

To track down the family, I spent hours searching through newspaper archives and phone books at the Dallas Public Library. As it turned out, there were several families who lived in Highland Park that owned hardware companies.

But which family had a son the right age? I started asking people, "Do you remember a guy from a hardware store family who was active in debutante circles in the 1960s?" One name rose to the top.

There was indeed a person whose family owned hardware stores and was highly active in social circles.

His name was John Taylor Higginbotham Jr., known to some friends as Johnny.

When I heard the name, my first thought was, *Uh, no!*

The Higginbotham family was one of the most prominent in the city. Several redbrick buildings in the heart of downtown had the Higginbotham name on them. The family businesses included Higginbotham-Pearlstone Hardware; Higginbotham Bailey, a wholesale dry goods firm; and Higginbotham-Bartlett Lumber. At one time, there were branches across Texas and the South.

Multiple generations of the Higginbotham family had married into other prominent families, so they were woven through Dallas society. I would be poking a hornet's nest to raise the possibility that a Higginbotham was the jewel thief.

Now I understood why McCaghren was reluctant to name names.

Instead of a seasoned criminal whose mailing address was the penitentiary, the jewel thief might be one of Dallas's very own.

It didn't take much searching to find out that the suspect's father, John T. Higginbotham Sr., was a highly respected business leader. A member of the powerful Dallas Citizens Council, he also served on the boards of the Dallas Chamber of Commerce and First National Bank. He was one of the VIPs invited to the ill-fated luncheon for President Kennedy.

Higginbotham's son, John Jr., was prominent in a different way. Unlike many other sons in dynastic families, young Higginbotham did not become a leader in the family business. He did not follow his father onto civic boards. He was more attracted to the social whirl.

John Jr. served as president of the Idlewild Club that selected debutantes and was a member of the Terpsichorean Club that presented them. That meant he was a constant presence at social affairs from the late 1940s through the 1960s. Even when Higginbotham was nearly two decades older than the young women being honored, he showed up in society news as an escort. He seemed to thrive on the glamour.

Everything I could find confirmed that Higginbotham could be the mystery man. He lived in Highland Park, not far from the Dallas Country Club. And he would have been in his early thirties when the burglaries were at their peak, just as the police's psychological profile predicted.

◆

I invited McCaghren to lunch again at Bugatti's, the Italian restaurant he liked. By this time, we were more accustomed to each other. We had talked many times on the phone and developed a cordial working relationship.

I asked McCaghren point-blank about Higginbotham: Did he follow the footprints to John Higginbotham Jr.'s house?

McCaghren seemed surprised that I had figured out the name, but answered directly:

"Yes. We all thought it was him."

Trying to stay calm, I suggested, "Walk me through what happened."

After following the footsteps, McCaghren and several detectives went to one of the family's hardware outlets. They asked an employee if he sold galoshes like the ones the jewel thief wore. When the employee realized they were cops, he asked them to leave. To avoid a scene, they left.

But McCaghren did not give up. Working with Sgt. Henry Gardner from Highland Park, he set up stakeouts at Higginbotham's house. Several times a week, they hid in the alley at night. To their disappointment, the stakeouts produced little but sore backs and mosquito bites.

Gardner and McCaghren thought there were good reasons to believe young Higginbotham was the thief: He fit the profile. And a number of the burglary victims told police that they suspected Higginbotham.

"So why didn't you arrest him?" I asked.

"We couldn't get the warrant from Highland Park to search his house," McCaghren replied. "Said it was too risky. We figured they didn't want to embarrass one of the city's leaders."

So, that was it.

Higher-ups in Highland Park had blocked the burglary investigation.

Now I understood why McCaghren kept saying that his hands were tied.

Highland Park, whose per capita income made it one of the wealthiest enclaves in the nation, was known for pampering its residents. The small suburb was like Mayberry with money. If residents asked police to watch their homes or collect their mail while they were gone, they did. Some residents left a key with the department when they went out of town. Sixty residents had a direct line to the police station.

If there was a domestic disturbance—and there were some—police kept it quiet. And if someone wanted to rummage through a home to look for stolen jewels, they would need the equivalent of a red-hot smoking gun in their hands to get permission.

The catch-22 was that Gardner and McCaghren needed to search the house to find the smoking gun. But Police Chief W. H. Naylor said no.

Officers who worked with W. H. Naylor described him as a good chief who was "old school." To some, that meant "You took care of your people, your city. If they didn't want it in the paper, you did your best to keep it out." To others, "old school" meant Naylor had seasoned instincts. "He could see a guy walking down the street and call a squad car to check out a possible burglar. Sure enough, it would be a burglar," remembered Officer Jim Oakkerson.

"Bud" Naylor had started as a clerk in 1928 and worked his way up the municipal ladder. When he became police chief, he kept crime low by insisting that streets be constantly patrolled. Before the King of Diamonds came along, the round-the-clock patrols in Highland Park kept burglaries down. People said that if you called to report a break-in, a squad car was there before you could hang up. The burglary rate in Dallas was five times higher. Violent crime in Highland Park was even more rare—only three murders in twenty years. "You spent most of your time looking after the flowers and trees in the parks," an officer told the *Dallas Morning News.*

When the jewel thefts interrupted the tranquility, Naylor was in his sixties and white-haired. He had been around long enough to know that several members of the Higginbotham family lived in Highland Park. They served on the boards of the opera, symphony, and art museum. The Higginbothams didn't just know "the right people"; they *were* the right people.

Naylor understood that there would be an awful scandal if the police stomped into a Higginbotham home and didn't find anything. And it darn sure would be a scandal if they *did* find something.

So, was Naylor shielding a prominent resident by opposing a search warrant?

Or trying to follow the law?

I asked several attorneys their opinion. A noted criminal lawyer said Naylor's caution was understandable. "You would have to prove that somebody told you about *specific stolen items* in this residence. Somebody reliable has to tell you this. It's the Fourth Amendment for good reason. You don't want people going through anyone's house without good cause."

However, since police had followed the thief to Higginbotham's house and had descriptions of missing jewels, a former president of the Criminal Bar Association said, "It's a close call—but search warrants are granted more often than not."

When I asked McCaghren again about the incident, he repeated, "The authorities did not want to embarrass one of the city's leaders."

When I asked him to put that in writing, he qualified his remarks slightly, adding that Naylor "did not say the family was too prominent for us to investigate. That was the assumption made by Gardner and myself."

Either way, the investigation was stopped at John Higginbotham's door.

36

The Nice Guy

McCaghren remained convinced they had found their man: socialite John T. Higginbotham Jr.

They just couldn't get to him.

Besides being a perennial escort—the kind of guy who hangs around the party too long—what was Higginbotham like? Did he have what it took to be a burglar?

To find out, I began contacting Higginbotham friends and family members to get descriptions of him. Some weren't pleased he was considered a suspect in the jewel thefts. One relative warned, "You will be sorry if you do this."

Yet some Higginbotham relatives went out of their way to be helpful. One shared family cookbooks that had historical information about the clan. In vintage photos, Higginbothams posed in their touring cars or gathered around dining tables. They were handsome people. To the eye, they looked prosperous and proper, the epitome of respectability. But as detectives will tell you, every family has secrets.

I asked a respected attorney who did legal work for the family, could John T. Higginbotham Jr. have been the thief? "I wouldn't doubt it," he said. "He was a very attractive young man, had a pleasant personality, trim and handsome—a *bon vivant*. He had access to all the big homes at one time or another. He had the means to case a place. Later on, he was on hard times and needed money. He wasn't always flush."

A former Idlewild president who knew Higginbotham from deb party days said he had harbored suspicions for years that Higginbotham could be involved. "Absolutely. He had a snarky side not everyone saw."

"His name came up a lot," a school friend remembered.

"I could see John doing it as a dare, a lark, to see if he could do it," a friend who vacationed with him said.

Yet others expressed surprise and disbelief that anyone would suggest Higginbotham was the thief: "I would pass out if it were John Higginbotham," said former debutante Carol Taylor. "I would just find it hard to believe."

Frances Martin Flaig, a longtime friend from high school, agreed. "I would never think in a thousand hundred years that he could be the King of Diamonds."

A cousin, Nina Works, said, "I can't imagine Johnny as King of Diamonds. We were all crazy about him. Besides," she said, "he had big feet. All Higginbothams have big feet. I can't see him as a cat burglar."

A former fraternity brother, Julian Talichet, was adamant: "No way. I would bet my bottom dollar it wasn't him. It didn't seem his personality."

I knew from years of interviewing that if you ask three people to describe someone, you are likely to get three different impressions. Sure enough, when I asked what Higginbotham was like, a cousin said he was "very sweet" and dressed up as Santa Claus at Christmas gatherings to hand out gifts to children. A man who attended parties at his house thought he was "pretentious" and had an air of entitlement. And a man who vacationed with Higginbotham found him "exotic, handsome, chic." All those things could be true and still not add up to a whole. Or a thief.

Yet one aspect of Higginbotham came up repeatedly: many people mentioned there was "something odd" about Higginbotham. He could be strange, one person said, "kind of a character." Another said, "He was definitely eccentric." And one said, "He was odd, but his family was odd." A relative went further and said, "It was a weird branch of the family."

This turned out to be important.

◈

I checked to see if Higginbotham fit the profile that psychologist Robert Stoltz made, and most of the boxes checked:

He was a "mama's boy." Higginbotham had a special attachment to his mother, Verda Nelle. Neighbors said she was a beautiful but unstable woman. She was stricken with a neuropathic disease that gradually destroyed her fingers and toes. As her condition worsened, she was unable to care for her children. A neighbor told me that Verda Nelle spent most of her days on a chaise longue or in bed, dressed tastefully but incapacitated. "She was always upstairs," one of the children's friends remembered. Her death certificate stated she died from "self-administered barbituric poisoning" when she was thirty-eight. She reportedly was found by her son.

He was a latent homosexual at a time when such things had to be deeply repressed. In the 1950s and early 1960s, being openly homosexual was not merely frowned on, it was illegal under Texas law. "Coming out" would have been risky. Two of the women who dated Higginbotham had differing impressions about his sexuality. One said she went out with Higginbotham so much that they were considered "an item." But after a while, she realized he never tried to kiss her. "Eventually, I decided something is wrong with this guy and moved on," she said. The other date said she never suspected he might be homosexual. "He made me feel he was in love with me—and seemed smitten with several other women in those days," she said. But after a moment's pause, she mused, "He might have been bisexual . . ."

Other contemporaries thought Higginbotham was homosexual, but no one spoke of it. The social accommodation was an early version of "Don't Ask, Don't Tell." Gay men sometimes concealed their sexuality by marrying women from prominent families. Those who remained bachelors—like Higginbotham—often continued to escort debutantes to social events. It was a polite masquerade.

Higginbotham kept himself fit. Though he didn't participate in robust sports like football and basketball, Higginbotham played tennis and golf.

He was slender but muscular, "like a high school wrestler," a contemporary said. As an adult, he worked out to stay in shape.

He was the right height. Estimates of the thief's height varied: Witnesses who got a glimpse of the thief guessed he was between five foot seven and five foot nine. Police said he might be as tall as six feet, based on his footprints and stride analysis. Higginbotham claimed to be six feet tall on his passport. His draft records indicated he was five eleven. The draft record was probably closest.

He had the kind of social connections that would have been helpful for the thief. "Early in his life, he was friends with *everyone* and belonged to *everything,*" a friend recalled. When he became president of Idlewild in 1956, he gained access to party details and the addresses of prominent families.

He escorted debutantes until 1967–68, when he was thirty-nine. He was less visible in society coverage, but remained in the Hesitation Club, an exclusive dance club, and attended fundraisers for the Dallas Opera and TACA, the arts organization championed by Evelyn Lambert.

Higginbotham collected jewelry. In fact, he displayed beautiful gems and art objects in his homes. A friend remembered Higginbotham put a large topaz next to a metal-and-leather clip used to hold marijuana cigarettes. The clip was shaped like a giant spider. "He was crazy about jewelry," a former date said. "He would look at my things and admire them, more so than the average man would." Later in life, he gave Nancy Hamon a two-inch amethyst with a gold mounting to wear to her birthday party—with the caveat she return it.

Another friend recalled that Higginbotham bought semiprecious stone boxes of lapis, malachite, or tiger eye, and decorated them. "He would superglue a piece of jewelry on it like a clasp. He had a way of putting stuff together and creating a juxtaposition that was amazing."

Higginbotham's fascination with jewels was known in wealthy circles. News accounts in 1967 noted he was among the Dallas socialites who went to see a preview of David Webb jewelry in Fort Worth. The contingent included Ginny Murchison, Sharon Simons, and the Glenn Turners. Some went to a dinner at the home of Anne Windfohr and some to a dinner party hosted by billionaire Perry Bass.

As I talked to more people, other characteristics surfaced:

Higginbotham wasn't afraid to take what he wanted. He collected planaria—also known as frangipani. On trips to Mexico and California, he scouted out exotic varieties in nurseries and private gardens. If he spotted a type he didn't have, he took a cutting, even if the plant was behind someone's wall.

Like the jewel thief, Higginbotham smoked cigarettes. As an adult, he also smoked marijuana. One visitor recalled ringing his doorbell and being shocked when he answered in a marijuana haze, too giddy with laughter to carry on a conversation.

He liked to travel and live first-class. He traveled to the Hamptons and La Jolla for social events. When he turned twenty-one, Higginbotham sailed first-class on the RMS *Queen Elizabeth* to Europe with three friends. After a summer of touring, he returned with eight bags, compared to his friends' three or four. Winn Morton, a Highland Park classmate, ran into Higginbotham at the Plaza Hotel in New York after his trip. "He bragged about how much money he had spent," Morton said. "He spent lavishly."

He had refined tastes. Over the years, he became highly knowledgeable about rare furnishings and accumulated expensive antiques for his homes. Visitors remembered he had Chippendale chairs, rare Sarouk rugs, and vintage French cabinets that were "exquisite." He acquired Egyptian artifacts and Roman antiquities. He liked to visit art galleries and attended the opera. At times, his friends said, he played opera recordings in his home.

He was a gracious host who liked to entertain lavishly. For his dinner parties, he sometimes placed a large silver bowl in the entryway that was filled with seventy-five roses. A cousin remembered, "When he gave a party, you wanted to be there. He had a great eye for art and furnishings. And he was good company."

In fall 1962, Higginbotham and his closest friends—Gerald Hargett, Currie McCutcheon Jr., and Harrell Harrison, an SMU classmate—hosted a black-tie dinner at Higginbotham's new residence on Edmondson Avenue. The Virginia colonial house had a living room with a beamed ceiling, a garden in back, and servants' quarters.

According to society coverage, Nancy Hamon came in a long black dinner dress with a white ostrich wrap. Nancy Ann Smith arrived in a shimmering silver-blue cocktail dress.

The party was a graduation of sorts: After his father married the widow of one of his cousins, Higginbotham moved out of the family home on Bordeaux. He no longer listed his occupation as a vice president at a Higginbotham company but as "investments." He was thirty-four and on his own.

He may have harbored a grudge because of increased animosity toward homosexuals. In addition to the "Red Scare" campaign against communists, Senator Joe McCarthy and others had launched a parallel vendetta against homosexuals in the 1950s called the "Lavender Scare." Thousands were booted out of civil service jobs and the military, often based on rumors. Senator Alan Simpson would later observe that while the Red Scare got more attention, the Lavender Scare harmed more people. Homosexuals already lived in fear of being beaten up or thrown in jail. Now they had the additional risk of being unemployable and shunned as deviates.

Businessman Buddy Macatee, who had known Higginbotham since elementary school, told me he remained a friend even after he realized his classmate was homosexual. "I really appreciated the burden on guys like him who were gay," Macatee said. "Most guys wouldn't even wear a pink shirt because they didn't want other guys to tease them for being a 'pansy.' It could get very ugly. So they kept it in the closet. That's just the way it was."

Higginbotham's sexuality may also have created a barrier between him and his father. His father was a quiet and conventional man who spent his weekends waxing his Cadillac in the driveway or watching Dallas Cowboys games at a friend's house. His way of coping with the problems in his household was not to talk about them. "He was a man of few words," a neighbor recalled. "A nice man, but sort of aloof, very proper, very upright." In his will, he dutifully gave John Jr. the same share of his estate as his sisters, but remained distant. "His father loved him," a family attorney said. "He just didn't want anything to do with him."

Higginbotham Jr. may have felt rejected in another way. In 1958, the year he turned thirty, Higginbotham thought he had a picture-perfect match: He got engaged to a pretty, blonde debutante. Newspapers announced the engagement. Friends hosted parties. Arrangements were made for a fall wedding. Then, a month before the ceremony, Higginbotham's fiancée broke off the engagement and returned the diamond ring he had given her. Friends said Higginbotham was devastated. The rebuff ended his dream of a perfect family. He displayed the spurned engagement ring in a glass case for a long time.

Did his personal rejections fester into resentment? And revenge? Police noted that in one burglary, the jewel thief took one earring with a large blue-white diamond and left the other behind. It looked as though he was deliberately spoiling the set. When he broke into oilman Ed Cox's home on Gaywood, he took one earring from two sets, ruining both.

People also noticed there was something oddly vindictive about the thefts. "He was depriving women of something they loved, just like he was deprived," a former classmate said. "It was almost as if he was thinking, *I'll show them.*"

◆

One of Higginbotham's most unusual quirks was that he collected animals. Lots of them. In addition to a succession of dogs, he had coops full of birds when he was growing up. Children in the neighborhood came to see his banty hens pecking around the yard. He also had a few roosters and a hawk or two that he enjoyed showing off.

His friend Buddy Macatee remembered that when they were students, Higginbotham raised guinea pigs and gerbils, then sold them to a hospital for testing. Somewhere along the line, he added an alligator, nicknamed "Ally." Though small, the reptile had a habit of wandering out of the backyard, which panicked the neighbors.

When he was older and had houses of his own, Higginbotham raised pigeons and sometimes dyed them pink. Over time, his menagerie included parrots that he taught to do tricks and canaries that filled the house with their song.

Visitors to his home remembered seeing Doberman pinschers, Jack Russell terriers, golden pheasants, and a peacock that wasn't pleased to be part of an eccentric zoo.

And then there were the snakes.

Higginbotham collected snakes. He accumulated dozens of them, big ones, small ones, poisonous ones. Even a boa constrictor.

One woman remembered that Higginbotham brought out his snakes at dinner parties to show them off. Sometimes he turned them loose to unnerve the guests. He would laugh as the women shrieked and men backed away.

One of his favorite pranks was wrapping his boa constrictor—which was ten feet long—around the shoulders of an unsuspecting visitor. He seemed to enjoy making others uncomfortable.

A friend told me that Higginbotham liked to tell the story about the time he was driving through Oklahoma. He saw a house with a sign out front advertising Free Kittens. He knocked on the door and told the woman who answered that he was interested in her kittens.

"Which one?" the woman asked, pointing to the kittens.

"I'll take all of them," Higginbotham answered.

"Oh, do you love kittens?" she asked.

"No," he said, "I have snakes."

Higginbotham always laughed harder than anyone about the story.

Several visitors noticed that some of his art seemed calculated to shock. For example, Higginbotham placed a dildo on the wall next to a framed drawing by John Lennon and claimed it was a replica of the rock star's penis. It wasn't. "He just liked pranking people," a friend said.

Others were taken aback by his proud display of an ancient Roman brazier he had restored. He had taken the brazier to an art restorer to have missing penises reconstructed on three tall satyrs that held up the bronze container. When he picked up the restored work, he handed it back with the instruction: Make the penises bigger. He then displayed the enhanced brazier in the middle of a coffee table, where it was sure to draw a reaction. It was surrounded by his jewel-covered boxes.

◆

As Higginbotham aged, he saw his old friends less and less. They heard he had become more sexually adventurous. A neighbor on Edmondson told me there were comings and goings from his house at all hours. "There were quite a few late-night fights," she said. "Doors would slam and somebody would leave in a cab."

Another side of Higginbotham was emerging. Social friends who were also homosexual confided Higginbotham gravitated to practices known as "rough trade." Some of his new associates were not genteel, they said.

One of his high school friends told me that he asked her to go with him to a private gathering at the home of millionaire John Gillin. Higginbotham said he didn't want to go alone.

To her surprise, some strange men were there with Jasper Kirksmith. They seemed to know Higginbotham, she said. "They were all in dark suits," she remembered, "and they were scary. Very rough looking. They came stag without dates and stayed together like a pack. They frightened me," she said. "I was scared. There was something ominous about them." She asked to go home.

Though she did not believe Higginbotham was the jewel thief—and adamantly said so—she worried that he was associating with dangerous people.

◆

What did these descriptions add up to? I went through my notes over and over, trying to find the core truth about Higginbotham. Could he really be the one? There was more ambiguity in real life than in the detective stories. I wanted some kind of Sherlockian breakthrough that shouted, "There's your man!"

I decided to follow McCaghren's example and reached out to a psychologist: Dr. Sarah Feuerbacher, a professor at Southern Methodist University. I gave her all the information that I had gathered about Higginbotham and asked, Could someone like that have pulled off the burglaries?

"Yes," she said, without a trace of hesitation. Dr. Feuerbacher explained that Higginbotham might have had what's called a "narcissistic personality disorder." Such a disorder could have compelled him to steal beautiful things as prizes, either as a soothing mechanism for his conflicted feelings or an adrenaline high during low periods. Stealing could have been a fetish, an inner compulsion that might not make sense to someone else, she said, but that satisfied a deep-seated need to possess beautiful things. Taking the jewels could have given him a charge and provided revenge for feeling spurned individually and culturally.

How could someone described so often as "nice" steal from people he knew?

Lack of empathy for the people they harm is very common for people with antisocial or narcisstic disorders, Dr. Feuerbacher explained. In Higginbotham's case, his need for gratification blinded him to the harm.

Would a pattern of mental illness in his family help explain his behavior?

Yes, his manic-depressive tendencies could have been a genetic inheritance, she said. On top of that, at the time when young Higginbotham needed his mother's nurturing to develop trusting relationships, she was struggling with her own health issues. She was unable to relate to him during his formative years—and he was not able to help her "be well." His extended adolescence in the debutante circle would have been a temporary escape from family problems that he could not fix.

"What about the snakes?" I asked. Sigmund Freud believed snake dreams were phallic symbols related to sexual energy. Were Higginbotham's snakes a Freudian clue?

Dr. Feuerbacher suggested Higginbotham might have kept snakes as pets because controlling them made him distinctive and masterful. To the outside world, he could be charming; inside, he felt compelled to find ways to remove feelings of inadequacy and hurt, ways to seem powerful and daring. He had a deep-seated need to control things—like animals and, perhaps, sex partners.

Although it was just a brief sketch, Dr. Feuerbach's analysis fleshed out the profile Dr. Stoltz had developed fifty years before. The combined assessments fit. They reinforced the possibility that the best candidate for the King of Diamonds was a social insider who felt like an outsider. The surge of adrenaline from his risky behavior made him feel powerful and superior—a man to be reckoned with.

New England police gave a similar description of Blane Nordahl, the brainy silver burglar who stole from celebrities like Ivana Trump and Bruce Springsteen in the 1990s and early 2000s. Like Higginbotham, he got a kick out of sneaking into homes while the occupants were asleep. Nordahl told authorities he stole for the excitement, not just money. "It's like a natural high," he said. "It fills a void. A lot of times, life can be very mundane, very tedious. You want something different."

Nordahl, too, had a difficult home life. His parents divorced when he was young, so he was shuttled between them. And like Higginbotham, he enjoyed the attention he received from the press as "Burglar to the Stars."

Journalist Michael Finkel recently uncovered a similar profile when he researched a masterful art thief in Europe. Stephane Breitwieser stole an estimated $2 billion in artwork—and kept the treasures to admire in his home. Experts told Finkel that such "unhealthy collecting" occurs most commonly in people who are prone to depression and feel out of place in society. The obsessive collecting offered "a magical escape" into a private world.

Breitwieser's family was ruptured when his parents divorced, much as Higginbotham's family was ruptured by his mother's illness and death. Neither had a close relationship with his father. And like the Dallas thief, the European thief was proud of his skills. He left empty art frames as "calling cards."

According to experts consulted by author Finkel, obsessive collectors have a heightened "aesthetic desire" for beautiful things. Translation: they fall in love with them. Brain studies show that pursuing coveted objects releases an intoxicating flow of brain chemicals. Afterward, the collectors don't feel immoral because they believe that they appreciate (and deserve) the objects more than the owners.

All this rang true about Higginbotham.

Higginbotham's friends and relatives acknowledged a skein of mental illness ran through his family. Besides her physical ailments, they said, his mother was "kind of crazy." One described her as "certifiable." His older sister Rose Nelle was afflicted with other troubles.

When I brought up Rose Nelle's name in interviews, I noticed that people tended to mumble vaguely that she "had problems" or "was a mess." One said tactfully, "She was the sweetest thing, but she was seriously off." I wasn't sure what to make of her until one of Higginbotham's friends blurted out, "She was a nymphomaniac!"

I cringed when I heard the word. Doctors rarely use that term anymore—it is loaded with judgmental baggage, implying some kind of depravity rather than mental illness. Today, the problem is called a "sex and love addiction" or "hypersexuality." Recent research has shown a correlation between such behavior and mania and bipolar disorders. But back then, people found it awkward to discuss oversexualized behavior in a woman. In fact, they were uncomfortable discussing mental illness at all.

In private, family friends confirmed that Rose Nelle's manic behavior got more sexual in nature as she got older. Fraternity boys took advantage of her. A prominent woman remembered Rose Nelle stood on her head without underwear at one party and kissed a social beauty on the mouth at another. A friend of her younger sister's said she came home drunk with strangers in tow.

Word got around about Rose Nelle's conduct. "People talked about her," a contemporary said. "It took a toll on the whole family."

A relative agreed. "They suffered," she said. "Oh, they suffered."

Rose Nelle's family tried to help her. As a last resort, her father sent her to the University of Texas Medical Branch in Galveston to undergo shock treatments. The psychiatric hospital had become the state's leading practitioner of electroconvulsive therapy. Being "sent to Galveston" was synonymous with having no other recourse.

The treatments were harsh medicine. At its most effective, sending small bursts of electric current through the brain can relieve depression and mania. Yet the process was still being fine-tuned in the 1950s. Shocks were administered without anesthesia. Some patients broke limbs as they thrashed about. Afterward, they might not remember large parts of their lives or the names of family members.

Even so, the Higginbothams were desperate. They hoped Rose Nelle could start over if she came back less erratic, more governable. But she didn't. She eventually was taken to a nursing facility. Her brother John visited her when others didn't.

At his point, I felt sincerely sorry for young Higginbotham, his sister, the whole family. I had to remind myself: there's no feeling sorry in detective work, like no crying in baseball. Detectives can't be soft.

And yet.

It was a terribly painful situation.

I could see why so many of Higginbotham's friends were protective of him. He grew up with a sick mother, distant father, troubled sister. Uncomfortable as the idea seemed at first, it began to make sense that

Higginbotham, with his manic highs and despondent lows, could have taken the jewels. When he was on an even keel, there would be a lull in the burglaries. When he was on a downswing, there would be a rush of burglaries to boost him.

Higginbotham was able to hide his conflicts behind the mask of a well-mannered young man in a tuxedo. He kept up a façade of social conformity, while in private he led a different life. Beautiful things were his weakness, so he searched out the most desirable treasures and took them.

Many people mentioned to me that the King of Diamonds reminded them of the Phantom of the Opera. Both felt misunderstood and were determined to have the objects of their desire. They had a point. The jewel thefts were crimes of passion—of a very different kind.

◈

As the thefts continued, talk increased that Higginbotham was involved. School friends asked one of his younger sisters, "Is your brother the jewel thief?"

"I don't know," she answered. "I'll ask him."

"Are you the jewel thief?" she confronted her brother.

He thought it was funny, she told her friends. He laughed. But he didn't say he wasn't the thief.

There were other possible suspects, but the most plausible leads pointed to the same person: John T. Higginbotham Jr. Though police couldn't get material evidence, the psychological indicators were overwhelming and unique, like a psychic fingerprint.

As it was, the detectives tracked the thief to John Higginbotham's door, and no farther. "We all thought we knew who it was," McCaghren said to me multiple times. "We just couldn't get to him."

But that was not the end of the story. No. The possibility of an accomplice surfaced unexpectedly.

And the thief targeted one of the richest women in the world.

37

The Heiress

When financial publications listed the richest Americans in 1957, J. Paul Getty was at the top. H. L. Hunt was close behind—and in the company of the Mellons and the Rockefellers. Getty said Hunt was actually the richest.

When lists of the wealthiest women were added, Hunt's eldest daughter, Margaret Hunt Hill, made the list with more than $1 billion in assets. She trailed Queen Elizabeth but placed in the top tier with Philippines First Lady Imelda Marcos and the female heirs to L'Oréal and Mars candy bar fortunes.

Her father had shot to the top with a bold gamble: He persuaded seventy-year-old Columbus Marion "Dad" Joiner to sell his East Texas oil leases in 1930. Hunt had a hunch the oil under the hard-scrabble farms was worth a lot more than Dad Joiner realized. He bought Joiner's leases with his poker winnings and a loan. That gamble paid off spectacularly. The giant East Texas oil field created more wealth than any other mineral discovery in the continental US.

◆

Hunt didn't grant many interviews. I was fortunate that he gave one to me—and it was a lulu.

While I was working for the Associated Press in 1972, I read about the unusual exercise Hunt thought would prolong his life. It was called "creeping." Intrigued, I left a message at his office that I would like to talk to him about the benefits of creeping. To my surprise, Hunt called me back. He said to be at his house at six A.M. the following day. I showed up the next morning and waited in the dark on his doorstep with the AP photographer who was assigned to go with me, Ferd [sic] Kaufman. Ferd was not happy to be out in the cold at such an early hour—and said so.

The door suddenly opened. We were face-to-face with a white-haired man with strangely intense blue eyes. Come in, he said, it's time for breakfast.

Hunt invited us to sit at the dining table and share a breakfast of dried apricots, nuts, dates, and not much else. In addition to creeping, Hunt had adopted the diet of Himalayan tribesmen who lived to be a hundred. I chewed on the same dried apricot for five minutes while Hunt scooped up a second helping.

Then he abruptly pushed back his chair and started crawling around the house on his hands and knees. It was amazing how fast the old guy could go at eighty-three.

As Hunt crawled full-speed around his living room in his pin-striped suit, I followed, asking questions while trying to take notes. The photographer struggled to keep up behind me. Hunt's second wife, Ruth Ray Hunt, warned sweetly, "Poppy, be careful," and followed the three of us, catching vases and straightening the rumpled rugs. Hunt chortled, "I am a crank about creeping!" and barreled on.

After fifteen or twenty minutes of scooting around and around the furniture, which left all of us a little breathless, the richest man in the world stood up, grabbed my arm, and announced he wanted to show us his ten-acre estate. He insisted that I sit in the front seat with him, the chauffeur, and his wife Ruth. That meant four of us were squeezed together, while the photographer sat by himself in the back seat. One slow drive around

the house, a replica of Mount Vernon, would have been enough to appreciate the views, but Hunt insisted his driver keep circling. I was wedged
so close to Hunt that I could feel him breathing. I politely insisted several
times that I needed to go to work. Yet Hunt pressed on. I could hear Ferd
Kaufman chuckling in the back.

As we circled, Hunt pointed out a two-story brick house on the grounds.
"That's Hassie's house," he said softly. His oldest son, Haroldson Lafay-
ette Hunt III, was rarely seen in public. Diagnosed with schizophrenia,
his behavior had become so dangerously erratic that he was sent for shock
treatments, like Rose Nelle. Still uncontrollable, he was given a lobotomy.
Afterward, he had limited capabilities. He spent the rest of his life as a
recluse. His condition was a constant tug at the heart of the father who
had hoped his namesake would run his empire.

Years later, I found out that Hunt had adopted the creeping exercise
as a way to help Hassie. The technique, part of the Doman-Delacato
method, was supposed to improve connections in the brain. Hunt was so
determined to help his son, he donated money to launch the therapy at a
local university. Yet Hassie did not improve. As we drove repeatedly by his
house, I wondered if he was watching from the window.

That morning with H. L. Hunt remains one of the strangest interviews
I ever did. I can still remember his hard grip on my arm and the intensity
of his gaze. Hunt was a forceful man, used to getting his way.

People who sat next to Hunt at dinners told me he was one of the
smartest men they ever met. But he was grandly eccentric. In a departure
from his lifelong enthusiasm for Baptist hymns, he became a passionate
fan of opera and, in particular, of the petite and pretty opera singer Lily
Pons. Hunt financed an entire performance when she had the lead role in
The Barber of Seville. Opera fans got free tickets, but during intermission,
they had to endure a sales pitch by the millionaire for his "Gastro Majic"
health elixir and a reading of his anti-communist views.

Hunt was so fervently anti-communist that he funded dangerous
elements in the John Birch Society and radical politicians like General
Edwin Walker. History shows he also helped J. Edgar Hoover smear

Martin Luther King Jr. His vision of democracy was giving rich people like him—citizens in the kingdom of money—more votes than others.

Hunt's best idea may have been that eating too much meat, sugar, and white bread is bad for you. He was ahead of the times on that. He often took his lunch to work in a sack because he believed fruits and vegetables were healthier than processed foods.

Nevertheless, dried apricots and creeping didn't extend Hunt's life to one hundred. He died two years after our encounter at the age of eighty-five.

◆

Though he remains known primarily for his gargantuan oil discovery, the richest man in town was also the biggest gambler. After his winning bet on East Texas oil, Hunt never stopped gambling. He walked from his office to the Southland Hotel to roll craps, sometimes all night. He drove to Top O' Hill in Arlington, where food was free. He even played dominoes at the dodgy Redman Club with hitman R. D. Matthews.

Before World War II, Hunt devoted several floors of a downtown building he owned to a full-blown betting operation, with board boys posting horse race odds and results. Bookies were stationed at desks with phones to take bets. The police seemed not to notice.

When his bets grew too big for local bookies, Hunt turned to New York bookie Frank Erickson and his protégé Gil "the Brain" Beckley. During the 1960s, Hunt thought nothing of betting $50,000 on a single sports event. Some weeks he bet on every game in the Southwest Conference.

Dallas mayor Erik Jonsson occasionally played cards with Hunt at the Petroleum Club. Jonsson told local historian Darwin Payne that Hunt once fanned out a deck of cards on the table, looked at them for a minute, and handed the deck to Jonsson to keep overnight. Hunt called Jonsson the next day and named all the cards in order.

Although he had a phenomenal memory, Hunt might not have been as good a gambler as he thought. Palm Springs gambler Ray Ryan won $240,000 from him in a marathon gin rummy match. His granddaughter

Lyda Hill beat him at dominoes. And a handsome newcomer named Jack Kirksmith deliberately sought Hunt out at the Petroleum Club for card games, so he could win oil leases from him.

Though his gambling didn't make the news, his love life did. Scandal erupted when it was revealed Hunt had hidden two secret families for many years. His daughter Margaret sometimes worked as her father's assistant, so she was the first to discover the other families. Sensing trouble ahead, she suggested her amorous father create trusts for the children in his "first family" to protect their interests. As a result, when *Forbes* magazine published a new list of the wealthiest Americans in 1982, Hunt's first family dominated the list: Margaret was No. 4, Caroline was No. 5, Lamar was No. 8, Herbert was No. 9, and Bunker was No. 10.

Margaret Hunt Hill wasn't in the news as much as the others, and she preferred it that way. Her brothers Herbert and Bunker made headlines when they tried to corner the silver market. They lost over a billion dollars, but the family fortune survived. Their younger brother Lamar had better luck: He launched the Kansas City Chiefs, a pro tennis tour, and major league soccer. Margaret's shy younger sister Caroline Rose transformed the former home of a cotton millionaire into a five-star hotel. Under her careful hand, The Mansion Hotel became the flagship of a global luxury hotel company.

It was a remarkable group of siblings. Margaret and her husband, Al, an avid tennis player and skier, made shrewd investments in Colorado real estate. In the 1950s, they turned 1,300 acres of giant sandstone formations near Pike's Peak into the "Garden of the Gods," a popular tourist destination. Then they added a $15 million resort with tennis courts and golf courses.

The Hills' friend John Gillin served as the first president of the Garden of the Gods Club. When the resort opened, he brought top socialites like Nancy Ann Smith to Colorado for the festivities. And when the Hills' daughter Lyda made her debut, Gillin served as one of her escorts. So did John Higginbotham. They were veteran escorts; the family trusted them.

Unlike her father, Margaret Hunt Hill had become an accepted figure in Dallas society. As a bigamist, he wasn't welcome in the powerful Citizen's Council or the best country clubs. But society usually forgave family scandals after a generation—if the fortune was still intact. The Hunt fortune was still growing.

◇

When the thief broke into the Hills' home in 1964, he seemed oddly comfortable in the house. Police suspected he had been there before.

The Hills' older children, Lyda and Al Hill Jr., were away at college when they got the news about the burglary. According to Al Jr., his parents had recently added an office for Mrs. Hill in the master bedroom upstairs. The office balcony overlooked the pool area. As an afterthought, the Hills added a spiral staircase to the balcony so they could reach their bedroom from the backyard. This proved a mistake.

"Whoever the burglar was, he sat in a rocking chair on that balcony for quite a while," Al Jr. remembered. "He must have been smoking while he waited for them to turn the lights out, because he put several cigarettes out by his chair."

After the Hills fell asleep, the intruder slid open the door to the bedroom and tiptoed into the dressing area. In a departure from his pattern, he took some of Al Hill's expensive watches and cufflinks. Then he pulled out a jewelry drawer from Mrs. Hill's vanity table and carried it down a hall, walking by their daughter Alinda's bedroom. The teenager thought she heard a noise and threw her pillow on the floor, half-awake. The thief paused, then walked on.

Stepping softly down the stairs, he made his way to the breakfast room. He placed the drawer on the table, sat down, and sorted through the contents. If a piece didn't interest him, he discarded it on the table or left it in the drawer. The thief seemed to be looking for something in particular—and was in no rush to leave. It was as if Goldilocks dropped by and helped herself to the family jewels instead of porridge.

The thief was astonishingly bold. "He got one of the plastic cups we used around the pool and had a drink while he sorted through the jewels," Al Hill Jr. remembered.

When the Hills discovered the burglary the next morning, Margaret Hunt Hill was distraught. In addition to some of her favorite jewelry, the thief took a pearl necklace that her mother had bequeathed to her sister Caroline. Caroline had loaned the pearls to her for the social season. Now they were gone.

Mrs. Hill was only grateful that the thief did not find her engagement ring. Before she went to bed, she had placed the 12-carat diamond in a pink plastic container for cleaning jewelry. The ring was still inside when Margaret Hill rushed to look for it. She wondered, Was the thief searching for the big ring?

Her husband theorized the thief was paying off someone in the insurance business to get the appraised value of jewels and the addresses of owners. But the police could find no connection to insurance companies.

Much later, people would wonder, Why didn't the police test the DNA left on the water glass and cigarettes at the Hill house? If DNA samples had been taken, the police might have made a case against someone. Unfortunately, DNA analysis didn't exist at the time. DNA testing was not used in criminal cases in the US until 1987. By then, the Hill evidence had been thrown away.

At the time of the burglary, University Park police were stunned. What kind of burglar would smoke cigarettes a few feet from his victims? Who would sit at a table to sort through his spoils, knowing he could be discovered any minute?

In an unprecedented move for the suburb, Police Chief Forrest Keene distributed hundreds of wanted posters around the community. The posters promised a $1,000 reward for any information leading to the capture of "Dallas County's most wanted criminal—the master jewel burglar."

Yet he remained at large and at work.

38

Puzzling Behavior

A t times, the jewel thief seemed to be flaunting his prowess. He pried open windows that were painted shut. He jumped from the second floor of a house, diamond bracelet in hand, and sprinted past a startled paperboy. At another home, he climbed up a trellis in the patio.

When the thief discovered the master bedroom door was locked at one home, he didn't give up—he went outside, found a ladder, reached through the bedroom window, and grabbed the jewels from a box on top of a dresser.

The Varel burglary provided a textbook example of his skill, five years after the Graf burglary. Though the Dallas police were saying the thief wasn't active, he was.

That November evening, Barbara Varel regretted saying yes to a dinner at Evelyn Lambert's penthouse. Since the Varels were flying the next morning to their home in Paris, she had second thoughts about going out. It was cold and drizzly. But Mrs. Lambert had insisted they come.

The Varels were an artsy power couple. Barbara Varel supported the theater and the opera, while her husband, Dan, who was sixteen years older, supported what she wanted. Brown-eyed and honey-haired, Mrs. Varel had been on the covers of *Seventeen* and *Mademoiselle*. She grew into a savvy force on arts boards.

For his part, Dan Varel had a genius for inventing mechanical equipment. The Air Force purchased several of his inventions. When he moved to Dallas, he started a company that manufactured drill bits he designed. Within a decade, the company went from three to three hundred employees and was shipping drill bits worldwide.

One of his manufacturing plants was in France, so the Varels made Paris a second home. That fall, they were planning to stay at their Paris apartment until Christmas. But first, they had to go to the Lamberts' dinner.

The dinner conversation was lively, but the service seemed awfully slow. By the time the Varels got back to their house, it was after midnight. As Mrs. Varel headed up the stairs, she thought she heard the sound of a door closing, a click. It seemed to come from their bedroom.

She called down to her husband, "Honey, have you locked up?"

"I am now," he replied. "Be up in a minute."

"Good," she said, relieved.

She looked around the bedroom; nothing looked disturbed. On instinct, she opened her closet door to look inside, thinking the click came from that direction. Nothing seemed amiss, so she closed the door.

Mrs. Varel was looking forward to being in their Paris home because fall was so lovely there that time of year. Yet she did not sleep well. She half awoke around two A.M., then went back to sleep.

When she got out of bed in the morning, she noticed her closet door was wide open. *That's funny*, she thought. *I remember closing it.*

Unsettled, she went into her dressing room. The red travel bag she had packed with essentials to carry on the plane—her *"necessaire"* bag"—was gone. Some of her favorite jewels were inside.

A quick check showed jewelry also was missing from her dresser. In all, someone had stolen a diamond necklace, two diamond bracelets, a set of diamond earrings, several jeweled bracelets, a pair of pearl-and-diamond earrings, and a pearl necklace.

Her husband called the Highland Park police. Within minutes, Sgt. Henry Gardner arrived and searched the house. He found her red bag in a toolhouse out back. It was empty, and there were waffle footprints in the courtyard.

◈

Mrs. Varel immediately suspected Evelyn Lambert had something to do with the break-in. She thought Evelyn acted oddly that night and dragged the dinner out. Was she purposely stalling to give the thief time to hide inside? Barbara Varel thought so. She had observed Evelyn's behavior over the years. But she kept her thoughts to herself.

Sgt. Gardner thought the break-in had all the hallmarks of the King of Diamonds:

One, the thief had carefully planned the break-in. He knew the Varels were going out and their next-door neighbors would be gone. He smoked a pile of cigarettes while waiting in the house next door for the Varels to leave.

Two, the weather was bad, so he had worn his trademark galoshes.

Three, the thief pushed a wrought-iron patio chair up to a bathroom window that was high off the ground. With impressive dexterity, he squeezed through the small window and dropped silently to a toilet below.

Four, the thief was not heard by four children or their nanny.

Five, he was not interrupted by family dogs.

Six, the thief hid behind Mrs. Varel's clothes in the closet and waited for the couple to go to sleep. Then he took what he wanted and sneaked out, like clockwork.

When I talked with her years later, Barbara Varel said it had haunted her that the thief was in her closet while she changed into her nightgown and was asleep, totally vulnerable. "This was the traumatic thing—he was so close," she said, her voice growing tight with emotion even fifty years later.

Since then, she admitted, she hesitates before she reaches for her closet door at night.

◈

Fannin continued to downplay the burglaries to reporters. He told them the thief might be in prison somewhere else. He said the King's break-ins stopped the summer of 1963.

But in truth, the thefts had not stopped. The 1964 thefts at the homes of Barbara Varel and Margaret Hunt Hill fit the King's pattern to a T.

When reporters pressed him, Fannin shot back, "No jewel thief has a monopoly on overshoes and a screwdriver. They caught three in Beaumont—all wearing overshoes."

Fannin's frustration was understandable. He had been taking the heat about the jewel thief since the Graf burglary in 1959. He got constant needling. After someone stole his best jacket from the back seat of his wife's car, the local press wrote about it.

In 1965, when Los Angeles police arrested a career burglar with jewels from two Dallas break-ins, Fannin traveled to California to quiz him. "Why are you here?" the burglar taunted Fannin. "You should be back in Dallas, catching the King of Diamonds!"

Fannin had to bite his tongue. He knew why the case couldn't be closed, but he couldn't say it.

In exasperation, he told reporters the burglaries might never be solved. "I don't think I'm the only one who regrets not solving it," he said. "All of us dreamed about it. But it's a lot like the Kennedy assassination. None of us wanted that to happen, and we all wanted to solve it. It just won't ever be solved."

I understood that the way had been blocked in Highland Park, but it puzzled me that Fannin and McCaghren gave up without a fight. Why didn't they find another way to get evidence on Higginbotham?

I asked McCaghren why he didn't call in Higginbotham for questioning to see what they might learn. "You interviewed other socialites," I reminded. "Why not him?"

McCaghren stayed tight-lipped. He would only say, "Our hands were tied."

◆

Pressing the issue got more difficult as his health wavered. Sometimes, he would say in a hoarse voice, "Why don't you call me back next week." I worried I might lose my best source.

When McCaghren had surgery on a leg damaged in Korea, I took him some balloons to cheer him up. He had lost thirty pounds. He hated the physical therapy, so he told his doctor to just cut his leg off. "He said that would be worse—HAH!" he said. The pain was an ever-present reminder of his war experience. McCaghren had a tattoo on his arm that said, "Lest We Forget," but there was no way he could. Still, he was always courteous when I dropped by. "How's your book coming?" he would ask.

One day, I tried again. "After Highland Park vetoed a search, why didn't you find another way to look for the evidence? You looked in Jim Kirksmith's suitcase without a warrant. You put a video camera in Jasper's apartment without a warrant. Couldn't you find another way?"

After a pause, McCaghren admitted, "We could have." From his resigned tone, I could tell he had always known we might arrive at this moment.

"We could have gotten a search warrant from a Dallas County judge. It would have been good anywhere in the county—including Highland Park," he said. "Chief Naylor wouldn't have liked it. Once, when I was working with a task force on organized crime, we made the mistake of staking out a house in Highland Park without telling him. Naylor made a big fuss about it—a *big* fuss. He wouldn't like it, but we could have gotten a county warrant to look at the house. Justice of the Peace Bill Richburg used to leave us a stack of signed search warrants when he went on vacation. He'd say, 'Thought you boys might need these.' So, we had plenty of search warrants."

I couldn't believe what I was hearing. I asked again to make sure, "You mean you could have searched the house?"

"We could have," he said.

"But you *didn't*?"

"No."

"*Why* didn't you?"

"Politics," he said, with one of his sighs. "There was a lot of politics back then. People were afraid of trouble."

We sat in silence as I absorbed what this meant. McCaghren and Fannin had been told to back off.

I pressed McCaghren: *Who* put on the brakes?

He wouldn't say.

Was it Police Chief Jesse Curry?

No, it wasn't Curry.

City Manager Elgin Crull?

No, he said.

Fannin?

No, no, he shook his head. "Just politics."

He would say no more. I realized that McCaghren wasn't going to snitch on anyone. It wasn't part of his ethos. I noticed he didn't look at me when he responded, and pretended to flick something from his trouser leg.

Was this a masterful deflection? Or the truth? It was hard to tell. The traditional "blue wall of silence" meant the police kept their dirty linen private.

While the dead end was frustrating, I now understood why the biggest jewel theft case in Dallas history was never solved: higher-ups wanted to avoid a controversy.

Some people might call that a cover-up.

39

The Frito Bandito

The pressure on Fannin and McCaghren eased when the King seemed to disappear in 1967. The only jewel thief in the news that year was Jack "Murph the Surf" Murphy. New York police arrested him for stealing the "Star of India" and twenty-three other priceless gems from the American Museum of Natural History.

But the next year, the King of Diamonds reappeared. Maybe he needed money. Maybe he wanted to show he was still someone to be reckoned with. In October 1968, he broke into the home of Herman Lay, the founder of the Lay's Potato Chip empire. Lay had what he thought was a state-of-the-art alarm system. The King got away with $51,000 in jewels anyway.

When the burglary alert came in that Sunday morning, Detective Sgt. John Chism was on call. He hurried the twenty miles from his home in Irving to Lay's home. Chism knew who Herman Lay was. He'd enjoyed plenty of his chips.

As he drove up the long driveway, Chism marveled that the place looked like something out of *Gone with the Wind*. That was by design. When the Lays moved to Dallas from Atlanta in 1961, Amelia Lay wanted a house that resembled the antebellum mansions of the Deep South. So the Lays built a house on Radbrook Place with white columns across the front and oceans of flowers all around. The house was just across Bachman Creek from 9400 Rockbrook, the home designed by Frank Lloyd Wright for John Gillin.

When Chism pulled up to the Lay House, he saw a man walking toward the creek in back of the house. Chism assumed he was a yardman because he had on old tennis shoes and rumpled khakis with a hole in the knee. Chism walked over to ask if he had seen any footprints. The rumpled man was Herman Lay. And yes, he had found footprints. He showed Chism the waffle-sole tracks. They led from the creek to the house.

Lay told Chism he was surprised that the thief had singled them out. He said his wife didn't have much jewelry compared to people like Mrs. Murchison, who had diamonds "as big as golf balls."

The two walked around the house to find where the thief entered. They found a footprint on top of an air conditioner by a bathroom window. As he had before, the thief pried open the window and took some gems while leaving others.

But there was a surprising difference: in addition to choosing jewels from Mrs. Lay's dressing table, the thief took jewels from a safe. This was a departure—the King was not a safecracker. Could this be a different burglar with waffle-print shoes?

Several people were on the property at the time. The Lays' son Ward had a broken leg and had fallen asleep on a sofa. He said he didn't hear anything. A butler and his wife had a room above the garage, but they didn't hear anything, either.

Chism wanted to interview the butler and his wife, but Lay asked him not to. He explained his wife had always wanted a French butler and maid. The two were already upset about the burglary. "If they get offended and go back to France," Lay said, "I'll never hear the end of it."

Chism agreed with the condition that he get full access to everyone else. He liked Lay. He was a very wealthy man yet had a down-to-earth manner. He confided to Chism, "It's been five years since I've driven a car—and I have five of them."

Lay's success was one of the great American business stories. He had started his first business when he was ten, selling cups of Pepsi for a nickel in his front yard in South Carolina. The house was across the street from a ballpark, so Lay sold lots of Pepsi to thirsty fans. He opened a bank account, bought a bicycle for himself, and hired assistants to tend the stand.

Pretty soon, the ballpark invited young Lay to come inside and sell. His sales pitches showed a natural gift for marketing: "Hey, get your nicely roasted, nicely toasted California sun-dried, long-eared, double-jointed peanuts! Five a bag!"

Lay became one of the park's top salesmen. He left college early to start a career at Sunshine Biscuits, only to be fired during the Depression. In desperation, Lay wrote two hundred letters to prospective employers. He received one response. It was from a potato chip distributor in Georgia. Lay turned down the offer because he felt there was no future in little slices of potato. When he still didn't have a job a week later, Lay took the job and delivered bags of chips from his Model A Ford. He began to see a future in little slices of potato. He borrowed $100 and started a chip company in Atlanta. Five years later, Lay's potato chips were sold nationwide.

When H.W. Lay & Co. merged with the Frito Company in 1961, Herman Lay moved to Dallas to run the largest snack food company in the US. The underestimated chips became a global phenomenon with the tagline of "Betcha can't eat just one." And after Frito-Lay merged with PepsiCo in 1965, Lay's snack empire included Doritos, Cheetos, Tostitos, Ruffles, Pringles, Fritos, Sun Chips, Pita Chips, Pepsi, and more.

Resettled in Dallas, the Lays became known for their warmth and philanthropy. "Mimi" Lay was churchy and loved organ music, so they donated an organ for the new symphony hall. She also loved flowers, so they donated two acres of garden for the Dallas Arboretum. The Lays not only had money, they donated money.

Chism felt pretty sure the King of Diamonds was involved in their burglary, but the inclusion of the safe puzzled him. How did the thief know how to open it?

◈

Fifty years later, I tracked down the Lays' daughter Dorothy to see what she remembered. "I do remember it broke my mom's heart to have so many valuables taken," she said.

She recalled her mother thought at first the thief might be a woman in a group that met in her house the day before. I asked, was Evelyn Lambert in the group? "Why yes," she said. "They were best friends. Joe Lambert did their landscaping."

Who was her mother's hairstylist? Mr. Jack, she said. She went to his salon.

Did she know the Higginbotham family? "Yes, or I think my father did. There was a young man who hung around our house, doing errands and odds and ends."

Could his name have been Higginbotham? "Why yes, I think it might have been. Had brown hair . . . nice-looking. There was some relationship with my father, or maybe my brother. He would do my mom a favor and take me to a birthday party, things like that. I never questioned it enough to ask, 'Who is he?' He ran errands for Mom if Dad was out of town. I accepted him as a friend of the family."

When I mentioned the exchange to detective Chism, he told me that at the time of the break-in, he intentionally asked the Lays' twenty-three-year-old son Ward if he knew John Higginbotham. Yes, the son said, he knew Higginbotham from social circles.

Chism suspected Higginbotham was involved in the burglary, but after a few weeks, the trail went cold. The press took little notice of the theft. The King of Diamonds was yesterday's news.

The investigation lost more momentum when Walter Fannin was promoted to deputy chief. Fannin had been the skipper for the search; now he steered several departments. McCaghren also got a promotion to director of intelligence. He had his hands full tracking vice and homicide.

As a result, the hunt for the King of Diamonds fell to a few determined officers, like Sgt. John Chism.

And took a last, unexpected twist.

40

Sgt. Chism

After our talks about the Lay burglary, I met with Sgt. Chism several times. Chism looked like central casting's idea of a Texas cop: he wore gimme caps, drove a Ford truck, and was a little on the burly side from his days of enjoying chicken fried steaks. He was a good ol' boy in the best sense of the word—the kind of guy you would want around if you had a wreck on the highway or a gunman in the convenience store.

Chism spoke the way people in Texas used to talk before being homogenized by TV. He described a colleague as "the best thing since peanut butter" and a conman as "sweet as two donuts."

He grew up in Cooper, a small East Texas town called a "long taw" community because oxen and people stopped there in early days to rest on the way somewhere else. Chism's dad was a cotton farmer and rancher. When times got lean in the 1930s, and the local bank failed, his family moved to Dallas. His father found a job at Best Foods, which became famous for its mayonnaise when women no longer made their own. His mother went to work as a nurse.

Because of the Depression, money was always a concern. "I went into the Army so I could get more than one pair of shoes at a time," Chism said, only half joking.

A big, broad-shouldered guy, Chism played guard on his high school football team. As a result, when he joined the Army, he was assigned to the armored division's football team. Eventually, he was dispatched to the security police in West Germany, where he worked on criminal investigations. He began thinking police work might be a good career after the war, better than farming.

When a slot opened at the Dallas Police Department, Chism jumped at it. He was put on patrol in a neighborhood where fights over the jukebox or women were usually fatal. For the next few years, he earned his stripes investigating liquor store stickups, rapes, domestic violence, and shootings in bars.

When he was assigned to Fannin's squad, Chism was eager for the change. He'd heard about the King of Diamonds for years; now he could hunt him. He knew there was a suspect who was off-limits. But maybe he could avoid the political repercussions if he caught the thief in the act. Or maybe there might be a breakthrough on someone else.

One of Chism's first assignments gave him the chance to show Fannin he had the right stuff for the job. Someone had broken into the Orchid Shop, a boutique dress store owned by S. L. "Cash" Cashion. The store catered to women who could afford designer fashions—and men who could afford French lingerie for their mistresses.

In the 1960s, the shop became infamous for selling "topless" swimsuits by Austrian designer Rudi Gernreich. Though the suits were generating excitement in the fashion world, Neiman Marcus had turned down the risqué bathing gear.

That meant Cash Cashion's little store on Oak Lawn Avenue got an exclusive opportunity. With a name like "Cash," you can be sure he made the most of it.

He put a mannequin in the window wearing a fire-engine-red bottom with no top. The bare-breasted dummy stopped traffic. And brought pickets with signs saying, In the name of Christ, NO! A local minister complained to the press that the suits were a "trend toward further moral decay."

Police Chief Curry announced his men would arrest anyone wearing the X-rated suits in public. But the brouhaha died down quickly after the store sold out of suits in one day, even the red suit on the mannequin.

Cashion got a lot of publicity and bawdy jokes out of the episode, but it was no laughing matter when someone broke into the store and walked off with several racks of clothes. On top of that, a burglar broke into his home the same week and stole his wife's jewels. Cashion was irate. He called Capt. Fannin, an old friend, and demanded, "Do something! Catch the damn crooks!" Cashion had owned a bar called the Spindletop, and like most men who have been kings in their own realm, he was used to having his demands obeyed.

Fannin was in a bind. Cashion's wife, who ran the Orchid Shop, was a close friend. She gave him good deals on lingerie for his wife. Fannin called Sgt. Chism into his office and told him not to come back until he found the thieves. "This is your case," he said, "and I don't want to see you until you clear it up."

Chism stayed away from the office for several weeks. Working from his car, he tracked down the stolen gems at a pawnshop and found the clothes at a resale shop.

Fannin was happy. Chism got to come back to the office—and the search for the jewel thief.

Chism knew more about the jewelry trade than most detectives because his in-laws were in the jewelry business. Plus, he had taken gemology courses in college. He knew what to look for.

A burglary that fit the King's pattern came along soon. A thief broke into a ranch-style home on Strait Lane, the "Millionaires' Row" of houses where teenager Marvin Moore had come face-to-face with the thief.

According to Chism, a married couple had been to a party at the home of Clint Murchison Jr. After an evening of drinks and talk, the couple came home and went to bed. Before they fell asleep, they had sex.

The next morning, the husband walked out the sliding glass door in the bedroom to have a cigarette on the patio, which overlooked a creek. After a few puffs, it dawned on him that the patio door had been *closed* when they went to bed. He asked his wife, "Did you open the patio door?"

"No," she said. "Why would I?"

A check of the house showed their walk-in closet had been disturbed. And some of her jewelry was gone.

The couple suspected the thief was hiding in the closet when they came home. That meant he eavesdropped on their sex play, then sneaked out when they fell sleep.

The two were concerned about the loss of the jewels, Chism remembered, but they were more concerned that the burglary might be reported in the newspapers. They didn't want their friends to find out the thief listened while they were having sex. They would be teased mercilessly. Please, they beseeched the police, keep quiet about the incident. And they did.

When I asked the name of the homeowner, Chism said he didn't remember, although his memory usually was better than most of the policemen in their eighties. I put the thought aside for the moment. Many months later, I discovered that Clint Murchison Jr.'s right-hand man and party companion—Robert F. Thompson—lived at 10010 Strait Lane. In fact, Thompson's construction company built the house along with several other houses in the area.

I called Chism: Was the man on Strait Lane tall and balding?

Yes.

Could his name have been Bob Thompson?

Maybe. Sounds right. I'll check.

Though he was retired and lived some distance away, Chism drove in from his home in Irving. He went up and down Strait Lane looking for the house that fit his memory—and found it, a ranch-style home with a pool and creek in back, close to Walnut Hill Lane. It was the Thompson house.

Thompson's name had come up frequently in my interviews. He had served with Senator Joe McCarthy during World War II, and they looked so much alike they were often mistaken for each other. After the war, Thompson got a job with the Murchison companies through a family connection. He was happy to introduce his old war buddy, now a Wisconsin senator, to his rich boss. Soon, Murchison was supporting McCarthy—and McCarthy was supporting the depletion allowance.

By the time of the break-ins, Bob Thompson was executive vice president of Tecon, the Murchison construction company. But his portfolio was much deeper, like a trunk with a false bottom. All manner of things were concealed beneath the cover.

◈

When Thompson first joined the Murchison companies, Clint Sr. put Thompson and Clint Jr. in charge of building houses out of cement to provide affordable housing for veterans. Despite the need, no one wanted the houses. They were ugly. Besides that, Thompson and Murchison spent more time doing the town than checking city regulations. Roads for the houses had to be torn up and repaved.

Clint Jr. recovered by taking a page from his father's playbook—he bought another construction company, then leveraged that company's assets to buy another. Pretty soon, Clint Jr. and his friend Bob were running a major construction firm.

They made a good team. While Clint Jr. was introverted, people said Bob Thompson could talk "partridges out of a mesquite tree." He smoothed the way for Murchison projects around the world and painted the town with his boss along the way.

As a core member of the "Rover Boys" party crowd, Thompson joined Clint Jr. and Bedford Wynne in their late-night revels with friends like Gordon McLendon. They consumed women and drinks with abandon.

Thompson was a big man, so he could drink prodigious amounts, but when he had too much, friends said, it was wise not to poke the bear.

He courted famous people like actor John Wayne and liked to show off his connections. Sometimes, Thompson would pick up the phone and dial Hollywood stars to impress people. "Want to talk to Elizabeth Taylor?" he would say and hand the phone to an astounded friend.

With his receding hairline, Thompson didn't look much like a ladies' man, but he had a Marine machismo that gave him a rugged appeal. One contemporary compared him to former Senator Fred Thompson, gruff but attractive. Women and men were impressed by his take-charge confidence.

A singer at the Cipango Club recalled seeing Bob Thompson come in with some friends one night. From the bandstand, she caught sight of a small flight bag that he had placed on the chair next to him. She thought it odd that Thompson would bring the airline bag with him into the club. Later in the evening, he invited her and her husband to come to an after-hours party at a hotel not far away. When they entered the hotel room, she noticed the same airline bag sitting on a bed.

There was lots of drinking, she recalled, and the crowd included some women with bright red nail polish and visible cleavage who would not be mistaken for Garden Club members. One of the women opened the flight bag and discovered it was stuffed with cash. She began pulling out wads of bills and throwing the money into the air. Pretty soon, money was flying all over the hotel room.

At that moment, Thompson received a phone call from Clint Jr. He listened, nodded his head, and said, "I'll be right there." After he hung up, Thompson told the people in the room, "Clint said to bring the money. He wants it right now." They scrambled to pick up the money and put it back in the bag.

Where did the money come from? What was it for?

Thompson wouldn't say.

♦

The burglary at Thompsons' house was a fitting bookend to the break-in at Clint Murchison Sr.'s home in 1961. The Murchison burglary had opened my eyes to ties between Dallas gambling and organized crime. The Thompson burglary provided the rest of the story—Dallas ties to corrupt politicians.

Besides serving as the wingman on late-night prowls, Bob Thompson functioned as the consigliere in many Murchison business affairs. He was the go-between. For example, Thompson was the link to union leader Jimmy Hoffa, who kicked in millions from Teamsters pension funds for Murchison projects. Thompson became so close to Hoffa that when the union leader's daughter got married in 1961, Thompson and his family were invited to the wedding.

When Thompson celebrated his birthday the next year in Washington, D.C., it drew press attention. President Kennedy and Lyndon Johnson attended, along with seven cabinet members, some 30 senators, and 200 other VIPs.

Less publicly, when the Murchisons needed political favors, who treated powerful figures to a rowdy night on the town? Bob Thompson. In particular, Thompson made it his business to befriend Lyndon Johnson's special assistant Bobby Baker. Baker acknowledged in his autobiography that he often went "helling" with Thompson and Thomas D. Webb Jr., a former Hoover assistant who became a lobbyist for the Murchisons.

Then in 1964, a scandal erupted about Bobby Baker's side deals. His stake in the notorious Quorum Club set off the alarms. Located in the Carroll Arms Hotel, the club was a two-minute walk from the Capitol. It had the reputation as a convenient place for lawmakers to enjoy a drink with a lobbyist or a dalliance with an attractive woman—without missing a vote. Murchison's team found the club useful.

One of the most alluring waitresses became infamous: Ellen Rometsch. News accounts say she looked like Elizabeth Taylor, but may have been an East German spy. Some of President Kennedy's pals arranged for him to meet Rometsch. The introduction became a series of trysts. After word leaked that the president was fooling around with a Soviet sexpot, Rometsch was put on a plane back to East Germany.

When the scandal hit the headlines, Congress started asking questions about Bobby Baker—and friends like Bob Thompson. The Senate Rules

Committee launched an investigation into Baker's use of the Quorum Club to entertain members of Congress.

Was Baker arranging sex for lawmakers to get their votes?

It certainly seemed so.

Senate members also suspected Baker was steering government contracts to wealthy donors like the Murchisons in return for payoffs. They noticed that Thompson arranged for Baker to profit from stock in an insurance company without investing money of his own. Thompson testified that he got a $300,000 loan for Baker to buy the stock with one call to Dallas bank president Robert Stewart. "That's the way we do business in Texas," Thompson boasted.

The Senate committee also asked Thompson about his connection to the Carousel Motel in Maryland, which Baker owned. The motel reportedly was used as a rendezvous for high-priced call girls and politicians. When the Carousel got into financial trouble, Bob Thompson offered to buy it for $1.5 million to help Baker out. Just doing a favor for a friend, Thompson testified.

Baker eventually was convicted of tax evasion and fraud. When he wrote a memoir about his wheeling and dealing days, Baker dedicated the book to his new friends in prison—and his old friend Bob Thompson.

The Baker scandals weren't the only times Thompson skated away from trouble. There were several more congressional inquiries into Murchison contracts. One of the inquiries exposed a deal in Haiti that literally smelled.

You see, American money was pouring into Haiti to keep the country from turning communist. US companies were jumping at the chance to establish factories on the island because labor was cheap. But it was risky business. Haiti had become one of the most corrupt countries in the world.

Dictator Francis "Papa Doc" Duvalier was holding on to power with the help of Tonton Macoute enforcers who used their machetes to reduce opposition, a hand at a time. People and money disappeared with disturbing regularity. Add drugs and voodoo to the gumbo, and you have what writer Graham Greene called a "nightmare Republic."

This did not deter Clint Jr., who established a flour mill and cattle ranch in Haiti. According to the US ambassador at the time, Roy Davis, Murchison paid $200,000 to $250,000 in graft to obtain the right to build the flour mill. Haitian leaders got stock in the company while Murchison got a monopoly on the flour market. Thanks to connections, his Caribbean Mills got surplus American wheat at a low price and ground it into coarse gray flour that was sold at a high price.

Since the Murchisons had large cattle herds on the island, it made sense to add a meat-packing plant. They called it the Haitian-American Meat and Provision Company (HAMPCO). The key players included Clint Jr. and Bob Thompson. The other partners were a stained crew: Washington operative I. I. Davidson, LBJ aide Bobby Baker, and Las Vegas gambling power Ed Levinson.

With a crime figure like Levinson involved, this clearly was not a humanitarian mission. And when Russian Georges de Mohrenschildt showed up in Haiti, too, it confirmed nothing good was afoot.

The HAMPCO deal turned out to be especially foul business. Sanitary conditions were so bad that the plant had to be shut down several times. Haitians wouldn't buy the spoiled HAMPCO meat. Latin American countries refused shipments. The US wouldn't accept the rancid products either.

Baker used his White House clout to get a permit to export the HAMPCO meat to Puerto Rico, where it could be shipped into the US. Fix-it man I. I. Davidson and lobbyist Thomas Webb then arranged to sell the meat to a "friendly" wholesaler in Chicago.

To disguise its poor quality, the meat was ground up and sold to unwitting consumers as sausage, frankfurters, bologna, and hamburger.

Documents showed that Clint Jr. and Bob Thompson approved the meat deal.

So perhaps it's not surprising that Bob Thompson wanted to keep it quiet when the King of Diamonds invaded his personal territory. He didn't want scrutiny. While he looked like just another balding, middle-aged guy in the construction business, Thompson had a hand in some very dubious doings.

◆

Such were the undercurrents in the King of Diamonds story:

Political corruption and graft.

Sports corruption and illegal gambling.

Prostitution and sex trafficking.

Organized crime.

They flowed below the surface of the jewel thefts like a dark river below ice.

Many a night I stayed awake, pondering what I had learned about the hidden side of Dallas and wondering, Who were the real thieves in the story?

41

The Surprise Twist

After seven years of research, my list of burglaries showed the King of Diamonds stole the equivalent of $6 million in jewels today.

The police had stopped updating their spreadsheet in 1963 after forty burglaries. I had found twice as many thanks to some shoe leather, the internet, and interviews.

I was wrapping up my research when a new twist turned up.

Actually, it was more like a whiplash.

At one of our lunches, Sgt. Chism mentioned something that had puzzled him. He liked to meet at a place called Wonderful World of Cooking. I could see why: The restaurant served chicken fried steaks with cream gravy and homemade pie. The coffee mugs were refilled every few minutes by waitresses who treated Chism like an old friend ("More coffee, hon?").

Trying to watch his weight, Chism always ordered salads, but he couldn't help glancing at the enchiladas on the next table. As he pecked at his salad, he mentioned he and Sgt. Charlie Dellinger resumed their surveillance of Higginbotham in the late 1960s.

"I thought the top brass wanted you to back off," I said.

"Well, we didn't have to tell them everything," he said.

Chism explained that he and Dellinger had cultivated sources in the gay community who gave them a new lead. They said some guys from Highland Park were stealing stuff—including jewels.

For months, Chism and Dellinger staked out the bars that Higginbotham and his friends frequented in the Oak Lawn area. As they peered through the smoky haze, they noticed that Higginbotham's group often included Jasper Kirksmith.

This surprised them. Why did Jasper spent so much time with Higginbotham's crowd? Was Jasper gay? Or working with Higginbotham?

Although Fannin and McCaghren had suspected Kirksmith and Higginbotham individually, they had not connected the two.

Like they say on TV, this sent the investigation in a whole new direction. Could Jasper Kirksmith and John Higginbotham have partnered in some of the jewel thefts?

Yes.

When I looked into the possibility, I discovered the two had been close for a long time.

- *They attended the same parties.* Newspaper accounts show their names at the same debutante events from the late 1940s to the 1960s. They would have seen each other regularly.
- *They also attended racy pool parties together.* In the late fifties, Higginbotham went with Jasper to private parties at a North Dallas home. According to witnesses, the other participants included Jasper's brother Jack, who gambled heavily with the host, and Russian Georges de Mohrenschildt, who came to play tennis and prey on women. Even Jack Ruby, who provided women for the host, showed up at times.
- *Higginbotham also lived with Jasper.* After his father remarried, Higginbotham moved into Netta Kirksmith's house at 4521 Edmondson. Then he bought a house down the block at 4544 Edmondson.

- *Higginbotham later bought Netta Kirksmith's home.* Because his house was being demolished to make way for a tollway, Higginbotham bought Netta's house after she died. Jasper arranged the sale.
- *Higginbotham and Jasper associated with sinister characters.* According to one of Higginbotham's dates, he met with Jasper and a menacing group of men at John Gillin's home. They seemed to know each other.

John Gillin was a wild card in the story. Very early in my research, a long-time friend mentioned that his father was convinced that Gillin was the jewel thief. His father was in a position to know: he was the top financial executive at Gillin's company and close to the Gillin family. He saw and heard things that made him suspicious.

At the time, I put the thought aside because Gillin didn't fit the thief's profile. At six feet four, he seemed too tall to squeeze through tight places and hide in closets. As time went by and Gillin's name kept coming up, I began looking online for mentions of him in FBI documents. And there he was: in 1961 and 1962, the FBI listed John Alexander Gillin as a jewel thief suspect. In fact, the FBI categorized both Gillin and Jasper Kirksmith as "TJT"—Top Jewel Thieves. The feds believed they were transporting stolen jewels across state lines.

This was an ah-ha moment. Fannin had pegged it right when he said one person probably started the signature thefts, then others got involved. It looked increasingly likely that John Higginbotham started the signature burglaries by stealing jewels he coveted—then Jasper Kirksmith and John Gillin got in on the act, for profit or kicks, or both.

Sgt. Chism began to suspect the same thing as he watched Higginbotham and Jasper in Oak Lawn bars.

At long last, a Sherlockian solution seemed at hand, a solution based on obser-vation and deduction, like the Holmes cases. I tested the new hypothesis:

How did Jasper and John Gillin fit in?

Both could have scouted targets. Jasper knew wealthy families in Fort Worth and Dallas from his deb escort days. Gillin moved in social circles and did business with oil families. Five of the burglary victims lived close to Gillin's house.

When necessary, Jasper could have driven a getaway car. A car resem-bling his mother's cream-colored car was spotted a few blocks from the Sam Wallace burglary. Police chased the car at high speed, but lost it.

Jasper also could have fenced jewels that Higginbotham didn't want to keep. He gambled with pawnshop owner Arthur Bishop and had connec-tions to criminal circles in Florida as well as Las Vegas.

Could Jasper have pulled off some jewel thefts on his own?

Yes. Though he was too big to have crawled through windows, Jasper knew how to pry open doors and could have simply walked into some homes. He lived at the Crest Park apartments in the 1950s when doors were forced open and jewels stolen. The thefts stopped after he moved out. Jasper also was registered at several Dallas hotels when jewel thefts took place. The possibility also remains that Jasper and some rough friends were involved in the violent burglaries later on that didn't fit the King's classic pattern.

Why would John Gillin get involved?

Gillin didn't need money, but he was dependent on Jasper Kirksmith to bring women and excitement into his life. In the fall of 1961, the company that Gillin founded, National Geophysical, changed direction and he stepped down as president. That meant Gillin had more time on his hands. The FBI suspected Gillin transported jewels out of state; he could have done so on business trips without arousing suspicion.

◆

Sgt. Chism kept an eye on Higginbotham and Jasper through the late 1960s. Chism could see that Jasper's excesses were catching up with him.

He was ticketed for driving while intoxicated multiple times and arrested for possession of marijuana.

Police also arrested Jasper for shoplifting a can of tuna fish late one night at a grocery store in Oak Lawn. Another night, police picked him up for stealing coins from a newspaper rack. It was penny ante stuff, signs of a life out of control.

"I think he was probably drinking or high both times," Chism said.

When he wasn't running rigged card games or living off women, Jasper made money by selling fake prescriptions for drugs. His friends called him "Dr. Kirksmith." He swiped blank prescription pads from a society doctor, then sold them to students, party girls, and pals. If marijuana or cocaine were needed for Gillin's bacchanals, Jasper knew where to get it.

Chism brought Jasper Kirksmith in for questioning several times in 1968 and 1969.

"He was gabby, *real* gabby," Chism remembered until he challenged Kirksmith about specific jewel thefts.

"He said, 'Prove it!'" Chism remembered. "He didn't say he didn't do it. He just said, 'Prove it!'"

The police still couldn't prove it, but they felt sure he and Higginbotham were involved.

And that's exactly when the King made his last appearance.

On New Year's Day 1970, the King of Diamonds sang his swan song.

For the second time, he broke into the Park Lane home of Murchison oil executive Frank Schultz. In the first burglary, the thief took $9,000 in jewels in the wee hours of New Year's Day in 1963. Exactly seven years later, someone using the same method got away with $60,000 in jewelry.

"It was like reading the same report over again," remarked Sgt. Behringer.

Both times, the thefts occurred after the couple returned home from a New Year's Eve party. The thief pocketed some jewels and left some. No one in the family heard or saw anything. Their dog didn't bark.

After the second burglary, police found a trail of overshoe prints outside the house. The thief apparently went from window to window, peering in to watch members of the family who didn't go out that night. The Schultzes returned about one A.M. When Mrs. Schultz awoke, she noticed the door to her dressing room was closed. She usually left it open. Then she discovered the jewelry that she had worn was missing, a ring and bracelet valued at $25,000 each and a $10,000 jeweled clip.

It was the last known appearance of the King of Diamonds.

His distinctive burglaries stopped.

People were left to wonder what happened. Had the King died? Moved away? Retired?

Detective Chism believed the King knew the Dallas police were watching him—and his friends—very intensely. "Maybe he thought we were close enough to be afraid of getting caught," Chism said. "He didn't want to go to prison."

McCaghren suggested the same thing: "He knew that we knew who he was."

After the final burglary in 1970, people continued to speculate about possible suspects—a caterer, an architect, the maître d' at a posh restaurant.

Yet nothing significant surfaced to tie anyone besides John Higginbotham and Jasper Kirksmith to the jewel thefts. Nothing.

The path always led back to them. They remained the most plausible suspects.

Perhaps there was something I missed. Or got wrong. Could it have been one of the others in the Clue game? That's possible. But after six years of following every possible lead, I came to believe that John Higginbotham started the thefts, then fell in with Jasper Kirksmith and, to some extent, John Gillin.

You may disagree.

But if they didn't steal the jewels, *who did*?

Epilogue

By the end of the King of Diamonds era in 1970, the culture that shaped the jewel thefts had changed dramatically.

In one decade, the country had gone from Mamie Eisenhower with her square-cut bangs to Mary Tyler Moore, who wore pantsuits and had a career of her own. Patti Page and the prep school fashions of the fifties were out—bikinis, bell-bottom jeans, and the Rolling Stones were in. By 1970, the gay liberation movement had been launched and Neil Armstrong walked on the moon.

When the jewel thefts slowed to a stop, anxiety about the King of Diamonds died down. People moved on with their lives.

❖

John Higginbotham Jr. found a career apart from his family's hardware and lumber business—real estate. He and his friend Harrell Harrison built several motels in West Texas and the Wayfarer Inn in East Dallas. Buoyed by that success, Higginbotham developed some small shopping strips and bought houses in Highland Park and Oak Lawn to remodel.

However, with his expensive tastes, Higginbotham tended to spend more than he made. When the economy collapsed in the 1980s, Higginbotham lost most of his properties. He started over with a landscaping business and introduced innovations like "pleached" trees that were sculpted into shape. When commissions became fewer, Higginbotham got by with a lawn care service. Society friends looked the other way when they saw him driving through his old neighborhood with his lawnmower crews.

As time went on, Higginbotham drifted away from his society friends and they drifted away from him. Most got married and had families, while he surrounded himself with younger men. He became more flamboyant about his sexuality.

Though his resources dwindled, Higginbotham managed to entertain with style from time to time. His houses overflowed with beautiful objects and rare plants that he collected. A friend recalled that Higginbotham had a way of showing how to appreciate beautiful things. "He would point to a stunning flower and say, '*Look* at that *color*! Have you ever seen a flower this color?' Or he would make you smell something two or three times and say, 'Isn't that *unbelievable*?'"

Higginbotham's menagerie of snakes grew—he had albino snakes and poisonous blue mambas as well as boa constrictors. He kept them in stacks of boxes, like spice boxes, only bigger. To feed the snakes, he defrosted rats and mice that he stored in a freezer.

He also kept canaries in the house, so when visitors entered, they heard birds chirping. In a way, Higginbotham had gathered a new family around him. Over the years, he kept two Doberman pinschers, some Jack Russell terriers, peacocks, golden pheasants, orange-footed African ducks, and dozens of roller pigeons. The ducks had their wings broken or clipped so they could only fly in circles. The roller pigeons got their name from their ability to rise a hundred feet in the air, dive toward the ground, and soar back up. Friends said Higginbotham liked to go out in the afternoon, release the roller pigeons from their cages and fly them. Then he would let the African ducks out. Soaring, flapping birds filled the sky in an aerial rodeo that was mesmerizing to watch. When the performance was over,

Higginbotham herded the birds back into their coops with two bamboo poles. He was the master of his own odd world.

Even at middle age, friends said, Higginbotham tended his domain in shorts and flip-flops, with a thin brown cigarette dangling from his lips. When he built a house on Midway Road, he imported stone from Mexico for arches across the front, giving the house a hacienda look. An array of palm trees ringed the house. A neighbor told me that when temperatures dropped steeply one winter, Higginbotham rushed out to buy all the electric blankets he could find, then wrapped the blankets around the tree trunks, and plugged them in. The palms survived. The image stayed with me of a man out in the cold wrapping blankets around his trees to keep them warm.

When his funds got short, Higginbotham sold the house on Midway and moved to a less expensive neighborhood. His new house on Betty Jane Lane was modern and had lots of glass, a friend recalled, plus a large greenhouse in the back. Once again, Hollywood photos and memorabilia were juxtaposed on the walls with animal trophies and art. His houses were all like overstuffed cabinets of curiosities, people said, yet he made the miscellany look sophisticated.

I asked several of his friends if Higginbotham ever talked about his family problems. Did he mention his mother's suicide? His sister's mental problems? No, they said, he kept the past to himself. Did he ever mention the rumors that he was a jewel thief? "No." Not even for a laugh? "No." Instead, he focused on the unusual and beautiful things he gathered around him, his life's work.

When he was in his sixties, Higginbotham called a former deb he had dated. He said he wanted to talk to her. When he came to her house, he said he wanted to write a book about how to win the lottery and asked for her help. She assumed he was looking for a way to make money, but explained she couldn't help. She had written five books, but they were novels. They chatted a bit, then he left.

Higginbotham worked out to stay in shape, friends said, but had a heart condition that eventually required a pacemaker. While he was recovering from surgery, his friend Kevin Fox came to his house to take him to a movie. Higginbotham didn't feel well, so Fox drove him to the nearest emergency room. Higginbotham died of heart failure shortly after they arrived. He was sixty-nine.

Relatives said family members divided up or sold everything in his house, the antiques, the art. Did that include the jewels he collected? No one seemed to know. His birds were given to an avian society and the snakes to a herpetology society. Per his wishes, Higginbotham was buried next to his sister Rose Nelle, in the shade of a large oak tree.

In contrast to the days when he was featured regularly in society coverage, I could find no obituary for John T. Higginbotham Jr., not even a few lines in the back of the newspaper. In the end, he kept his secrets to himself.

◆

After Jim Kirksmith's death, the remaining Kirksmith brothers struggled with their own demons. When he was fifty-six, gigolo-playboy-pimp **Jasper Kirksmith** married a woman who was nineteen years younger. Relatives said she was pretty and worked as a hostess at hotel lounges and restaurants. The police believed that Jasper lived off her income, rigged card games—and stolen jewels.

His wife lived with his excesses for many years before divorcing him. Four years later, Jasper Kirksmith killed himself at her home. As a belated courtesy, he climbed into the bathtub before he shot himself, to reduce the mess. He was seventy-eight.

There was one last, tantalizing wrinkle to Jasper's story. I had filed a Freedom of Information request with the CIA to see if the agency had any records on him, since the FBI had destroyed theirs. For months, I waited for a reply, then forgot about it. A year and a half later, I received a strangely worded response. It said any public records on Kirksmith had been released—and any private records were classified.

When I mentioned this to McCaghren, he guessed right away, "He was probably an informant." That seemed possible. Jasper made money as a pimp, jewel thief, and crooked gambler, so ratting on his colleagues would have been in character. But which ones? Dallas hoodlums? Las Vegas mobsters? Florida traffickers?

I may have gotten a clue when McCaghren called to tell me something he had forgotten. In the late 1960s, the FBI contacted him. The feds asked him to put the Zuroma Club on Skillman Avenue under surveillance. The members included known figures of La Cosa Nostra. The FBI thought some members were fencing jewels and Jasper was involved.

Specifically, the FBI suspected Jasper was still in cahoots with Joseph Merola, a Cuban jewel thief and gun trafficker linked to Florida hotel thefts. Merola was close to the Mannarino crime family in Pennsylvania, which had owned casinos in Cuba. To protect himself, Merola snitched on other crooks to the FBI, the DEA, and the CIA. Sometimes he claimed he worked for the CIA. He was a tricky operator, so brazen he stole guns from a National Guard armory. Merola reportedly kept a speedboat docked at the Garden of Allah Hotel in Miami Beach, ready to move contraband of all kinds. Now the FBI had reason to believe he was moving stolen jewels through Dallas—with Jasper's help.

McCaghren's men watched the comings and goings at the Zuroma Club for a month. They recorded the license plate numbers of everyone who entered, then ran criminal checks on them. Besides local Mafia leader Joseph Civello, the guys playing cards included a mobster from Chicago who had a record for jewel theft. Another had Mafia ties and owned several bars and restaurants on Greenville Avenue where jewels were known to be fenced.

Yet the FBI investigation seemed to stop there. Did the FBI—or CIA—shield Jasper from charges in return for information?

As McCaghren often said, I wouldn't be surprised.

The youngest Kirksmith brother, **Jack Kirksmith**, left Dallas in 1963. Behind on his house payments, Kirksmith moved to Corpus Christi to try the oil business there. Charming but unlucky, Jack struggled with the ups and downs of the oil business—and other risky business—for the rest of his life. When he was summoned to testify before a grand jury, he bragged to friends that he talked his way out of trouble.

Could the fox-like brother have been involved after all? In 1963, just before Jack Kirksmith left town with his family, police received a curious call. Just before dawn, a man driving a beige-gold station wagon like Jack's family car was seen driving repeatedly by a house on Gaywood. The owners were out of town, but a house-sitter noticed the car. She called police to report the man walked onto the porch and began looking in windows before she asked through the intercom what he was doing. He left hurriedly and drove off. A coincidence? Or a clue?

In the 1980s, Jack Kirksmith worked on oil leases for a North Texas banker who was later indicted on ten counts of conspiracy and banking fraud. The banker went to jail, while Kirksmith hunkered down at his small farm in North Texas. In his last years, he struggled with the ravages of a lifetime of heavy drinking and died at the age of eighty-one, the last of the ill-starred Kirksmith brothers.

◆

Like his pal Jasper, **John Gillin** married late in life. He was fifty-seven when he fell for a woman thirty-one years younger who was a former beauty pageant winner and worked as a hairdresser. Because of her interest in art, he paid for her to attend Parsons School of Design in New York and take classes at Columbia University. Tongues wagged that he wanted to gloss up her background for their wedding announcement. Still, she was personable and was soon playing tennis at the Dallas Country Club.

When they moved to Beverly Hills, Dorothy Gillin drove Dallas visitors to see movie stars' homes in her Rolls-Royce. Gillin died there in 1975 after a heart attack. He was sixty-four.

◆

Paul McCaghren and **Walter Fannin** had dramatically different finales to their careers.

McCaghren remained a controversial figure in the Dallas Police. He had a knack for ruffling feathers, especially when they needed to be ruffled. At thirty-four, he became the youngest captain in the department. Many in police ranks hoped McCaghren would become chief. Instead, he was passed over in 1970 for Frank Dyson, who promised to modernize and reform the department. Dyson extended a peace offering by making McCaghren the head of intelligence and vice operations. He even gave McCaghren an office a few doors from his own, a privileged position.

Yet McCaghren made headlines more often than Dyson. In the spring of 1971, he okayed a raid on Lee Park, which had once been a popular site for sock hops and graduation parties. The park had deteriorated into a hangout for hippies and runaways. There was open drug use and sex on the front lawn. Several murders occurred.

McCaghren's officers cleared the park. Hopped-up hippies were hauled away as TV cameras recorded the melee. Hundreds of arrests resulted, including a few outraged neighbors who were just out for a walk. McCaghren was pilloried in the press by defense attorneys who claimed the raid violated the civil rights of people in the park. Afterward, Lee Park became a safer place, but McCaghren paid a price with Chief Dyson, who was incensed that he learned about the raid on the evening news.

McCaghren was back in the news later that year when he contended in a widely publicized speech that organized crime was costing Dallas "more money than all the burglaries, robberies, and thefts combined." He warned that small bets made at service stations, barber shops, or grocery stores found their way up the organized crime ladder, and the consequences were serious. Five "mob killings" had taken place in the last five months, he reported, one involving a power struggle over the heroin market. It was getting harder to stem the influx of organized crime, he said, because criminal elements were investing in "legitimate fronts" to hide their activities. City leaders, who tended to downplay organized crime, dismissed his talk as publicity-seeking.

McCaghren rattled the status quo again in early 1972 when he helped expose the head of the crime commission as a fraud. John McKee had turned his role at the commission into a stage for himself. He pounded podiums and raised alarms about crime and communism, stabbing the air with his cigar for emphasis.

Reporter George Carter discovered McKee was a fraud, but his editors at the *Times Herald* spiked the story to avoid angering powerful figures on the crime commission. *Newsweek* reporter Hugh Aynesworth took up the story but had trouble getting McKee's fingerprints to check his records. McCaghren agreed to help. Although McKee was his mentor in the Masonic order, he felt duty-bound to see if McKee was hiding something. McCaghren tricked McKee by handing him a piece of paper to read, then had the fingerprints traced. The results showed McKee was a Navy deserter—and a thief. What's more, he had been embezzling money from a children's hospital and the Masonic order while leading the crime commission. He was a crook.

Yet when the story came out, McKee's defenders blasted McCaghren for making the city look bad. They claimed McKee had done more good than harm.

McCaghren became persona non grata in his Masonic lodge. He shrugged and moved on.

Rather than lower his profile for a while, McCaghren began pushing for a federal investigation of organized crime in Dallas. The Justice Department was considering a strike force in either Dallas or Houston to probe sports betting. Secret meetings with Justice Department lawyers were held before dawn in an undisclosed hotel in Dallas.

Reporters found out about the hush-hush meetings and asked McCaghren point-blank if he had asked for the strike force. McCaghren replied, "We didn't ask, we *pleaded* for them to come to Dallas."

However, the feds didn't choose Dallas. They went to Houston. District Attorney Henry Wade had supported the strike force in public and acknowledged that the huge volume of betting in the city would not be possible without organized crime. Privately, he disparaged McCaghren and the DPD to the feds.

Was Wade's opposition a case of one alpha male outmaneuvering another? Or did Wade have some grounds for his criticism? Whatever the reason, the chance for a major probe of organized crime in Dallas went south.

With every new controversy, McCaghren's political capital shrank. Eighteen months after elevating McCaghren to assistant chief, Dyson sent him to the basement.

Some said he was demoted because higher-ups were not informed when the FBI raided Dallas bookmaking operations. In a massive sweep, the FBI targeted the service station owned by Joe Civello and Philip Bosco, bookie Bobby Joe Chapman's car lot, and Joe Ianni's Vesuvio restaurant. Chief Dyson claimed McCaghren helped the FBI set up the wiretaps, then didn't keep him in the loop. He reassigned McCaghren to a room without a telephone. His new job was approving parade permits.

Not one to sit quietly in exile, McCaghren approved a request from a gay liberation organization to hold a parade. It was the first gay pride parade in the city. They say outraged residents jammed the City Hall switchboard for days.

To McCaghren's surprise, when he requested reassignment, the chief gave him a worthwhile assignment. Dyson named him second-in-command of the tactical unit. McCaghren was pleased. The tactical squad was where the action was.

An explosive situation soon gave McCaghren the chance to show his mettle. A series of police shootings in minority areas had stirred protests. A crowd of more than 1,200 protestors—mostly Black citizens—gathered across a freeway from the city's skyscrapers. The protestors wanted to parade through downtown with the body of a young Black man shot by police.

Chief Dyson ordered McCaghren's unit to prevent a riot. Thousands were watching on live TV as tensions mounted in the street. The crowd of protestors vastly outnumbered McCaghren's thin blue line of officers. As their taunts grew louder and protestors tried to shove the officers aside, McCaghren stepped forward. His goal was to keep lives from being lost on either side of the line, Black or white or blue.

Standing military parade straight, McCaghren walked between the crowd and his men, pushing protesters back to clear the way. As he walked by the apprehensive policemen, he looked each man in the eye. Don't over-react, he advised, stay professional. He paused to straighten their ties and flicked imaginary specks of lint from their jackets. They got the message: hold the line but stay cool. They did, and the crowd dissipated. Racial problems continued, but that day, violence was avoided.

The next time McCaghren hit the headlines, he was lauded as a hero. He saved the lives of two dozen hostages by talking two armed robbers into surrendering.

Around ten P.M. on a Monday night in 1973, the gunmen barricaded themselves inside the Inner Circle Lounge in East Dallas. One had escaped from a mental hospital and was possibly suicidal. He and his partner opened the bar so their hostages could enjoy a final Happy Hour—and prepared to shoot their way out. The men had a .30-caliber submachine gun, a sawed-off shotgun, and a revolver. They demanded a car, a tankful of gas, and a plane at Love Field to make their getaway.

More than 125 police officers blockaded a twenty-five-block area around the Greenville Avenue bar. McCaghren found a phone booth in a fire station and called the gunmen. He told them, "You're not going to just get out of there, jump into a car and fly into the wild blue yonder. This is the first day of the rest of your lives—or the last—it depends on how you want it."

Chain-smoking cigars and shifting his weight from one foot to the other, McCaghren stood in the booth for eight and a half hours and kept the gunmen on the line. "Don't let this phone go dead," he warned, "or I'll think something bad has happened in there, and we'll have to come in."

With equal doses of blarney and parental firmness, he told them, "Let's stay cool. I have no desire to hurt you . . . This blaze of glory stuff is no good." McCaghren bought time by asking, "Who's your favorite brother?" "Have you ever received counseling?" At one point, the gunmen sent out a cigar for McCaghren.

Eventually, it worked. The gunmen surrendered at eight thirty in the morning. None of the hostages was harmed. Exhausted, McCaghren went home.

The *Dallas Morning News* printed an editorial praising McCaghren for using persuasion instead of guns to defuse the situation. It concluded that Captain McCaghren had proved to be "a real man."

The afterglow did not last long.

McCaghren was demoted again. He had angered higher-ups by testifying in private to a city council probe of corruption in the DPD. Then he objected in public to Chief Dyson's plan to use federal money to hire more policemen. McCaghren told reporters that "putting officers on the federal payroll" might jeopardize local control.

This time, Dyson banished McCaghren to the property room, a windowless space in a building across town. It was known as "the graveyard." McCaghren made light of the humiliating treatment by joking that Dyson put him in charge of "counting shirts."

He sabotaged any hope of returning again to meaningful work when a TV reporter came to his farm to ask how he felt about being demoted. When a bull in the pasture behind McCaghren made a loud noise, he quipped on camera, "Hush, Frank!"

That finished him.

Realizing he had ended his career, McCaghren began operating a private security company while supervising the property room, his way of giving the raspberry to higher-ups one last time.

McCaghren took off Badge No. 886 in November 1974 after serving twenty-one years. He told reporters he decided to go when secretaries began asking how to spell his name.

McCaghren's resignation generated a wave of press coverage because he was widely recognized as the most colorful Dallas police officer in recent history. He brought personality to a largely faceless institution in the city.

"I doubt if his type of cop will pass this way again," said public information officer Bob Shaw. "A little bit of history died with the resignation of Paul McCaghren."

Police reporter Jim Ewell wrote that officers who worked with McCaghren described him as a "policeman's policeman," who "doesn't believe in apologizing for good police work." On the other hand, Ewell wrote, McCaghren's bluntness came across as arrogant to some officers. They said McCaghren's bold manner made his demotion inevitable. "His type don't usually make chief," one said.

At forty-three and still in his prime, McCaghren built up his security firm, benefiting from the contacts he had made as a detective. From then on, he led the life of a successful businessman, gambling without qualms, and enjoying weekends at his farm.

Then in 1978, he hit the headlines again.

During an interview with the House Select Committee on Assassinations (HSCA), McCaghren made a stunning revelation: he had the original Dictabelt recordings taken from dispatcher transmissions during critical minutes of President Kennedy's assassination. They were the only audio record of gunshots fired that day.

How did McCaghren get the recordings? Police Chief Charles Batchelor had entrusted McCaghren with the tapes and other documents in 1969. Apparently, former Chief Jesse Curry had gathered the materials for a book and left them behind in a file cabinet. Batchelor feared the records might fall into the wrong hands or be destroyed, so he gave them to McCaghren.

McCaghren transferred the recordings to a trunk in his garage. When asked why he didn't reveal the tapes earlier, McCaghren replied, "No one ever asked me."

The recordings became critically important as the HSCA investigated whether three or four shots were fired at the president's motorcade. A panel of acoustic experts identified what sounded like four gunshots. That tended to support the theory that some shots could have been fired from the grassy knoll in front of the president's motorcade, not just the Texas Schoolbook Depository. Based partly on that acoustic evidence, the HSCA concluded that a conspiracy could have been involved in the assassination, possibly including the Mafia.

Yet the Justice Department did its own analysis of the tapes with a different set of consultants, who came to a different conclusion. They declared there were only three shots recorded on the audiotapes, and the fourth sound was probably a motorcycle backfire. A third review panel agreed with the first analysis, but by that time, the old tapes were in such frazzled shape, the dispute was never resolved.

McCaghren continued to lead his private security firm for several decades. As his war injuries limited his mobility, he turned over daily operations to his longtime colleague, Brad Smith.

When he and his wife were in their mid-eighties, they moved into an upscale assisted living facility with valet parking, a concierge, tasteful artwork, and happy hour. When I went by to continue our interviews, I could see that McCaghren's health was declining, but not his gruff charisma.

By this time, we had developed a cordial but mutually wary relationship. Then something came up that nearly torpedoed our conversations.

Several of my sources had tipped me that there were rumors McCaghren had "gone rogue" toward the end of his career and did things he shouldn't have done. The internal affairs department put out word that McCaghren was hanging around with bad apples in the force, gambling with people he shouldn't, and sleeping with women he shouldn't. He wasn't doing things by the book, they said, and had some rogue officers around him. They were called "McCaghren's Gang."

I was not surprised that there was mean-spirited talk about McCaghren because the police department was known for its cutthroat politics. But could it be true? I knew McCaghren wasn't a saint, but I thought he was a talented, serious cop. Now, I worried, Could I trust his version of events?

I checked with several old-time reporters. Yes, they said, there had been some "rogue" rumors. They had brushed the talk aside because the men who worked with McCaghren continued to respect him. One reporter suggested internal affairs powers were angered when McCaghren talked about corruption in the department, so they were painting him with the same brush.

I decided to ask McCaghren directly. When I went to see him again at the retirement home, he had lost more weight and seemed worn down.

His wife was ill. I hesitated to bring up something negative so late in the process, but I did.

Did he know about the rumors? Was he cheating on his wife? Playing cards with the wrong crowd? Had he gone rogue for a while?

It was an awkward moment.

McCaghren looked down at the floor. I held my breath.

"Womanizing?" I prompted.

"I had some relationships, yes," he answered. "I'm not proud of it. I didn't think other people knew." He paused. "The police department's the worst for rumors."

A rogue?

"I liked to be the first on the door when we busted it in, yes. Might not have had a search warrant."

Gambling?

"I went to Shreveport quite a bit. Sometimes they comped me at hotels because I was a police officer. I was always afraid to drink too much over there. Too risky. But in Dallas, the people I played cards with were all police officers. Just police officers."

I knew McCaghren wasn't telling me the whole story. Still, I had to give him credit for answering at all. Admitting you've made mistakes is difficult for anyone; admitting you've made mistakes to someone writing a book took nerve. If McCaghren concealed parts of his life, he wasn't the only one.

A year later, after his wife died, he confided to me that he'd had a serious affair with debutante Margaret Otis. I had suspected as much. Yet it was the kind of unlikely romance—an heiress and a hard-knocks cop—that could only work in movies with couples like Spencer Tracy and Katherine Hepburn. In real life, the affair ended. They talked about marriage, one of her friends told me, but it didn't work out. McCaghren stayed with his wife, and Miss Otis went on with her life.

McCaghren also acknowledged he had been struggling with post-traumatic stress disorder. What he experienced in Korea still dogged him, along with the anxieties of his police work. He had started therapy at the Veterans Hospital and it was helping. He rarely missed the support group sessions. He even wrote a letter to the new Dallas police chief, encouraging him to make sure policemen got care for PTSD. I admired him for that. He had come a long way from our first conversation when he brushed aside my questions about his wartime experiences and joked about his fall from power. At eighty-nine, he was facing his real wounds.

During the COVID quarantine, McCaghren left the assisted living facility and moved in with one of his daughters and her family. When he was riding in his motorized wheelchair to physical therapy, he met a new lady friend. At ninety, he moved in with her and started work on a memoir.

In contrast to the disputes that tripped up McCaghren, **Walter Fannin** was an uncontroversial figure for the rest of his career. He remained the kind of man who doesn't get his name on the outside of a building but is well-regarded on the inside. He dutifully served as secretary-treasurer of the FBI National Academy Association for twelve years, handling the unglamorous chores. He stayed a member of his Masonic Lodge for fifty years, and Casa View Baptist Church for forty-five years.

When Fannin retired in 1976 with the rank of deputy chief of police, he had been with the Dallas Police Department for thirty-six years, six years longer than his grandfather. He and his wife, Betty, had been saving money a long time for a trip to Disneyland after he retired. Joe Cody led an effort to collect money for a farewell party and a trip; so much money was contributed that Fannin and his wife went to Europe for twenty-one days.

As his health faltered, the men who worked for years with Fannin—McCaghren, Jim Behringer, Joe Cody, Charlie Dellinger, Jack Davis, John Chism—came to visit him in the hospital. They teased him again about the time he backed his RV into a creek and had to get their help pulling it out. He still didn't think it was funny.

McCaghren gave the eulogy at Fannin's funeral. He recalled complaining to Fannin one day, "We take the bad guys off the streets, but after we are gone, no one will remember what we did." Fannin didn't buy the self-pity. They could only do their best, Fannin advised his hot-blooded friend, "and make room for others to follow."

I asked Fannin's children if their father regretted not capturing the jewel thief. "He liked to get things buttoned-down," his daughter Delores said. "So yes, he didn't like things unfinished."

Her brother John added, "He wished things had turned out different, but this was a single case—and he knew from all his cases, if we don't get you today, somebody will, even if it takes a hundred years."

Josephine Herbert Graf, whose burglary put the jewel thefts on the front page, married again after Bruno Graf's death. She chose Emilio Chomat, a Cuban educator who spoke five languages. They divorced a few years later. She continued to host elegant dinners around her floating dinner table and died in her home at ninety-two. Her house on Park Lane, the only Dallas private residence designed by Edward Durell Stone, was given landmark status.

"My mother was an amazing woman," her daughter **Dr. Joanne Stroud** told me. "She was married five times, twice to the same man, and the last time when she was in her seventies to a man who was twenty years younger. She was simply remarkable."

Following her brief and unhappy marriage to Jim Kirksmith, **Nancy Ann Smith** married Dr. Buck Wynne, the man she wished she had married. They divided their time between Dallas and Rancho Santa Fe in California, where they raised racehorses. After Wynne died of cancer, Nancy Ann married Alfred W. "Hap" Chandler, a retired Navy captain. They moved into penthouse 22A at 3525 Turtle Creek, the same penthouse Evelyn Lambert once occupied.

Interior designers Loyd Taylor and Paxton Gremillion transformed the penthouse into a showplace that surpassed even Evelyn Lambert's efforts.

Visitors remember with awe that the living room looked like a movie set, with shimmering white mirrored walls, white marble floors, and white furniture.

Little did they know the designers achieved the unique effect by painting the wall panels with opalescent nail polish. After they depleted every bottle of the Revlon polish they could find in stores, Taylor and Gremillion ordered it in fifty-gallon containers.

In another sensational touch, the round master bedroom featured a domed ceiling with a chandelier that came from the Palace Theater. The dome was so heavy, it had to be lowered by helicopter.

Other designers quipped that Nancy Ann's interior designers had been given an unlimited budget—and exceeded it.

As Nancy Ann Chandler, she remained an influential figure in Dallas society for many years. By this writing, the Crystal Charity Ball that she founded had raised more than $150 million for children's causes.

After a series of strokes, Nancy Ann Chandler died in 2017 at the age of ninety-three. Those who read the obituary closely, or attended her memorial service, noticed there was an omission: there was no mention, not a word, of her marriage to Jim Kirksmith, an unfortunate chapter in her life that she preferred to put behind her.

◆

In 1968, **Candy Barr** received a pardon from Governor John Connally, which freed her from the parole restrictions that had kept her from performing. Short on money, she returned to stripping a few times, even doing a stint at the downtown Colony Club where she became famous. For a $5,000 fee, she posed for *Oui* magazine at the age of forty-one. The fact that a grandmother had posed naked set tongues in Dallas wagging again. After that, she lived in relative seclusion as Juanita Phillips. She'd had enough limelight and controversy.

In her last interview in 2001, Phillips told *Texas Monthly*'s Skip Hollandsworth that she had several regrets: making the pornographic film that made her famous, not getting to go to college, and her marriages. Those regrets aside, Phillips said she did what she did to survive.

At sixty-six, she was getting by on her disability check and cooked her meals on a hot plate. As she put on her sunglasses to leave the interview, she warned Hollandsworth, "Now don't you let anyone know where they can find me. Let the world find someone else to talk about. I like being left alone."

She died four years later of pneumonia. *Playboy* magazine saluted her as one of the twentieth century's most desirable women. After she died, the possession of two ounces or less of marijuana became a misdemeanor punishable by up to 180 days imprisonment in Texas, far less than the 15-year sentence Candy Barr received for having four-fifths an ounce of marijuana.

◆

Restaurateur and alleged Mafia foreman **Joe Campisi** died at the age of seventy-three in 1990, after having a heart attack while chasing an employee he thought was stealing money from the restaurant's cash register. New Orleans crime boss Carlos Marcello reportedly paid for the funeral arrangements.

◆

J. Edgar Hoover served as director of the FBI until his death in 1972 at the age of seventy-seven. He had controlled the nation's top law enforcement agency for nearly half a century—thirty-five years as director of the FBI and eleven years as head of its predecessor, the Bureau of Investigation. Hoover was buried in the Congressional Cemetery in a lead-lined coffin that weighed a thousand pounds to prevent desecration. He left most of his estate to his longtime associate, Clyde Tolson, who was buried not far away.

◆

After decades of faithful service to the community, burglary victim **Ruth Collins Sharp Altshuler** became known as the "Godmother of Philanthropy" in Dallas. Her generosity outshined the rowdy oil barons in town who did far less for the community.

After many years as a widow, she married a distinguished psychiatrist at Southwestern Medical School, Dr. Kenneth Altshuler. When she was eighty-eight, Dallas Mayor Mike Rawlings asked Mrs. Altshuler to organize a dignified ceremony to commemorate the fiftieth anniversary of the Kennedy assassination—and raise the funds to do so. At first, she said no. She was nearly ninety. Surely it was someone else's turn.

But the mayor persisted: the world would be watching. Then he added an entreaty she could not resist: "Do it for Dallas." Once again, she said she would do her part. "I'm over the hill," she told him, "but I'll come back over the hill."

The resulting ceremony recognized the 1963 tragedy with gravity and decorum. Historian David McCullough gave an address. Navy jets performed a flyover salute. And the Naval Academy choir sang "America the Beautiful." Thousands of Dallas citizens stood in the November rain for hours to show their respect, including Ruth Altshuler, bundled up against the cold and rain, but standing straight. The burden the city shouldered for so long was settling into history. She died peacefully five years later.

❖

Evelyn Lambert died at the age of ninety-seven in a Cuernavaca hospital in 2004. Well into her nineties, she entertained regularly and enthralled guests. "Evelyn Lambert is still utterly dazzling, an irresistibly eye-catching presence," one visitor wrote when she was ninety-three.

At a time when most of her peers had died or were in nursing homes, Evelyn Lambert tried to establish a Guggenheim Museum in Mexico. She convinced thirty-two Mexican governors to support the idea and chose a triangle of land in Morelos. Her vision included an architecture school and the preservation of ancient sites. But the complicated land and government approvals dragged on. Guggenheim director Thomas Krens chose a different site. Her hopes also fizzled for a show of her art collection at the Peggy Guggenheim Museum in Venice, which she had helped restore. As her health and influence faded, so did support.

Evelyn had hoped that after her death, her home would become a museum to preserve her art collection. But the buyers of Casa Leon were not interested in her art. Her collection was sold by her friend Alma Shon's children, her sole heirs.

Not long before her death, she told a writer with typical amplification, "I think I've had a very good life. I've had highs and lows. The highs were accomplishing things I set out to do, like bringing contemporary art to Dallas. To be the wife of the man who beautified Dallas. To bring as many Texans to Venice as there are Venetians."

When it came to regrets, Evelyn insisted, "I have a very bad memory for regrets."

And that seemed to be the truth.

◆

Nancy Hamon was never robbed by the King of Diamonds, thanks to the DPD surveillance at her house—or because John Higginbotham was a good friend and sometimes lent her jewels. When she hosted an Arabian Nights costume party, most guests wore elaborate turbans. Higginbotham came dressed as a beggar with a ragged turban and blacked-out teeth. She laughed harder than anyone.

Hamon's jewels were eventually stolen, but by several armed men. One evening in the 1980s, they forced their way into her house while she and her husband were watching TV. As they rushed through the door, Nancy Hamon slipped her 18-carat diamond ring under a sofa cushion.

It was not a polite visit. The burglars roughed up the couple and demanded the "good stuff" at gunpoint. Mrs. Hamon said she had placed the jewelry in a bank vault that day.

"Too bad," one of the burglars said.

She replied coolly, "That depends on your point of view."

After rummaging through the house, the intruders found some jewels and fled.

Not long afterward, the Hamons ran into Vegas kingpin Moe Dalitz at the La Costa Country Club in California, which Dalitz and his partners built with Teamsters help. Dalitz told the couple he had heard some of her jewels were stolen. He scolded them, "Why didn't you call me? I might've gotten some back for you!"

After the conversation, Nancy Hamon asked her husband to see if Dalitz could still find some of her pieces. But her husband said no. "You don't want to owe these people a favor," he said.

When her husband died in 1985, Nancy Hamon found herself at the helm of one of Texas's great oil fortunes with little experience to draw on. She quipped that she didn't know anything about oil except as a good salad dressing.

She proved particularly good at giving her husband's assets away and became one of the leading philanthropists in the city. She wanted her "last check to bounce"—and gave it a good try, donating millions to education, the arts, and medicine.

In 1988, Hamon gave a unique thank-you party for friends who offered support during the painful periods when her husband, her only son, and her stepdaughter had died. She chartered the luxury ocean liner *Sea Goddess II* for five days and hosted 110 guests for a well-lubricated cruise to Spain and Morocco. She danced the flamenco; Louis Armstrong played "Happy Birthday." The party cruise became known as "The Ship of Fools," a nod to Katherine Anne Porter's novel about human foibles. Few knew that while most of the guests slept late, Evelyn Lambert and Sharon Simons slipped ashore to attend church.

Ten years later, Hamon invited three hundred guests to a costume party themed "Midnight in the Garden of Good and Evil," echoing John Berendt's novel about decadence and deception in Savannah.

She lived out her days in a penthouse at the Mansion on Turtle Creek, across the street from the former Cipango Club. Her parties were still lively as guests played boogie-woogie on her two grand pianos into the wee hours.

Per her wishes, no services were held after Nancy Hamon died at ninety-two. Everyone agreed she was a tough act to follow.

◆

After a series of strokes, **Clint Murchison Sr.** passed on management of his companies in 1960 to his sons, Clint Jr. and John. By the time the King of Diamonds sneaked into his house the next year, Murchison was devoting most of his time to playing cards. In 1965, he was relegated to a wheelchair. He encouraged his younger wife, Ginny, to carry on her active lifestyle in Dallas while he stayed at his ranch. For entertainment, he had his chauffeur drive him around the property.

Murchison's business empire remained dogged by controversy. According to author Dan Moldea, his companies were investigated by nine federal agencies and two congressional committees during a ten-year period after 1955. The committees brought to light questionable dealings with organized crime and the Teamsters. But no charges resulted.

When Clint Sr. died at the age of seventy-two in 1969, his fortune was estimated at $500 million. The *New York Times* described him as a one-man conglomerate who "devoted his entire life to making money."

Murchison's passing did not leave a lasting mark on Dallas. He had received requests for donations from all over the world—but was not known for major philanthropy. When Stanley Marcus asked Murchison for a donation for the opera, he replied, "You keep up the aesthetics, and I will keep up the broken-down gamblers."

Murchison could be compassionate, handing down cash from his office window to a homeless man and helping an elderly Black man start a hog-raising business. But his blind spots—a tendency to ignore the rules and do business with bad actors—were passed on to his namesake son and became a curse.

As for Murchison's prized Del Mar racetrack, the state of California bought the property. The state currently leases the track to the Del Mar

Thoroughbred Club for the racing season. The Del Charro, Murchison's glamorous hotel, was torn down in 1977 to make room for a condominium complex.

◆

After their father withdrew from day-to-day operations, **Clint Murchison Jr.** and his brother **John Murchison** expanded the family business into real estate and a host of other projects.

Following John's death in 1979, a legal dispute over his estate led to the sale of the Dallas Cowboys football team, a painful loss to Clint Jr., who considered the team his greatest accomplishment. He had selected Tom Landry to coach the NFL team and Tex Schramm to run the organization, then wisely let them make the day-to-day and play-by-play decisions. Behind the scenes, Clint Jr. pioneered the use of computers to analyze players. After he built a futuristic stadium with a partially open roof, fans bragged it was "so God can watch his favorite team play." The football team turned out to be his best financial decision. When he bought the franchise in 1959, he paid $600,000. When he was forced to sell in 1984, it was worth $60 million.

While he prided himself on his 140-plus IQ, Clint Jr. lacked personal skills. One observer described him as being so introverted he would not stand out in a crowd of two. He expressed his humor in pranks—like releasing chickens during a Washington Redskins game—and his writing. He was a good enough writer that he sometimes subbed for local sports columnists when they went on vacation.

Yet with all his assets, the younger Murchison struggled to prove himself. He was living proof of the Texas adage, "It's hard to grow grass under a tall tree." He overreached, trying to outdo his father. Addicted to debt and over-leveraged, he ran into crippling financial difficulties in the late 1980s when the real estate market crashed and oil prices dropped. Dozens of deals, each financed by another, fell apart. The hole got too deep to climb out.

Clint Jr. filed for bankruptcy protection in one of the nation's largest bankruptcy cases. Some $500 million in liabilities piled up against $254 million in holdings. One of Texas's great fortunes ended in a scrap sale, including Clint Jr.'s 1974 silver Rolls-Royce and his twenty-six-acre home on Forest Lane.

Though he built a phenomenally successful sports franchise, Clint Jr.'s other dealings tarnished his legacy. Congressional committees probed corruption in his contracts for federal housing and a desalination plant. They investigated favors he traded with LBJ aide Bobby Baker and his dubious deals with gangsters like Ed Levinson. Yet like his father, he avoided legal consequences.

Clint Jr.'s association with alleged Mafia figures raised more uncomfortable questions. After he bought the Tony Roma restaurant franchise in 1976, information surfaced that Roma's real name was Tony LoPresti and he was connected to the New York Mafia. Agents with the Bureau of Alcohol, Tobacco, and Firearms, who had Roma under surveillance, reported that Murchison appeared firmly entrenched with "individuals who are proven national crime figures."

Two years later, according to the FBI, lobbyist I. I. Davidson tried to broker a meeting for Clint Jr. with New Orleans Mafia boss Carlos Marcello. Davidson claimed Murchison wanted to buy some land from Marcello. Though the request ended up a footnote in the FBI sting operation known as "Brilab" (bribery-labor), FBI tapes of Marcello's conversations revealed Murchison's name came up multiple times regarding real estate and bank deals. It also came to light in court filings that Clint Jr. had partnered in two Dallas banks with Louisiana banker Herman K. Beebe, who reportedly had ties to Marcello. The banks had been drained by risky loans and failed.

Clint Jr.'s longtime friends lamented privately that he had lost his bearings personally as well as professionally. He jumped into the *Playboy* era with abandon, reveling in temptations from cocaine to cocktail waitresses. His free-wheeling days and nights ultimately cost him his marriage to his first wife, Jane Murchison.

After his second wife, Anne, became a born-again Christian, Clint Jr. followed suit. Murchison gave up his reckless ways but was struck by a degenerative nerve disease that required round-the-clock care. Months later, he died at sixty-three.

Moves to have Murchison named to the NFL Hall of Fame resurface from time to time. His family members would like to see his significant contributions to the sport of football remembered rather than his mistakes. A new book, *Hole in the Roof*, which describes Murchison's innovations in stadium architecture and computerized systems, has been well-received.

Most of Clint Jr.'s party friends—the "Rover Boys"—died in their sixties, too. **Robert Thompson** died at sixty-four of lung cancer. **Gordon McLendon** died at sixty-five of esophageal cancer. And **Bedford Wynne** died of a heart attack at sixty-six. Wynne's later years were a notable departure from his glory days as a Cowboys part owner. He sold his stake in the football team in the late 1960s to pursue other ventures, like Bravo Smokes, a non-nicotine cigarette made out of lettuce. Unfortunately, customers complained they tasted like "old socks." Wynne also tried raising racehorses, but his thoroughbreds didn't win and his track debts mounted. After he got a warning from hitman R. D. Matthews to pay up, his family had to lay low. Somewhere along the line, Wynne's second marriage broke up. He became active in Alcoholics Anonymous and reportedly was speaking at the podium when he recognized someone coming in the door. Wynne collapsed on the spot and died of a heart attack. Some say the man looked like R. D. Matthews.

George W. Owen Jr., the Guy Friday for Clint Murchison Jr. and his party friends, remained an avid sports booster until his death in 2000, just before his seventy-fifth birthday. Having been investigated repeatedly for illegal gambling, Owen would probably find it ironic that sports gambling was later legalized in thirty-eight states, though not in Texas. Legal betting was booming around the country and so was illegal betting, thanks to the internet.

After 1970, **Jim Ling** no longer ran the company that carried his name. He was forced to move out of his $3.2 million house. H. L. Hunt's son Lamar bought the mansion and kept the gold "L" on the front gate.

Before he could make a comeback, Ling was struck with Guillain-Barré syndrome. Within a week, he was completely paralyzed, requiring a tracheotomy, a respirator, and intravenous feeding. He could only move his left eyelid. His heart went into wild fibrillations. A priest gave him last rites.

Thanks to extensive physical therapy, he was able to walk again, although his stamina was never the same. Visitors noted he had difficulty getting up from his desk.

Undaunted by his setbacks, Ling refused to speculate on what he might have done differently to save LTV. What if he hadn't expanded so fast? "I don't play if-sies," he said. Ling continued to make deals, mainly in the energy business, until his death in 2004 of esophageal cancer.

◆

And what happened to the city of Dallas, the backdrop for the King of Diamonds? Dallas became a much different city.

The Old Guard that had been synonymous with the social set was not as influential. Dallas elected two female mayors, two Black mayors, several Black district attorneys, a Hispanic police chief, a gay Hispanic female sheriff, and a Black female sheriff. Gay people lived more openly.

H. L. Hunt's name is rarely mentioned, but several of his descendants became instrumental in moving the city forward. His granddaughter, Lyda Hill, became one the leading philanthropists in the nation and launched major initiatives in science and medicine. His grandson, Ray Hunt, created his own success in the oil business and became a respected city leader.

The debutante ritual that had dominated the life of the jewel thief now played a much smaller role in social life. The daily newspapers stopped providing extensive coverage of the parties. The list of debutantes became more diverse, but fewer people paid attention other than the deb families and their friends.

After the Cowboys won the Super Bowl in 1971, the team got the nickname "America's Team." People began to identify the city with football more than tragedy.

And when the TV show *Dallas* lit up TV screens in 1978 with an opening helicopter shot of gleaming glass skyscrapers, the city got its glitz back. The throbbing, upbeat theme song became the city's new anthem. For thirteen seasons, the TV show turned old oil into new gold, thanks to Larry Hagman's portrayal of the scheming tycoon J. R. Ewing. When the TV character was shot to death in a cliffhanger episode in 1980, everyone from President Carter to Queen Elizabeth was asking, "Who shot J. R.?"

As the twenty-first century got underway, oil fracking and high-tech companies brought a new batch of billionaires to town. Bentleys and Teslas replaced Cadillacs as show cars. A telecommunications CEO owned Justify, the Triple Crown Winner. Another tech mogul spent $7 million a year keeping a seventeen-member crew busy on his two-hundred-foot yacht. Not to be outshone, Dallas Cowboys owner Jerry Jones bought a $250 million super-yacht that included a spa, a gym, a sauna, and two helipads.

There were still grand parties, but the New Rich tended to celebrate causes more than frivolity. When they hosted parties, they were usually fundraisers for charity or a politician. As Jack Roach, an attorney for "Old Oil" families, put it, "There are a lot of people in Dallas now with greater fortunes—but they're not as much fun."

When people look back on the King of Diamonds era, they don't remember the excesses—and inequalities—as much as they remember the great flair and style. They remember the larger-than-life characters who lived with gusto, partying as if there were no tomorrow.

Now and again, the long search for the King of Diamonds comes up, and people wonder, Who was he?

The answer is that he was next door the whole time.

Acknowledgments

S ince this project took more than seven years and involved hundreds of interviews, there are more people to thank than I can possibly list. But I hope everyone who took the time to talk with me knows that I am deeply grateful.

Special thanks to the staff at the Dallas Public Library and the SMU libraries, who provided invaluable help. Likewise, Delores Fannin, Paul McCaghren, Kevin Fox, and Rob Kendall provided essential research materials.

And special mention is owed to Jan Hart Black, who helped start this project and remained supportive in many ways.

Thanks also to those who served as early readers and provided helpful feedback, including Henry Tatum, Carolyn Barta, Ellen Kampinsky, Mary Jalonick, Mary Suhm, Regen Horchow, Jeremy Halbreich, Caren Prothro, Mary Lois Leonard, Connie Copley, Libby Norwood, Rita Cox, Laura Onsgard, Nancy Kruh, Joyce Saenz Harris, Janie Paleschic, Bob and Laura Ikel, Diana Clark, and Jean Ables Flatt. Hand over heart thanks to you.

In addition, I am forever grateful to Cindy Keever, Virginia Carmichael, Susan Elliot Hamm, and Leslie Wells, who helped me trim what was a whale of a manuscript into a more readable length.